HILLARY
(AND BILL)

THE MURDER VOLUME

PART THREE OF THE CLINTON TRILOGY

CROCODILE TEARS? Hillary listens glumly while husband President Bill Clinton wipes away tears at a memorial service for U.S. Commerce Secretary Ron Brown. The plane on which Brown was traveling crashed on a hillside in Croatia in 1996. Problem is, Brown's head had a bullet hole in it when inspected by more than a few rescue workers and medical professionals—a wound like none other found on the 35 fellow passengers who died that day. Chances are, someone murdered Brown to prevent him from testifying against Bill and Hillary. RICHARD ELLIS/AFP/GETTY IMAGES

HILLARY (AND BILL)

THE MURDER VOLUME

PART THREE OF THE CLINTON TRILOGY

BY VICTOR THORN

Published by
Sisyphus Press
in conjunction with
American Free Press

HILLARY (AND BILL)
The Murder Volume
Part Three of the Clinton Trilogy

ISBN 0-9785733-8-2
ISBN 978-0-9785733-8-6

SISYPHUS PRESS
P.O. Box 10495
State College, PA
16805-0495

Copyright 2008 by Victor Thorn

All rights reserved, including the right of reproduction. For permission, write the author at the address above.

First Edition: September 2008: 1,000 copies

Manufactured in the United States of America

In conjunction with
AMERICAN FREE PRESS

645 Pennsylvania Avenue SE
Suite 100
Washington, D.C. 20003

www.americanfreepress.net
1-888-699-NEWS toll free

WING TV
www.wingtv.net

DEDICATED TO:

*Danny Casolaro,
William Cooper,
&
Hunter S. Thompson*

*Independent researchers, journalists,
and truth-tellers who were taken
well before their time*

> "*Whenever another being is not experienced as human, the act of destructiveness and cruelty assumes a different quality.*"
>
> —Erich Fromm
> *The Anatomy of Human Destructiveness*

TABLE OF CONTENTS

HILLARY (AND BILL)
The Murder Volume
Part Three of the Clinton Trilogy

Chapter One:
- **THE BOYS ON THE TRACKS** 1
  - Arkancide 1
  - Dr. Fahmy Malak 3
  - Dan Harmon 14
  - Dixie Mafia: Murder, Inc. 21

Chapter Two:
- **MASSACRE AT WACO** 27
  - Hell on Earth 27
  - Police State 32
  - Hillary Clinton: Baby Killer 39
  - FBI & Delta Forces 43
  - Motive 44
  - Waco: A New Revelation 47

Chapter Three:
- **THE MURDER OF VINCE FOSTER** 57
  - Mainstream Media Cowardice 57
  - The Arkansas Group 59
  - The Actual Murderer Revealed 66
  - No Malice or Forethought 75
  - Another Stain 77
  - Fort Marcy Park 84
  - Hoaxed Suicide 87
  - The Crime Scene 88
  - The Park Police (Keystone Kops) 90

TABLE OF CONTENTS (CHAPTER THREE CONT'D)

    Eyeglasses 93
    Shoes 93
    The Gun & Bullets 95
    Wound 99
    Witnesses 102
    Patrick Knowlton 104
    Murder at the White House 107
    Hillary's Plumbers Break In 109
    The Fake Suicide Note 117
    The Fiske-Starr Cover-Up 121

Chapter Four:
    THE MURDER OF JERRY PARKS 135

Chapter Five:
    OKLAHOMA CITY BOMBING 151
    Bombs Inside the Alfred P. Murrah Building 151
    The Elohim City Connection 167
    Brig. Gen. Benton Partin Speaks Out. 193
    Addendum to Dipole Might 196
    Collateral Damage 197
    The Murder of Officer Terence Yeakey 200

Chapter Six:
    CHINAGATE & THE MURDER OF RON BROWN 205
    America Betrayed 205
    The Riady Empire 208
    Hubbell, Huang and Hillary's Treason 212
    Dead Men Walking 222
    Spoofing, Suicide & Survivors 235
    A Lead Snowstorm 242
    Cover-Up du Jour 245

TABLE OF CONTENTS (CONT'D)

Chapter Seven:
    THE MURDER OF DANNY CASOLARO 253

Chapter Eight:
    THE CLINTON BODY COUNT 263
    110+ & Counting 263
    Actual Cases: Read 'em & Weep 266

Chapter Nine:
    PRESIDENTIAL PARDONS 291
    Free the Criminals 291
    Marc Rich 298

Chapter Ten:
    THE POWER BEHIND THE THRONE 305
    Human Reconstruction & Remolding Society 305
    Masons, Jesuits & Rhodes Scholars 313
    Vernon Jordan & the Bilderbergers 325
    60 Minutes & Ross Perot 336
    The CFR, Trilateral Commission & Greenspan 344
    Rockefeller Connection 348
    Conclusion 353

About the Author 354

Endnotes 355

Bibliography 372

Index 378

THEY SAW TOO MUCH: When two teenage boys were caught snooping around the CIA drug and weapons smuggling operation in Mena, Arkansas, they were killed and their bodies placed on a railroad track. Despite overwhelming evidence that the deaths were homicides, a pliable Clinton-crony coroner, Dr. Fahmy Malak, ruled them accidental.

CHAPTER ONE

The Boys on the Tracks

ARKANCIDE

The most controversial notion surrounding Hillary and her husband is a concept which has come to be known as the Clinton Body Count. In a nutshell, the underlying premise is as follows: a significant number of people close to or affiliated with the Clintons have met untimely and questionable deaths over the years, especially those in positions to expose or damage Bill and Hillary. The odds are so astronomical in regard to these multiple fatalities (via homicide, supposed suicides, or alleged freak accidents) that it cannot be written off or explained as mere coincidence.

Before proceeding, let me clarify. Am I purporting that Bill and Hillary killed all of the people listed in the following chapters with their own hands? Absolutely not. That would be preposterous. But what I am contending is that a string of deaths has occurred which are so suspicious and have so much evidence pointing in the direction of Clinton involvement that the preponderance of evidence makes them the number one point of focus. Whether they utilized Dixie Mafia hit men, CIA-hired "mechanics," or good old-fashioned thugs to perform their wet jobs, this many people do not die at random. There must be a driving force behind their demise.

In addition, when you finish reading this book, do a simple calculation. How many suspicious, highly unordinary deaths have occurred in *your* life to people close to you? How about to all of the people you've met in your life? Do they have these highly irregular deaths surrounding them? As you'll see, the Clinton Body Count is off the charts, and the inordinate percentages defy logical explanation. This many people simply don't die in such questionable manners, and the common denominator in all of them is the Clintons.

Lastly, skeptics will ask: if the Clintons were responsible for so many deaths, why haven't they been convicted or imprisoned for them? As pointed out in chapter 9 of Volume Two of this trilogy, the Clintons have escaped justice for three reasons:

> 1) They have been protected by some very influential people over the decades who have a vested interest in their advancement and survival.
>
> 2) They've been able to rig the system in such a manner that judges, prosecutors, and grand juries have all been "in the bag," so to speak, in both Arkansas and Washington, D.C. In the nation's capital, Bill and Hillary were able to successfully protect themselves by firing every U.S. attorney, then replacing them with their own hand-picked cronies. The situation was even worse in Arkansas.
>
> 3) The corporate media has too often been a lapdog rather than a watchdog by either not seriously investigating this phenomenon, or giving it short shrift in their dutiful acceptance of, and adherence to, the Clinton party line.

The result is a dark, morbid, troublesome entity which has taken on a life of its own. Some call it the Clinton Body Count, while others couch it in equally ominous terms: "A great many people associated with William Jefferson Clinton and/or politics in Arkansas have, over the years, died of unnatural causes or rather suddenly under circumstances that have come to be known in folklore as 'Arkancides.'"[11]

Anyone who has investigated these Arkancides comes away with an eerie feeling, similar to that of the O.J. Simpson trial. *Something just wasn't right*; and it's hard to stomach somebody getting away with murder (quite literally, over and over again). With Bill

CHAPTER ONE

Clinton and his wife, one writer laid forth the following sentiment. "For all his bright promise and fine beliefs, he long ago made a deal with a benighted political organization that had thugs among its operatives. If you wonder why people hate him, it's because they recognize that training, they sense those crude values, that ruthlessness and lack of moral center. And they want an old-fashioned accounting."[2]

If we believe in anything in this country, it's that people must pay for their crimes. It's time the Clintons were held to the same measure as everyone else.

DR. FAHMY MALAK

The Boys on the Tracks, the subject of both a full-length book by Mara Leveritt and a documentary (*Obstruction of Justice*), is one of the most gruesome examples ever of how depraved the Dixie Mafia is. "On the night of August 23, 1987, two teenaged boys, Kevin Ives and Don Henry, said they were going deer hunting. At 4:25 am, August 24, the crew of the northbound Union Pacific train saw the boys lying side by side on the [railroad] track. They could not stop in time. Arkansas State Medical Examiner Fahmy Malak ruled the deaths 'accidental,' saying that the boys had passed out on the tracks after smoking too much marijuana."[3]

Actually, Dr. Malak produced quite a number of variations to his story. First he ruled it "a double suicide. When the parents claimed that was not possible, he changed it to a modified suicide—that they were under the influence of marijuana and fell asleep on the tracks."[4]

The parents of these boys didn't believe that explanation either. "When a sheriff's deputy met with Don's father to inform him of the 'suicide,' Curtis Henry told the sheriff, 'You're crazy as hell.' Linda [Ives] and her husband were equally as astounded. There was no way that Kevin, 'happy as could be' that day before the body was found, would have willingly sat down on those tracks."[5]

But Malak stood by his "THC intoxication"[6] story, saying that "the boys had smoked 20 marijuana joints and fallen into a trance on the railway tracks."[7]

His decision was met with resistance and outrage at every turn. The principal of Bryant High School stated the obvious. "How many times would two boys pass out at the same time, and in the same position?"[8]

Another problem surfaced which completely destroyed Malak's initial assessment. Dr. Joseph Burton, Atlanta's chief medical examiner, "indicated that the marijuana reading was totally invalid. Incredibly, Dr. Malak had used a urine drug test on the boys' blood instead of the necessary blood drug test. His choice to use this incorrect procedure produced Malak's incredible statement about the boys."[9]

Realizing that he was up a creek without a paddle, the coroner continued to modify his story. "When Malak learned that the boys were known to be 'clean,' he changed his opinion to 'suicide.'"[10]

So, it went from accidental to modified suicide to drug overdose back to suicide. If that wasn't bad enough, Malak next targeted the train operators—blaming them for possible murder.

Malak added what many considered his most offensive statement. "Could it be a homicide?" he asked rhetorically. "There is one condition that fulfills the criteria of homicide. If the engineer is lying, he could stop and he wouldn't, if he was under the influence of marijuana or alcohol."[11]

So now, at least according to Malak, the crew members were at fault for being stoned? The train's conductor, Jerry Tomlin, was understandably irritated by the medical examiner's audacity. "All I've got to say about Dr. Malak's testimony is that I will go with him and be tested any day, any time he chooses. Then we'll go to the state hospital to have him tested for a brain."[12]

What has been presented thus far would be enough to make anyone scratch their head, but we're just getting started. Try this on for size. "One of the boys' severed feet was left at the scene (Malak never even realized it)."[13]

It wasn't found until the next day, and "Dr. Malak never mentioned in his autopsy that one of the feet was missing."[14]

CHAPTER ONE

Plus, there was no way to reenact the crime scene because, "in a classic case of investigative ineptness, the officer who took all the measurements used the train as a reference point each time. The train, of course, pulled away later in the day, leaving no benchmark for further investigation."[15]

If you think the above description is simply official incompetence, consider: "'Mistakes' made in the case were more planned than accidental. The case file had no transmittal sheets indicating where the existing crime scene evidence was preserved. Another major item missing from the file was a set of crime scene photos. There was a list detailing the photos in the file, but the photos themselves were gone. There were few actual witness statements, and the leads mentioned in the file had never been followed up."[16]

The obstruction went further. "Three members of the train's crew said they saw a 'green tarp' made of cloth, which had partially covered the boys' bodies before impact. Another crewman remembered seeing the tarp lying in the ditch beside the train tracks. But the tarp—evidence that someone may have covered the [already] dead boys to ensure that the train engineer wouldn't see their bodies in time to stop the train—was never listed on the crime scene evidence sheet. It disappeared."[17]

This tarp may have contained blood residue, fingerprints, DNA, hair or clothes samples; but it was discarded and never presented into evidence.

The biggest blow of all, though, was to come the following year. Hang on tight because after the bodies of Henry and Ives were exhumed, the entire case blew wide open. In April 1988 a second autopsy was conducted by the Atlanta medical examiner Dr. Joseph Burton. He found a "V" shaped "penetrating wound" into the "thoracic and left lower chest cavity" of Don Henry. He showed an enhanced photograph of the wound to six other forensic investigators. They all concurred that it was a stab wound consistent with it having been inflicted by something such as a large cutting edge knife.

He also found that Kevin Ives had been smashed in the head with a rifle butt, probably Don Henry's .22 caliber hunting rifle.

There was "considerable reaction within the lungs of both boys" indicating that they had not died immediately.[18]

Another man, district deputy prosecuting attorney Richard Garrett, told reporters that "the pathologist had found wounds on the bodies 'not consistent with being struck by a train.'"[19]

These boys didn't die by accident, suicide, by being run over by a train, or because of the "psychedelic influence of marijuana."[20]

What we had here was murder. "To the astonishment of experts who later conducted a second autopsy, Dr. Malak failed to notice clear evidence of beating marks and a stab wound."[21]

The whole thing was a deliberate cover-up. The preponderance of evidence in this case indicates "Kevin Ives and Don Henry sustained injuries prior to the impact of the train that were inflicted on them by another individual or individuals, [and] that their bodies were placed on the track."[22]

Here's the bottom line: "Don Henry had been stabbed in the back, and the skull of Kevin Ives had been crushed. The conclusion was that both boys were murdered before being lain across the railroad tracks in the dead of night prior to a freight train's passage through the backwaters of the Sad Sack State."[23]

The proof was so overwhelming that "a grand jury was convened in 1989 and concluded that it was not just a train accident. The boys had been murdered!"[24]

After they were killed, their bodies were "then transported to the tracks to make it look like a suicide."[25]

Further, "bloating of [their] facial tissues indicated the beatings had taken place well before the train collided with their bodies."[26]

We're going to disclose very shortly who was responsible for these murders—and what their motive was—but first let's take a closer look at Dr. Fahmy Malak, one of the men responsible for covering up the Train Death Murders. Who was Fahmy Malak? The short answer is that he was "a crony of Bill Clinton and his Arkansas Mafia."[27]

He was "an Egyptian with poor command of English"[28] who "repeatedly lied about his credentials, misconstrued his findings, and misrepresented autopsy procedures. In the lab, he misplaced bodies and destroyed evidence."[29]

Rather than simply *editorializing* about how incompetent and corrupt Dr. Malak was, here's a list of his "greatest hits."

> - "In his most creative ruling he concluded that James 'Dewey' Milam had died of an ulcer and then been decapitated by the family dog. According to Malak, the animal had eaten the entire head and then vomited, leaving traces of half-digested brain matter. To Malak's chagrin, however, the man's skull was later recovered. No bites were taken out of it. The man had been decapitated with a sharp knife."[30] Initially, Malak had ruled the "headless corpse case *a death by natural causes*."[31]
> - In a "suicide" diagnosed by Malak, the dead man was found to have been shot five times.[32]
> - In another murder case, Malak used the DNA material from the wrong corpse to ascertain at what distance a gun was fired.[33]
> - In still another case, one of his own technicians testified that Malak had him manipulate a photographic image of a rifle butt to fit the size of an injury to support Malak's faulty conclusions.[34]
> - Over a five-year period, Malak had been challenged in court at least 17 times by other pathologists; the National Association of Medical Examiners says this is an unusually high figure.[35]

Malak was so despised and distrusted, and his "misjudgments became so notorious that a group of families formed a pressure group called VOMIT (Victims Of Malak's Incredible Testimony) to picket his public appearances and pressure the governor [Bill Clinton] to remove him."[36]

The situation was dire beyond description, and apparent to anyone paying attention. Clearly, "Malak caused the Clinton administration more embarrassment and more grief than anyone else; yet he managed to hang onto his job."[37]

Not only did Malak retain his job despite wild protests, but Governor Clinton "ignored VOMIT's complaints [and] raised Dr. Malak's salary, giving him the second biggest salary in state government."[38]

Bill Clinton was so cowardly in his support of Malak—and in his lack of concern for the truth—that he "steadfastly refused to even meet with Linda Ives and other families around the state who were victimized by Dr. Malak."[39]

But Clinton certainly had time for the corrupt medical examiner. "Malak boasted that he was one of the few in the state who could see the governor on fifteen minutes' notice."[40]

Not only was Malak crooked, he was also borderline crazy. "Several departing employees cited as their reasons for leaving Malak's bizarre behavior and paranoia. Law enforcement officers familiar with the crime lab, including FBI agents and sheriff's deputies, underlined that charge, complaining about Malak's insistence on photographing all visitors to his office. This included not only families, but police officers as well."[41]

Still, Malak hung on, even when the usually docile Arkansas press savaged him. Meredith Oakley of *The Arkansas Democrat* wrote about Fahmy Malak: "He didn't know a marijuana high from a stab wound. Before his scalpel, suicides looked like accidents and murders looked like natural causes. He couldn't keep his testimony straight from one minute to the next. He treated evidence like a four-year-old treats a jigsaw puzzle; when the pieces didn't fit, he tried to pound, push and mold them into place. Malak's tenure in the state Crime Laboratory was one fiasco after another."[42]

Furthermore, "'that Malak survived in Arkansas is a testament to Clinton's power,' wrote Meredith Oakley in her dispassionate Clinton biography, *On the Make*."[43]

Despite all this outrage and embarrassment, "Clinton remained

Malak's staunchest defender. For reasons known only to him, the governor chose to ignore the criticism of Malak's abilities as a forensic pathologist, criticism leveled by colleagues in the field as well as by citizens."[44]

Governor Clinton wasn't the only one running interference for this pathetic excuse for a medical professional. "Malak was well protected. The head of the State Medical Examiner Commission, Dr. Jocelyn Elders, refused to take action. She would later become the nation's Surgeon General. You see, cover-ups are like cancer. They just keep growing, involving more people, more payoffs, and sometimes more deaths."[45]

Another one of Malak's "chief defenders was Max Howell, a powerful veteran state senator who had headed the legislative committee formed to review Dr. Malak's work. Howell had announced at the start of the review that he 'had an admiration' for the way Malak had handled his job."[46]

The public and professional outcry became so intense that Malak was forced to resign. But lo and behold, the malignant doctor was saved at the last minute because "he would immediately move into a new job under the direction of Dr. Jocelyn Elders at the Arkansas Health Department. The job was created especially for him."[47]

Who, you may ask, conjured this post for Malak? "A Clinton spokesman confirmed that a member of the governor's legal staff had helped to bring Malak's lawyer and health department officials together."[48]

Of course, the Clintons don't want you to read too much into this turn of events, for Bill told reporters, "'We didn't make any deal.' He added that it was 'almost coincidental' that the health department job opened up just as Malak became available."[49]

Still, why would normally astute politicians like Bill and Hillary latch onto an obvious liability like Fahmy Malak? It didn't make sense. He was so repulsive to people that they actually showed up at his court appearances wearing VOMIT t-shirts. In addition, the media was accusing him of "lying on the stand, tampering with evidence, and manufacturing of convictions."⁵⁰

The Clintons weren't stupid. Why align with a public relations nightmare? It didn't just happen by accident. There had to be something more.

Well, like most everything else in Arkansas and with the Dixie Mafia, there *was* more to the story. First, "In many states a coroner is an appointed official who doesn't have to be a doctor or have any medical training."⁵¹

Plus, secondly, in May 1992, "*The Los Angeles Times* ran an article about Clinton's relationship with Dr. Malak. Titled *Clinton's Ties to Controversial Medical Examiner Questioned*, the piece reported how, for several years, Clinton had refused to dismiss the doctor whose controversial decrees had included a ruling that helped Clinton's mother, a nurse-anesthetist, avoid scrutiny in the death of a patient."⁵²

Undoubtedly, there was something rotten in Arkansas, and now we're closing in on pinpointing the reason why Fahmy Malak was retained amid gross incompetence and corruption. For years, "the popular theory was that Malak 'had something on Clinton' that made the governor loath to fire him. That is mere conjecture, but more than likely based on two medical controversies involving Clinton's mother in the early 1980s."⁵³

The first controversy involved the death of Laura Lee Slayton, a woman in her twenties who had recently given birth. During surgery, the young mother died from cardiac arrest, and "shocked staff members at the hospital pointed an accusing finger at [Virginia] Kelley [Clinton's mother, then using the surname Dwire]."⁵⁴

Why? Answer: because "Laura Slayton was on the operating table under anesthesia when her oxygen supply, being administered by Virginia Dwire, was abruptly cut off."⁵⁵

After an investigation, Dr. Robert King testified that "Virginia Dwire had not adequately monitored Slayton before transferring her to recovery after surgery."⁵⁶

Lawsuits were filed, and soon, "by the late 1970s, physicians had begun refusing to work with her [Mrs. Clinton]."⁵⁷

CHAPTER ONE

Why had Virginia Kelley become anathema to them? Doctors objected to the fact that "she wore inappropriate costume jewelry into the operating room, was not always attentive to patients, filed her nails, wiped her shoes, and left patients unattended during surgery."[58]

More brazenly, "when the horses were running at Oaklawn, she had a reputation for reading the daily racing form during surgery."[59]

With questions of blame still lingering after Laura Slayton's "bungled anesthesiological procedure,"[60] an even bigger disaster hit Clinton's mother. Here is what transpired. On June 27, 1981—after a yelling match—22-year-old Billy Ray Washington hurled a chunk of concrete through the car window of some teenagers who had told him, "Why don't you shut your ass, mother f***in' nigger?"[61]

> At Billy Ray's feet lay a hand-sized hunk of broken sidewalk concrete. He picked it up and hurled it at the car [of the teens]. The slab flew through the passenger side's open front window. It was her good fortune that the young, mini-skirted occupant of that seat was snuggled against the driver, for otherwise it would have been she, not Susie Deer, who'd be screaming now in frenzied anguish.

The concrete projectile hurtled to the back seat and smashed against the dozing Susie's face, rendering her mouth and nose a bloody pulp.[62]

Susie was rushed to the hospital, where she "half-walked and [was] half-carried into the emergency room."[63] The surgery performed on Ms. Deer was not life-threatening; the physicians—William Schuelte, James Griffin, and William Johnson—"set the broken jawbone, reconstructed her torn and lacerated lips and mouth (restoration of her broken teeth was to come later), and stitched her gashed left cheek."[64]

Also on the scene was Virginia Dwire, who "hovered over the patient, monitoring the liquids flowing through the I.V. tubes inserted in her arms and stabilizing the windpipe supplying air to Susie's lungs."[65]

When Susie's aunt, Diane Cox, asked one of the doctors about her condition, he replied, "She'll be perfectly all right."[66]

As mentioned earlier, "Susie's injuries, grotesque as they seemed, weren't life threatening."[67]

But Susie would not live another day, for something went horribly wrong on Virginia Dwire's part.

Dr. Schuelte directed Mrs. Dwire to remove the breathing tube supplying oxygen to the anesthetized patient's lungs from her nose and insert it into her mouth.

"I watched the procedure," the physician said. "She tried to slip the tube into the girl's mouth and feed oxygen down her lungs two times, maybe more."

As Mrs. Dwire struggled vainly to restore the supply of oxygen to the patient, Dr. Griffin admonished her:

"For God's sake, force air into her. She's showing signs of being starved for oxygen."[68]

Moments later, "the patient had suffocated. 'She stopped breathing,' was how Dr. Schuelte put it. . . . She was pronounced dead on the operating table."[69]

Did Bill Clinton's mother deliberately try to kill the young girl? Of course not. It was obviously an accident due to incompetence or negligence.

But here is where we get down to the nitty gritty "because Susie Deer had been struck by a rock and expired in surgery, the cause of death had to be determined by Dr. Fahmy Malak."[70]

Prior to dying, Susie Deer "was sitting up and chatting before surgery at the Ouachita Memorial Hospital. During the operation, however, Virginia Dwire fumbled the breathing tube with disastrous results. Deer died from lack of oxygen. It was a clear case of medical malpractice, but Fahmy Malak concluded that the patient had died of 'blunt trauma' to the head."[71]

CHAPTER ONE

You read that correctly. Malak "ruled the death a homicide. His autopsy report contained no mention of the difficulties the doctors had reported over the insertion of the breathing tube."[72]

Susie Deer died "during non-critical surgery performed hours after the original injury,"[73] yet the man who threw the chunk of concrete—Billy Ray Washington—"was arrested and charged with homicide. He spent two and a half months in prison for [Virginia Dwire] Kelley's mistake."[74]

While these events were transpiring, Bill Clinton's mother was understandably nervous. She "was also being sued at the time by another family after a young mother had died during minor surgery due to problems relating to her anesthesia. Kelley's drinking problem was well known in Arkansas and was thought to have contributed to her ineptness."[75]

To help her cause, something very peculiar took place. Bill Clinton's mother "was given access to the autopsy report."[76]

The most obvious question was: "what kind of clout did Virginia Dwire have, to be shown a report the State Crime Laboratory does not release to anyone except prosecuting and defense attorneys for evidentiary purposes in homicide trials?"[77]

Incredibly, "permission had to have come from the very top of the State Health Department—the office of the director, Dr. Jocelyn Elders."[78]

She was the same woman who hired Fahmy Malak after his forced resignation, and the woman who Bill Clinton later named Surgeon General of the United States. What resulted from Ms. Elders' actions was clear. "Virginia Dwire was given access to the medical examiner's report so as to allow her to better defend herself against disciplinary procedures by the hospital."[79]

After the smoke cleared, no real consequences befell Bill Clinton's mother. Her "privileges as a nurse at the hospital were revoked, although no one saw fit to tell the public the real reason why the young lady had died."[80]

Up until that point, however, staff at Ouachita Hospital whispered that "she was 'an untouchable,' that she had 'immunity' and couldn't be dumped as the hospital's nurse-anesthetist [at a salary reported to be in the six figures]. Her son was a powerful politician."[81]

With this further information now at hand, a few questions can be answered. First, "why, despite all the controversy around him, was Malak kept in office? Could this be an explanation?"[82]

Fahmy Malak was directly linked with the Clintons in a series of events that had drastic consequences for the politician. The suspicions about Bill's mother were confirmed in 1992 when NBC's *Dateline* interviewed Jesse Chandler—a former top aide to Dr. Malak that investigated the Susie Deer case—who "claimed that Malak had mounted 'a cover-up to protect Clinton's mother.'"[83]

Now is it evident why Fahmy Malak remained so long? Not only did he protect the governor's mother, but he was a ringer for the entire Dixie Mafia. If they needed a case obstructed, Malak was there to do their dirty work.

DAN HARMON

Now that we've traveled along this circuitous route, let's return to the murders of Don Henry and Kevin Ives—the "Boys on the Tracks." Why were these two seemingly innocuous teens so brutally killed in the middle of rural Arkansas? For starters, their "bodies had been found [near] a drug drop location which drug traffickers called 'A-12'."[84]

State police sergeant Barney Phillips confirmed this information in March 1989 when he wrote, "The area where the two boys died is a drop zone for dope coming out of Texas."[85]

Likewise, Jean Duffey, a highly respected prosecutor for the Saline County Drug Task Force, connected the deaths to Arkansas's most infamous criminal operation. She cited a pilot/operative who told her "he had flown the Saline County drop which was known as 'A-12,' and that he took orders from CIA operatives out of Mena."[8]

As you can tell, the rabbit hole is getting deeper, with bought-off Arkansas officials now entering the picture. According to the above-referenced pilot, "then-Sheriff Jim Steed gave protection to drug traffickers, and Roger Clinton and Skeeter Ward, Seth Ward's son, often picked up drug drops in the area."[87]

Richard Garrett told Robert Stack of NBC's *Unsolved Mysteries* that at the time, "Saline County and the central Arkansas area were overrun with drug traffickers—and it was drug trafficking at a high level that extends to other states and other countries."[8]

It all comes back to Mena, CIA drug smuggling, and Iran-Contra. As one video on the subject declared, "Clinton had integrated a number of corrupt cops, judges, and politicians into high-level positions to ensure the continued success of the drug-smuggling and money-laundering operation. All was going well until a fateful night in the fall of 1987."[89]

Russell Welch, a state police investigator, alleged that "higher-ups in the state were linked to a major narcotics trafficking operation,"[90] and if one began "looking through the police files and news clippings, it was evident that the deaths were linked to organized crime, what federal authorities have called the Dixie Mafia. The Dixie Mafia is a loosely knit group of thugs who are found throughout the South."[91]

Another person's testimony which will become important is that of Sharlene Wilson, a woman who—on December 10, 1990—"walked into a U.S. District Court in Little Rock and blurted out in front of an astonished grand jury that she had provided cocaine to Bill Clinton at Le Bistro nightclub during his first term as governor."[92]

She also "testified about seeing Bill Clinton get so high on cocaine he fell into a garbage can."[93]

Wilson was so well acquainted with the Arkansas drug scene that "she had even done a stint for three or four months unloading bags of cocaine at the Mena Airport in the mountains of eastern Arkansas. If there was anybody who knew the business inside out—where the aircraft made their drops at night, who picked up the deliveries, who laundered the money, who ordered the hits—it was Sharlene Wilson."[94]

Wilson also recounted her cocaine days with Roger Clinton

(who played in a rock band, appropriately titled, Dealer's Choice), and Bill Clinton's cocaine use at the Coachman's Inn near Little Rock during the late 1970s. She continued: "I was, you know, the hostess with the mostest, the lady with the snow. I'd serve drinks and lines of cocaine on a glass mirror."

People shared sexual partners in what amounted to a Roman orgy. They were elite gatherings of ten to twenty people, mostly public officials, lawyers, and local notables, cavorting in a labyrinth of interconnected rooms with women that included teenage girls. Bill Clinton was there at least twice, she said, snorting cocaine "quite avidly" with Dan Harmon.[95]

Momentarily, you will discover that Dan Harmon is a central figure in the train track murders, and Sharlene Wilson has stated that she "made her first drug deal by selling an 'eight ball,' or 3.5 grams of cocaine, with Dan Harmon and Roger Clinton at a Little Rock nightclub."[96]

Wilson was also very candid about what took place at Mena. "She used to pick up cocaine deliveries on the railway tracks near the little town of Alexander, thirty miles south of Little Rock. 'Every two weeks, for years, I'd go to the tracks, I'd pick up the package, and I'd deliver it to Dan Harmon, either straight to his house, or at my house.'"[97]

She added, "Roger the Dodger [Clinton] picked it up a few times."[98]

With the names that you've been reading, it's obvious that "despite blatant bungling and cover-up by authorities, the crime [the Boys on the Tracks] would be linked to drugs, the murder of six figures implicated in the first killings, and allegedly to Mena."[99]

Scores of people knew the truth, including one boy's father, Larry Ives. "I think the main reason we didn't get a thorough investigation to start with is that there's a big drug ring operating in Saline County and a lot of people in the know are involved, and they didn't want an investigation because they thought it would mess up their little party."[100]

One of the most intriguing pieces of this puzzle can be found

CHAPTER ONE

in a man named Dan Harmon, who was the prosecuting attorney for Arkansas's 7th judicial district. According to Keith McKaskle, who would eventually wind up on the Clinton Body Count list with a slit throat, Harmon "was one of Saline County's largest suppliers."[101]

Others substantiated this information, such as Pulaski County narcotics investigators who had "begun hearing from informants living near the Saline/Pulaski border that Harmon was buying and selling drugs and providing drug dealers with protection."[102]

Nearly a decade later, Harmon would pay for his crimes (at least *some* of them),

The temblor hit on June 11, 1997 when a Little Rock jury convicted Dan Harmon on five counts of racketeering, extortion and drug dealing. . . . Harmon was one of the commissars who had enforced a politicized criminal justice system during the tenure of Governor Clinton.[103]

Is it just me, or is nearly every single person in Bill Clinton's inner circle associated with drugs in a very big way? Don Tyson, Roger Clinton, Dan Lasater, Jackson Stephens, Dan Harmon, Seth Ward, Finis Shellnut . . . these guys weren't pillars of the community; they were down 'n' dirty mobsters and narcotics traffickers who killed people that got in their way.

Which leads us to the night of the murders: The CIA pilot referred to earlier in this chapter told investigator Jean Duffey that in regard to the 'A-12' drug site, "drop number 46 was a money drop that came up missing. He said the cops in charge of picking up the drop hid out for subsequent drops to see who might steal another drop. [The pilot] said Kevin and Don were in the area of drop number 50 and were ambushed. They were beaten and killed and their bodies were placed on the tracks."[104]

Before continuing, it's important to note that "although [Barry] Seal was assassinated a year before Kevin and Don were murdered, the drug drop they stumbled upon was originally part of Seal's operation."[105]

This point is key because some researchers imply that the

Mena operation died off when Seal was killed; but as can now be seen, it was still very much in operation.

Here's the nitty-gritty. According to Sharlene Wilson, "she had accompanied Dan Harmon and Keith McKaskle to the tracks on the night the boys were killed. She said that two other men had been there, as well, and that all of the men were agitated because there had been a small band of kids that had tried to already rip off the drop. There was supposed to be a drop of three to four pounds of coke and five pounds of weed. Several of the boys had gotten away, but they had caught two—Kevin Ives and Don Henry."[106]

Dr. Joseph Burton, whose opinion we heard earlier, stated, "Don had been stabbed twice in the back, and the back of his head was crushed, with the imprint of a gun butt. Kevin had been severely struck on the side of the head with a heavy blunt instrument—possibly a gun butt."[107]

In addition, an "ambulance crew had reported very dark blood at the scene, indicating the boys had died long before their bodies were found."[108]

Others also stepped forward to present eyewitness testimony. Detective John Brown discovered a teen "who had been out with two friends that night looking for a marijuana patch. The witness had been about sixty feet away, hidden below the bank, watching a group of men talking on the tracks. 'One of them I definitely recognized as Dan Harmon. Then I noticed two more people, Kevin and Don, walking down the railroad tracks.' At first it looked as if Harmon was just talking to the boys, but then a shot rang out. The witness turned and ran."[109]

Sharlene Wilson, a former DEA informant, said that "Dan Harmon, the prosecutor, was present when the boys were killed and that they were killed by police. High-ranking officials were said to be involved."[110]

Wilson continued to fill in blanks about that tragic evening.

> Sharlene was supposed to make the pickup that night but she had been 'highballing' a mixture of

cocaine and crystal and was totally strung out. They [some of the men Harmon had sent to watch the delivery] told her to wait in the car, which was parked off Quarry Road. It was around midnight.

"It was scary. I was high, very high. I was told to sit there and they'd be back. It seemed forever. I heard two trains. Then I heard some screams, loud screams."

When Harmon came back, he jumped in the car and said, 'Let's go.' He was scared. It looked like there was blood all down his legs.

She later learned that a group of boys had been intercepted at the drop site. According to Sharlene, some of them had managed to get away, but Kevin Ives, 17, and Don Henry, 16, were captured. Harmon's men interrogated them as they were lying on the ground, face down, hands tied behind their backs. They were kicked and beaten, and finally executed. One of the boys was stabbed to death with a survival knife. The bodies were wrapped in a tarpaulin, carried to a different spot on the line, and placed across the railway tracks so that the bodies would be mangled by the next train.[111]

There is more testimony linking Dan Harmon to the crime scene. Sharlene Wilson "said her car had been used by Harmon to deliver a green tarp, which was, as she described it, just like the tarp that disappeared from the crime scene."[112]

One other woman, Katherine Brightop, "testified that she was told by her former boyfriend, Paul Criswell, that he, his father Finnis Criswell, [used car dealer Davis] Calloway, and another man whose name she didn't know had carried the boys' bodies to the railroad tracks, covered them partially with a tarp, and left them there."[113]

Lastly, "three men were also reported to have been in a truck near the scene when the ambulance crew showed up. They said they were from the 'Alexander Fire Department.' But, there was no fire department in Alexander."[114]

Now, with this much evidence and testimony, don't you think there was enough information to move forward in arresting and/or convicting the guilty parties? Not in Razorback country. Thankfully for the citizens, "Dan Harmon, the Arkansas investigator who concluded there was no murder, [went to] prison on drug charges."[115]

Similarly, "Bill Clinton played a suspicious role in the cover-up. As governor, Clinton shielded his medical examiner, Fahmy Malak, who remained in office until 1992. As president, Clinton hamstrung the Train Deaths investigation for good [by] ordering the resignation of all ninety-three U.S. attorneys."[116]

Freelance investigative journalist Philip Weiss summed it all up. "There is plenty of evidence of political obstruction of justice in the case, obstruction reaching to state officials. At the very least, Governor Bill Clinton looked the other way. He protected the obstructive; he refused to meet with Linda Ives."[117]

This case was—quite possibly—the most blatant example on record of a concerted effort to obstruct justice in order to protect the Dixie Mafia, "an informal association of white gangsters that constitutes one of the largest, most deadly and least-known gang systems in the United States, blanketing sixteen Southern states."[118]

We aren't merely talking about drug trafficking or money laundering; but murder. "Several witnesses to a local grand jury were rubbed out, and no one was charged in any of the widening circles of violence. It went beyond the county. 'This goes deep,'"[119] one relative said knowingly.

It certainly did, and officials such as Sheriff Judy Pridgen of Saline County knew it. Her words are riveting: "We know where this leads. Do you really want to take down the president [President Clinton] of the United States?"[120]

The stakes were that high, and as a result, drastic action needed to be taken to protect the Clintons. "[Dan] Harmon had prevented the grand jury from calling witnesses. Already, people associated with the case were beginning to die in what amounted to a reign of terror among young people in Alexander, Arkansas."[121]

As a reward for his despicable services, Harmon received a light sentence in what should have been first degree murder charges. Linda Ives—a Benton, Arkansas housewife and mother of one of the murdered boys—was fully aware as to why "the Justice Department's prosecution of Dan Harmon in June 1997 was confined to racketeering when they knew perfectly well—or so she had to assume—that he had murdered her son."[122]

Why was this miscarriage of justice allowed to occur? The answer leads directly to the heart of Arkansas's Dixie Mafia. "Linda Ives, Jean Duffey, and [Saline County detective] John Brown all came to the same conclusion. They were pitted against Dan Lasater—the Dixie Godfather, and the friend of and provider for the Clinton brothers."[123]

DIXIE MAFIA: MURDER, INC.

By 1990, only three years after the murders of Kevin Ives and Don Henry, at least eight people connected to this case died in highly suspicious manners.

"In the summer of 1988, Keith Coney was speeding on his motorcycle down Highway 40 when he crashed into a truck and died. Witnesses said he was being chased. Some police have said that Coney's throat had been cut before he fled on his motorcycle. There was no autopsy and his death was ruled a traffic accident."[124]

"One police officer said that Coney's throat had been cut before he jumped on his motorcycle to evade being killed; that he was chased by another vehicle and passed out from blood loss before running into the truck."[125]

"Coney told his mother he knew too much about the railway deaths and feared for his life. . . . [He] had been with the boys a few hours before their deaths. Linda Ives now believes that they met up again at the tracks. 'I'm sure now that there were three of them out there, at least, and he was one who got away.'"[126]

"Two days before his death, Coney told a friend, Boonie Bearden (who later mysteriously disappeared), that he knew that the police were involved in the death of the boys. Others have testified that Coney was selling drugs for a man who had links to one of the 'Alexander firemen,' the ambulance crew encountered on the night of the deaths."[127]

"Jeff Rhodes, who had information on the Henry/Ives murders—was found with his hands and feet partly sawn off and shot in the head, then thrown in a dumpster and the body burned."[128] "Rhodes' father told the press that his son called him shortly before his death, explaining that he had to go into hiding because he had information about Kevin's and Don's murders, as well as McKaskle's."[129] "His body had been burned so badly investigators at first couldn't determine if it was a man's or woman's body."[130]

"Danny 'Boonie' Boonie Bearden, a friend of the boys, disappeared. His body was never found."[131] "It is rumored he knows exactly what happened at the tracks."[132] "An anonymous caller told police he had been killed. Police found a piece of Bearden's clothing in the Arkansas River in the vicinity of where the caller said he had been murdered. . . . Boonie's officially listed as 'missing.'"[133]

James Milam was found decapitated; nonetheless, the state medical examiner, Fahmy Malak—who also called the Ives-Henry deaths accidental—was declared the death to be of natural causes.[134]

In January 1989, Gregorie 'Fat Greg' Collins, aged 26, was found killed by a shotgun blast to the face, in rural Nevada County. Collins had been subpoenaed to testify before a Saline County grand jury in the Henry and Ives case. He had also joined Boonie Bearden on occasion in burglarizing houses for drug money.[135]

"Keith McKaskle is also said to have had information on the murders. He was found stabbed to death."[136] "McKaskle, manager of The Wagon Wheel—a bar not too far from where the boys were found—was a police informant and had been cooperating with the investigation of the boys' death. He told Kathy Pearson that the prosecuting attorney, Dan Harmon, was involved in drug trafficking; in fact, that Harmon 'was one of our biggest suppliers.' McKaskle was murdered in his garage late one night after returning home. Five men, dressed in black and wearing hoods, stabbed McKaskle—known for his fighting prowess—one hundred thirteen times.... According to several witnesses, McKaskle said weeks before his death that his life was in jeopardy because of his knowledge of the Henry-Ives murders."[137]

Another grand jury witness, Richard Winters, was killed in the summer of 1989. Winters was apparently murdered in a set-up.[138]

"In June of 1990, Jordan Ketelsen allegedly killed himself in his truck using a shotgun. His girlfriend was the only witness. The police did not conduct an investigation of the death despite the fact that Ketelsen was a known drug dealer widely believed to be linked to the murder of Keith McKaskle. No autopsy was conducted, and Ketelsen's body was quickly cremated."[139] "Ketelsen's father, Ron, was a known drug dealer in Benton [Arkansas] at the time of his death. It's also rumored that Jordan had information about the Henry and Ives case."[140]

Of course the Clintons want everyone to believe that these throat slittings, dismemberments, arson, homicides, and "suicides" are all coincidences; not that they had anything whatsoever to do with all of the deceased parties being directly linked to the Boys on the Tracks murders. On top of that, the primary witness—Sharlene Wilson—was locked away in "the Women's Unit of the Arkansas Department of Corrections, where she had been sentenced to 30 years."[141]

If the above murders took place in *your* community, would you think it all just happened by chance? Of course not; but in Arkansas, it's all standard fare.

Try to imagine what horrible human beings would first of all take part in importing millions of dollars of drugs into this country—most of them in an "official" status. These men are crooked, corrupt, and totally devoid of morals. Then, when their little racket is exposed, they first kill two high-school boys; then brutally snuff at least eight others. These are disgusting, vile creatures; and they were all a part of the same Dixie Mafia to which Bill and Hillary belonged. "The deeper the undercover officers looked, the more certain they became that the operation was protected at the highest levels of law enforcement in Saline County, Pulaski County, and Little Rock."[142]

At its most basic level, this entire phenomenon was a direct result of the Dixie Mafia, which is referred to in a book entitled *Gangs USA* as "one of the largest, most deadly gangs in the country."[143]

According to this book, "the gang had its beginnings in bank robberies and interstate theft. As it evolved, the members began using their profits to buy public officials through campaign funding. It wasn't long before the Dixie Mafia moved to drug dealing, which brought money laundering and contract murders."[144]

These killings were a sick aftershock of Mena, which was one of the darkest, most soulless episodes this country has ever had to endure. To bring it all home, "[Bill] Clinton was groomed and brought up the political ladder by the Arkansas good-old-boys. [Political insider Larry Nichols] claims they own him and he does their bidding."[145]

As a result, "That's what you can do when you control every aspect of government in a small pond. That's organized crime. Ask the FBI. The kingpins are absolutely ruthless and unpredictable. They kill people, and nobody can do anything. That's who's running your government right now."[146]

CHAPTER ONE

IRAN-CONTRA BUSTS WIDE OPEN: With the 1986 crash of a C-123 Fairchild cargo plane and the subsequent capture of Eugene Hasenfus, a CIA gun runner, the Nicaraguan government finally had the smoking gun to prove that the United States was arming the Contra rebels seeking to overthrow the Marxist regime of Daniel Ortega. (Hasenfus had worn his parachute that day, disobeying the "no parachute" order for the mission. The two pilots died.) A black book of phone numbers in the wreckage tied the plane to an operation run out of Ilopango Airbase in El Salvador, supported by anti-Castro Cuban exile Felix Rodriguez. Profits from the sale of weapons to Iran were used to partially pay for the operation but a large portion of the funding was generated by the sale of cocaine. Gun runners would drop off their guns and fill up the cargo hold with cocaine. This cocaine was then flown back to several small airports in America, one being Mena, Arkansas. Bill and Hillary were fully aware their state was being used as a mini "narco-republic," but found the hush money they received for allowing such activities came in handy in Bill's election campaigns.

WACO—A MASSACRE OF WITNESSES: Vernon Wayne Howell (a.k.a. David Koresh (1959–1993)) was the leader of a Branch Davidian religious sect in Waco, Texas. He and his followers may have been massacred by order of the Clinton administration to hide their involvement in manufacturing weapons ultimately bound for the Contra rebels in Nicaragua. Despite claims he was molesting children and forcing women in his church to engage in sexual relations with him, a government psychiatrist who interviewed members from the church found there was no evidence to support claims Koresh inappropriately touched any females in his congregation. Most of the claims the public heard about the Branch Davidians were flat-out lies.

CHAPTER TWO

Massacre at Waco

HELL ON EARTH

April 19, 1993 in Waco, Texas has been described by some as hell on Earth. Early that morning, federal agents stormed a religious compound where, subsequently, an enormous inferno broke out, consuming the structure in a fiery blaze. Millions watched live on television as flames engulfed the isolated building. "Eighty-six men, women, and children were killed in the fire."[147]

The horror was unimaginable, for at that moment in time the U.S. government was attacking its own citizens as "FBI tanks went smashing through the walls of Mount Carmel."[148]

The inhabitants at Waco were incinerated, and "the death toll added up to the worst tragedy precipitated by government action on American soil."[149]

Although the mainstream media and White House spokesmen spewed a litany of lies, the reality was far different. "Infants too young to use [gas] masks were subjected to six hours exposure to CS gas, a weapon banned in warfare under the Paris Convention of Chemical Weapons."[150]

The inhabitants were tortured, chemically poisoned, and ultimately murdered in what amounted to a government-sponsored holocaust. "The bodies of most of the women and children were found huddled together in a concrete storage area near the kitchen, where they had apparently been trapped by falling debris."[151]

Blame for this savage attack reached all the way to the upper echelons of the U.S. government, including Bill and Hillary Clinton.

Fifty-one days earlier, another travesty occurred which ignited this gruesome situation. "On Sunday morning, February 28, 1993, about one hundred heavily armed Bureau of Alcohol, Tobacco and Firearms agents (ATF) invaded the residence of a religious group in Waco, Texas, attacking the building with loud shouts as if they were attacking a drug cartel. There were about one hundred people inside the residence, primarily women and children."[152]

Who lived at this rural site? "The religious group resided in a large building on property known as Mount Carmel. Known as the Branch Davidians, they were a relatively peaceful group, harming no one, wanting to be left alone. As is common in Texas, and to earn extra money, the group frequented gun sales and had accumulated a large cache of various types of weapons."[153]

[By the way, such commerce was, and still is, legal under the Second Amendment of our Constitution.]

When government forces storm-trooped Mount Carmel "to serve the warrants, the ATF arrived at the Branch Davidian compound with truckloads of heavily armed agents and helicopter backup. The government agents, according to the *Waco Tribune-Herald*, 'leaped out of the cattle trucks, throwing concussion grenades and screaming, "Come out!"'"[154]

As their invasion began, "Wayne Martin, a Harvard-trained attorney who belonged to Koresh's group, called 911 from inside the compound for help: 'There's 75 men around our building and they're shooting at us! Tell 'em there's women and children in here and to call it off!' Martin asked the police at least 25 times to stop the ATF attacks."[155]

But nothing could impede their bloodlust at that point. "The search warrant was served by a virtual army of more than 100 heavily armed men clad in body armor, breaking windows and kicking down doors. The Gestapo-like approach to serving a search warrant was likely to trigger a defensive response, even if the agents were wearing shirts that said ATF."[156]

A gunfight ensued, and "in the initial raid, four ATF agents were killed and twenty wounded, while six Branch Davidians were fa-

CHAPTER TWO

tally shot, with four others wounded [including David Koresh]."[157]

After the initial onslaught, "the BATF initiated a siege of the Mount Carmel compound that lasted fifty-one days."[158]

Although the raid, siege, and apocalyptic nightmare inferno were bad enough, the truth about this event was not provided to the American people. Within these pages, I will relate what *actually* took place in Waco, concluding with an analysis of an excellent documentary entitled *Waco: A New Revelation*.

To begin, we must ask: why would the ATF engage in such a reckless escapade when all they seemingly wanted to do was serve a warrant to David Koresh? Below are a few of the circumstances which allegedly led to this disastrous event.

1) Prior to the Waco assault, female ATF agents "claimed they were sexually harassed by male colleagues,"[159] creating a public relations disaster for the agency.

2) These charges were further magnified when *60 Minutes* did a damning expose on them.[160]

3) The raid "occurred just days prior to an annual appropriations hearing that would be crucial to determining the agency's budget—a well-executed raid could only have enhanced the agency's prospects for funding."[161]

As you'll discover near the end of this chapter, however, these explanations pale in comparison to the real reason for the raid. But for the time being, let's examine a few of the inflammatory lies told by the government, as well as a very intriguing Clinton Body Count anomaly. One writer has even gone so far as to declare, "Every salient fact put forward by the Clinton administration about Waco is a lie."[162]

The primary form of propaganda pounded into the public mindset was that David Koresh was sexually abusing children inside his home. Janet Reno, the newly appointed Attorney General, even went so far as to say "that the Branch Davidians were beating babies inside the compound."[163]

But are these statements true?

Dr. Bruce D. Perry, chief of psychiatry at Texas Children's Hospital and associated with the Baylor College of Medicine, who had examined girls who had been released between the ATF raid in February and the April 19 FBI assault, found no evidence that Koresh had sexual intercourse with children or even young women.[164]

The day after the raid, [FBI Director William] Sessions appeared on national television and explained that there had been "no direct evidence of contemporaneous child abuse" at the compound, all of which was true if FBI intelligence is accurate.[165]

After the ATF raid, "the Department of Justice issued a 'clarification' stating that in fact they had no evidence of child abuse during the fifty-one day siege.[166]

"Texas Children's Protective Services thoroughly investigated the child abuse charges in 1992 and dismissed them for lack of evidence."[167]

Their director, Bob Boyd, said that after the ATF raid, the children who left the compound were "healthy, happy, and cared for."[168]

The children at Waco were not beaten, sexually abused, or mistreated. Yet again the Clintons lied; and, in all honesty, it seems they rarely—if ever—tell the truth about anything. They're habitual liars. Even if the children had been traumatized, "child abuse is not a federal offense. If it were, it would not fall within the jurisdiction of the Bureau of Alcohol, Tobacco and Firearms."[169]

So, why did the ATF pull a blitzkrieg on the Branch Davidians at Mount Carmel? A second excuse they gave was that there were firearms housed at their compound; but as I mentioned earlier, David Koresh and his counterparts were well within their Second Amendment rights to possess these weapons. Now, there *was* something fishy taking place at Mount Carmel that involved weapons (think Iran-Contra); but that issue will not be addressed until later in this chapter.

Rather, since the Clinton Body Count is the premise of this volume, let's focus on the four federal agents whom were killed during the initial ATF raid on Mount Carmel in February, 1993. For starters, "all four had been hand-picked to serve in Bill Clinton's security detail during his 1992 presidential campaign."[170]

Then, even more coincidentally, "between the fall 1992 election and early 1993, the four were transferred from that Secret Service detail to regular ATF field service."[171] Even more amazing was that they were "hand-picked for the Waco raid."[172]

Here is where the matter turns truly bizarre. The American Justice Federation possessed a videotape of the first Waco raid taken from a hidden camera. It showed:

> [F]our government agents climbing a roof. Three of the four enter the compound through a window. The fourth agent, after waiting until the others are inside, throws what appears to be a grenade into the window. He also fires his weapon in their direction. The three agents who entered the compound were listed among the four ATF agents who died as a result of the raid. They were not killed by the Davidians in self-defense. They were murdered and it was an obvious set-up."[173]

"The alleged former bodyguards were actually killed by a fourth ATF agent, either deliberately or with reckless application of the 'spray and pray' method of gunfire used after the three had entered a roof-top window."[174]

Further, "combine that statement with the video showing the three ATF agents . . . climbing into Koresh's bedroom, and then, after the three have entered, the fourth agent who had been posing as a lookout, suddenly starts firing IN—yes IN—to the room where the three agents have entered."[175]

Think about it: What did the three agents have in common?

They all had been recently transferred to that same Bureau of Alcohol, Tobacco and Firearms unit. They all, coincidentally, drew the same unfortunate assignment of climbing through the window (no other agents took that particular entrance).

They were all murdered under the same circumstances.

And all three had been Clinton bodyguards during the 1992 presidential election.[176]

POLICE STATE

The most pressing question at this point is: "What, if anything, did [agents] McKeehan, LeBleu, Willis, and Williams know about Bill Clinton? Why were they the only ones to die in the ATF raid?"[177]

These men were forced to take their secrets to the grave, but a flow of clandestine information was certainly available to the ATF before they ever made a move on the Davidians. The source was an informant whose role we'll address in a moment. But by having a mole inside Mount Carmel, the authorities knew a few key details, such as the fact that there would be little resistance from Koresh and his followers if they executed their initial raid on February 28 because "most of the Davidians' guns were packed up in boxes in preparation for a gun show in Austin [the following day]."[178]

This information is confirmed by another source. "The ATF went ahead with the raid on February 28 [because] they knew that most of the arsenal (a licensed gun shop, by the way) had been taken to Austin for a gun show that morning."[179]

The inhabitants were essentially defenseless because "according to the affidavit filed supporting the search warrant, ATF knew nearly all the guns in the compound were locked up and only Koresh had the key."[180]

The ATF source inside Mount Carmel was forty-two year old Special Agent Robert Rodriguez, who had showed up about ten days prior to the raid "for target practice on the makeshift rifle range in back of the house."[181]

Amazingly, the ATF wasn't too bright in regard to their informant because the gun he brought to the compound was an AR-15 sniper rifle. According to David Koresh, Gonzalez was no rank amateur, and he knew it. "There's one thing you can never fake," he said. "Experience. You can never act like you don't know how to drive a car when you do."

Gonzalez acted as if his weapon were a new toy. "He's talking about how he just bought this, you know, AR-15 and all that, and anyway, it's a one and seven twist, which is a military spec twist, you know," Koresh said. "It's for the stabilization of tracers, the higher grains. And the thing is—the thing had a trigger job on it. The pull on it, it was probably, probably about—at the, at the max, a pound and a half, maybe two pounds at the max. You know, a good four pounds is considered good for ARs [automatic rifles]. I took it and I was plucking these little stones off, you know, just right off the iron-sights. And he says, 'Well, what do you think about it, you know, Dave?' And I said, you know, in your line of work, this is a sniper rifle."[182]

Gonzalez' status as a rat wasn't the only indication that authorities had targeted the Branch Davidians long before the February raid. Nearly a year earlier, "in March 1992, neighbors had watched men dressed in SWAT team uniforms practicing forced entries at a rural house nearby. A few months later, they spotted lawmen setting up a surveillance camera—an ATF 'pole camera'—to watch Mount Carmel."[183]

Additionally, "a couple of Koresh's followers had seen two mysterious men in white medical smocks standing on the property of an adjoining ranch, fiddling with beepers on their belts. When two men from Mount Carmel approached them, the pair turned, ran back to their car, and sped off."[184]

As time went by, the surveillance increased dramatically in Waco. "During the summer of 1992, helicopters had flown low over Mount Carmel, apparently taking photographs; the 'copters had returned again in late fall. In the weeks preceding February 28 [1993], they'd seem to always be in the sky. Residents of Mount Carmel had noted low-level overflights on December 16, January 6 and 14, and on February 3, 18, and 25. On January 27, a long-haired unkempt young man—an ATF agent—came to Mount Carmel in the guise of a UPS delivery assistant. He had shown up asking to use the bathroom at Mount Carmel, and had aroused the suspicions of David Jones. Jones had given him a roll of toilet paper and sent him to use the men's outhouse; then he'd talked over his suspicions with Koresh, who called the sheriff's office to ask why it was sending people to spy on him."[185]

Despite being under their watchful eye, the local authorities never tried to arrest David Koresh. They easily "could have served the warrant to Koresh when he was away from the compound, perhaps while he visited his favorite hangout, the local Pizza Hut,"[186] when he went to the post office in Waco, or took his daily jog. Koresh wasn't hiding, he wasn't on the run, and he wasn't using a fake identity. Rather, he was completely out in the open. Moreover, Koresh was no angel, and "in the past [he] had peacefully submitted to warrants when approached in a normal fashion, without an attack force of a hundred heavily armed men breaking into his home while helicopters hovered overhead."[187]

Obviously, the ATF didn't want to peacefully apprehend Koresh or serve him a warrant in a responsible way; they wanted a confrontation, and the 'sinful messiah,' as the local media labeled him, had a bull's eye plastered on his chest. In other words, when they raided Koresh's compound, their primary purpose wasn't to serve a warrant; they wanted the leader killed in the guise of a gun battle which they would naturally blame on him. The only problem was: the ATF couldn't keep their mouths shut. For starters, knowing that they were intent on seeing bloodshed, the ATF contacted a local ambulance who "knew when the raid would take place. An ambulance service employee [then] tipped KWTX-TV, who sent a reporter and a camera crew to cover the raid."[188]

Ironically, a fateful turn of events allowed the Davidians to know precisely when the ATF was about to strike. "At 7:00 am, on Sunday, February 28 cameraman Jim Peeler was roaming the countryside, looking for the huge Mount Carmel compound. Peeler claims to have become lost and at 8:00 used a cellular telephone to call in for directions. Incredibly, he claims to have gotten lost again and happened upon a mail carrier, who politely gave him directions."[189]

Here's the twist. "As soon as the camera truck pulled away, the mail carrier, a Branch Davidian named David Jones, sped back to the compound and alerted Koresh. The Davidians were thus armed and ready when the ATF teams arrived."[190]

If it weren't for this tip, it's almost certain that Koresh would have been murdered that morning by ATF agents.

If that wasn't enough, "the ATF had leaked the story to local television stations, who the ATF invited to videotape its original assault."[191]

I guess when bullies flex their muscles; they want the lights and cameras there to catch all the glory.

By this time, secret agent Rodriguez's cover had been blown. Rodriguez swore under oath that Koresh "turned and told me the ATF and the National Guard were coming."[192]

Now, let's pause for a moment and analyze the situation. David Koresh was portrayed in the media and by the government as a gun-nut, religious fanatic, and terrorist; yet when he discovered that the ATF had sent yet another mole into his midst and that they were prepared to invade his home, what did he do? Kill the agent? Shoot him in cold-blood like the ATF did to him and others only a few hours later? No, Koresh approached Gonzales and said, "It's up to you now . . . we know they're coming."[193]

But there was no murder or bloodshed. Instead, "Koresh wished him [Rodriguez] good luck as he walked out the door."[194]

The ATF agent was an infiltrator, a betrayer of the Davidians' trust, yet Koresh didn't act like a psychopath. He knew the government was going to strike, yet he bid a peaceful farewell to the informant. After his departure, "Rodriguez rushed back to the undercover house across the road and informed James Cavanaugh, ATF's deputy tactical coordinator for the ATF operation, that Koresh knew they were coming. Apparently unfazed by the news, Cavanaugh asked Rodriguez only whether he had seen any guns. When Rodriguez said he hadn't, Cavanaugh told him to report the news to Chuck Sarabyn, the tactical coordinator for 'Showtime.'"[195]

Koresh and his counterparts didn't intend to assault government forces; it was the other way around. "If the Davidians had really been planning to ambush the raiders, the Branch Davidian gunners would have deployed in such a way as to be able to direct fire on the vehicles, annihilating the attacking force before it could exit the trailers. As an attorney for the Branch Davidians later put it, 'If the Branch Davidians intended to ambush those people with .50 caliber machine guns and they came up in unprotected cattle cars with nothing but tarps on them, they would have blown them away.' The FBI's Waco commander, Jeffrey Jamar, told a reviewer from the Department of Justice that the Branch Davidians 'could have easily killed all of those agents before they even got out of the cattle cars with the kind of weapons they had.'"[196]

But they didn't.

On the other hand, how did the government act? They sent "Bradley M-728 combat engineering vehicles (tanks) to punch holes in the walls of the buildings in which the Davidians lived, and to pump poisonous tear gas into their homes at 15 second intervals, while FBI loudspeakers proclaimed, 'This is not an assault.'"[197]

While the 51-day siege was under way, the FBI "pumped loudspeakers with sounds of dental drills and screaming rabbits being slaughtered"[198] at their compound. "Federal agents ordered electricity cut off to the compound"[199] and "turned off the community's water supply and cut off its sewers."[200]

To prevent them from sleeping, the FBI "blasted him [Koresh] and the other members of his community with ear-shattering noise and aimed powerful electronic spotlights into their windows at night."[201]

Here is how bad it got. "Among the items blasted on the loudspeakers were the sounds of dentists' drills, locomotives, helicopters hovering, loud obnoxious music, Tibetan Buddhist chants, previously recorded negotiations, squawking birds, cows mooing, clocks ticking, telephone busy signals, the cries of rabbits being killed, and the song *These Boots Are Made for Walking*, hinting that they would be burned and stomped on."[202]

This particular last entry—the song *These Boots Are Made for Walking*—is especially sinister because of the following lyrics, which were prophetic of what the government intended to do: "You keep playin' where you shouldn't be playin'; And you keep sayin' that you'll never get burned; Hah! Well, I just got me a brand new box of matches!"²⁰³

As we all know, shortly thereafter, the Davidian compound was set ablaze.

After word of their tactics got out, a magazine editor wrote, "For the first time in history, a president attacked American children with tanks and got away with it,"²⁰⁴ while Larry McMurtry, author of the bestseller *Lonesome Dove*, said with disgust, "The most Orwellian aspect of the final day was the FBI's attempt to convince the Branch Davidians that they weren't under assault, even as tanks were knocking the compound to splinters and pumping in the gas."²⁰⁵

Columnist R. W. Bradford labeled the phenomenon, "mass murder, American style,"²⁰⁶ after concluding "Janet Reno, the nation's top law enforcement agent, is a mass murderer."²⁰⁷

Even jurors who sat on the Branch Davidian trial were appalled. Jury foreman Sarah Bain commented, "The federal government was absolutely out of control here. We spoke in the jury room about the fact that the wrong people were on trial, that it should have been the ones who planned the raid and orchestrated it and insisted on carrying out this plan that should have been on trial."²⁰⁸

These words are powerful, but certainly well justified when taken in the context of how many children (let alone adults) were massacred inside that compound. "Over 200 tear gas canisters were thrown into the building,"²⁰⁹ but "the FBI did not use what is commonly referred to as tear gas, technically known as chlorodcetophenome, abbreviated CN. It used something much more powerful: a white powder, technically known as o-chlorobenzylidene malonitrile, more commonly known as CS. CS is described by *The Hazardous Chemicals Desk Reference* as 'moderately toxic by inhalation' when dispersed into the air. Within seconds, it incapacitates its victims, causing extreme burning, tearing, coughing, difficulty in breathing and chest tightness, blindness, dizziness, vomiting, and nausea."²¹⁰

This substance is so lethal that "the manual used by the U.S.

Army for training military police sternly warns: CS gas projectiles are not designed for the direct introduction of a crowd control agent into barricaded buildings. Do not use around places where innocent persons may be affected. Do not use where fires may start or asphyxiation may occur."[211]

Yet scores of innocent children were inside the Mount Carmel compound without electricity or water and the FBI's "tanks [at 6:04 am] began punching holes in the house and inserting CS gas. Within thirty minutes, a white flag appeared waving outside a window of the compound."[212]

But by this point the FBI was intent on murder. Incidentally, "CS gas is banned under the Paris chemical weapons convention, under which the United States is a party as of January 1993."[213]

Also, "over [FBI Director William] Sessions' objections, [Janet] Reno had given orders to storm the compound with Abrams M1-A1 tanks using CS gas."[214]

A white flag from the Branch Davidians didn't stop Bill Clinton's storm-trooper onslaught, for "FBI tanks inserted more CS gas while FBI marksmen fired canisters of tear gas into the compound."[215]

At 9:55 am, "a government tank rammed through the front door,"[216] then "at 11:47 am, another tank assault was launched. Minutes later, fire burst out and spread quickly."[217]

Meanwhile, as the Davidian house was being incinerated in a blatant act of government-sponsored arson, they were also taunting its leader.

"A loudspeaker blared, 'David, you have had your fifteen minutes of fame. Vernon [Koresh's given name] is no longer the messiah. Leave the building now. You are under arrest. The standoff is over.'"[218]

As you will soon see in my overview of *Waco: A New Revelation*, it was not an option for the Davidians to leave their structure, for they were being shot at by FBI and Delta Force agents when they did so. "Federal officials stated many of the bodies had bullet holes in them."[219]

HILLARY CLINTON: BABY KILLER

With the possibility of residents *inside* the compound being shot by federal agents, the labyrinth of deception and official criminal action gets even murkier. The obvious question is: who was ultimately responsible for this outrageous slaughter? Rather than merely being a local issue in rural Texas, the ATF became involved. Then, after the initial shootout, "the FBI and the Department of Justice took control of the operation from the Department of Treasury's ATF. This transfer of responsibility put Attorney General Janet Reno in direct control of the Waco operation."[220]

Here's the enigma, and the real shame. Although Janet Reno was the U.S. Attorney General who was supposedly in charge of the Waco operation, her actions seem strangely inexplicable. As an inferno was blazing in Waco, Texas on the morning of April 19, 1993, "nearly five hours into the operation, which was escalating by the minute, Reno left the command post in Washington to keep a speaking engagement at a conference in Boston."[221]

That's like a Navy commander going to a luncheon during the attack on Pearl Harbor. It doesn't happen. Although Reno appeared peculiarly uninterested, there were others in D.C. who had their eyes focused on Waco; namely the Clintons. For starters, Bill Clinton sent one of his closest associates to Texas for two days before the initial raid even took place.

At the time of the February 28 raid on Mount Carmel, Bill Clinton's close friend, Roger Altman, was deputy Treasury Secretary and was instructed to ensure that things went smoothly when the warrants were served on the Davidians. Altman even made a special trip to Waco, in furtherance of his duties, after a briefing on February 26.[222]

Why, one wonders, was somebody in the Treasury Department dispatched all the way to Texas to oversee what appeared to be a simple case of either child abuse, or a weapons violation? Since when do the Feds get involved in such seemingly "localized" matters? Or, was something much more damning involved; something that directly affected the Clintons and their superiors?

Even though the Branch Davidian compound was located on the outskirts of Waco, Texas, other agents from neighboring cities and states also became involved. For instance, in the following passage, notice how the Koresh raid was being planned by the ATF *months* in advance—proving that this matter had reached the upper corridors of power way in advance of the now-infamous February, 1993 blitzkrieg.

When the plans for the raid on the compound began to seriously take shape, sometime in December 1992, a meeting was called in Houston by assistant special agent in charge, Chuck Sarabyn. The meeting was attended by Phillip Chojnacki of the Houston office; Ted Royster of the Dallas office; William Buford, resident agent in charge of the Little Rock office and co-team leader of the New Orleans Special Response Team. Three other agents from Albuquerque, Dallas, and New Orleans attended.[223]

Ask yourself: why would somebody from Bill Clinton's Little Rock get involved in what seemed like solely a Texas matter? After all, since when did Texans need anybody else to solve their problems for them? Didn't they have the Texas Rangers down there? Why get Bill Clinton's people involved unless something of great importance was going down? Then, when the day of infamy arrived, "President Clinton sent [Roger] Altman to Waco when the raid took place and had acting U.S. Attorney General Stuart Gerson [Janet Reno's predecessor] contact him to give him an update as the raid progressed. According to Gerson, the White House had expressed an interest in staying informed."[224]

Are we to infer that every single time a warrant was being issued in every small town across the nation for child abuse and/or gun violations, Bill Clinton personally sent his people to keep an eye on the situation and to be personally apprised of it? Such a notion is ludicrous, but Clinton sure as hell was concerned with what was happening in rural Texas. In fact, Attorney General "Gerson advised FBI Director William Sessions of the president's request, early on the morning of the ATF raid. Gerson called Clinton personally at 7:30 am to give him an update, as requested. That was two hours before the ATF attempted to serve warrants on Koresh."[225]

Clinton was so fixated on this unknown guy in Texas named David Koresh that no one had ever heard of that he was getting calls about him before the warrant was even attempted to be served. Don't you think there's something very fishy going on with this situation? "During the raid, Clinton received two calls from White House Communications Director George Stephanopoulos, advising him about what was happening. When the raid was completed, the president was again briefed on what had taken place."[226]

This raid at Waco—on a seemingly obscure religious cult—went all the way to the top. "From the very beginning of the standoff the Justice Department kept the White House informed of events at Waco."[227]

Then, when the ATF's overkill tactics blew up in their faces, the White House became even more involved. After the raids, Attorney General Stuart Gerson met with:

- Webb Hubbell—assistant attorney general
- Bernie Nussbaum—White House counsel
- Bruce Lindsey—presidential advisor
- George Stephanopoulos—communications director
- Mack McLarty—White House chief of staff

That's a pretty impressive lineup for little 'ol Waco, Texas. Then, on April 12, 1993 after Janet Reno became Attorney General, she "had a meeting with Hubbell, Nussbaum, Sessions, and other FBI and White House officials."[228]

That same week, another interesting figure officially entered the loop. "Hubbell attended a meeting at the White House, in Nussbaum's office, to talk more about the plan. Others who attended that meeting were Bruce Lindsey and Vince Foster."[229]

Once Vince Foster enters the picture, you know that another person isn't far behind: Hillary Clinton. Here is where events turn wild. "Appearing on CNN's *Larry King Live*, [Linda] Tripp suggested that [Vince] Foster, at Mrs. Clinton's direction, transmitted the order to move on the Branch Davidians' Waco compound."[230]

Was Hillary Clinton actually behind the Waco massacre? "When asked how the decision to move on Waco was transmitted, [Linda] Tripp said: 'Foster, Mrs. Clinton, [deputy Attorney General] Webb Hubbell, (Attorney General) Janet Reno.'"[231]

This information is substantiated by a man named T. March Bell, a former House Waco investigator. In the film *Waco: A New Revelation*, he states, "We in fact received anonymous phone calls from Justice Department managers and attorneys who believe the pressure was placed on Janet Reno by Webb Hubbell, and pressure that came from the first lady of the United States."[232]

Bell went on to explain: "Mrs. Clinton, Foster, and Hubbell worked together on Waco. . . . [T]here were calls from the first lady and Vince Foster to Hubbell's office during the Waco crisis."[233]

Maybe it's just me, but since when was a first lady directly involved in policy and decision making?

Bell concluded by adding that "Mrs. Clinton grew more and more impatient as the Waco standoff came to dominate the headlines during the early months of the Clinton administration. It was she who pressured a reluctant Janet Reno to act. Reno, on the other hand, was not enthusiastic about launching the assault. 'Give me a reason not to do this,' she is said to have begged aides."[234]

As you can tell, the Waco assault has taken on an entirely new complexion, with yet again Hillary Clinton manning the reins. A perfect illustration of how Hillary reacted with inhuman iciness was described by someone directly on the scene. "[Linda] Tripp said she was with the former deputy White House counsel [Vince Foster] when the news of the Waco assault broke on television. 'A special bulletin came on showing the atrocity at Waco and the children. And his face, his whole body slumped, and his face turned white, and he was absolutely crushed knowing the part he had played. And he played the part at Mrs. Clinton's direction,' charged Tripp. 'Her reaction, on the other hand, was heartless.'"[235]

Obviously, the Waco compound was extremely important to the Clintons. There was only one problem: Hillary's secret police made it nearly impossible for investigators to discover precisely why they placed such emphasis on Waco because three weeks later—after Vince Foster's murder—they stole everything from his office. "We may never know what was on the computer [at Mount Carmel]. Foster's Waco files could tell us, but they ended up in the possession of Mrs. Clinton after his death."[236]

Journalist Ambrose Evans-Pritchard verifies the existence of this top secret data. "Foster kept a Waco file in a locked cabinet that was off limits to everyone, including his secretary."[237]

This event was of such importance to the first lady that Steve Barry, Special Forces expert, stated that "Hillary set up a special 'crisis center' in the White House to deal with Waco. Serving with her in the center was Vince Foster who, according to his widow, was subsequently fueled by horror at the carnage at Waco for which the White House had ultimately been responsible."[238]

FBI & DELTA FORCES

Prior to disclosing the true motive for the government assault on Waco, a few more loose ends need to be tied up. One, as you'll see shortly, is my overview of *Waco: A New Revelation*, which has some gruesome disclosures. "Davidians who had run out of the back of the flaming building—the side not covered by television cameras—had been killed by FBI sniper fire."[239]

This point is crucial because Waco was not a self-induced 'mass suicide' initiated by David Koresh or the Davidians. Rather, it was murder—plain and simple—initiated by the federal government, with Hillary Clinton in control of operations.

Secondly, although the Davidians were charged with the murder of four ATF agents during their initial February raid, another very real possibility exists which contradicts the official story. In a documentary entitled *Waco: the Big Lie*, "video footage of the raid appears to show three ATF agents being killed by 'friendly' fire. We see the agents enter the window, leaving a fourth agent on the roof. He then [throws a grenade and] sprays the wall with machine gun fire. Many believe this was when the three men died, and many think it was deliberate. These three dead agents had all been personal bodyguards of Clinton during the presidential campaign."[240]

Lastly, a third documentary, *Waco: the Rules of Engagement,* includes footage "in which infrared video taken by a surveillance helicopter clearly shows sniper fire, as well as tanks firing incendiary devices into the building."[241]

If anyone watches the three above-listed documentaries, it will become obvious that the Davidians did not set the Mount Carmel fires. Rather, the inferno was deliberately precipitated by FBI helicopters and tanks via incendiary devices that engulfed the compound, which was already a powder keg to start with. Don't believe the lies. Watch the videos with your own eyes and determine the truth for yourself.

As Congressman Jim Traficant said later, "When you have one hundred TV crews but not one fire truck, that's not a well thought out plan. That's box office."[242]

Only "after the fire started, the local fire department was called. When the firefighters did arrive, Jeff Jamar, the FBI person in charge at the scene, wouldn't let the trucks near the burning structure. He explained that it was too dangerous because the Davidians were shooting. FLIR and video tapes showed no evidence of Davidian gunfire, and it would seem quite preposterous to think they had shooting on their minds when they were being engulfed in an inferno. Nevertheless, Jamar was commended for his handling of the matter."[243]

MOTIVE

So, let's get to the bottom of what happened at Waco. "Since it can easily be established that the Davidians did not set themselves on fire, but rather were burnt to death and shot by order of the Clinton administration, the next question is why. What was the motive for this atrocity? The answer is one that boggles the mind. The Waco compound was incinerated—and David Koresh killed—

because it held damning evidence linking it directly to CIA arms-dealing and the operation at Mena. Yes, again the ghost of Mena rears its ugly head. Over the years, "many have said that Mount Carmel was some sort of intelligence front."[244]

In addition, "the minister of a rural Davidian church in Waco [said] that Koresh had worked for the CIA."[245]

Another added element of intrigue is the precise time when the Davidians were initially targeted—prior to Bill Clinton even being nominated as the Democratic candidate for president. That means George Bush Sr. was still in office when Waco appeared on the radar screen as a hot button issue. Still, the question remains: why would the government care about this seemingly obscure cult in Texas? Why did the Clintons exert so much energy—and endure the public relations nightmare—for a rural religious sect?

The investigation of the Branch Davidians actually began in May 1992 when a McLennan County deputy sheriff informed the ATF office in Austin of suspicious UPS deliveries to a Davidian-owned mechanic shop and storage building they called the Mag Bag, located a few miles from the compound. The deputy noted that several shipments of firearms worth more than ten thousand dollars had been delivered to the Mag Bag....

Koresh was also buying powdered aluminum, thousands of 7.62 millimeter rounds for AK-47 semiautomatic rifles, and hundreds of M-16 E-2 conversion kits used to convert the lower receiver housing of semiautomatic Colt AR-15s into fully automatic M-16s.[246]

Are you starting to see where this explanation is going? Think back to Terry Reed and the machine shops he established in Arkansas.

Here's the hook: Koresh used some of the same supply houses that furnished parts to the CIA's arms-smuggling operation in Arkansas in the 1980s. These included Nessard Gun Parts, an Illinois company; Sarco, Inc., a New Jersey company which sold conversion kits in Arkansas and Texas in the 1980s; Olympic Arms, Inc., a Washington retailer; Center Fire Systems of Kentucky; and Shooters Equipment, a South Carolina manufacturer.[247]

On top of that, "some of the kits came from companies operating in Arkansas at the same time the CIA gun-smuggling operation, Centaur Rose, was in full swing."[248]

Further proof can be found in the fact that "the ATF also discovered that the Davidians had bought more than $40,000 worth of arms, including more than a hundred 'upper receivers' for AR-15 rifles. The ATF suspected that the Davidians planned to combine those upper receivers with lower receivers to convert the semiautomatic AR-15 weapons into machine guns."[249]

Was Waco nothing more than a gun manufacturing and/or modification facility for the CIA? Is that why the Clinton administration focused so much energy on it, despite the fiasco that resulted? Was the Mount Carmel compound akin to other clandestine arms plants that worked on the sly for the CIA, such as Seth Ward's POM? And, most importantly, did David Koresh have a falling out with the Agency, such as what happened to Richard Nixon, Manuel Noriega, or Saddam Hussein? After this split-up, or difference of opinions, was Koresh able to link George Bush Sr.'s gun-running directly back to similar operations in Arkansas, all of which were financed by Mena drug smuggling money? Was Koresh getting ready to blow the whistle, and is that why he *had* to be killed and the compound had to be burned—to destroy all the evidence? The possibility that Koresh was supposed to have been killed (instead of simply wounded) in the initial February raid becomes increasingly real the more we learn.

If such conjecture is too far-fetched for you, ask: why did interest in this small, obscure cult reach all the way to the uppermost levels of the Clinton White House, even before warrants were served? Also, why were plans for the invasion already being made when George Bush Sr. was still president? Something very damning was taking place there which—if brought out in the open—would have affected many high-level politicians whose hands were dirty from drug and illegal weapons money. Koresh had to be killed to keep him quiet.

WACO: A NEW REVELATION

In a riveting documentary—*Waco: A New Revelation*[250]—directed by Jason Van Vleet and narrated by seventeen-year FBI veteran Dr. Frederic Whitehurst; Special Forces, FBI, and former CIA operatives step forward in a bold way to proclaim that the government's story about Waco is simply not believable, and that the American people have not been told the entire truth. Below is a list of anomalies, inconsistencies, observations, and previously undisclosed facts that went unreported in the mainstream media interwoven with outside source material which verifies the above-mentioned documentary.

The initial Waco raid was the largest shootout in American law enforcement history, and it was initiated by the United States government. Attorney Jack Zimmerman, who visited Mount Carmel during the siege, later testified, "It was very compelling that the ATF fired first.... I saw the bullet holes in the front door. Almost every bullet hole was an incoming round, and what I mean by that, it is a metal door. You could easily tell that the bullets were incoming rounds: they were punched in."[251]

A recorded 911 call between two Davidian members and Lt. Larry Lynch confirms that government forces initiated the raid.

> **Wayne Martin:** Another chopper with more people; more guns going off. They're firing. That's them, not us.
>
> **Steve Schneider:** There's a chopper with more of them.
>
> **Lieutenant Lynch:** What?
>
> **Schneider:** Another chopper with more people and more guns going off. Here they come!
>
> **Lynch:** All right, Wayne, tell ...
>
> **Schneider:** We're not firing. That's not us. That's them!
>
> **Lynch:** All right. Stand by. I'm tryin' to reach 'em. Stand. Don't return fire, okay.[252]

According to the ATF, they had three or four video cameras pointed at the Mount Carmel front door to record their raid. But, when events didn't turn out as expected, they claimed that none of the cameras could be found—they all vanished. Likewise, their on-site log books either disappeared or had pages ripped out of them.

David Koresh went into Waco nearly every single day to run errands or to jog. He could have been peacefully arrested or served a warrant at any time, but instead the government opted for a massive attack. "Logs kept at the undercover [ATF] house showed that Koresh had left Mt. Carmel on January 28. During the San Antonio trial, defense lawyers called to the stand an auto machine shop operator who brought signed invoices showing that Koresh had been in his place of business on January 29. A rustic character named Tommy Spangler testified that Koresh had come to the junkyard where he worked on February 24, just four days prior to the raid."[253]

When ATF agents attempted to serve a warrant to Koresh, they didn't use a bullhorn, nor did they try to notify Koresh beforehand with a knock at the door. The following testimony transpired at the Davidians' San Antonio trial between defense attorney Dan Cogdell and a Special Agent King:

> **Cogdell:** If David Koresh had welcomed the front door team that wouldn't have changed anything about your mission and tactics? You still would have thrown in flash-bang grenades and completed your "dynamic entry"?
>
> **King:** That is correct.[254]

What many people have asked over the years is: why weren't the Texas Rangers, the Texas State Police, or even the local Waco Police Department used to serve this warrant? It's their jurisdiction. Why the ATF—a federal agency? In addition, consider how the compound was approached. "The ATF agents arrived in their cattle trailers, screaming like Marines storming a beach, not identifying themselves or asserting a search or arrest. Koresh opened the door and told them, 'Get back! There's women and children here. Get back. I want to talk.' Then, according to Koresh, he was shot immediately, barely getting out that last word, along with his father-in-law, Perry Jones, who died from his wounds."[255]

After the initial raid, Branch Davidian Michael Dean Schroeder was killed by ATF agents while he was returning home through the woods to the compound. His body was left in a ravine for five days. It had seven bullet holes in it, two behind the ear at point-blank range. He was murdered, and "there was never any question that he was shot by the [ATF] during the siege. Davidian Michael Schroeder was not attacking anyone. His crime? He had been away at the time of the first raid and was approaching the compound, trying to get in and join his family."[256]

Joyce Sparks of Texas social services stated very plainly that the children who had been released from the compound appeared well cared for, and there were no signs of physical or sexual abuse.

During the 51-day standoff, an FBI negotiator told Branch Davidian representative Steve Schneider that "no one was authorized to come out of the compound for any reason or they would be dealt with in a severe manner." The implication was that the government wanted the Branch Davidians dead inside and unable to speak with the press. During negotiations, it was made clear that Koresh and his cohorts were willing to negotiate. According to spokesman Steve Schneider, "a lot of people would be willing to come out if led by an intermediary, such as talk show host Ron Engleman."[257]

There was also another option. Defense Attorney Dick DeGuerin stated, "Koresh told him that he would surrender to the Texas Rangers. The Rangers said they would accept such a surrender if DeGuerin arranged it with the FBI. But, as usual, the FBI rejected any such third-party efforts, no matter how credible or promising."[258]

The FBI wanted so little to do with any type of outside party getting involved that "after KRLD radio host Ron Engleman began broadcasting sympathetic coverage of the Branch Davidians, FBI Special Agent in Charge Jeff Jamar pointedly reminded KRLD management that the Federal Communications Commission licenses radio stations. So, FBI Commander Jeff Jamar manipulated media coverage by threatening the radio station with the removal of their license."[259]

FBI Director William Sessions requested a flight to Waco where he sought face-to-face discussions with David Koresh. His request was directly impeded by the Justice Department, which refused to let him board a plane.

In March 1993, the FBI cut off all electrical power to the compound. Their water tanks were also shut off.

Waco was the first instance ever in which the U.S. government used tanks against its own citizens.

It was the FBI's position not to do anything that was seen as *provocative* when they unleashed their forces on day 51 of the standoff. Are tanks bashing through the walls of someone's home with their booms not considered provocative?

After the Mount Carmel compound was burnt to the ground, FBI spokesman Bob Ricks stated that his agents did not return any gunfire against the Davidians the entire day. This statement is an unequivocal lie. For starters, Attorney General Janet Reno granted permission to the FBI to return fire. Secondly, the FBI had three "Blue" sniper teams located at positions near the compound named Sierra One, Sierra Two, and Sierra Three. The man in charge of one outpost, Lon Horiuchi, was actually the FBI agent who shot and killed Vicky Weaver at Ruby Ridge while she held her infant child. He was charged with manslaughter, and according to internal law enforcement documents, his deadly shooting of Weaver was called "unconstitutional." Horiuchi is known to have fired shots at the Davidians on April 19, 1993. His role that day was nothing more than a government-hired hit-man.

When autopsies were performed on the Davidians who tried to leave the compound *before* fires broke out, their lungs contained no smoke or soot (i.e. they didn't die from asphyxiation). But they were found to have bullet holes in their hands and torsos. These individuals were shot while leaving the residence. Some people have asked: why didn't the Davidians simply leave on day 51? It's because they were getting shot at by FBI and Delta Force agents, and "autopsies revealed [26 Davidians] had died by gunshot."[260]

In a government videotape of the event, flashes are seen emanating from a helicopter hovering over the compound. Dr. Edward Allard—a video and FLIR image expert—stated that these flashes were machine gun fire at 600 rounds per minute. He further stated that it would be *impossible* for these shots to be sunlight reflections. Also, in this same video footage, a machine gun mounted on a pedestal can be seen in the open doorway of a helicopter as it loomed over the roof at Mount Carmel.

In another government video filmed at the back of the compound away from network cameras, two men are seen dropping out of the escape hatch of a tank, then opening up with automatic gunfire at the compound. Dr. Allard states that there is "nothing in nature that causes thermo flashes to within 1/30th of a second." It's gunfire, plain and simple. Then, after the tank crushes the compound's roof, gunfire is seen in the courtyard emanating from FBI agents. Remember: this video was taken by the government! Lying through his teeth, recently appointed FBI Director Louis Freeh stated, "No shots were fired outside the compound," while the Justice Department deceived the public by saying that this gunfire was merely the "reflected light off of something shiny."

Here are a few words of wisdom: if somebody lies to you, they presume you're stupid. Don't fall for their chicanery any longer. Once again, Dr. Allard refuted their deception by using basic physics: it was *impossible* for the FBI's gunfire to be reflected sunlight. With the government's own footage serving as proof, the ten flashes/second is exactly the same rate as that of machine gunfire. The flashes could have only been caused by gunfire, and since the only people *outside* the rear of the compound were federal agents, where do you think it originated from, and against whom was this gunfire directed? They were killing the Davidians who tried to flee to safety.

The government's FLIR video also revealed that at 12:10 pm, automatic weapons were being fired into the compound at the only exit not on fire. Fifteen people were subsequently found shot to death at this exit. An anonymous FBI agent wishing to protect his identity appeared in this documentary and stated that the Davidians who were shot to death were "clear-cut homicide victims." The government was guilty of murder in the first degree. The government did no ballistics tests whatsoever on any of the weapons possessed by the agents present at Mount Carmel. Zero.

Bodies of the deceased Davidians were stored frozen in trailers for later examination. But, conveniently for the government, somebody cut off the electrical power to these units, so the bodies decayed to the point of being useless as medical samples. In addition, many of the corpses were either bleached or destroyed at the crime scene before being transported off the premises. No evidence, thus no chance to determine foul play.

During testimony, former FBI fire expert Rich Sherrow asked some extremely valid questions of his former employer: why was evidence disappearing; why was the FBI destroying evidence; and why were they tampering with the crime scene?

Texas authorities and U.S. Marshals refused to let the local Waco coroner turn over autopsy evidence from the Waco victims to investigators. The obvious question is: why? What were they hiding, and what evidence was tampered with?

Following the Waco inferno, President Bill Clinton appeared on national television and said that the compound was set ablaze by David Koresh and his followers in a mass suicide. Bill Clinton is a habitual liar, and he lied that day. The residents at Waco desperately wanted to live. Government agents burned them alive in what can be categorized as nothing short of cold-blooded murder.

The FBI originally brought enough CS gas canisters to last (supposedly) for 48 hours. By 10 a.m. on the first morning, they had already depleted their *entire* supply and had to have more canisters

CHAPTER TWO 53

flown in from Houston. As stated earlier, CS gas is much more lethal than standard tear gas.

The FBI gassed the concrete bunker for two hours straight with CS gas. This area (where the women and children congregated) was totally enclosed, and these innocent victims were sprayed at point blank range with no ventilation whatsoever. The inhabitants were thus tortured for upwards of three to four hours. Worse, the filters in their gas masks quit working after awhile and the toxins were like acid or napalm on their flesh. The Davidians' skin began peeling off in whole layers at a time. "Retired Army Colonel Rex Applegate, one of the world's foremost authorities on riot control"[261] is on record as saying, "It is reasonable to assume that individuals in the Waco building were subjected to such CS gas concentrations that they were incapacitated to the point where they were physically unable to exit the gassed areas."[262]

Further proof that federal agents started the Waco inferno came from a government video showing a detonation in the Mount Carmel courtyard, followed by more machine gunfire emanating from the tanks.

April 19, 1993 was the windiest day of the year in Waco, and there is corroborating government videotape proof that accelerants were used at all points where fires broke out. The film footage shows projectiles being shot from the grenade launcher of a tank into the compound. These Mach 651 projectiles used by the FBI are pyrotechnic devices which started the fires. Also, investigators discovered in a Waco evidence locker pyrotechnic rounds that were pulled from the rubble at Mount Carmel which passed through the wooden structure (i.e. they were shot externally through the walls to start the fires).

Additionally, pyrotechnics were found at all points of origin where the fires began. Colonel Jack Frost, an ordnance engineer for the United States Air Force, surmised that these devices could have started the fires at Waco.

Firsthand accounts from a rare survivor of the inferno proved that the women and children were not suicidal. After fleeing to their concrete bunker when the fires began, they doused themselves with water to live longer. The documentary also contends that a deadly explosion occurred at the compound, after which FBI agents entered the compound, shot the residents, and then lit another explosive. Shortly thereafter, a huge hole was blown in the roof. Brigadier General Ben Partin, a military explosives expert, said without hesitation that a "demolition charge went off in the roof." The result, as can be seen from the government's footage, is the detonation of a high explosive through the roof. The walls of this bunker were constructed of G-8 concrete (i.e. rebar reinforced). Partin went on to declare that the compound was destroyed by a *shaped charge*. Ask yourself: what are the odds that David Koresh crawled from his residence, hopped inside a helicopter, and then used one of his personal 'shaped charges' to bombard his own house? The probability isn't even remotely conceivable. The only entity capable of dropping shaped charges through that roof was the federal government.

Further evidence that there was direct government involvement at the highest levels can be derived from the fact that five days before the Waco showdown, a secret meeting took place between Attorney General Janet Reno and members of Delta Force. U.S. Army Sgt. First Class Steven M. Barry actually said that the official name of this entourage was the Combat Applications Group.

In mid-March 1993, Gene Cullen of the CIA special ops group, revealed that a meeting was held at CIA headquarters in which representatives from Delta Force and the Justice Department discussed their plans for Waco. Although they had first denied it, the government later admitted that, indeed, over ten Delta Force operatives were at Waco inside tanks and at sniper points. In other words, they were not merely advisers, but were instead deployed. This information is confirmed by James B. Francis Jr., an official of the Texas Department of Public Safety, who noted, "There is some evidence that may corroborate the allegation that Delta Force participated in the assault."[263]

The CIA's Gene Cullen elaborated, saying that certain Delta

Force members admitted to not only being deployed, but actually engaged in gunfire against the Davidians. Cullen told the *Dallas Morning News* that "he estimated that up to ten [Delta Force members] were actively involved in the assault."[264]

Lastly, Steven Barry added that Squadron B of Delta Force was there, pulling triggers. Such use of U.S. Army personnel is a crime under the Posse Comitatus Act which forbids military force against U.S. citizens.

Last but not least, on April 14th and 15th a meeting was convened between Bernard Nussbaum, Vince Foster, and Webb Hubbell where they discussed the use of military force at Waco. Vince Foster became the point man for the operation; and once it turned disastrous, he uttered sadly, "the FBI lied to me." In a confidential 302 report, Lisa Foster said that Vince Foster was very troubled by the deaths of dozens of children at Waco, as well he should have been. The cover-up was even more appalling. "Dr. Alan Stone, a Harvard law and psychiatry professor, characterized the Justice Department's self-investigation as a 'total whitewash.' 'The Department,' wrote Stone, 'proclaimed the Waco operation a success even though all the patients died.'"[265]

Please note that all three individuals at the above-mentioned meeting were exceptionally close representatives of Hillary Clinton. Bernard Nussbaum was nicknamed "Hillary's Brain"; Webb Hubbell was her right-hand man/operative at the Rose Law Firm; and Vince Foster was her closest advisor, confidant, and sometime lover. What were they discussing? Answer: the use of military force at Waco. Now, I challenge anyone to convince me that Hillary wasn't directly involved in the brutal, illegal murder of those innocent men, women, and *children* at Waco. This lady is a cold-blooded killer. The government killed children at Ruby Ridge; the government killed children at Waco; and as you'll see shortly, the government killed children inside a day-care center in Oklahoma City.

NOT SO SQUEAKY CLEAN: Vince Foster was a confidant of the Clintons for many years and was up to his neck with their corrupt activities dating back to his Rose Law Firm days, when he may first have fallen in love with Hillary Clinton. Whatever the truth, Vince Foster most assuredly did not commit suicide in Fort Marcy Park, Virginia as federal authorities insist.

CHAPTER THREE

The Murder of Vince Foster

MAINSTREAM MEDIA COWARDICE

"Vince Foster was the highest U.S. government official to meet a violent death since the suicide of Secretary of Defense James Forrestal in 1949 and the tragic assassinations of two members of the Kennedy family."[266] The official story is that Vince Foster was so despondent that he killed himself in a fit of depression. But an unending set of questions—that demand answers—persist. "Was Foster murdered? If he did commit suicide; why? Do the answers lie in what Foster knew about the president and first lady? Were documents hidden or destroyed? Did top officials tell the truth? Was there a conspiracy to obstruct justice? If the Clintons had nothing to hide, why did they so often act like they did?"[267]

After all, "he was Hillary Clinton's closest friend, the one person in the world that she would entrust with the most sensitive problems."[268]

Regrettably, "official" answers were not easily forthcoming because "the Foster case is taboo for American journalists. In private, many concede the official story is unbelievable, but they will not broach it in print."[269]

Other journalists—those who don't bow and cower in the presence of their corporate overlords—realized "that Foster was a man who moved in the shadows."[270]

Because of his enigmatic, man of mystery stature, his death too was shrouded in intrigue with the official explanation being nothing more than a preposterous smokescreen which has become part of our culture's phony consensus reality.

But Vince Foster didn't take his own life. In fact, "this was not a marvelously well-planned fake suicide—if it were not for the president and politics, an average detective would have considered the thought of suicide laughable."[271]

Of course, considering that Hillary Clinton was positioned at the center of the storm, stories emanating from her spin machine changed numerous times in the days following Foster's death.

> 1) In a pronounced shift, statements coming out of the White House no longer praised Foster for his strength or expressed surprise over his suicide. The "Rock of Gibraltar" line was dropped. Instead, top White House personnel started characterizing Foster as confused and overwrought.
>
> 2) White House officials seemed to want to avoid the scrutiny that would follow if it were widely believed that Foster had killed himself due to work-related burdens or troubles.
>
> 3) Eventually, it was decided that "Foster's suicide stemmed from personal depression and personal problems.[272]

Just like that, Vince Foster offed himself not because of anything related to the Clintons, but instead it was solely 'personal' in nature (i.e. Vince's own fault or doing). Bill and Hillary (as well as their power brokers who lurked behind-the-scenes) knew it couldn't be any other way, for "If Foster didn't die the way [Independent Counsel Robert] Fiske said he did; then it is likely the president is somehow involved, and if he is, the democratic process simply can't survive such a disclosure."[273]

That's why the mainstream media had to circle the wagons, close ranks, and float the ludicrous "suicide" story. If they didn't, murder charges would have been leveled straight into the White House's heart, and the power elite who had spent so many years grooming Bill Clinton for his position did not want to see their investment be so readily disposed of.

The murder of Vince Foster equals the bottom dropping out—impeachment, economic panic, a lack of confidence in the very fabric of our government, and a closet full of skeletons opened to the world (i.e. Mena, etc). To ensure that the press corps and U.S. Senate stayed in line (even the "conservatives"), an overriding fear factor was put into full effect. An aide to Senator Jesse Helms said of the cover-up: "Since the Clinton White House was capable of resorting to murder, people were afraid to mount a challenge."[274]

Thankfully, those in the know with the courage to stand up and speak their convictions stated otherwise. James Dale Davidson, co-editor of *Strategic Investments*, mentioned a concept that still haunts the Clintons today. He wrote in October, 1997, "I am convinced that Foster is not alone in meeting an untimely death in recent years. He is probably just one of fifty or more who have been murdered for various reasons during the Clinton administration."[275]

THE ARKANSAS GROUP

Most books or articles debunking the subject of Vince Foster's "suicide" present a plethora of evidence which contradicts the "official" version of events. This information is invaluable, and we'll certainly broach it later, but for the time being I'd like to confront some of the "whys" of Vince Foster's murder, along with the happenings which led to it, especially those involving his Arkansas cohorts.

So, without beating around the bush, why was Vince Foster killed? A slew of individuals in the Clinton inner circle had been imprisoned during the late 1980s and early 90s, or were facing impending legal action. These included Roger Clinton, Dan Lasater, Dan Harmon, Jim and Susan McDougal, Webb Hubbell, and Don Tyson. Hillary Clinton's closest confidant was also in hot water, for if there was ever a protector of secrets, it was he. "Clinton and Foster were on the phone the evening of July 19

[1993] discussing the impending federal investigation. It was no friendly chat. Foster told Clinton in no uncertain terms that he would not destroy evidence; that he was not going to jail to protect the Bill 'n' Hill gang."[276]

These simple yet extremely complex words were the crux of why Vince Foster was snuffed. When one became part of the Arkansas Group, it was expected that they would do anything to protect the Clintons, even go to jail. That understanding was priority number one, and there would be no deviation whatsoever from the plan. If trouble arose, those close to the Clintons were expected to fall on the sword. Once these individuals accepted blame and were severely tarnished in the process, they were left behind like yesterday's garbage. Look at how many people the Clintons have used, abused, discarded, and left lying in ruins over the course of their political careers. Loyalty is only a one-way street; Bill and Hillary must be protected at all costs.

Vince Foster was slaughtered as another sacrificial lamb at the altar because he refused to become the next Clinton jailbird. Sure, he'd been there every step of the way until 1993—through Whitewater, the cattle futures windfall, Mena, ADFA, and Madison Guaranty. But now—only weeks after Waco—Vince was facing a major league hornet's nest, and he knew it. That's why he was getting ready to bail out and blow the whistle. It was either his hide or theirs, and Foster didn't feel like being another scapegoat for the Clintons' sins.

At a dinner engagement a few days prior to his murder, "Foster announced his intention to resign his position as deputy counsel to the president. His family members, however, talked him out of doing it, suggesting that things would get better."[277]

He was serious about protecting his own interests, though, and "the day before his death, Foster had left his office to visit a Washington, D.C. law firm where he engaged the services of two lawyers."[278]

Such a move made the Arkansas Group skittish beyond comprehension, for if Foster talked, their entire house of cards would crumble. All of a sudden, the drug running, money laundering, embezzlement, misappropriation of funds, bribes, kickbacks, cronyism, murder, and tax evasion would spill out into the open.

To prevent such a disaster, the Clinton inner circle began working hard and heavy on their ticking time bomb. Their first course of action was when "[Webster] Hubbell and his wife spent the weekend before Foster's death with Foster and his wife, Lisa, vacationing on the eastern shore of Maryland."[279]

Although Hubbell later related that it was an enjoyable weekend, "Lisa Foster told the Park Police that 'it had not gone particularly well.'"[280]

In fact, it seems that Hubbell actually "tracked them down at the Tidewater Inn, [and] for the rest of the weekend the Fosters were corralled by Hubbell and his friends Harolyn and Mike Cardoza [head of Clinton's legal defense fund]."[281]

Apparently nothing was settled, even though "the Arkansas Group—as the insiders called themselves at the White House—were very interested in the outcome of that weekend, as if something were riding on it."[282]

So much so that "Bruce Lindsey and [an unidentified] Washington lawyer paid a personal visit to Foster."[283]

Still, Foster told them something they didn't want to hear: "he was going to cooperate with the investigation."[284]

Hillary sent in other reinforcements to try to change his mind, for "during the week before his death, Foster had a private dinner with Susan Thomases [a top White House aide]."[285]

Foster appeared to be adamant in his decision. "Marsha Scott, the White House correspondence director and Clinton's ex-girlfriend from the 1960s, had met privately with Foster in his White House office. She told investigators she thought Foster had 'come to a decision.'"[286]

Panicked and running out of time, the big gun was sent in. "Clinton himself called Foster the night before his death, ostensibly inviting Foster to join Bruce Lindsey and Webb Hubbell at the White House residence to watch a movie. (Foster declined.)"[287]

It seems "on July 19, [Clinton] invited Foster to come to the White House to watch a movie with a small group of Arkansans—Clint Eastwood's *In the Line of Fire*, about a Secret Service agent trying to thwart an assassination. Foster, by now joined in Washington by Lisa Foster, begged off, saying he wanted to spend the night at home."[288]

Other authors have confirmed that "Clinton had one last 20-minute conversation with Foster the Monday night before his death."[289]

What did they discuss? "Some in the Clinton inner circle speculated that Bill had said something to Foster, perhaps suggesting that he had to hang tough. That may have tipped Foster over the edge."[290]

Foster wasn't about to be another Clinton fall guy. "One of Foster's last phone conversations on the morning of his death was with Brantley Buck, the Rose Law Firm partner assigned to investigate Webb Hubbell and Park-O-Meter."[291]

As we know from previous volumes, once you start scratching the surface with POM, it isn't long before one uncovers Mena, ADFA money laundering, and the Clintons' ties to George Bush's Iran-Contra drug trafficking. Vince Foster was ready to lay his cards on the table. Obviously, the Clintons weren't accustomed to being fingered for their crimes. Rather, they preferred others to serve as their proxies. A fitting example was Webb Hubbell.

Hillary Clinton suddenly found her billing records for the Rose Law Firm under her bed at the White House. But she only found those records *after* her senior partner at the firm, Webb Hubbell, *agreed to go to jail* rather than testify against the Clintons.[292]

That's the way Bill and Hillary liked it. They relied on their minions to bite the bullet and go down with the ship. But when Bill asked Vince to meet with them and presumably watch a movie, "Foster refused the invitation."[293]

At that moment, Foster was a dead man, for his "rebuff was read by the Arkansas Group as an indication that he was no longer on the team."[294]

CHAPTER THREE

In other words, his usefulness to the Clintons was exhausted and he had become expendable. Case closed.

The only problem was: how could they eighty-six him, especially with his wife Lisa in the picture? Not surprisingly, the Arkansas Group did their duty to save the day. How so, you may wonder? Well, to make it appear as if Vince Foster committed suicide, the killers had to get inside his house to (a) get a gun that he supposedly used to blow his brains out, and (b) create some type of 'suicide' note or handwritten document.

But how could the intruders do that if Mrs. Foster was at home? Enter David Watkins, Hillary's fall guy for the Travelgate fiasco who was eventually fired from the White House for "using government helicopters for joy rides."[295]

After discovering that "Mrs. Foster had lunch that afternoon with Donna McLarty, Mack's wife,"[296] she still needed to remain *incommunicado* for awhile. Lo and behold, "it was revealed during the Senate hearings . . . that Mrs. Foster had been playing tennis with Mrs. David Watkins."[297]

This point is crucial because from the day of Vince Foster's murder onward, Lisa Foster reacted completely out-of-character for the grieving wife of a high-profile, very dramatic 'suicide.' Or, more accurately, forces were set in motion to insure that Lisa Foster adhered to the game plan. For starters, a lawyer named James Hamilton was appointed as Foster's handler. Guess who set these wheels in motion. Hamilton was "hired by Associate Attorney General Webster Hubbell to handle the fallout from the death."[298]

Hamilton was also "a member of the elite, very expensive K Street firm of Swidler and Berlin"[299] who, very conveniently, "had befriended Hillary Clinton and Bernie Nussbaum."[300]

Also of interest, Hamilton had "worked on the Clinton transition team."[301]

Once again, we see Hillary's fingerprints all over an operation. Of course Hillary, always in control, handled the transition details when they moved into the White House, whereupon she worked with James Hamilton. A year later, he was co-opted again to keep

Lisa Foster in her place. By all appearances, Hamilton handled his duties expertly. First of all, "he did not let the Park Police get anywhere near the grieving family. 'We did not interview any of the Foster children. Mr. Hamilton would not make them accessible to us,' said Park Police Captain Charles Hume. This is an astounding comment. Foster's children were grown adults, perfectly able to answer questions by the Park Police. Two of them, Laura and Vince III, accompanied their father to work on the morning of his death. Their insights were critical to the investigation."[302]

But no questions were allowed.

Foster's wife fell into the same category. "Captain Hume then goes on to say that Lisa Foster had obviously been coached. . . . We had a hard time getting started because Hamilton wanted to lay out the ground rules. *Lay out the ground rules?*"[303]

As one investigator commented, "Lisa Foster surrendered herself totally to the political agenda of James Hamilton."[304]

Mrs. Foster even resorted, according to script, to contradicting her own stories. Initially she spoke about the troublesome weekend in Maryland with Webb Hubbell, but then changed course midstream. "Lisa Foster's insistence that her husband had been 'so happy' seemed [to be] forced."[305]

In a sense, Lisa Foster repeated the *Stepford Wife* response of Jackie Kennedy after her husband was murdered in broad daylight; his brains splattered a crimson red across her pink dress. If these killers could commit such grievous acts against their spouses, what would prevent *them* from being offed? Since the Clinton crowd-Dixie Mafia was famous for *Arkancides*, Lisa Foster didn't want her children waking up to read the headline: Despondent Wife Commits Suicide.

Lisa Foster stayed loyal to the Arkansas Group to such an extent that *New Yorker* magazine carried an article in September, 1995 entitled *Life After Vince*. Author Michael Kellett gives an update of what happened post-Vince for Mrs. Foster: "I hope I don't sound like I'm trying to deprecate the level of her [Lisa Foster's] grief or her sincerity, but she has been Clinton's best ally, by far, in this affair. She is engaged to be remarried to a Clinton-appointed Arkansas federal judge. He and his former wife had been friends with the Fosters and attended Vince's funeral. A few months later, his wife died—suddenly—in her sleep. No mention is made of her having been ill."[306]

Could this death have been another Arkancide? The question is valid because those closest to Vince Foster—at least initially—knew without a doubt that he didn't take his own life. Most dramatic of these reactions was that of Webster Hubbell.

Phillip Carroll, described as Vince Foster's mentor and a Rose Law Firm senior partner, "reported that Webster Hubbell, then-Associate Attorney General, telephoned him the night of Foster's death: 'Webb called me at midnight the night it happened. He said: don't believe a word you hear. It was not suicide. It couldn't have been.'"[307]

These words originated from the ultimate Arkansas Group insider—a man in the know. He was telling Foster's mentor that Vince didn't do himself in. It was murder. Hubbell had momentarily strayed from the script, but obviously someone got to him shortly thereafter. "Carroll and Hubbell were thrown together several times the next few days, but Hubbell never voiced his doubts again."[308]

The Arkansas Group closed ranks, with many luminaries making high-profile appearances in the days following Vince's murder. These were the ultimate handlers *paying their respects*, similar to Mob bosses attending the funeral of a rival godfather who they had just whacked. "More people poured into the Foster home: David Gergen, a White House advisor; Vernon Jordan, the Washington lawyer and close friend of the Clintons; [and] Arkansas Senator David Pryor."[309]

Crying crocodile tears, they were laughing inside; they'd covered up another one.

THE ACTUAL MURDERER REVEALED

The keeper of every deep, dark secret; the hidden heart of darkness; the man who knew too much—these are all fitting descriptions for Vince Foster. Even more titillating, the purported highly moral attorney straight out of *To Kill a Mockingbird* was furtively having an affair with the governor of Arkansas's wife, Hillary Clinton.

Still, what did Vince Foster know that merited putting a bullet into his head? If he spoke with government investigators and spilled his guts rather than being placed in a federal penitentiary, what would he tell them? Instead of simply conjecturing on what Vince Foster knew, I'll use a few direct quotes to illustrate how much dirt could have come forward had Foster started to sing.

"The troubled lawyer from Little Rock was not simply the keeper of the Clintons' most sensitive files on Whitewater and other matters, but also a crucial figure in their sub rosa 1992 campaign funding."[310]

"In the Clintons' 1984 and 1985 tax returns, Foster wrote, they took personal interest deductions for debt that should be corporate. If these documents got out, the Clintons could easily have found front-page headlines about not paying their taxes, or worse."[311]

"All three of Clinton's top financial contributors have been implicated with drugs at some level."[312]

There was Don Tyson, Worthen Bank (owned by the Stephens family), and the infamous Dan Lasater. Further, Lasater's top aide was Bill Clinton's director of administration in the White House. A very sticky can of worms, indeed, especially when we consider that "by 1989, Charles Black, the Deputy Prosecutor for Polk County which covers Mena, had collected over 20,000 pages of evidence in his criminal file for Mena."[313]

"Vince Foster served as both Deputy White House Counsel and personal attorney to the Clintons. In these capacities, he was involved in more Clinton controversies than perhaps any other individual aside from Bill and Hillary Rodham Clinton."[314]

Few could dispute that "Foster was totally trusted by the Clintons as the guardian of all their family secrets,"[315] and we haven't even

CHAPTER THREE 67

mentioned his knowledge of Jim McDougal and Madison Guaranty, the trooper allegations of his affair with Hillary, the $100,000 commodities bribe, and ADFA money laundering. Foster knew this couple intimately and his world was crashing down around him. Worse, Hillary looked guiltier every day as scandal surrounded her. Attorney Allan Dershowitz commented on how clients behave:

> In my 30 years as a criminal defense lawyer, I have noticed one general distinction between the actions of innocent and guilty clients. The innocent save every scrap of paper in the hope and expectation that somewhere in the boxes of files, bills, phone logs, and diaries they will find some proof of their innocence; the guilty, on the other hand, destroy as much as they can, in the fear that somewhere the prosecutor will find something incriminating.[316]

Hillary was guilty as sin, and as such she shredded her past with the precision of an exterminator. So did Oliver North, for that matter. Since so many others had already taken the fall, Vince Foster saw the writing on the wall; he had a legal bull's eye painted on his chest. He was expected to be the next to go on trial, bite the bullet, and spend time behind bars—or sing.

There was only one problem. Vince Foster wasn't exactly a choir boy either. In fact, he'd been up to his eyeballs in intrigue and illegal activities for many years. He may have been able to get by unscathed in backward Arkansas, but the heat was closing in once he reached D.C. The first sign of trouble was a *Wall Street Journal* article entitled *Who is Vince Foster?*

The most noticeable drawback to this piece was that it only skimmed the surface and didn't delve into Foster's real shenanigans. On the other hand, a man named James R. Norman wrote a blockbuster column for *Forbes* magazine that was fact checked by the editor and ready for press when it was cancelled at the last minute. It appeared later in the less well-known *Media Bypass*.

What was the establishment press trying to conceal about Mr.

Foster? A good place to start is where Bill Clinton and George Bush first worked together: Iran-Contra. Of course this endeavor—as we have shown—was directly tied to the drug trafficking network in Mena, Arkansas. In a lawsuit brought by Army Special Forces member Bill Tyree, the plaintiff stated that "Vince Foster, a good friend of Governor Bill Clinton, often shuttled vast sums of money around the world that related completely to 'The Enterprise' formed by Oliver North and George Bush."[317]

Tyree also asserted, "Between 1971-72 BCCI was conceived and born primarily as a bank for the U.S. Intelligence Community to go around Congress in funding so-called 'black operations.'"[318]

Obviously, what we're now discussing transcends simple political graft that was performed at a state level. Instead, Vince Foster became involved with the big boys, and in the months leading up to his murder, Foster believed he was a marked man. According to Webb Hubbell, "Foster even believed his phone was tapped."[319]

So, get ready, hold on tight, because this ride is as wild as it gets—the *real* reason Vince Foster was murdered!

Two weeks before his death on July 20, 1993, White House Deputy Counsel Vincent W. Foster went into a deep funk. The official cause of death, given by former Independent Counsel Robert Fiske, Jr. was suicide driven by depression over, among other things, several newspaper editorials. But Vince Foster had a much bigger and darker reason to be seriously burned out. He had just learned he was under investigation for espionage.[320]

Espionage. Spying against the United States government? It's hard to imagine more serious charges. Or, as James Norman asked in the first line of his article: "Was White House Deputy Counsel Vince Foster selling U.S. secrets to Israel? The CIA suspects he was."[321]

Prior to delving into the Mossad's role in this matter, let's step back and examine the events that led up to their involvement. We know that the CIA and NSA were running the Iran-Contra/Mena deals, and that billions of dollars of dirty money had to be laundered. In Arkansas, there is "this company, Systematics, which

CHAPTER THREE

[was] owned by Jackson Stephens of Stephens, Inc."[322]

You remember Stephens, Inc, right—the Arkansas kingmakers? Well, they "had an attorney who was kind of off the record doing work for them, named Vince Foster."[323]

What was his specific role? "Foster was a trusted deal guy for Stephens at the law firm. Although Foster never shows up officially as an attorney of record for Systematics, he was definitely in the loop, basically smoothing out things between Systematics and the NSA, which was the main government agency that was contracting for a lot of this stuff."[324]

I'll provide a fuller description of Systematics in the next few pages, but for the time being, Foster was undoubtedly a man lurking in the darkest of shadows. "Foster is at the Rose Law Firm. Think of him as a high-level marketing guy between Systematics and the NSA. NSA—they have all these spooky contracts that they are trying to find contractors for. Foster would have been a go-between there."[325]

Where Vince is, we know Mrs. Clinton can't be too far behind. "Hillary was actually an attorney of record for Systematics in 1978 when Stephens tried to take over the Financial General Bankshares in Washington. These holding companies later became First American—Clark Clifford, Robert Altman, all that crowd."[326]

These individuals and institutions were instrumental in the operation of one very important rogue financial entity—BCCI. Who, pray tell, was lurking behind the scenes? "Stephens was fronting for the BCCI crowd,"[327] trying to take over banks and install Systematics as its data processor [i.e. money launderer]. All the while, "Hillary represented Systematics in that."[328]

Where these individuals worked also enters the picture. "The Rose Law Firm was reportedly a CIA asset, in which partners included Hillary Clinton, Webster Hubbell, and Vince Foster. Insider reports indicate that Assistant Attorney General Webb Hubbell [was] the real power in the office of U.S. Attorney General, and that Attorney General Janet Reno [was] a front carrying out the dictates of the group from the CIA asset, the Rose Law Firm."[329]

Of course once you start speaking about Arkansas in the 1980s, drugs are always a factor. "Then we have Bill Clinton himself. He was ensnared by CIA arms and drug traffic by protecting this large operation that existed at Mena Airport, plus his connections with scandal-plagued financier Stephens. What a team!"[330]

The entire picture is now coming into focus. "The key player in the Rose Law Firm money laundering was allegedly Vince Foster. Working as a cut-out under Hillary Clinton and Webster Hubbell, Foster worked through an off-shoot company called Systematics, Inc., allegedly to wire transfer deposits to various small banks around the country, then to a larger bank in Chicago. The funds were then transferred to offshore accounts in the Cayman Islands and Switzerland. At this time Foster allegedly set up a personal numbered Swiss account to handle his 'cut.'"[331]

All of a sudden, Vince doesn't appear to be so squeaky clean, does he? "Since at least the late 1970s, Foster had been a silent, behind-the-scenes overseer on behalf of the NSA for a small Little Rock, Arkansas bank data processing company. Its name was Systematics Inc., launched in 1967 and funded and controlled for most of its life by Arkansas billionaire Jackson Stephens, a 1946 Naval Academy graduate along with Jimmy Carter. Foster was one of Stephens' trusted deal makers at the Rose Law Firm, where he was partner with Hillary Rodham Clinton, Webster Hubbell and William Kennedy (whose father was a Systematics director). Hubbell also played an overseer role at Systematics for the NSA for some years according to intelligence sources."[332]

What role did BCCI-scoundrel Jackson Stephens' company play in this puzzle? "Systematics has had close ties to the NSA and CIA ever since its founding, sources say, as a money-shuffler for covert operations. It is no secret that there were billions of dollars moving around in 'black' accounts—from buying and selling arms to the Contras, Iran, Iraq, Angola, and other countries to paying for CIA operations and laundering money from clandestine drug dealing. Having taken over the computer rooms in scores of small U.S. banks as an 'outsourced' supplier of data processing, Systematics

CHAPTER THREE

was in a unique position to manage that covert money flow."[333]

Systematics was the cyber-money launderer that, at least partially, kept funds flowing through the network. "One man who uncovered the link between Systematics, Foster and covert money movements from arms and drugs was Bob Bickel, who was an undercover Customs investigator in the 1980s. 'We found Systematics was often a conduit for the funds' in arms and drug transactions, says Bickel. 'They were the money changers.' His story is corroborated by a former CIA employee who says it was well known within the Agency in the late 1970s that Foster was involved with Systematics in covert money management."[334]

Due to his highly valued role, "When Bill Clinton went to Washington as President he took Foster and several other associates with him. Foster was named liaison to NSA—a remarkable feat since few of Clinton's staff members could reportedly pass a security background check and therefore receive a security clearance."[335]

So, the Arkansas drug and money laundering network moved from Little Rock to D.C., with Vince Foster holding a key role in the operation. But here's where they hit a snag. Being that Hillary Clinton was never seen as a friend of Israel, and since she was the hands-on manager of personnel, policy, and direction, Israel got worried. To keep Hillary in line, they needed potential information by which to blackmail her. "In Arkansas, the Mossad is said to have found out about Vince Foster's payoff role in the drugs-and-guns-and-money Mena operation, and so the Israelis blackmailed Foster for information on other FOBs (Friends of Bill Clinton—who by this time had made it to the White House)."[336]

The rabbit hole gets deeper. "Sometime in the early '80s, he [Foster] developed this relationship with the State of Israel. In fact, some of the same handlers were involved in the Jonathan Pollard case. They basically nurtured him and groomed him for many years and then bingo, they hit the jackpot—he ended up in the White House."[337]

Take a moment to appreciate what we have here. Israel has a Pollard-type spy directly in the White House who has not only had an affair with the president's wife, but knows *all* their dirtiest secrets. In 1986, Pollard was convicted of spying for Israel, and the damage he did to our national security is incomprehensible. Now the Israelis had another asset even closer to the reins of power. So, the Mossad learns all of Vince Foster's underhanded schemes; then compromises him for their own benefit. "The deal, according to insiders, was simple: Foster was to leak codes and secrets to the Israelis in exchange for their promise to not expose him, his connections with drug running and money laundering for Clinton, and in addition, the Israelis would add to his Swiss bank account—which they had already discovered by means of their very special computer software given them by someone in the U.S. government."[338]

The software being alluded to was called PROMIS, and in time it would become associated with the INSLAW scandal involving Edwin Meese, the Reagan administration's Department of Justice, and a variety of sleazy deals involving the Israeli government, computer back doors, and its sale to foreign governments, terrorist organizations, and a host of corrupt bankers.

The newly relocated Rose Law Firm lawyer was obviously in a pickle, for "the CIA had Foster under serious investigation for leaking high-security secrets to the State of Israel."[339]

What we are now seeing wasn't child's play by any stretch of the imagination. "A lengthy investigation had located over a dozen sources with connections to the intelligence community who confirm a shocking story of money laundering and espionage connected to the highest levels of the White House."[340]

Since the Clintons had fired all the U.S. Attorneys except one (Michael Chertoff) and replaced them with hand-picked cronies, they caught wind of what was happening with Vince Foster and knew that it could lead to a world of trouble. Soon, "Foster is called by a member of the upper echelon of the White House and advised that 'the CIA is on to you—something about spying for Israel.'"[341]

All hell is now breaking loose. "Foster panics. He cannot turn to the White House as they want to divorce themselves from his activities, which would be disastrous if known by the public—especially in relation to the Clinton staff having such difficulty with security clearances in the beginning—and he can't turn to other federal agencies for help. It would only be a matter of time before he was 'visited' by the FBI for questioning, and he had no idea how much information they had on him, supplied by this cell of CIA which had no part in Iran/Contra or drug smuggling and money laundering through Arkansas."[342]

At this point, as previously noted, the Arkansas Group began frantically trying to see what Vince Foster was going to do. The possibilities were a lose-lose situation for them. If Foster revealed all he knew about Mena, Iran-Contra, and ADFA money laundering, the entire cabal would be imprisoned. On the other hand, if Foster copped to espionage charges, the scandal would ruin the Clinton administration.

Sensing no other alternative, "Foster decides to 'resign' and hopes the Clintons can work out the details to keep him out of harm's way."[343]

However, he *did* have an ace-in-the-hole: a secret Swiss bank account that was being fed by his various illegal endeavors. In fact, Foster had been nurturing this nest egg for quite some time. London's *Sunday Telegraph* reported on May 21, 1994 that "investigators discovered that during the five-year period prior to his death, Vince Foster had made secret international travels, including at least two virtual overnight trips to Geneva."[344]

Then, with his life unraveling before his very eyes, there were "numerous secret trips Foster made abroad, the last less than three weeks before his murder."[345]

So, with millions at his disposal, Foster decides to resign his post at the White House, then "leave the country, pick up his money in Switzerland, then disappear for an undetermined amount of time until things blew over."[346]

But again, events didn't turn out as planned. The problem "is that the CIA team had [PROMIS software's] 'back door' to empty Foster's bank account, transferring the money to the U.S. Treasury.

When Foster calls Switzerland to prepare the bank for his arrival and withdrawal of a large amount of cash, the bank explains he now has a zero balance."[347]

Double-crossed, Foster had to have known the gig was up. "Broke and with no place to turn, Foster calls the only people he can turn to: the Mossad."[348]

Craig Roberts, a 26-year veteran with the Tulsa Police Department, where he served in the patrol division, undercover assignments, SWAT (Special Operations), and as a police helicopter pilot with the Air Support Unit for fourteen years, lays it all out: "Speculation at this point would probably follow the line that Foster's Mossad contact asks who has talked to him, then if he has been interviewed by the FBI or CIA, and when he reports to the negative, he is told to 'meet us tonight in the parking lot (or the 'apartment') and we'll take care of everything.'"[349]

Vince Foster didn't kill himself, and—as surprising as it may seem to most researchers in the alternative media—the Clintons didn't snuff him either. In fact, although Vince was up the creek without a paddle, he wasn't even aware that he would be killed on that specific day. Neither were the Clintons, for they had ample opportunity to murder him when Foster spent the previous weekend at a lake resort with Webb Hubbell. If they had intended to Arkancide him, a convenient little boating accident a la William Colby would have sufficed. But they didn't do it, which can be determined from how frantically they broke into his office to steal certain files. Had the Clintons been behind his murder, they would have had already taken care of those details.

Therefore, if Vince didn't commit suicide and the Clintons weren't responsible for his murder; then who killed him? Answer: those with even more to lose than any of them—the nation of Israel. After the fallout from Jonathan Pollard's extremely damning spy case—not to mention all the other instances of illegal Israeli spying against the United States—a definite backlash would have occurred if the American public had become aware that one of the highest-ranking members of the Clinton cabinet had been passing secrets to them. Further, had Foster turned state's evidence and revealed Israel's role in the October Surprise scandal, arms sales to Iran, Iran-Contra, and their theft of the PROMIS software by super-spy Rafael Eitan, head of the IDF's [Israeli Defense Force] anti-terrorism intelligence unit; America's supposed "ally" might no longer have been the recipient of billions of dollars in foreign aid each year, not to mention unlimited protection by the U.S.

It is for this reason—to safeguard their vested interests (i.e. the U.S. cash cow)—that the Mossad murdered Vince Foster.

NO MALICE OR FORETHOUGHT

Suicide has often been compared to preparing for an extended vacation: a slew of details must be wrapped up; plans made; arrangements taken care of; and final loose ends tied. The same applies to killing oneself; one doesn't take it lightly, especially a person as meticulous as trial attorney Vince Foster. It is painfully clear by his actions during the final days and hours of his life that he had no intention whatsoever of ending his life. Sure, Foster was in serious trouble on numerous different fronts; but taking the big plunge wasn't his solution. On top of that, Foster didn't act like someone who thought they were about to be murdered.

According to Foster's secretary, approximately six hours before his death, Foster mailed a letter to his mother. He has frequently been described as a "'Southern gentleman' with extremely genteel manners. He was especially courtly with women. He seemingly had a healthy relationship with his mother. Despite this, the letter to his mother, sent only hours before he allegedly killed himself, does not contain a single expression of feeling. There is no hint whatsoever this would be his last communication with his mother."[350]

All indications are that Foster deeply cared for his sister Sharon Bowman. Sharon still lived in Arkansas [and] she traveled one thousand miles to Washington to visit her brother, only to arrive the day of her brother's death. Consider that Vince had talked to Sharon and promised her an exciting personal tour of and lunch at the White House. It seems apparent he was looking forward to seeing his sister. Yet he supposedly killed himself on the day of her arrival. Such an incredibly cruel way to miss his date with Sharon is not consistent with the affection Foster felt for her.[351]

To begin his last day on Earth, Vince Foster "dropped off two of his children on his way to the White House that final morning. What were his final words to his children? Any last words of advice? Anything dramatic? Nothing is in the report which suggests that the last contact with his children was more emotional or intense than usual."[352]

During the morning hours at work that fateful day before leaving for lunch, "Foster worked quite conscientiously. He actually maintained a telephone log that morning preceding his death. Is there any purpose other than *future* reference for keeping a record of calls? Why would a man who is going to kill himself care about the future? Here is a man who is [supposedly] distraught and tormented to the point of suicide. Yet he is sufficiently organized, composed, and future-oriented to keep a phone log.[353]

There is much in Foster's behavior during the days preceding his death that indicates he had no intention of killing himself. Only days before his death, he called James Lyons, a friend and trusted advisor in Denver. He told Lyons he needed him in Washington. They made plans for Lyons to fly to Washington on Wednesday, July 21 (the day after Foster allegedly killed himself). Foster called Lyons again on Sunday to confirm their Wednesday appointment. It seems clear Foster was planning on meeting Lyons. It also seems highly unlikely he intended to kill himself the day before the arrival of his friend.[354]

How about this one. According to all reports, Vince Foster left work at the White House at 1:00 in the afternoon. Now, if he truly is suicidal, how does he want to spend his final moments on Earth? "We are to believe that sometime after 1 pm when he was last seen, Foster got an 80-year-old gun, and wishing to experience the exhilarating D.C. weekday afternoon traffic just one last time, he got in his car and set out for Fort Marcy Park."[355]

That's what we're to believe: Foster wanted to spend his final moments in some of the worst traffic in the nation—on Washington, D.C.'s roads?

Finally, "people choosing suicide often make additions or changes in their will, make gifts of valued personal items, leave notes or instructions to a spouse regarding investments, and so forth. Yet, he made no such personal arrangements. At the time, he was working on putting the Clintons' assets into a blind trust, which was quite complicated. Yet, he did not leave any final instructions or information for his successor relating to the trust, or for that matter, to the Whitewater investigation. . . . He [also] did some 'cleaning and straightening' and paid a couple of bills."[356]

Do the above actions sound like those originating from someone about to end his life forever? Vince Foster wasn't making any plans to kill himself. Hell, even though Foster desperately wanted to flee his mounting legal problems, at the time he wasn't planning on making a trip. Vince Foster wanted to stay alive; it was *others* who had different plans for him.

ANOTHER STAIN

> "*Hillary Rodham loved Vince Foster.*"[357] "*It is absolutely inconceivable to me that Vince would have killed himself without first saying goodbye to Hillary.*"[358]
> —Observations of trooper L.D. Brown

I'd like to reiterate a point made in the previous section. If the Clintons had wanted to, they had every opportunity to murder Vince Foster the weekend prior to his death. Joined by Webb Hubbell at a Maryland resort, they could have easily had Foster "drown" while falling over the side of his boat, then claim it was a tragic accident. Meanwhile, they could have calmly entered his office and cleaned out any incriminating files. But they didn't do that.

Instead, Vince had no idea that his time was short, nor did the

Clintons. They were all caught by surprise. When the Mossad took him out, it was done quickly, and *very sloppily*. The job was botched, but they had to do it then—with a sense of urgency—because Foster was getting ready to talk. Once federal officials who weren't controlled by the Clintons realized they had another Jonathan Pollard-style spy case on their hands, the nation of Israel would have come under intense scrutiny. The Pollard case would no longer be an anomaly, especially when we consider their involvement in the October Surprise, Iran-Contra, theft of the PROMIS software, and arms sales to Iran.

In addition, there were plenty of non-corrupted federal officials who despised the Clintons and wouldn't mind seeing them take a fall; not because of a right-wing conspiracy, but because of the way Bill and Hillary acted during their first year in office. There was Travelgate, Filegate, the firing of nearly one hundred U.S. attorneys, shoddy treatment of Secret Service agents, and the horrific massacre at Waco. They didn't hate the Clintons because they were Democrats; they couldn't stand them because they were arrogant, sleazy, deceptive, and immoral.

Vince Foster would have been the perfect vehicle to bring them down, and he was ready to spill his guts. But in a bizarre twist, Israel had as much to lose as the Clintons, and since they were paying Hillary's right-hand man money to divulge state secrets, they were looking at Jonathan Pollard II. Israel could not withstand another scandal, so they moved with urgency and offed Foster. Haste makes waste, however, and they botched the job horribly—possibly worse than just about any fake suicide in history. It was a joke, an embarrassment, and a complete laughingstock.

Vince Foster worked at his White House office that morning, then at "about one pm on July 20, 1993, Foster stopped by [Linda] Tripp's desk, lifted some M&Ms from a bowl and said, 'I'll be back.' He never returned."[359]

At that time—prior to the Monica Lewinsky hoopla—Linda Tripp was still an unknown who hadn't been caught up in the D.C. media circus. She was also called by some "the last known person to see Foster alive."[360]

Actually, many researchers have reached the above conclusion, but in reality there was one other individual *after* Tripp to see Foster. "Secret Service Security officer John Skyles was guarding the gate that Foster exited shortly after 1 pm. In other words, *he was the last known person to see Foster alive.*"[361]

Officer Skyles testified at a Senate hearing that "Foster did not appear to be at all depressed or preoccupied as he walked by,"[362] and that he half-smiled after saying hello.

The story (i.e. propaganda) about Foster being massively depressed is nothing more than another dose of Clinton deceit. "If there is one item of valuable information that can be gained from all the one hundred twenty-five interviews, it is this: not one person could recall Foster contemplating or making any statement in which he specifically mentions any intention to commit suicide."[363]

Further proof can be derived from the following passage:

Foster's brother-in-law, former Congressman Beryl Anthony, was asked about a report that Foster had been despondent for two weeks and that he had discussed this with him. Anthony's response was, "That's a bunch of crap. There's not a damn thing to it." The same day, Dee Dee Myers (born Margaret Jane Myers), White House spokesman, told reporters, "There was no reason to believe he was despondent." Communications Director Mark Gearan said he had seen no changes in Foster's demeanor and that he had never indicated that "anything was out of the ordinary." Betsy Pond, the White House counsel's personal secretary, said she had "noticed nothing strange about Foster."[364]

The depression angle only arose later when the Clintons had to come up with an explanation for his death beyond "murder." When Linda Tripp learned of his death, "her grief was mixed with stern disapproval at the actions of White House aides during the chaotic days that followed."[365]

When testifying before a grand jury, Tripp expounded upon her doubts. "'I am afraid of this administration. I have what I consider to be well-founded fears of what they are capable of.' When asked to elaborate, Tripp explained, 'I had reasons to believe the Vince Foster tragedy was not depicted accurately under oath by members of the administration. I knew based on personal knowledge, personal observations, that they were lying under oath!'[366]

Here is where circumstances begin to get very strange. We know that Foster "walked past the guard desk at Entrance E-4"[367] of the White House and spoke with Officer Skyles, but "there is no record in existence that Foster left the White House under his own power that fateful day of July 20. No video of his exiting the building exists—or so we are led to believe."[368]

In the Senate Manuals, Skyles "described Foster as *walking*. In order to leave the White House parking area by car, one has to pass a guard. Very conspicuously missing was the statement by the guard monitoring the drive-through gate."[369]

Further, "there is no log book entry that shows he ever checked out of the White House through a uniformed Secret Service post."[370]

How could this be, since the White House is "the most secure building in the world? It is equipped with the most sophisticated exit and entry control and video surveillance system available today."[371]

Two possibilities exist—either the surveillance tapes and log book entries were destroyed to prevent incriminating evidence from surfacing, or Foster didn't leave the White House parking lot under his own power. After all, "there is no report, record, note, or anything mentioning his departure at an exiting gate."[372]

He didn't simply vanish into thin air like a magician. Then how did he leave? One researcher has speculated that, "He didn't drive. To walk out of the White House area one must pass through a turnstile which is activated by a card. There is no guard. Foster walked out."[373]

Obviously something was awry, but I don't necessarily agree with the above analysis for the following reason. According to Trooper Larry Patterson, he left work in Little Rock at 4:30 pm on the day that Vince Foster was killed. After returning home twenty minutes later, he received a phone call. "It was [Trooper] Roger Perry. He said that he had just received a call from Helen Dickey that Vince Foster had blown his brains out in the parking lot of the White House."[374]

Helen Dickey was a White House aide who, according to Roger Perry, "called from the White House early on the evening of Foster's death—well before the White House claims to have known of the death—to advise that Foster had shot himself in his car in the White House parking lot."[375] ["Helen called crying, and she said, 'Vince got off work, went out to the parking lot and shot himself in the head.'"[376]]

Helen Dickey was also Chelsea Clinton's former nanny, and "she is on record as having made a phone call to a state trooper in Little Rock around 4:48 pm on the afternoon of the murder, saying Foster had shot himself in his car in the White House parking lot."[377]

If we round-off this call to 5:00 pm Arkansas time (central time zone), then "Dickey knew about Foster's death about fifteen minutes before Park Police even found—about 6:15 Washington time—the body at Fort Marcy Park in suburban Washington. It also means that the official account, that the White House was informed sometime around 8:30 pm, or after, is not true."[378]

An even odder aspect of this time discrepancy is that "two Arkansas State Troopers claim [Kenneth] Starr's investigator attempted to have them change their testimony as to when they were notified of Foster's death."[379]

Specifically, Coy Copeland, a retired FBI agent, attempted to have both Patterson and Perry alter their accounts to coincide with the Clinton timeline. Roger Perry said clearly, "Copeland acted like he wanted me to change my story."[380]

Why would Kenneth Starr be siding with the Clintons when, supposedly, he was their mortal enemy? The truth, as you will soon see, is that the Clintons actually *celebrated* when they discovered that Kenneth Starr was going to head the "independent" investigation. Starr was part of the cover-up despite all the Clintons' feigned objections to his role as prosecutor. Kenneth Starr was in the bag 100 percent.

There are other glaring inconsistencies with the "official" (smokescreen) timeline. "The president and White House officials say that he was not notified of the death until 10 pm."[381]

How are we to account for the events witnessed by the CNN makeup artist sent to prepare the President for his appearance on *Larry King Live* that night? As she was putting the final touches on the President's blotchy yellow skin in the White House Map Room, a man walked in and announced that a note had been found in Vince Foster's office. She was not able to identify the aide, but remembered Mack McLarty was in the room. It must have been about 8:50 pm."[382]

According to Communications Director Mark Gearan, "confirmation came at 9:55 pm"[383] that Vince Foster was dead, and the purported suicide note was not located until the following day. Yet Bill Clinton was notified at least an hour beforehand of a supposed suicide note, while Helen Dickey was making calls in the late afternoon. As usual, the Clintons were lying through their teeth.

Anyway, let's return to July 20, 1993. We know that Linda Tripp saw Vince Foster leaving his office, and that a security guard witnessed him leaving the White House. But beyond these two events, the picture goes black. One point is certain: the actual killing "couldn't have been done inside the White House. So Foster had to be lured to some place out of public view, by someone he trusted, where he was murdered."[384]

Many researchers have speculated that this individual had to have been Hillary Clinton because of two intriguing factors. First, "the FBI lab found a three to four inch stain of semen on the inside front portion of Foster's underwear,"[385] while there were "blond and light brown hairs on Foster's undershirt, pants, socks and shoes."[386]

This disclosure is crucial, for Foster had slightly graying black hair and was, by all accounts, a fastidious dresser. So why would he be found with a semen stain in his undershorts?

Naturally, rumors reemerged about Vince's affair with Hillary, which has been established quite credibly. "Hillary indeed had an affair with her law partner and close friend Vince Foster dating to the mid-1980s."[387]

But once they all moved to D.C., circumstances became stickier. Due to their high-pressure lifestyles, the public spotlight, and scandals galore, "Foster's relationship with Hillary, always complex, was now strained and fraught with tension."[388]

Among other things, there were "Hillary's violent fits of temper about how everything was going wrong,"[389] while "Vince's loyalty to Hillary kept putting him in positions that forced him to choose between compromising his principles or failing to be a stalwart protector of Hillary."[390]

From what we've since discovered about Hillary's lover, I seriously question Foster's 'principles' due to his involvement in Mena, ADFA, money laundering, etc; but still, their relationship was rocky and "many close to the situation have said Foster had been pressing Hillary for a resumption of their liaison that had abruptly ended in Little Rock upon the election."[391]

A second point of conjecture revolved around rumors that "Vince Foster was killed in a love shack and was there with Hillary."[392]

A number of researchers wrote articles with sensational headlines such as, "Foster's Secret Hideaway Apartment Revealed"[393] where, purportedly, "Foster and other women or men in the White House maintained a secret apartment in suburban Virginia and that's where the death actually took place."[394]

These theories are sexy and provocative; but there's one glaring problem. Even if Vince and Hillary were privy to a secret rendezvous love shack, there hasn't yet been any credible evidence proving that he was killed there. The blond hair and semen in his shorts are certainly teasers with, admittedly, quite a bit of circumstantial merit. But by all accounts, Hillary wasn't even near Washington, D.C. on the day of Foster's murder. She was in Little Rock that day. Of course the Clintons lie, but as I stated earlier, had they wanted to kill Vince Foster, they would not have done it in such a frantic, haphazard way.

Upon hearing of Foster's death, Hillary immediately did what she had been groomed a lifetime for—she went into "fixer" mode and ordered Foster's office to be cleansed of any incriminating evidence. Her actions are indicative of what Hillary considered the first and only priority at that moment of crisis. "Hillary did not call Lisa Foster to offer words of sympathy. Instead, just four to five minutes after [Mack] McLarty's call, she phoned Maggie Williams and dispatched her to Vince's office. If there was anything there that might prove embarrassing to the Clintons—like a suicide note in which he claimed his undying love for Hillary—they had to get their hands on it before the police did."[395]

Obviously there was other potentially incriminating evidence lying around Foster's office; but as Hillary reverted to form in her role as fixer, so did her husband Bill who, on the night his childhood friend Vince Foster was murdered, shacked up with his former girlfriend. "White House staffer Marsha Scott would tell David Watkins's wife Ileene [she] spent the night 'with Bill in his bed.'"[396]

Even in the shadow of death, the Clintons are utterly despicable people.

FORT MARCY PARK

"Vince Foster's body was found deep inside the wooded Fort Marcy Park, a well known gay 'cruising' area,"[397] that is "described as 'a deserted park.' The Virginia state map doesn't even list Fort Marcy. Virginia publishes a 168-page vacation guide which includes descriptions of 56 state parks, but Fort Marcy is not even mentioned—not once. DeLorme Publishing produces a huge 80-page map book listing and describing numerous parks and recreational facilities in Virginia. Fort Marcy is not mentioned."[398]

Park Police were quick to reiterate that this secluded park "was known for gay activity."[399]

Vince Foster wasn't a homosexual, but his killers were certainly aware of this little haven for alternative lifestyle quickies. In fact, by the time of his death, Foster had lived in the D.C. area for a year and a half at best and probably didn't know of the place. As one author noted, "to get to Fort Marcy, one has to be purposeful."[400]

In other words, it's not like the Washington Monument which anyone could find in the snap of a finger. By being hidden and obscure, however, Fort Marcy was the perfect place for dumping a body.

Strangely enough, even though "the first Park Police officer on the scene made an instant determination of suicide,"[401] and we've already established that Vince Foster supposedly wasn't identified until 9:55 pm, "what was the Park Police SWAT team doing at Fort Marcy at 7 pm on July 20, 1993, attending to a routine suicide?"[402]

On the other hand, what are we to make of Vince Foster's purported *final* decision in life—his choice of where he was going to die? Foster was a man of taste: a mannered, well-bred attorney accustomed to lavish political dinner parties and living in style. If his existence had become so chaotic, burdensome, and intolerable, wouldn't he want some peace during his last moments on Earth?

But not Vince Foster (or so we're led to believe). First of all, we know that he dropped off his children before going to work, but somehow "he did not park [his car] in his reserved slot inside the White House ground, number 16 on Executive Boulevard West. It was never logged in and never logged out"[403] [or at least this is what we were told by official sources]. But on the morning of "July 20, Vince and his two children bustled down the steps of their house in Cambridge Place at about 8:30 am and piled into the Honda [his personal car]. Vince the father dropped Vince the son at the Metro—the son was a staff aide to Arkansas Senator Dale Bumpers—and dropped Laura at work."[404]

Later, at the murder scene, "Park Police detective Cheryl Braun took five Polaroids of the Honda at Fort Marcy. Time 7:30 pm. But it is impossible to make anything out except that the license plate is redacted—yes, redacted—it's just a white box. The close-up shots of the car taken later at the Park Police impoundment lot reveal that there was no White House pass on the windscreen."[405]

Was this car even Vince's? Further, if Foster truly intended to kill himself, why not—after dropping off his kids—find a beautiful place to relax, contemplate, and prepare for this monumental decision? Instead, he goes to work, tediously logs telephone calls, then "wishing to experience the exhilarating D.C. weekday afternoon traffic just one last time, he got in his car and set out for Fort Marcy Park."[406]

Anyone that has ever driven in D.C. knows that it's positively one of the most hectic, congested, and frustrating cities in America to navigate. Is engaging in such a mind-wracking activity how Foster wanted to spend his final hours?

Let's get real. The entire premise is preposterous. Fort Marcy is an unkempt Civil War-era park that nobody even knows about except adventuresome gays and a few Civil War buffs. It's plagued by mosquitoes, and hardly tranquil or majestic. Consider: "The scenery takes an abrupt and dreary turn as you enter the park. In July, it looks like you have just entered a jungle. The view of the Potomac is obscured. If someone wants to spend his last moments amidst a beautiful or peaceful setting, this is not the place."[407]

The paths are described as 'harsh,' while "there are just no clean areas with soft grass or gentle slopes to lie or sit down on."[408]

After encountering the first clearing inside the park, Foster supposedly went even deeper inside the insect infested area. "The second clearing had to be the most secluded, most private place in the D.C. metropolitan area."[409]

Let's pause for a moment and analyze that statement. Vince Foster is an Arkansan. He'd only lived in D.C. for little over a year. But of all the places inside the Beltway, he by chance happens to select the most secluded, private place in the entire area—one that's not even on a map? What are the odds? It defies belief. Yet that's where his body was found. "How secluded is it? Let's put it this way: it's so secluded that someone could carry the body of a man, unwrap it, lay it out, put a gun in his hand, press his finger against the trigger to make it look like a suicide, put some gunpowder on his hand and in his mouth, and leave without being seen—all in broad daylight."[410]

There is not a single account from family members or friends of Vince Foster ever going on an outing to Fort Marcy Park, or having ever even heard of it. It was an a little-visited Civil War park, not a tourist attraction or a place where one would picnic on a Sunday afternoon. But *someone* was certainly aware of it—homosexuals, and those who murdered Vince Foster, then dumped his body.

HOAXED SUICIDE

Entire books have been written about the Vince Foster murder, and they prove beyond any reasonable doubt that the official version given for this unexpected death was an unabashed lie. In addition, the police work and subsequent medical inquiries were reminiscent of Dr. Fahmy Malak's obstruction of justice-style practices in Arkansas. Well-known murder expert Vernon Geberth commented that "this is the most sloppy death investigation I have ever heard of."[411]

Why would this renowned authority issue such a statement? Essentially, because after looking into this matter he found "missing evidence, witness tampering, falsified testimony, a forged suicide note, forensic evidence that contradicted official finding, and much, much more."[412]

In other words, when it came to the Clinton Body Count, the White House counsel's murder was more of the same modus operandi. "Foster did not die where his body was found—his corpse was moved after death for unknown reasons, [while] the Clinton White House systematically obstructed every investigation into Foster's death."[413]

Lastly, similar to the Arkancides which occurred during his tenure as governor, the media was a willing accomplice to the cover-up of these murders. "The major networks proved by their actions that their goal was not to unveil the truth, but to protect the White House at all costs."[414]

Officially, the Clinton-corporate media deceivers claimed "that Foster had killed himself after taking a 1913 Colt .38

revolver, pressing the four-inch barrel deep against the back of his mouth, and firing."[415]

Oddly, even though Foster's body was discovered in Fort Marcy Park, "no one came forward to claim they had seen him alive at the park; or even around Washington that fateful afternoon. From the time he left the White House, five hours of his life are simply, and inexplicably, unaccounted for."[416]

As you'll see, there are so many irregularities with this case that it screams of foul play; yet the wool continues to be pulled over our eyes. What inconsistencies am I referring to? For instance, "the bullet and skull fragments not being found, the carpet fibers, and relatively small quantity of blood all suggest that the shooting occurred elsewhere. The other fingerprint, the blond hair, and another's gun powder, all suggested foul play. No dirt on the shoes, the blood contact stain, the blood drain tracks, and the blood distribution all suggested that the body was transported. Finally, the gun remaining in the hand, the body lying flat, the erratic distribution of powder, and the first observation that saw no gun in Foster's hand, all supported the contention that an effort was made to create an appearance of suicide."[417]

THE CRIME SCENE

Right from the get-go, irregularities abounded once Vince Foster's body was discovered. Some initial reports filtering in "had Foster draped over a cannon, others had him lying in a ditch. He was all over the place. There was no hard information at all on the crime scene."[418]

The most fundamental basic tenet of any murder-crime scene is to determine the precise location of the body; yet the medical examiner—Dr. Donald Haut—and Park Police both described the wrong death scene. They initially spoke of Foster's body being in a completely different area of Fort Marcy Park than what was later agreed upon. The obvious question is: "why would officials lie about one of the most elemental aspects of any death investigation: the placement and location of the body?"[419]

The answer is simple—Vince Foster didn't *choose* a location to kill himself. He was murdered, and his body was moved at least three different times. Since this homicide was performed in haste, the outcome was slipshod and haphazard. On top of that, various officials weren't all on the same page in their reporting (i.e. a finalized script hadn't been passed around to all the participants). Thus, gaping errors emerged. First, it was obvious that others were present on the scene, for "vegetation at the bottom of the body had been tramped down like somebody had been walking or messing around that area."[420]

Officially, Foster died alone, yet "the underbrush from the body down to the ditch and up the other side of the ditch had been trampled down . . . the swath looked like it had been created by several people climbing the slope."[421]

Why was that area so heavily trampled? Because as we'll see later, there is an old cabin at the rear of Fort Marcy Park—with a separate roadway leading to it—and that is where Foster's body was originally brought before being finally deposited. "Foster's body had been brought in via the old road and carried over this trampled path by several men."[422]

Therefore, we now have *multiple* individuals at the crime scene, not just Foster. Further, not a single person heard gunfire in that area, even though a notable dignitary lived nearby. "The Saudi Arabian ambassador's residence is just across Chain Bridge Road from the park, approximately 100 yards, as the crow flies, from where the Fiske report placed Foster's body. Also nearby was the mansion of Prince Pandar bin Sultan of Saudi Arabia."[423]

Clearly we can see why this detail matters. "The ambassador's residence is protected twenty-four hours a day by five trained security guards, three of whom routinely roam the property and periodically check Fort Marcy Park. No one heard a gunshot on the afternoon Foster allegedly shot himself at Fort Marcy."[424]

They weren't the only residents in the area. "There are five homes within 570 feet of the spot where Foster's body was found. One of them, 1317 Merrie Ridge Road, belongs to Senator Bennett

Johnston of Louisiana. The closest is 660 Chain Bridge Road. It is 300 feet away. With a sand wedge you could pitch a golf ball over the top of it. . . . Nobody heard a shot."[425]

The closest home was 300 feet away. That's the length of one football field. Do you think if you stood at one goal line and somebody shot a gun at the other goal line, it could be heard? Residents *were* present that day, too. Amazingly, one couple that was home said "the FBI had never dropped by to learn if they had heard that .38 Special on the quiet, sultry afternoon of July 20, 1993."[426]

Do you think that is why FBI Director William Sessions was fired the day before Vince Foster's murder—because he would have checked on such matters?

Others, however, did take their responsibilities seriously, including Congressman Dan Burton, who "had a homicide detective recreate the shooting with an object of the same basic density as a human head. The shot could clearly be heard 100 yards away, even with an earthmover running in the background."[427]

Conclusion? No shots were fired that day at Fort Marcy Park.

THE PARK POLICE (KEYSTONE KOPS)

When Kevin Fornshill appeared on the Foster crime scene, it took him a mere two minutes to contact D.C.'s Park Police and tell them he had a 'suicide' on his hands. When asked later what contributed to this presumption, he replied that it was "based on the determination the person was dead."[428]

Fornshill obviously should have known better, for "standard police procedure is to first treat every suicide as a homicide. That wasn't done here. 'It seems to me that he made the determination prior to going up and looking at the body,' senior Park Police investigator Cheryl Braun said, admitting the police's verdict was reached before detectives had even inspected the death scene."[429]

How do you suppose Fornshill arrived at such a predetermined conclusion? Here's the answer. "The Park Service is a fine organization, but it works under the supervision of the Secretary of the Interior, not the Justice Department. The Park Service has neither the depth nor the experience to investigate a case of this magnitude, unless, of course, the White House meant to limit the scope of the investigation."[430]

Now remember, from all official accounts, the Park Police were investigating a routine, anonymous suicide when they arrived at "6:14 pm and 32 seconds."[431]

Also, as we've determined, the body supposedly wasn't even identified until two and a half hours later. Further, since homicide was immediately ruled out, there was apparently no reason to consider foul play. Then why . . . this question *really* needs explanation . . . why were "members of the Special Forces, an elite unit of the Park Police closely associated with White House security, at Fort Marcy Park—where Foster's body was found—by 7 pm on the night of the death?"[432]

So, on the one hand we have the Special Forces rolling in, and on the other a crew straight out of a Keystone Kops movie. Were the Park Police actually that inept? Decide for yourself. Here is their first report relayed to the Secret Service:

> On the evening of 7/20/93, unknown time, U.S. Park Police discovered the body of Vincent Foster in his car. The car was parked in the Fort Marcy area of Virginia near the GW Parkway. Mr. Foster apparently died of a self-inflicted gunshot wound to the head. A .38 caliber revolver was found in the car.[433]

For some inexplicable reason, I thought Foster was discovered near the second cannon at Fort Marcy Park; but the initial reports have him and a gun in his car! As you'll see, this miscue was only the first of many, such as, "the U.S. Park Police never took a crucial crime-scene photo of Vince Foster's body before it was moved."[434]

The reason no pictures were taken is because—at least in the beginning—there wasn't even a gun found on or near Vince Foster! "The first Park Police official to 'discover' Foster's lifeless body was Sgt. George Gonzalez. He continued to insist under questioning from the Federal Bureau of Investigation agents, and others, that there had been no gun near or on the body, or in either hand as a faked photograph, which surfaced later, attempted to illustrate."[435]

Two other witnesses, including Sergeant John Rolla, stated that there was no gun in Vince Foster's hand when they arrived, and that "the palms were up."[436]

Such testimony presents a huge obstacle to the official story, for later the public was shown a close-up photo of a gun in Vince Foster's hand. But this photo is verifiably fake, as we'll soon show, because every individual initially on the scene said there was no gun.

Also, since we mentioned how the Park Police initially reported that Vince Foster was found dead *inside* his car (then later near cannon number two); weigh this peculiarity. "Four different people searched Foster's pockets while the body was still in the park. There were no keys to be found. There were no keys in his Honda in the parking lot. Then, how could Foster drive to the park and shoot himself without car keys? The answer, of course, was some member of 'the gang who couldn't shoot straight' drove Foster's body to the park and left the car there—and forgot to leave the keys in the ignition, or place them in Foster's trouser pockets."[437]

Again, we seem to have magic tricks being played on us, because how could Vince Foster drive with no keys? Did he levitate there, or fly like a bird? Hardly. But alas, guess what conveniently happened. "The keys did eventually turn up at the morgue, where Foster's body was taken."[438]

How did they inexplicably rematerialize? Well, two of Hillary's primary operatives showed up at the morgue right before the keys were located: "Former Rose Law partner and Travelgate figure William Kennedy III, and the mysterious figure of the FBI files caper Craig Livingstone."[439]

You remember Livingstone, don't you? He was the man who Hillary Clinton swore *under oath* she had never met, and was not even aware of; yet it was she who hired him to be one of her Plumbers. Isn't it funny how he showed up at the exact location where Vince Foster's body was—then all of a sudden the car keys were located?

EYEGLASSES

One scintillating piece of evidence found near Vince Foster's prone body was his eyeglasses. In fact, they were "found nineteen feet down slope from Foster's head, a physically impossible result of the claimed gunshot."[440]

To register this claim, imagine that you're sitting in a park with a pair of glasses resting on your face. You then place a gun in your mouth and pull the trigger. Your head will obviously snap backward; but will the glasses be flung nineteen feet? To obtain an answer, let's do an experiment. Put a pair of eyeglasses or sunglasses on your face; then jerk your head back as hard as you possibly can and see how far the glasses fly. I guarantee you'll never get them to travel nineteen feet.

Yet we're to believe that Vince Foster's glasses sailed what would nearly be the equivalent of a two-story building? One man, author Michael Kellett, was so certain that this feat could not be reproduced that he offered a cash prize to anyone that could do it. The sum was $10,000 to become the World's Greatest Head-Snapping Eyeglass Thrower.

To receive the $10,000, all the believer must do is repeat the "obvious scenario." Sit with the legs outstretched. Remember that was the position that he must have been in—on the slope where Foster was found—and wear eyeglasses similar to Foster, or have them in the shirt pocket. Then, with a mighty and sudden backward movement, the eyeglasses will be dislodged, sail over the top of the berm, and bounce through and over the dense July foliage to the bottom of the hill. I will allow a hundred tries.[441]

SHOES

Let's strain the credibility of the government's story a little further. Despite walking deeply into Fort Marcy Park, past the first cannon to the second, through highly-grown summer vegetation, "the FBI lab found not a speck of soil on his [Foster's] shoes or clothing despite a 700-foot-plus trek through the heavily wooded park. No grass stains were mentioned. No soil—yet almost every garment of clothing, including his underwear, was covered with multi-colored carpet fibers."[442]

Ponder what has just been presented. Try to imagine walking the length of more than two football fields through dirt, grass, weeds, brush, and trees and not having even a microscopic trace of *anything* on your shoes, pants, or shirt. Nothing. Zero. "The lab found no dirt on Foster's shoes."[443]

Curiously, there were carpet fibers on every article of clothing; not that investigators on the scene seemed to care. The Park Police, on the other hand, "failed to test the bottom of Foster's shoes for residue. Such a test could have determined whether Foster had walked, or had been carried, to Fort Marcy."[444]

So, let's analyze this situation. Was the entirety of Fort Marcy Park blanketed with carpet fibers? No. Or, could we presume that Vince Foster "removed his shoes and socks, carrying them in his hands as he walked through the park to the sight of his suicide?"[445]

Such a scenario seems highly unlikely being that Fort Marcy was a neglected, overgrown, unkempt park. Could Foster have levitated above the ground for over seven hundred feet? Not unless he was David Copperfield.

If you're scratching your head, so was Congressman Dan Burton, who decided to retrace Vince Foster's steps that day. "This is what he reported on the House floor on August 2, 1993: Foster would have had to walk a long way from his car to the second cannon. I walked all the way from the parking lot up to the second cannon: it was a dry day and I had dust *all over* my shoes."[446]

Any reasonable person would concur with this assessment. Yet not a single speck of dust, dirt, grass, or leaves was on Foster's shoes. They looked as if they'd just been removed from a box at the shoe store. How could that be? "The hard evidence indicates that the crime scene was staged, period."[447]

In fact, "there is ample evidence that Foster never entered the park alive."[448]

How did Clinton's crony Robert Fiske explain this glaring inconsistency? He stated that "foliage in the park that July day was particularly dense, preventing Foster from encountering even a smidgen of exposed soil."449

When you're finished laughing, try to comprehend how stupid they must think we are. Not even a kid who still believes in Santa Claus would buy that line. Of course, what *did* happen is obvious. Vince Foster was killed elsewhere; then his body was wrapped in a carpet to prevent a blood trail. It was carried to Fort Marcy Park, where the corpse was unrolled from the carpet and placed near the second cannon. No dirt or dust or grass on his shoes, but carpet fibers on every article of clothing. The reasoning used above is simple Forensics 101 at its most basic.

Vincent J. Scalice agrees. He's a "former homicide detective for the New York City Police Department . . . [who] had been a Consultant Member for the House Select Committee on Assassinations."450

What follows are his discoveries.

The so-called Scalice Report, released in April 1995, concluded that "a high probability exists that Foster's body was transported to Fort Marcy Park." It homed in on the fact that no traces of soil could be found on Foster's shoes, under a microscope, even though he had supposedly walked seven hundred feet through the overgrown park. The investigation did two simulation walks to see what residue was left after walking to the crime scene. Both models had visible soil all over their shoes.451

THE GUN & BULLETS

Beyond belief, when official reports were released, they stated that the gun which Vince Foster supposedly used to kill himself was *still in his hand* upon death. Understandably, some readers are not familiar with weapons, so let's allow the experts to speak on this subject. Army CID agent Gene Wheaton commented, "In my 25 years of investigating homicides, I have never seen a gun remain in the suicide's hand."452

So sure was he of himself that "Wheaton makes the grave charge that the gun was 'put in Foster's hand' by someone: the event was staged."[453]

Vernon Gerberth, author of the highly touted book *Practical Homicide Investigation: Tactics, Procedures and Forensic Techniques*, agrees. "Under ordinary circumstances, after the firing, the gun is away from the person."[454]

In simplest terms, using basic physics, "the gun's recoil normally throws the weapon free,"[455] and "handguns used in suicides often are catapulted . . . away from a body."[456]

But then again, when it comes to the Clinton Body Count and their Arkancides, everything defies description and logic.

How about the way Foster was holding the gun: "There's also the matter of the bizarre grip Foster supposedly used; his right thumb was found in the trigger guard, indicating that he fired the gun by pressing the trigger with that thumb."[457]

Suicide is the biggest decision a person ever makes in his life. Do you think a rational man like Vince Foster would risk botching the job by twisting his arms and hand into a completely convoluted, unnatural position and placing his thumb on the trigger? Hell no. What's even worse than a suicide by firearm is *a botched suicide by firearm* where you only blow off half your head and end up being a disfigured, brain dead vegetable for the rest of your life.

But Vince Foster purportedly used his thumb to pull the trigger, then let his arm fall pristinely along his side. Sorry, but I'm not buying it. Another detective added, "It's hard to explain how he shot himself—putting the barrel in at a right angle to his arm—fired it, and had it land in his hand at his side."[458]

Another eyewitness concurred. "Richard Arthur, who had attended to 25 or 30 gunshot deaths in his nine years as a rescue worker, believed it was a homicide. 'I've just never seen a body lying so perfectly straight after a bullet in his head.'"[459]

As stated previously, that the gun was even still in his hand was remarkable. One detective said, "In my 30 years in dealing with homicides, I've never seen someone shoot themselves in the mouth and still hold the gun perfectly at his side."[460]

This point brings us to another. "Although the gun's barrel was supposedly placed deep in his mouth, no teeth were even damaged, let alone broken."[461]

On top of that, "the revolver's sight on the muzzle would be especially destructive. In this event, there would be severe cuts and probably broken teeth."[462]

But not with Vince Foster. More amazingly, "that there was no blood on the gun or flame burns in the mouth disputed the contention that the shot was fired with the gun very deep in the mouth."[463]

But wait; any sane person would know that it'd be easy to prove that Vince Foster killed himself with the gun in his hand. All they'd have to do is show his fingerprints on it; then the case is closed. Any idiot could figure that out. There's only one problem. "No fingerprints were found on the Colt revolver retrieved from the scene. Likewise, there were no fingerprints on any of the twenty-seven pieces of the suicide note found by one of Foster's associates several days after his death."[464]

No fingerprints? How could there be "no fingerprints found on the gun even though the gun was found in his hand, lying neatly at his side"?[465]

How did the authorities explain the lack of fingerprints? "The FBI crime lab offers one of their deliciously bureaucratic observations about this. 'An individual who does not perspire readily might not have a print.'"[466]

So, there were no fingerprints because Vince Foster was perspiration-challenged—he wasn't sweating? But hold on. Didn't Foster supposedly take his own life in what is usually an extremely humid month? "July 20 was one of the hottest, muggiest days of the summer of 1993."[467]

Plus, Foster had reportedly just walked more than the length of two football fields to reach the second cannon; yet no perspiration, during a Washington, D.C. summer?

The Park Police didn't seem to care, though; for they "didn't even bother to send the gun for testing until a week after they ruled the death a suicide."[468]

Of course there were other anomalies, such as no gunpowder found on [Foster's] tongue."[469]

There were no skull fragments from the pistol shot.[470]

The bullet was never found.[471]

Let's examine these last few items more closely. First, "when a bullet is shot into a suicide's head, bone fragments from the skull will fragmentize and be scattered in the immediate area. None of the skull material, according to all reports from the scene, was ever found. Normally a .38 caliber bullet—according to police firearms experts at the LAPD—will blow a 4" or 5" hole, with blood and brains flying everywhere within the immediate area."[472]

Think of the assassination of President John F. Kennedy when one of the bullets penetrated his skull. It looked like a watermelon had been splattered with a sledgehammer, and that wasn't even done at point-blank range. George Gonzalez observed, "Usually a suicide is a mess,"[473] but that day at Fort Marcy Park, "Foster's body was laid out as if in a coffin."[474]

Further, "Fairfax County paramedic George Gonzalez told [journalist Christopher] Ruddy that he had never seen a gunshot victim like Foster in thirteen years on the job. All so clean, a pristine shirt, no blood to speak of. Then paramedic Kory Ashford said he picked up the body—which was lying straight, 'ready for a coffin'—and didn't see any blood."[475]

Here is how extremely bizarre the situation was. "Kory Ashford, the paramedic who placed Foster's body in the body bag, didn't even bother to use rubber gloves, there was so little blood."[476]

I'm sure you're probably getting the picture. "There were no visible powder burns inside Foster's mouth, and no signs of gunpowder on his face."[477]

Not surprisingly, "the bullet was never found,"[478] even though authorities did look. "Despite a sixteen-person search using metal detectors that yielded twelve modern-day bullets and a number of others from Civil War days, no bullet from the .38 caliber revolver was found."[479]

How peculiar—bullets from the mid-1860s still existed at Fort

Marcy Park, but none from Vince Foster's gun that was supposedly shot that afternoon.

No bullet, no fingerprints, no blood, and "no flame burns in his mouth."[480]

Plus, "Foster's wife Lisa could not identify the gun as having been Foster's,"[481] while "Foster's children did not recognize the gun as the one they had seen in their home."[482]

Similarly, "no matching ammunition was found in either of Foster's homes."[483]

Overall, "no member of the family was ever able to identify the gun found in Foster's hand. Not one. Ever."[484]

So, what happened?

1) Foster was not shot with the supposedly antique .38 revolver, but probably with a modern gun.[485]

2) After Foster was killed, his "6'4" frame was wrapped [in a carpet, producing all the fiber covering his clothing] and placed in the trunk or compressed in a way that restricted movement. The position was such that it caused blood to seep to the right shoulder and back. The chin was pushed against the right shoulder which caused the contact stain.[486]

3) It has been pointed out by Chris Ruddy, incidentally, that the revolver contained several components from different guns, giving it the characteristics of a "drop gun." The term is used to describe a non-traceable gun used by the underworld and commonly dropped at a death-by-gunshot scene to give the appearance of suicide.[487]

WOUND

The public was told Vince Foster killed himself with an antique 1913 Colt .38 revolver. By the government's account, Foster shoved the gun's barrel into his mouth and blew the top of his head out. But was this rendition of events true?

"Investigators noted no blood splatter or tissue above Foster's head, though the bullet is said to have exited the top of the back of his head while he was in a sitting position."[488]

One would imagine pools of blood, but paramedic Kory Ashford "did not even wash his hands after the task"⁴⁸⁹ of loading Foster's corpse into a body bag. Yet when Pennsylvania Senator Budd Dwyer killed himself at a televised press conference by placing a gun in his mouth and pulling the trigger, "blood poured out of his mouth like a faucet—which a number of pathologists have said is normal."⁴⁹⁰

Investigators also dug around to find other clues—"hand-sifting the soil to a depth of eighteen inches—no brain and bone fragments were found. Why?"⁴⁹¹

It seems fairly clear that a gun-related suicide should have produced certain results. "According to the autopsy, he would have been bleeding both from the mouth and from the gaping exit wound in the back of the skull."⁴⁹²

But let me repeat: there was "no blood on the ground. No blood on the corpse. No blood on anybody who had touched him."⁴⁹³

But wait, circumstances get even stickier. A confidential informant on the scene told British reporter Ambrose Evans-Pritchard, "There was no exit wound. Listen to me, and listen to me hard, 'cause I'm only going to say this once: Vince Foster was shot right here in the neck."⁴⁹⁴

This revelation was confirmed by "Richard Arthur, a medical technician at the death scene [who] observed what appeared to be 'a small caliber bullet hole' on the right side of Foster's neck."⁴⁹⁵

Such a disclosure directly contradicts Dr. James Beyer's original autopsy where he said "the bullet entered the back of Foster's mouth and then went backward and upward with an exit from the back of the head."⁴⁹⁶

Could Dr. Beyer be pulling another Fahmy Malak-style con job? When emergency personnel returned to headquarters after responding to the Vince Foster call at Fort Marcy Park, "One thing they could all agree on when they were recounting war stories back at Fire Station One was that nobody saw an exit wound. Kory Ashford didn't see it. Richard Arthur didn't see it. Sergeant George Gonzalez didn't see it. The head was intact."⁴⁹⁷

CHAPTER THREE

A gunshot to the neck completely and utterly changes everything. "Dr. [Donald] Haut reconfirmed the report to Reed Irvine of *Accuracy in Media*, and in that report confirms the presence of a gunshot wound exiting Foster's neck. This corroborates a sworn deposition of Emergency Medical Services Technician Richard Arthur."[498]

In addition, U.S. Assistant Attorney Miguel Rodriguez made "a set of five 'blowups' of the original [autopsy photos]. They revealed a dime-sized wound on the right side of Foster's neck about halfway between the chin and the ear. It was marked by a black 'stippled' ring—a sort of dotted effect, like an engraving—that was suggestive of a .22 caliber gunshot fired at point blank range into the flesh."[499]

Appearing before the Senate Banking Committee, Richard Arthur said in a sworn deposition that he saw "what appeared to be a small gunshot wound near the jaw line"[500] of Vince Foster. He then added proof of a cover-up. "Lt. Bianchi told me from orders higher up that I'm not allowed to talk to anybody about this if I value my job."[501]

This information is of the bombshell variety, for if we remember correctly, Foster was said to have killed himself with a .38 revolver; but now we have what appears to be a .22 caliber wound in the side of Foster's neck. Here's the clincher. A close friend of Vince Foster—"Little Rock criminal attorney Joe Purvis—viewed Foster's body at Ruebel's Funeral Home in the University Heights section of Little Rock."[502]

The following is what transpired: Purvis said he was allowed to see the exit wound, which he described as a small hole *in the back of the neck*. . . . Purvis acknowledged that he was permitted by the funeral home to actually see the exit wound. He confirmed that when Foster's head was lifted up he found a neat exit wound the size of a dime at the hairline of the neck."[503]

The real picture has now emerged. Vince Foster didn't shoot himself at Fort Marcy Park. There was no 'live' gun there. Some researchers have speculated that the antique Colt .38 was stolen later from Foster's residence; then placed in his hand. But even this scenario doesn't add up, for no one in Foster's family recognized the planted weapon. Meanwhile, Foster was shot elsewhere in the neck with what appears to be a .22 at point blank range. He was then "wrapped in something, probably a carpet that left fibers on his clothes, and he was laid on his back while being transported to the park [where] most of the blood would have seeped into the carpet."[504]

One last point before moving on: when homicides occur in outdoor venues such as parks or fields, forensic scientists often use entomologists (insect experts) to help them determine the time of death. They accomplish this task by using flies; or, more specifically, the eggs laid by flies on or inside the corpse. Without delving into a jumble of medical jargon or procedure, the lack of eggs laid on or inside Vince Foster "indicate that the body was in the park less than one and a half hours. All other indicators suggest that Foster had been dead longer. One of the central points of the murder hypothesis—that death took place somewhere else, and the body was then moved to Fort Marcy—is irrefutable. Flies don't lie."[505]

WITNESSES

In an extreme (and convenient) rush to judgment, Vince Foster's death was immediately classified a suicide. But "the initial reports by the Park Police from the scene where Foster's body had been found by a citizen, stated that he had been shot in the head execution style—a very strange way for a person to commit suicide."[506]

When coupled with the neck wound mentioned earlier, the scenario becomes clearer. How many people throughout history have killed themselves via an execution-style gunshot to the back of one's own neck? Also, yet another person on the scene stated that there was no weapon present. "A construction worker who routinely passed the park on his way home said he was stuck in traffic and had gone to that remote section of the park to urinate."[507]

There, he stumbled upon an unexpected sight: the corpse of

Vince Foster. The witness "has consistently maintained that, when he found the body, the man's head was looking straight up and his hands were at his sides, palms up with no gun in either hand."[508]

The observer was so confident that he swore in a deposition, "I am absolutely and totally, unequivocally sure the palms were up. I looked at both palms. There was nothing in his hands."[509]

Inexplicably, a gun *did* show up later, placed directly (and improbably) in Foster's right hand. But there were no fingerprints, no blood, no flame burns, and no powder residue. Obviously, the scene was later staged (very poorly) to give the appearance that Foster had taken his own life.

Additional witnesses stepped forward to claim that they saw others at Fort Marcy Park at exactly the same time as Foster's body was deposited. One woman arrived at the park between 5:15 to 5:30 pm and saw "a white male seated in the driver's seat of this particular vehicle [a tan Honda Accord]."[510]

The woman also added that "she believed the occupant had dark hair and could have been bare-chested."[511]

Two other witnesses—a Mr. Frist and Ms. Doody—saw "a man without a shirt"[512] in a car in that very same parking lot around the same time. As you will see shortly, this man was acting as a lookout while Foster's body was being carried to the second cannon.

The most pertinent question at this point has to be: from where was Foster's body being moved? This answer provides one of the final pieces to the puzzle. "There was a cabin about five hundred feet from where Foster's body was found. A path from the cabin leads directly to the site, and a private road leading to the cabin from another direction could easily be traveled unnoticed."[513]

The primary witness on the scene "told the FBI that when he found the body, the grass and weeds were trampled down in two areas: where the body was found and back through the trees and brush to the path leading to the cabin."[514]

Almost the entire picture has now become clear. While one man waited in the front parking lot off the George Washington Parkway, others took a back route into the park and stopped at a nearby cabin. There, Foster was either killed—or, more probably, it served as a staging area—before Foster's body, wrapped in a carpet, was carried 500 feet to the second cannon.

There was only one problem. Before the killers could finalize the last few steps of this hastily conceived hoax, they were interrupted. The man who accidentally discovered this matter of national security later said that he "suspected that he had disturbed the crime scene before it was 'ready' and thought that he was very lucky to be alive."[515]

PATRICK KNOWLTON

The individual who disrupted Vince Foster's crime scene at Fort Marcy Park was initially only identified as Confidential Witness, or "CW." In the spring of 1994, CW was finally revealed to be Patrick Knowlton, "an affable small businessman who sports a 'Clinton-Gore' campaign bumper sticker on the wall of his Washington apartment."[516]

The reason Knowlton needed protection was obvious: he saw things that day which the killers didn't want him to see. For example, in addition to what appeared to be Vince Foster's Honda, there was also another vehicle present in the Fort Marcy parking lot. Inside this car "was a male in his late twenties, probably Mexican or Cuban, with dark complexion."[517]

The man definitely didn't want Knowlton to be present, for "the suspicious-looking character made him feel 'nervous and uneasy.'"[518]

Knowlton added that "the character was downright scary. He didn't take his eyes off [me]."[519]

Who was this individual? Clearly, "the man's behavior was consistent with his acting as a lookout, as if his purpose was to prevent any passersby from venturing into the area of the park where Vince Foster's corpse was found eighty minutes later."[520]

As he glared in his direction, "the look made Knowlton feel like he was intruding, and appeared to him to communicate, 'get the hell out of here.'"[521]

But Knowlton wasn't one to flee without taking notice of his surroundings. For one, he "peered inside the vehicle where he observed . . . a leather briefcase or leather folder on the passenger side seat."[522]

As you'll ascertain later, Foster's briefcase becomes extremely vital in regard to his faked suicide note. This man's observations should not be taken lightly because "Knowlton has a superior power of recall. The doctors reported that Knowlton placed in the 90th percentile of what the general population would be expected to score. This result demonstrates Mr. Knowlton had unusually good powers of delayed recall of visually-presented stimuli and would be consistent with his ability to report accurately."[523]

More importantly, we need to look at certain times on the afternoon of Vince Foster's murder. "Four witnesses had seen an old brown mid-80s Honda parked in Fort Marcy Park between 4:30 and 5:45 pm. It was *not* Vince Foster's car. Foster's light gray 1989 Honda arrived later. There was another problem: Foster was already dead by the time his car arrived. His body was discovered at 5:30 pm."[524]

What does this information convey? "Autopsy data and estimates placed the time of death as occurring no later than 4 pm. If Foster's car had not yet been driven to the park by 4:30 pm, the time of Knowlton's observations, that certainly would contradict the notion of suicide."[525]

Knowlton wasn't the only person to corroborate these details. "All four witnesses gave consistent testimony. None contradicted the others. Their combined testimony plainly showed that Foster's body arrived in the park *before* his car. Naturally, this created a problem for investigators intent on proving that Foster committed suicide in Fort Marcy Park."[526]

Speaking of which, the FBI wasn't remotely pleased with these conflicting times, and did everything possible to have those at the park change them. "All four witnesses later complained that their statements to the FBI had been altered. Under FBI pressure, most agreed to change significant details of their stories. But one stuck to his guns. Patrick Knowlton alone refused to alter his testimony one iota."[527]

That didn't mean the FBI intended to play it straight with him. "In the spring of 1994, an FBI agent finally interviewed Knowlton, nearly one year after Foster's death. The agent later wrote a report quoting Knowlton as saying he would be unable to identify the man he had seen. Knowlton says this report is false. On the contrary, he had told the agent he remembered the man's face extremely well and was confident he could identify him. Why did the FBI lie about Knowlton's statement? Why wasn't Knowlton invited to look at police photos?"[528]

That was only the beginning. After Knowlton refused to buckle, "teams of agents harassed him 24 hours a day. Cars filled with four agents followed him. His phone rang in the middle of the night. Agents knocked on his door at 3 am."[529]

The FBI under William Sessions would have never acted in such a brazen way, but now rogue elements within the FBI became Hillary's personal attack dogs. Regrettably for Patrick Knowlton, they set their sights on him. Initially, Knowlton and his girlfriend noticed that "strange men were everywhere, one after another, growing more aggressive by the minute. They would cut right in front of Patrick, circle around him, even brush against him as they passed. Some were middle-aged white men, others Middle Eastern. They stared in Patrick's face with hard, hostile gazes."[530]

Knowlton contacted investigator and author Christopher Ruddy, who at first thought it was all his imagination. "When I learned of this, my immediate reaction was that Knowlton was under stress and perhaps paranoid."[531]

But after joining him one day, Ruddy witnessed their tactics firsthand. "There's a surveillance net of at least thirty people harassing Patrick. I've never seen anything like it in my life,"[532] he remarked.

Why were Hillary Clinton and her FBI pit bulls so intent on intimidating and destabilizing Patrick Knowlton? Because each had everything to lose if the American people ever realized how badly they'd been lied to. In addition, Hillary's neck was especially on the chopping block if the truth ever surfaced on a national level as to her vast involvement in the Vince Foster cover-up. Why? Because with everything he saw that day at Fort Marcy Park, we can only arrive at one verdict. Author "[Michael] Kellett concludes with this startling last word on the case: if Patrick Knowlton is telling the truth, the White House had to have been involved in the murder!"[533]

MURDER AT THE WHITE HOUSE

One of the most blatantly criminal aspects of the Vince Foster murder case was Hillary Clinton's direction of certain associates to break into the White House counsel's office and steal any potentially incriminating evidence contained in his files. As a prelude to this section, I'd like to present two introductory passages.

What really happened in Foster's office after his death and his files went missing? Who made all these calls to Arkansas that night, and what for? What did Hillary's chief of staff, Maggie Williams, do in Foster's office that night? What was Patsy Thomasson really looking for in Vince Foster's desk that night? Why in the world did friends of Hillary vacuum Foster's office and hold the Justice Department investigators at bay?[534]

The second excerpt harks back to a point made earlier where Clinton secretary Helen Dickey phoned Trooper Roger Perry and told him that Vince Foster had killed himself in the White House parking lot. The only difference is that instead of Foster taking his own life at 1600 Pennsylvania Avenue, he was instead murdered there; then left for the Clintons to decide what to do with him.

Shortly after Foster's death, his office was raided by White House personnel who carried off boxes of files and documents to upstairs bedrooms for examination. Several credible witnesses have reported this, even though it has been denied by White House staff personnel. It appears that if this occurred, it would be drug running and money laundering documents that would be of most concern. Even though most of these documents were burned and shredded at the Rose Law Firm during an all-night "house cleaning," certain players would be uncertain exactly what Foster kept out as personal "insurance." It has been speculated that Foster's body was left at the White House by his killers, but was moved after discovery by White House personnel to change the area of the "crime scene." If Foster was discovered in his car in the parking lot, the crime scene would encompass his office—and the files—which would be searched by police or federal investigators.[535]

Our analysis has now taken another dramatic turn. Could Vince Foster have actually been murdered while sitting in his car in the White House parking lot, somewhat confirming what Clinton aide Helen Dickey had told trooper Perry? The only difference to her story is that Foster didn't actually kill himself, but was instead shot in the neck by Mossad assailants before he could spill his guts to federal officials about their blackmail efforts (and much more). Foster's body was then left for Bill and Hillary to deal with (i.e. clean up the mess). Naturally, the Clintons didn't want a murder scene at the White House for two reasons. One, it would be a public relations disaster; and two, as noted earlier, they didn't want Foster's office and files to be part of an investigation, for they weren't sure what he had squirreled away inside his cabinets and safe.

So, panic struck the White House. Here they have the dead body of Vince Foster with a bullet hole in his neck. The nightly news would have a field day with this scenario; plus, they didn't want authorities on the premises before they could do some frantic housecleaning. Not knowing where else to turn, the Clintons fell back on their tried-and-true modus operandi: *Arkancide*. There's only one problem: suicides don't shoot themselves in the neck. So, they scurry Foster's corpse out of the White House parking lot and take him to the secluded cabin in Fort Marcy Park which is accessed via a secluded *back road*. There, they staged a more appropriate 'scene' (albeit very sloppily) of what they thought a 'suicide' should look like.

Sometime later, between 4:30 and 5:00 pm, Foster's body was rolled (or re-rolled) in a carpet and carried to the second cannon at Fort Marcy Park. Obviously, though, there are problems with such a scenario, including no gun at the scene (until one was planted later), no bullets, and no dirt or dust on Foster's shoes. Further, since Foster didn't drive his car from the White House parking lot, it had to be scuttled out later on the sly—thus no official record was ever made of its exit on the afternoon of July 20.

There you have it—the murder of Vince Foster on the White House grounds.

HILLARY'S "PLUMBERS" BREAK IN

The single entity who had more to lose than any other person in regard to the murder of Vince Foster—even more than the Mossad—was Hillary Clinton. Notwithstanding that his murder had to be made to look like a suicide, Hillary also went into hyper-fixer mode over the contents of Vince Foster's office. "The night of his death, Hillary launched one of the most shameful—and illegal—cover-ups of her entire career."[536]

What, precisely, are we talking about? "Within minutes after the news of Foster's death had been communicated to them, White House Counsel Bernard Nussbaum, First Lady Hillary Rodham Clinton's Chief of Staff Maggie Williams, and White House Director of Administration Patsy Thomasson were removing records from Foster's office."[537]

Not only were Hillary's Plumbers illegally breaking into and entering Foster's office, but they "were in there before 9 pm."[538]

This specific time is crucial because Vince Foster's body was not identified by White House staff members until after 10 pm. Therefore, the intruders were in Foster's office *before the positive identification*. In other words, "whoever dispatched the ghouls must have been *absolutely positive* that the body was Foster's."[539]

Here's the big question: "Whose idea was it to carry out the raid, and who had the authority to get Hillary's two top assistants, the director of the administration, and the White House counsel, to hop to it?"[540]

Let's face it: Nussbaum, Williams, and Thomasson didn't just break into Foster's office on a whim because they had nothing better to do that evening. They were directed to do so by someone in an extreme position of power. "Undoubtedly, it was Hillary Clinton who had orchestrated the purge of Vince Foster's office after his death."[541]

Why, one may wonder, were these burglars in Foster's office anyway? According to Maggie Williams, "She and Bernie were looking for a suicide note, or other clues to Foster's mysterious death,"[542] and they wanted to "feel the presence of Vince."[543]

While they were at it, they should have said they also wanted to meet the tooth fairy. Plus, if they merely wanted to locate a suicide note (which we'll elaborate on in a few moments), then why were they removing "armloads of files and loose-leaf binders"?[544]

What did Foster write, a suicide note that read like a novel, similar to Marcel Proust's *Remembrance of Things Past*? How many volumes did this supposed suicide note entail?

Incredibly, when asked about the stolen documentation, Clinton communications director Mark Gearan issued the following statement. "We know of no missing files."[545]

Yet "White House aides were scrambling like 'cats & dogs' to open Foster's safe on the night of July 20."[546]

Even more intriguing is the fact that "just after 7 pm, security officials cleared a 'MIG' group—a military intelligence group—into the White House West Wing. They met with presidential assistant Patsy Thomasson. Thomasson admitted to entering Foster's office later that night."[547]

Who, or what, was this MIG? "It appears that the unit is the Maintenance and Installation Group. It is part of the Technical Security Division, which handles alarms, locks, safes, surveillance, bugs, and the like. Very high tech. Very capable. If there was any unit in Washington capable of getting into Foster's safe, quickly and cleanly, these were the gentlemen who could do it."[548]

Officially, they were "logged into the offices of administration at 7:44 pm,"[549] over two hours before Foster was even identified! Obviously, the contents of Foster's safe were a high priority to the burglars, so, "did MIG assist her [Patsy Thomasson] by opening Foster's safe? Did MIG disable the entry alarm?"550

Or, was the MIG—a branch of the Secret Service—also there to merely "feel Vince's presence"?

At this point we know that Hillary's Plumbers made it inside Foster's office. What precisely did they filch?

> • Papers pertinent to the Whitewater project were removed from Foster's office during two searches—the first one, on the night of Foster's death (which went on for two hours rather than the ten minutes originally claimed), by Nussbaum, Maggie Williams, and Patsy Thomasson.551
> • A notebook Foster had kept on the travel office—which recorded Hillary's role—was removed from Foster's briefcase and concealed by Nussbaum.552
> • Copies of the Clintons' tax returns, a file marked 'Hillary Clinton Personal' and, for all anyone knows, documents relating to the Clintons' use of private investigators to track various women connected with Clinton in the past.553
> • The notes of Nussbaum's aide, Cliff Sloan, from the next day read, "Get Maggie—go thru office—get HRC [Hillary] and WJC [Clinton] stuff."554

Was the above information so damning that the Clintons would have gone to such great lengths to steal it; or could there be something more? As one writer asked, "What could have been in that batch of documents that was so incriminating, so abhorrent, that it was worth the extra measures? Was it so horrifying that it was also worth Foster's life?"555

Admittedly, the previous listed examples are pretty standard fare: Whitewater, Travelgate, adultery, and income taxes. The Clintons would most certainly be able to dodge those bullets. But there is one last item that few investigators have realized the significance of, or even mentioned. "Two separate intelligence agencies say documents relating to Systematics were among those taken from Foster's office immediately after Foster's death."[556]

Systematics, if you remember, was a software package pushed by Arkansas kingmaker Jackson Stephens which related to money laundering and the transfer of money between bank accounts. Why would someone like Hillary Clinton be concerned with Vince Foster's relation to these files? Because the money laundering led directly to Mena drug trafficking, ADFA embezzlement, and illegal campaign contributions. Now is it clear why Hillary's heaviest hitters were dispatched?

> [Bernard] Nussbaum so dominated the scene one would think that he, not the federal agents, was in charge. Nussbaum insisted that his own White House attorneys be present when staff witnesses were interrogated, a sure way of keeping people from talking frankly.
>
> The feisty lawyer also reportedly screened every piece of paper before letting the police see them. Nussbaum wouldn't let the police examine certain papers at all and wouldn't relinquish others. He carefully separated the papers out and gave the 'official' papers to the FBI. Foster's personal papers were sent to his attorney, and according to the White House, certain papers involving the Clintons were supposedly handed over to David Kendall, the First Family's personal lawyer.
>
> [I say "supposedly" because the White House has changed their story about the papers three times, and not until a year later did the truth come out.][557]

Maybe it's just me, but shouldn't this scenario be the *other* way around, with federal officials directing the investigation telling the

Clintons and their aides how things will be done, with White House personnel cooperating one-hundred percent? But yet again we see the Clintons acting as if they were a virtual law unto themselves. Imagine breaking into a jewelry store and stealing a box filled with diamonds, sapphires, broaches, and necklaces; then dictating to the police what you'll give back and what you'll keep. They'd laugh you out of the country; yet the Clintons did just that; then lied about it.

One FBI agent was aghast when hearing what took place. "The Secret Service agent asked me if I was aware that Foster's office had not yet been sealed. It was 10 am the morning after the suicide. My astonished reply was, 'What? You've got to be kidding me!' The office should have been sealed immediately after the White House learned of Foster's death, to prevent any accidental or intentional tampering of evidence."[558]

Also, let's take a look at exactly who served as Hillary's Plumbers. One of them was Patsy Thomasson. If you remember our previous analysis of Mena, "She spent the 1980s working for Dan Lasater, a Little Rock tycoon who went to prison for cocaine distribution. . . . Ms. Thomasson was his chief lieutenant."[559]

How did Ms. Thomasson end up in Foster's office? Was it of her own volition? Of course not. While eating at a restaurant, "she was beeped by David Watkins,"[560] one of Hillary's right-hand men at the time who helped her orchestrate the Travelgate firings and whose wife lured Lisa Foster out of their house so that Foster's gun could be stolen and presumably planted at the crime scene in Fort Marcy Park.

Another individual who contacted her was jailed Assistant Attorney General "Webb Hubbell, who directed her to look in Foster's office for a suicide note."[561]

But for some reason, Dan Lasater's cocaine sidekick Patsy Thomasson, the director of White House Administration, "was desperate to find the combination to Foster's office safe. She finally managed to get it open, apparently with the help of a special technical team signed into the White House in the late hours of July

20th. Two envelopes were reported to be in the safe by Foster's secretary which were addressed to Janet Reno and William Kennedy III. They were never seen again."[562]

Let's pause for a moment. If a person is going to take the plunge and they decide to leave a suicide note, they'd want to leave it in a location where *people can find it*. The last place they'd put a note is in a locked safe which needs a Secret Service MIG unit to open it. Yet, supposedly, this is where Patsy Thomasson sought Vince's final lamented words to the world. Hogwash. These people lie to such an inordinate degree that it boggles the mind. William Roemer, former head of the FBI's Organized Crime Strike Force, noted that this break-in, especially the entry into Vince Foster's safe, "raises the question of a cover-up."[563]

Another individual who became involved in the second part of looting Vince Foster's office was none other than Craig Livingstone, the dirty tricks operator and primary op behind Filegate in which nearly a thousand FBI files were stolen. A Secret Service agent revealed that "he saw Craig Livingstone, the director of personnel security, carrying documents out of the White House, first in a litigator's case and on a later trip in two cardboard boxes. Livingstone, too, would deny doing anything of the kind."[564]

In addition (the importance of this point will become clearer in the next section), "Secret Service agent Bruce Abbott testified that the next morning he saw Craig Livingstone carrying a brown leather or vinyl type briefcase, opening at the top, much in the fashion of a litigator's bag or lawyer's briefcase."[565]

As I've already pointed out, the Plumbers were "scrambling like cats & dogs"[566] to remove as much documentation from Foster's office as possible. The question now is: what did they do with these files—immediately relinquish them to official investigators? Not a chance. Rather, "some of the documents were turned over to Bill Clinton's personal attorney, Robert Bennett. Others were given to Foster's lawyer, James Hamilton."[567]

Others found a different path. "Several documents, including papers related to Whitewater, were removed from the safe and turned over to President and Hillary Clinton's personal lawyer, David Kendall."[568]

The secrecy was so pervasive that "some of the materials regarding the Clintons' personal affairs were sent to their Washington attorney. But the public wasn't told about that, or about their indirect route to the attorney."[569]

Hillary's control over the crime scene became so stringent that investigators weren't allowed . . . yes . . . weren't *allowed* to search Foster's office "until 10:00 am the following morning, July 21st."[570]

Remember, Foster was murdered on the afternoon of July 20— so they had to wait nearly twenty-four hours.

Hillary's paranoia stretched to incredible lengths, and no law could thwart it. After she discovered that Foster's wallet was found on his body, Hillary sent her Plumbers to the office of the Park Police where they "informed the police that they would have to break into the locked desk in which the personal effects were being held. The desk belonged to Sergeant John Rolla, who was off duty at the time; and since the White House couldn't wait until the next day, he had to make special arrangements to give up the keys."[571]

The search went beyond frantic to a point of crazed delirium: breaking into a Park Policeman's locked desk to obtain Foster's wallet. These people were horrified of what anyone else would find. Why? Here's an interesting clue. "Earlier that very day [of Foster's death], David Hale's office in Arkansas (he was instrumental in getting a fraudulent loan, much of which eventually wound up in the Clintons' partnership account) had been raided by justice officials, and a similar operation on Foster's office may have been imminent."[572]

Now can you see why Vince Foster *had* to be murdered? The walls were closing in, and he held all the secrets. Once Foster's files were accessed and he started to talk, a number of elite politicians, bankers, and intelligence operatives were going to take a mighty fall. Who, ultimately, was in charge of the cover-up and obstruction of justice in Vince Foster's murder? None other than fixer extraordinaire, Hillary Clinton.

How do we know? Well, at the time of the break-in, Bill Clinton was appearing live on Larry King's television show, so he obviously couldn't have been calling the shots. Further, Nussbaum, Williams, Livingstone, and Thomasson would not have taken such a highly illegal and risky task upon themselves. Therefore, "Hillary, it was said by many, directed the looting of Foster's office by cell phone from Little Rock."[573]

No doubt, Hillary was not only covering for others, but she also acted out of pure self-interest, for "given the nature of many of their dealings in Whitewater and other ventures back in Arkansas, her name was probably more exposed on the documentation in Foster's office than the former governor, and it is understandable that she would have been motivated to initiate and direct the raid."[574]

What a chaotic scene it must have been, and this is where I disagree with many Clinton researchers. Specifically, they lay out a scenario in which Bill and Hillary directed the murder. Then, when Patrick Knowlton stumbled upon Vince Foster's corpse at Fort Marcy Park, Hillary barked, "Okay, the body's been discovered. Let's go!"[575]

But in my view, that's not how events unfolded. With regard to Hillary, "undoubtedly she was involved in the early decision-making."[576]

But Foster's murder caught Hillary as much by surprise as anyone. That's why she went into such hyper break-and-enter mode. Time was of the essence. If they didn't snag Foster's files before the authorities did, they were sunk. If Hillary had commanded the hit on Foster, she would have already had a plan laid out to access his files. But as it stood, when Foster was killed in the White House parking lot, not only did she have to clean up the mess by having the body transported, but she also had to coordinate her Plumbers to do some frantic pilfering from his office.

Therefore, "throughout the crisis, Hillary kept a firm hand on the investigation."[577]

The reason why is obvious. "She did not want the Justice Department to have unfettered access to Foster's files"[578] [i.e. those who weren't directly under her thumb]. Thus, one of Hillary's most trusted aides, Maggie Williams, entered the picture as Ms. Clinton coordinated the break-in from her cell phone. "Phone records indicate that she [Maggie Williams] had been in contact with Hillary several times during the night."[579]

Further proof of Williams' direct link to Hillary during this caper can be found after Foster's Whitewater files were stolen. "What, then, happened to the Whitewater papers? Nussbaum had given them to Maggie Williams, who then quickly called Hillary Clinton in Little Rock, who in turn told her to put them in the safe in the family quarters on the third floor of the White House, where they sat for five days before being given over to Mr. Kendall [the Clintons' attorney]."[580]

To cover her tracks, Hillary lied about this matter for six months—saying that they had no files whatsoever—until "December 1993 [when] the White House finally admitted they had the Whitewater papers."[581]

THE FAKE SUICIDE NOTE

As noted earlier, a briefcase was initially seen in Vince Foster's car as it sat in the parking lot of Fort Marcy Park. In addition, one of Hillary Clinton's most notorious operatives, Craig Livingstone, was seen leaving Vince Foster's office with what appeared to be some type of leather briefcase. Were these the same items? Probably not, but a briefcase of some sort becomes an invaluable article of evidence when Foster's alleged "suicide" note enters the picture as another piece of the puzzle.

How so? Well, "several days after Foster's death, the White House produced a note, torn into 27 pieces and unsigned. They said it fell out of Foster's briefcase while they were gathering a package of his possessions to send to his wife."[582]

Stranger still, "the note never mentioned suicide, or anything close to it."[583]

According to the White House Pinocchio story, "this so-called suicide note was 'discovered' some days after Foster's death in his briefcase. However, there was only one problem with this discovery. Bernie Nussbaum, the leader of Bonnie & Clyde's locusts raiding Foster's office following the notification of his death, had shown the Park Police that same 'empty' briefcase with great playing-to-the-jury fanfare just two days before."[584]

So, once again the Clintons tampered with evidence in such a way that it defied the laws of our physical world. Like pulling a rabbit from a hat, the empty briefcase conveniently produced a torn-up suicide note only a few days later—completely out of thin air!

Others also found this amazing discovery hard to believe. "Although the torn-up note was reportedly found in Vince Foster's briefcase on July 26, a Park Police investigator said he had seen Bernie Nussbaum examining the contents of Foster's briefcase during Nussbaum's original July 22 search of Foster's office."[585]

This investigator continued: "During the July 22 search he had a clear view into the briefcase and was certain it was empty."[586]

Another member of the Park Police weighed in on this matter. Captain Charles Hume testified, "My opinion, if I looked in that bag, I would have seen a torn up note in it, especially if I had just pulled the papers out and put them out on the desk. I believe as a trained detective or if I was looking for that note or searching that bag for any evidence, I would have found that note, yes."[587]

Of course Bernie Nussbaum was not a trained officer of the law, but one of the police detectives present said, "Our oldest, blindest officer would have found that note."[588]

Backed up against a wall, especially when the *New York Times* voiced their suspicion of his story, "Nussbaum said he did not recall the briefcase."[589]

So, when the going gets tough and one's lies start catching up with them, all one has to do is conveniently fall victim to a dose of Hillary Clinton's 'amnesia' (i.e. forget everything by saying, 'I don't recall').

There's another curious twist. Similar to Vince Foster's gun which contained no fingerprints, we see the same phenomenon applied to his purported suicide note. "An FBI fingerprint analysis found no fingerprints—'a circumstance,' wrote the *New York Times*, 'that some investigators have found hard to believe.'"[590]

Again, the physical world is turned upside-down in Clinton-land—a place where objects disappear, reappear, and where fingerprints don't exist (at least in certain instances). Like so many other aspects of the Vince Foster murder, even those close to the case didn't believe Hillary's flimsy lies. Specifically, "Bernard Nussbaum's then-Executive Assistant, Betsy Pond, had reservations about the authenticity of the note."[591]

One investigator stated, "Betsy Pond's words and actions when she talked about the publicly released transcripts of the Vince Foster note strongly suggest that she had seen something that made her question the authenticity of the note. I believe she felt it was a forgery."[592]

Ms. Pond had every reason to be suspicious, for "three handwriting experts, including one from Oxford University, concluded the note was a forgery—a note which never mentioned suicide and [was] torn into 28 pieces and was found almost a week after his death."[593] [The 28th piece was missing.—Ed.]

No fingerprints, no sight of it in the briefcase, with experts determining that the note was a forgery. So, what precisely did this note declare? Of course, anyone that remembers this case knows the "official" line: Foster was depressed, events in Washington D.C. were overwhelming, and he just couldn't take it any longer. Or, as Bill Clinton told America, "He was profoundly depressed. You know, he left a note."[594]

But again, the truth was not being told to us. "The note to which Clinton referred was, in fact, a torn-up list of dubious origin, which made no mention of suicide. It was misleading of the President to tell the national television audience that Foster 'left a note,' implying it was a suicide note."[595]

The contents of this note weren't released "until August 10, 1993, when the Park Police officially closed their investigation of Foster's death. . . . The note consisted of a list of reflections, complaints, accusations, and exonerations. It did not mention suicide."596

The note concluded with this chilling declaration: "I was not meant for the job or the spotlight of public life in Washington. Here, ruining people is considered sport."597

But does one's displeasure or unease with one's job necessarily connote a death wish? Absolutely not, because in reality this alleged suicide note actually was Vince Foster's opening statements he planned on delivering to congressional investigators after he resigned his position at the White House and turned state's evidence rather than becoming another scapegoat who took a fall for the Clintons' crimes. What follows is a summation of Lisa Foster's testimony on May 5, 1994, taken from "Volume II, page 1646 of the Senate Manuals."598

> Lisa Foster then examined a photocopy of a handwritten note which has previously been identified as having been written by her late husband. Lisa Foster believes that the original note was written on or about July 11, 1993. Lisa Foster is not entirely certain of this date and believes the note was written sometime during the period between July 4 and July 20, 1993. She believes that the note was written by Foster in their Washington residence on a day when there were a number of young people in her house. . . .

Lisa Foster suggested to Foster that he write down everything that "they" did wrong. She suggested to Foster that he go on the offensive and not continue to take responsibility for every mistake which was made in the White House. Foster agreed with Lisa Foster's suggestion, and he sat up in bed and appeared energized. Foster told Lisa Foster that he had not resigned yet, and he said that he had already written his opening argument in his defense. Lisa Foster believes that the torn note which was found was (as indicated above) actually Foster's opening argument in the event he had to testify before Congress. Although Lisa Foster did not view or read the note on the day that Foster appeared to be energized by her remarks, she is confident that the comments written in the note were written on the same day.[599]

This article in question wasn't a suicide note; it was a plan as to how Vince Foster could protect himself against the Clintons after he resigned from their criminal madhouse and as he tried to stay out of prison. What he wrote was a defense—an opening statement—an attempt to go on the offensive before the Clintons put him behind the eight-ball, like they'd done to so many others before him.

Again, *it wasn't a suicide note!* Rather, "the note was written in his home, and the overwhelming likelihood is that it was obtained from his home."[600]

Then, after Foster was murdered and the Clintons had to create a cover story (i.e. he was "depressed"), Hillary's Plumbers broke into his house and stole his opening arguments. They then forged a new note, tore it to pieces, planted it in his briefcase (which was emptied days earlier and determined to contain no torn-up papers), and told the world this was his suicide note. Stated differently, "the note turning up several days later is now hard evidence that Clinton's goons were in Foster's home, obtaining the gun, the note, and whatever else they were looking for."[601]

THE STARR-FISKE COVER-UP

If one believes the conventional wisdom or popular mythology, 'independent' prosecutor Kenneth Starr was supposedly Bill and Hillary's fiercest nemesis—the bane of their existence. In actuality, nothing could be further from the truth, for Kenneth Starr served as "a passive accomplice in five years of Clinton cover-ups."[602]

Although the First Couple publicly sniped and complained about Starr being a partisan hit man and member of the vast right wing conspiracy, "privately the Clintons celebrated Starr's appointment. So says Nolanda Hill, longtime lover and business associate of late Commerce Secretary Ron Brown. 'When Starr was appointed, they were opening champagne bottles in the White House, they were celebrating.'"[603]

In addition, "according to Hill, Starr had actually been on Janet Reno's short list for the post of special counsel at the time she picked Robert Fiske. 'They would never have put him on the short list if they were worried about him,' she said."[604]

Why, we must wonder, was Kenneth Starr in the bag, so to speak? According to author Christopher Ruddy, who followed the Foster murder case for years, "the Clintons believed they had a hold over Starr, something with which to control, pressure, or blackmail him."[605]

How so? Whether they obtained this information via their theft of the 900+ FBI Filegate files, or via their control over the Justice Department, they found that "Starr shared some unlikely business partners with the Clintons."[606]

Similar to the Bush family being longtime business associates of the bin Laden clan, the Clintons and Starr had been doing business with certain nefarious Asians for quite a while. As you'll see in a subsequent chapter involving the murder of Ron Brown, Bill and Hillary were intimately linked with the Riady family for decades. Likewise, "During the time [he] was investigating the Clintons, Starr was working for a company wholly owned by China's People's Liberation Army and notorious arms dealer Wang Jun."[607]

In this sense, while the Clintons were wrapped up in Iran-Contra arms sales, Starr too had his skeletons. To what specifically am I referring? "Wang Jun was one of Starr's personal clients,"[608] and "in addition to being a major arms dealer, Wang Jun [was] also a high-level Chinese military intelligence operative and one of the major players in the Chinagate scandal."[609]

Worse yet, Nolanda Hill alleged "that Starr's entire investigative team had been infiltrated by Clinton operatives."[610]

Another individual close to the Clintons observed, "Half the people, or worse, that work for Starr are Clinton people—bad guys. They either report directly to the Clintons or worse."[611]

Such an assertion can be legitimately presented because "even

CHAPTER THREE

the FBI agents assigned to Starr were not working for Kenneth Starr in his Whitewater probe but for [Janet] Reno and the White House, giving the Clinton administration de facto control over the Starr investigations."[612]

The Clintons could have been brought down had a legitimate investigator actually handled the Vince Foster-Whitewater cases. Regrettably, as it turned out, Kenneth Starr was simply another straw man in their corrupt game. Christopher Ruddy rightfully sneered, "Starr was the sort of man who makes police states work."[613]

Ruddy continued, "He [Starr] was a coward, so paralyzed with fear in the face of naked evil that he would look the other way and pretend not to see it. He was just the sort of man that Bill and Hillary needed."[614]

Ruddy's anger continued unabated. "A weak, pathetic character, Starr has more responsibility than any other man in America for the woe the Clintons have wreaked, and will wreak, on this country. Starr has played out a role in the greatest Mutt and Jeff, Good Cop/Bad Cop routine ever perpetrated on the American public. Because of Kenneth W. Starr's complicity, the most corrupt administration in the history of the country continued with no end in sight."[615]

Editor James Davidson of *Strategic Investment* concurs. "When *The Decline and Fall of the United States* is written, Starr will merit a chapter. He will be seen as a weak, temporizing man who lacked the force of character to confront a corrupt system."[616]

This minion's lack of backbone was so pronounced that "Kenneth Starr refused to interview"[617] Patrick Knowlton, the most vital witness in the entire Vince Foster murder case.

The ugliness became so profound that "Miguel Rodriguez, Starr's lead prosecutor in the case of Vince Foster, resigned rather than be part of a cover-up. Starr's out-and-out cover-up of Foster's death began with his wholehearted acceptance of the report issued by Robert Fiske. Key witnesses, such as several Arkansas troopers who said they knew of Foster's death hours before the White House claims it did, were never put before a grand jury."[618]

Since we mentioned his name, let's take a look at the first "independent" counsel that was slated to investigate the murder of Vince Foster. "As president, Clinton approved Attorney General Reno's appointment of Robert Fiske Jr."[619]—a man completely on the take. So, right off the bat we have Janet Reno giving the nod to Fiske, which immediately discards any notion of *independence* in the investigation. Also, it seems the first family and their new "snoop" had quite an interesting past. "Fiske and Clinton go way back. It came out during the Senate hearings that it was Fiske who advised Clinton to fire William Sessions."[620]

This dismissal is crucial, and we'll examine it momentarily, but for now there are other Clinton-Fiske connections. When Bill and Hillary embarked on their real estate "career" via Whitewater, the land "was purchased from International Paper Company."[621]

Now, who do you think represented this entity? "The lawyer for International was none other than good ol' Fiske."[622]

Circumstances get even murkier in a big way when we learn of "Fiske's past association with the Bank of Credit and Commerce International which was involved in the laundering of drug money world-wide."[623]

Yes, BCCI—the Bank of Crooks & Criminals—rears its ugly head yet again. Plus, since Fiske was assigned to "investigate the various failed Savings & Loans in the Whitewater affair,"[624] venture a guess as to what they were associated with. "Many of these appeared to be involved in the laundering of drug money, particularly that which passed through Mena airstrip, a major entity in Clinton's candy store."[625]

There was other monkey business as well. One of the individuals who determined that Vince Foster committed "suicide" was Dr. Henry Lee. Who was he? Well, later he became "part of the defense team for the [O.J.] Simpson trial"[626] as well as being "the guy that was called in to do some work on the Danny Casolaro death down in Martinsburg, [West Virginia], way back in the early nineties."[627]

CHAPTER THREE

As you'll read in a subsequent chapter, Danny Casolaro was the first individual to start tracking the conspiratorial "Octopus" as an all-encompassing governmental organized crime syndicate. He was brutally murdered in 1991.

Even the congressional panel put in place to oversee Foster's murder was loaded to the gills with Clinton cronies. "The actual Senate investigation into [Foster's] death was being run by Michael Chertoff and Richard Ben-Veniste, a friend of the Clintons."[628]

We've already established Ben-Veniste's mob ties, while Chertoff was the *only* U.S. Attorney not fired by the Clintons when they did their slash 'n' burn purge of the Justice Department. Both Chertoff and Ben-Veniste later became members of the 9-11 cover-up.

To illustrate how rigged this "independent" investigation was, let's examine a point brought out a few pages earlier. "The Fiske Report says, 'the only vehicle entrance to Fort Marcy Park is from the Parkway.' Not true. Fiske unaccountably tries to ignore the existence of a back road. This road comes three hundred feet closer to the body site than the lot where Foster's Honda was parked. If Foster's body had been transported to the park, the killers would probably have used this back road because of its privacy and proximity."[629]

More importantly, there was a little-known cabin located near this back entrance that was probably used as a final staging area before Foster's body was dumped; yet there was no mention whatsoever of it in the Fiske report. He's lying by omission.

Many of these shenanigans could have been curtailed if someone "clean" had led the investigation, but "William Sessions, the honest director of the FBI, had been fired by Clinton the day before the death [of Vince Foster]."[630]

Who, in all creation, was cited to replace him? Louis Freeh, "friend of Bernie Nussbaum. Friend of Bob Fiske."[631]

You remember Bernie Nussbaum, don't you? He was one of Hillary's primary Plumbers that broke into Vince Foster's office and stole everything in sight. He—as well as Fiske—was friends with Louis Freeh.

Please don't take this dismissal lightly. "July 19, 1993 was a sad day for the FBI. Judge William Sessions became the first FBI director to be fired."[632]

This point is important in the larger scheme of American government because "the Director of the FBI is appointed for a ten-year term, somewhat like a judge, because it is always understood that a political FBI would upset the equilibrium of American government."[633]

Similar to their rape of the Department of Justice when they fired every U.S. Attorney except Michael Chertoff, "Director William Sessions had been defenestrated the day before Foster's death in a well-executed Washington putsch."[634]

Needless to say, this move created turmoil, and "it became obvious that the FBI agents who did the nuts and bolts work for the Fiske Report were engaged in a systematic cover-up."[635]

To prove how compromised Fisk was in regard to Vince Foster's murder, he explained that "a preliminary inquiry by the FBI failed to indicate any criminal activity, [thus] the FBI inquiry into this matter was closed."[636]

Even a ten year old child could tell that the Clintons were involved in it and their plumbers had broken the law numerous times; but still Robert Fiske came to the above conclusion. As a result, after Sessions had been unjustly canned, "the FBI was kept off as the lead investigative agency because of a power struggle between the FBI and the Department of Justice at the time of [the] Sessions firing."[637]

As we know, after the U.S. Attorneys were dismissed and Janet Reno became nothing more than a stooge of the grossly corrupt Webster Hubbell, It's no wonder that respectable elements of the FBI were squashed and superseded by the DOJ. The result was obvious: vital physical evidence and testimony was suppressed, ignored, and obstructed.

- "Four of the rescue workers testified in secret before the Whitewater grand jury in the spring of

1995 that they saw trauma to the side of Foster's neck or head."⁶³⁸ Of course, the official story has Vince Foster sticking a gun in his mouth and blasting a bullet through the *top* of his head. A neck wound changes everything. Kenneth Starr ignored this evidence.

• In "a folder of crime photos that had been deliberately withheld from the prosecutor . . . was the original Polaroid of Foster's neck. What it showed was something very different from the 'contact stain' in the fraudulent picture that had been circulating. Evidently, somebody had taken a photo of the original and then touched it up to disguise the incriminating evidence."⁶³⁹

• Speaking of which, "photographs were taken of the 'incident scene' but according to the 'independent' counsel, they were underexposed and hence, no photos were included in the report."⁶⁴⁰

• In this light, "the Park Police don't have a single photo of the whole crime scene."⁶⁴¹ Of those that did surface, none of them shows any context or perspective. "The only photos we know of are thirteen Polaroids showing only close-ups of Foster's body and the ground around it."⁶⁴²

• But wait a second. We seem to have another discrepancy. "The set of Polaroids that Officer [Franz] Ferstl took very early that night, recording the scene when the police first arrived, had disappeared."⁶⁴³ The whole situation is beginning to sound like a bad joke, or a twisted *Outer Limits* episode. Now you see it, now you don't. Bad magic at its worst. "Ferstl believes that he gave them [the photos] to Sgt. Bob Edwards. That was the last anybody saw of them. It has never been explained what Sgt. Edwards was doing at Fort Marcy Park in the first place. (The record shows that the Fiske investigative team never talked to him.) He was not the shift commander. He was not one of the detectives assigned to the case. Yet there he was, in the shadows, unaccountable, playing a critical role in the events of July 20."[644] This man, in all likelihood, stole some of the most valuable pieces of police evidence at the scene. Why was he even there at Fort Marcy? "Remember, this was supposed to be a 'routine suicide.' At that stage nobody was supposed to know that Foster was a top White House official."[645] But Sergeant Edwards was there confiscating prime photographs that never resurfaced again.

• The Park Police were obviously compromised. "Within hours of Foster's death, even before an autopsy was conducted, Park Police were disposing of crucial crime scene evidence. For example, Foster's White House assigned pager was given back to the White House on that very night, leaving us to wonder: who might have tried to call him that night? Were there any fingerprints other than his own on the device? We will never know."[646]

• The Park Police handling of this situation was so debased that "there is powerful evidence that the Park Police lied in their official reports as to the location of where Foster's body was found—changing its placement by a couple of hundred feet."[647]

• It seems evidence was tampered with in nearly every single instance. "The all important matter of the exit wound could have been easily resolved were it not for the missing X-rays (reminiscent of the missing crime scene photos). Oddly, the autopsy report clearly states that X-rays were indeed made. The Park Police report confirms this: Dr. Beyer stated that X-rays indicated that there was no evidence of bullet fragments in the head. Yet the Fiske report inexplicably states that no X-rays were made because the X-ray machine in Beyer's office was inoperable."[648]

The doctor himself clarifies this situation, but then he too drops the ball. "Beyer claimed to have taken at least twenty-seven photographs of the corpse, but a source close to the investigation believes that none were taken of that critical exit wound."[649] Imagine: a bullet wound in Vince Foster's neck completely ignored by the coroner (in addition to no crime scene photos or X-rays). Amazing beyond belief; an obviously transparent lie.

- In regard to Vince Foster's weapon, any first day rookie recruit at the police academy knows that tests are supposed to be performed on the weapon used in a crime, yet "the ATF was not asked to do a ballistics check on the gun until August 12, 1993, seven days after the Park Police had already issued its final report."[650]

- The strange gets even stranger. "The Clintons had ordered that one of the White House offices be completely re-carpeted shortly before the death of Vince Foster. The day following his death, a crew of workmen arrived at the White House and completely ripped up and removed what was nearly brand new carpet. They hastily piled the carpeting into a van and quickly left. The final destination of that carpet and why it was so hastily removed during the chaos and trauma following the death of Foster are mysteries."[651]

Let's put ourselves in the shoes of a detective for a moment and cast a keen eye on this revelation. We know for a fact that every article of clothing Vince Foster wore the day of his murder was covered with carpet fibers. Could a few remnants of carpeting have been lying around the office that were re-laid only days prior to the murder? In their haste, could White House cover-up artists have snagged one of these remnants and wrapped Foster's body in it? Then they realized that if someone who actually wanted to run a *real* investigation tested the fibers of this new carpet in comparison to the ones on Vince Foster's clothes, they'd be in serious trouble because they would match. So, they quickly covered their tracks by ripping up the brand new carpet and discarding it at an undisclosed location. But with a Fiske-Starr-DOJ-Park Police cover-up in full swing, nobody bothered to pursue this angle. How convenient.

I could continue listing these anomalies for page after page, but at this stage let's close with one last reexamination of Vince Foster's alleged suicide note. After all, the entire "depression" angle rests on this supposed document. Both Robert Fiske and Kenneth Starr should have examined this article with forensic precision. For starters, as mentioned earlier, three different handwriting experts declared the note a forgery. "One of them was Dr. Reginald Alton, emeritus fellow of St. Edmund Hall at Oxford University and former Chair of the English faculty, who had authenticated the C.S. Lewis diaries."[652]

His conclusion? "The note, he said, was a fake. It was the work of a 'moderate forger, not necessarily a professional, somebody who could forge a check or a pass in prison camp.'"[653]

Let's be clear: the note was a hoax. On top of that, it wasn't even a complete document. Instead, when "discovered" the note was torn into 28 pieces, with one of them missing. The public was told the torn sections were found in Vince Foster's briefcase. Again, another parade of lies.

> The briefcase had been searched four days earlier by Bernard Nussbaum in the presence of a team from the Justice Department. He had removed some files, peered into the briefcase from about two feet, and declared it empty. Twice.

> "It would have been impossible for him to miss that many torn scraps of yellow paper," said Sergeant Pete Markland, who was there representing the Park Police. By this stage Markland was convinced that Nussbaum was engaged in some sort of mischief. "It was absurd. I sat there shaking my head the whole time. I was disgusted."

When [Associate White House Counsel Stephen] Neuwirth picked up the briefcase the next week on Monday, July 26, the pieces of yellow legal paper that had been invisible before suddenly materialized.[654]

Conveniently enough, prior to the note's discovery, there had been a meeting between four individuals: Stephen Neuwirth, Bernard Nussbaum, White House spokesman Bill Burton, and Hillary Clinton. Even more interesting are some handwritten notes taken by Mr. Burton referring to how the Vince Foster "suicide note" would be found. Dated July 26, 1993, Burton wrote, "Far happier if discovered by someone other than Bernie."[655]

In other words, appearance-wise it wouldn't look very copasetic if Nussbaum found this note in the same exact briefcase which only a week earlier he'd personally inspected and had failed to find any such article inside. More importantly, with the first lady in attendance at this meeting, "Hillary Clinton was party to the deception."[656]

These same individuals were also quite guarded about letting anyone else see Foster's supposed note. "The Clinton circle was determined that no outsiders should get to see a copy of the original note. Webb Hubbell lobbied Phillip Heyman, the Deputy Attorney General, requesting that no photocopies of the note should be allowed to get out."[657]

Why do you suppose they would make such a strange request? Answer: because the note was an unadulterated, obvious fraud.

After experts examined the note, they opined that "at least two different hands worked on the note, suggesting that Foster's outline for the letter of resignation was 'modified.'"[658]

This forgery also created other problems. The faked note was originally torn into 28 pieces, but only 27 were found. What was contained on the "lost" section? "A botched attempt at a signature necessitated the strange "tearing" of the note and the loss of one piece just where the signature should have appeared."[659]

A suicide note with no signature; how precious is that?

Lastly, even though none of Vince Foster's fingerprints appeared on the note, there *was* one from somebody else. "The note had fingerprints on it and, officially, the origin of the fingerprints remains undetermined, but while testifying before the Whitewater Committee, an FBI expert reported that one palm print was identified as that of—guess who—Bernard Nussbaum."[660]

This is the same Bernie Nussbaum who reportedly missed seeing the 27 pieces of yellow paper torn up in Vince Foster's briefcase after he broke into his office on the night of his death.

In all honesty, I think Hillary Clinton and her Plumbers only told the truth about one detail in the entire Vince Foster murder—that he was dead. Everything else was unabashed, sloppily told lies. Any investigator worth their salt would have blown this case wide open in about two days time. But with Kenneth Starr and Robert Fiske at her disposal, Hillary covered-up another murder.

CHAPTER THREE

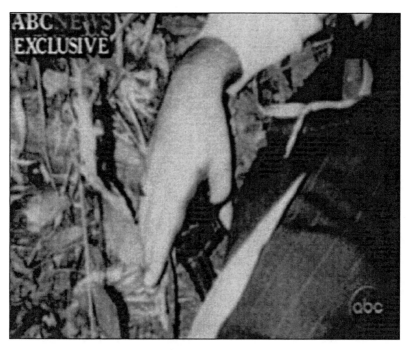

ODD GRIP: Here is a still video shot from some ABC News footage showing the odd way in which Foster supposedly gripped the "suicide" weapon.

PRETENDING IT'S SOMEBODY ELSE? A 1992 photo shows Bill and Hillary Clinton embracing at the time Bill was governor of Arkansas. The large number of close associates with damning information on the Clintons who have died in mysterious ways has led many researchers to speculate that the Clintons—or some powerful benefactors—have been eliminating any threat to the couple. Bill and Hillary's relationship is one entirely of political convenience.

AFP/GETTY IMAGES

CHAPTER FOUR

The Murder of Jerry Parks

E ven though Vince Foster was murdered on July 20, 1993, his presence continued to be felt into the future, especially in regard to the Clinton Body Count. Despite being portrayed as the most 'virtuous' of those in the Arkansas Group, Foster was undoubtedly a big-time player who posed more of a threat to the ruling elite than any political figure since Richard Nixon. Harvey Bell, a colonel in the Arkansas National Guard, had these words to say about Foster: "Vince liked to think of himself as a master chess player, moving all the pieces, controlling the game. He was always scheming in the shadows."[661]

As we've already determined, Foster was not a choir boy or the squeaky clean lawyer many portrayed him to be. Rather, along with Hillary Clinton and others, he was involved up to his neck in illegal activities.

This lifestyle, and his association with Bill and Hillary, directly led to Foster's murder. In addition, another man who became entangled in this twisted universe met a similar, even bloodier fate. According to his son (who we'll hear more from shortly), "on September 26, 1993, my father, Jerry Parks, the former head of security for Bill Clinton's presidential campaign headquarters, was brutally murdered."[662]

The hit, as you'll see, was classic Dixie Mafia; and even before his demise, Jerry Parks was being targeted as one of their victims. "A week or so after Foster's death, the Parks home was broken into, a highly sophisticated burglary in which phone lines and the alarm system were disabled. The files were stolen. Two months later, Parks was murdered."[663]

We'll address these files in a few moments, but first you should know how Jerry Parks was killed. "In September of 1993 while driving through a Little Rock intersection, his car was intercepted and stopped, and a lone assassin fired seven shots at Parks. At least three bullets were believed to be fatal."[664]

This incident was most certainly no accident. Here is what happened. Parks ate his "regular Sunday afternoon supper at El Chico Mexican restaurant. On the way back, at about 6:30 p.m., a white Chevrolet Caprice pulled up beside him on the Chenal Parkway. Before Parks had time to reach for his .38 caliber 'detective special' which he kept tucked between the seats, an assassin let off a volley of semi-automatic fire into his hulking 320-pound frame. Parks skidded to a halt in the intersection of Highway 10. The stocky middle-aged killer jumped out and finished him off with a 9 mm handgun—two more shots into the chest at point blank range. Several witnesses watched with astonishment as the nonchalant gunman joined his accomplice in the waiting car and sped away."[665]

As I said, this assault did not happen at random; nor by chance. "Parks was shot dead on the street. This was no mugging, but an out-and-out assassination, deliberate and determinedly thorough."[666]

To prove that this hit was intended for Parks, his family "later learned that the Caprice had been seen driving around the area of that intersection for three hours before the attack. [Jerry Parks] had been stalked."[667]

The gunman was described as being "a white male in his forties, six feet tall, with salt and pepper colored hair and beard."[668]

True to Dixie Mafia style, there is a strong possibility that the murder was linked to official sources: "An eyewitness told Mrs. Parks that he saw an Arkansas State Trooper leaving the scene of the crime. No charges have been brought."[669]

One of the most tragic elements of this case is that Jerry Parks knew the hit was coming. One day, while at home, everything became apparent to him. "'I'm a dead man,' whispered Jerry Parks, pale with shock, as he looked up at the television screen. It was a news bulletin on the local station in Little Rock. Vince Foster, a childhood friend of the President, had been found dead in a park outside Washington. Apparent suicide."[670]

Shortly after, "he muttered darkly that Bill Clinton's people were 'cleaning house' and he was 'next on the list.'"[671]

To protect himself, "he would pack a pistol to fetch the mail. On the way to his offices at American Contract Services in Little Rock he would double back or take strange routes to 'dry-clean' the cars that he thought were following him."[672]

Jerry Parks—a tough guy by anyone's standards—"ran a lucrative private security guard agency . . . one of Arkansas' most prestigious."[673]

He wasn't the type of guy who was easily scared, but he was now. Why? Because his agency handled Bill Clinton's security detail during the 1992 presidential campaign. A Clinton insider confided the following about their candidate. "He wanted Parks' guards to be his buffers when he did his screwing on the campaign trail."[674]

There were problems, however; many problems.

For one, "the Clinton campaign owed him more than $60,000 for work done by the firm"[675] which hadn't yet been paid. Secondly, "Parks decided to write an expose on aspects of Clinton's licentious life that was hidden from the public."[676]

Although we'll cover this subject in more detail, "Parks became so obsessed with his project that he expanded his efforts to chase down all reports that had surfaced about Clinton's infidelities since the beginning of his political career in 1974,"[677] thus establishing a motive for murder.

Whether it was revenge for not receiving the money owed him or simple disgust with Clinton's abject phoniness, his wife was "asked if it was possible that her husband could have played 'hardball' with the White House to recover his money. Mrs. Parks replied: 'He would never have been so stupid as to try to blackmail the president of the United States.'"[678]

In other words, Jerry Parks was well aware of the Dixie Mafia, Arkancides, and the Clinton Body Count. He also knew he was skating on thin ice.

Still, "On or about September 15 [1993], as Mrs. Parks recalled, 'our home was broken into. The phone lines were cut, knocking out our security system. When we checked around to see what might have been taken we found Jerry's files on Clinton were missing. I suppose they must have been stolen.'"[679]

The trauma and apprehension of living in the Dixie Mafia's bull's eye began having an effect on Mr. Parks. "Jerry couldn't sleep at night. He had nearly pulled out all the hair in his eyebrows. There was a great amount of stress. He was afraid. He carried a gun."[680]

Jerry's son, Gary, put the matter into even starker perspective. "Some very influential Arkansans have told me that my father was probably the only person in the state who could have brought [Bill] Clinton down. I have no doubt that Clinton himself, or people behind Clinton, had my father murdered."[681]

Mrs. Parks concurred. "I can't tell you that President Clinton ordered my husband to be murdered. But I can tell you that what Jerry had in his files could have unseated the President of the United States."[682]

Gary Parks continued, calling "his father's rub-out a 'premeditated, cold-blooded killing committed to silence him. I believe they had my father killed to save Bill Clinton's political career.'"[683]

Gary Parks didn't mince words:

> "'We're dealing with a secretive machine here in Arkansas that can shut anyone up in a moment.' It was a startling allegation. He was accusing the President of the United States of using a death squad to eliminate enemies."[684]

Needless to say, such statements are a bombshell, and some might dismiss them if they didn't know the entire story. Specifically, "Jane Parks went to visit a top official from the State Police whom she knew well from her church network. He told her outright that the murder was a conspiracy hatched in Hot Springs by five men who moved in the social circle of Buddy Young, the former chief of Governor Clinton's security detail and now the regional director of the Federal Emergency Management Agency for the south-central United States. She was given the names of five men, and was told that they had flipped coins to decide who would carry out the execution. And finally, she was told that nothing was ever going to be done about it."[685]

To ensure that the Clintons were protected, the same straw man who covered up Whitewater, the Vince Foster murder, and Mena entered the picture. Gary Parks snapped, "It's obvious to anyone with a brain that [Kenneth] Starr's job has been to make sure Clinton is not indicted and finishes out his second term."[686]

What type of information did Jerry Parks obtain and keep in his files that was so damning that it caused the Clintons to unleash their Dixie Mafia hit men? In essence, Parks collected data in three categories: Bill Clinton's womanizing, Roger Clinton's drug dealing, and Vince Foster's shadow network.

Let's start with Jerry Parks' surveillance of Bill Clinton's rampant prostitute-mongering. According to his son, one evening they "followed Clinton down to Roosevelt Road, a low-income area of Little Rock. Clinton circled the block a couple of times [riding in an unmarked state police car] and yelled over to a prostitute, a black woman. She got into Clinton's car."[687]

Other times, "they would stake out the haunts of the governor until the early hours of the morning. Quapaw Towers was one of them. That was where Gennifer Flowers lived."[688]

Bill Clinton's uncontrolled libido is tame compared to some of the other explosive information Parks collected; plus, others had already spoken out about this subject. So, there had to be more in the Parks family files that ultimately got Jerry killed. Another clue can be found in the information that Mrs. Parks had on Bill and Roger Clinton's activities at the Vantage Point Apartments, where she was employed as the manager.

> One time, Roger was so drugged out by the pool that [Mrs. Parks] had to take him physically by the arm back into his apartment. When they opened the door to the apartment, Bill Clinton was there. He was stoned. He wouldn't have known what was going on. He was basically sitting there on the couch with his arms down, just staring into the air. There wasn't anything but cocaine in the apartment. It was on the living room coffee table.[689]

With the drugs also came young girls—illegal, jailbait teenagers. According to Mrs. Parks, "What really started concerning me . . . was the young girls who came to the door. Roger would visit with them. These girls were young—fourteen, fifteen and sixteen years old. Roger constantly enticed the teenagers up to his place for parties with marijuana and cocaine."[690]

She also recounted why she believed Bill Clinton himself committed statutory rape. "One day Bill Clinton came to the apartment. He had an argument with Roger. Two men then came in two different state trooper cars. The girls were probably in their late teens. They couldn't have been 20. It wasn't 15 minutes before the noise started in the bedroom, and it was vulgar. It was Bill's voice and they were having some sort of sex party in that bedroom. The noise that came out of there I had never heard before. The 'f—' word was used real often. 'I'm going to screw your head off' was used too, but that was minor. God's name was taken in vain over and over."[691]

Roger's association with drug kingpin Dan Lasater was also an inflammatory issue because of Lasater's intimate contact with the governor. "By mid-1984, Roger spent virtually every waking hour getting high or trying to get high."[692]

Most anyone else would have been arrested years earlier, but since Roger Clinton was also one of the drug mules at Mena, he was afforded special protection from his brother's handlers. "He knew he was under suspicion but cockily assumed that he was untouchable. 'I've got four or five guys in uniform who keep an eye on the guys who keep an eye on me,' he explained."[693]

Still, when Roger Clinton spiraled so out of control (via drugs) that he became a political cancer, he too was served up as a sacrificial lamb and thrown in prison [all the while, of course, without fingering his brother's (i.e. the governor's) rampant drug use]. So, to have Jerry Parks murdered, there had to be more; which is where Vince Foster enters into the equation. We're getting into some real *Spy vs. Spy* skullduggery here, but this is the way the Clintons have always operated. Theirs is a realm reflective of *The Good Shepherd*, a movie that vividly illustrates a world where CIA spooks sleep with one eye open, never trust anyone, and constantly look over their shoulders. The Clintons aren't as much politicians as they are *operatives*.

Theirs is a world of paranoia and distrust. "In the late 1980s, Vince Foster—working on behalf of Hillary Clinton—hired Jerry Parks to do surveillance on her husband, Bill Clinton, like any faithful all-American wife would do on a daily basis."[694]

Yes, Hillary's secret police even spied on her own husband. While doing so, "Parks accumulate[d] thick files (with photographs) detailing the future president's pattern of womanizing."[695]

His efforts were quite extensive. "Parks had been working for Hillary Clinton, videotaping and cataloging the president's coming and goings and relationships with various females in Arkansas and elsewhere."[696]

Let there be no mistake who (as always) was calling the shots. "By the late 1980s Vince trusted Parks enough to ask him to perform discreet surveillance on the Governor. 'Jerry asked him why he needed this stuff on Clinton. He said he needed it for Hillary.' It appears that Hillary wanted to gauge exactly how vulnerable her husband would be to charges of philandering if he decided to launch a bid for the presidency."[697]

This information is confirmed by Jerry Parks' spouse. "Mrs. Parks' husband told her the operation was instigated by Foster's law partner, Hillary Rodham Clinton."[698]

Parks became such a Vince Foster-Hillary insider that he "went on to become chief of security at the Clinton-Gore headquarters during the presidential campaign."[699]

Thus, "Foster was using him [Parks] as a kind of operative to collect sensitive information on things and do sensitive jobs."[700]

However, Vince Foster didn't have a monopoly on these services. "It appears that Parks collected extensive surveillance files on Bill Clinton over the years—though not always for Foster. Some of it was clearly undertaken for other clients."[70]

According to his son, Arkansas political circles were teeming with intrigue. "The funny part is that the people who were paying Dad to photograph and document Clinton's illicit activities were supposed 'friends of Bill.' The deal worked like this. They gave Clinton money in return for favors, and then made sure Bill came through with the favors by reminding him of what they had on him. It really amazed Dad how Clinton was able to manipulate the people of Arkansas; but Clinton himself was also being manipulated."[702]

Primarily, though, "Jerry Parks had carried out sensitive assignments for the Clinton circle for almost a decade, and the person who gave him his instructions was Vince Foster."[703]

One of the jobs takes us to the heart of why Jerry Parks was a danger to the Clintons. "Foster and Parks had other operations running. The two of them had bugged the Clinton-Gore headquarters in Little Rock. 'Vince knew that somebody was stealing money from the campaign, and he wanted to find out who was doing it,' [Mrs. Parks] said. If her memory is correct, it suggests that Vince was far more deeply involved in the 1992 campaign than previously thought."[704]

How so?

Well, as you'll see, all roads once again lead to Mena, the single most glaring example of government criminality in the past fifty years. Foster was concerned because the entire phenomenon "raises extra questions about the bundles of cash coming through Mena. Was it campaign money? If so, how was it laundered? How could so much cash have been spread around without flagging the Federal Election Commission?"[705]

Sure, the telephoto lens photographs taken by Parks were embarrassing and could make Bill and Hillary jump through a few hoops, but Mena would drop them like a lead balloon. To show how deeply 'in' these guys were, "Parks had been a friend of Barry Seal, a legendary cocaine smuggler and undercover U.S. operative who had established a base of operations at Mena airport. Parks had even attended Seal's funeral in Baton Rouge after Seal was assassinated by Colombian pistoleros in February 1986."[706]

Parks also became a money-runner for the Mena operation, delivering the moolah to Vince Foster himself.

Once a cocaine shipment arrived, Parks "would leave his Lincoln at a hangar at the Mena airport, go off for a Coke, and by the time he came back they would have loaded the money into the trunk with a forklift. He never touched it. When he got back to Little Rock he would deliver the money to Vince Foster in the K-Mart parking lot on Rodney Parham Boulevard, a little at a time. They used a routine of switching briefcases, a 'flip-flop carrier' made of leather."[707]

What we're talking about is heavy-duty business: forklifts used to load the drug money, plus Vince Foster's direct involvement in Mena. Jerry's wife arrived at this knowledge in almost comical fashion.

In 1991, Mrs. Parks discovered what must have been hundreds of thousands of dollars in cash in the trunk of her husband's Lincoln car after he had made a trip to Mena airport in western Arkansas with Foster.

"It was all in $100 bills wrapped in string, layer after layer," she said. "It was so full I had to sit on the trunk to get it shut again. I took the money and threw it in his lap, and said, 'Are you running drugs?' Jerry said that Vince had paid him $1,000 cash for each trip."[708]

The shenanigans at Mena didn't end with the murder of Barry Seal, nor did it even end in the 1980s. Foster and Parks "appeared to have been involved [in] a variety of strange activities—including two mysterious trips the two men took to the town of Mena, western Arkansas, during the 1992 presidential campaign."[709]

So, not only were Dan Lasater, Dan Harmon, Don Tyson, and Roger Clinton directly involved with drugs, but so was Vince Foster—Bill Clinton's lifelong childhood friend and Hillary's lover. Plus, when Clinton's 1992 campaign was strapped for cash, Foster and Parks were zipping to Mena for some quick, readily-available dirty drug money.

Also, remember that Jerry Parks was notorious for chronicling his enterprises and storing the records in voluminous files. Now why do you think he was murdered by the Dixie Mafia in cold blood? Because of some pictures of Bill entering his girlfriend's apartment? Hell no. Parks had the down and dirty on Mena, including huge payoffs, money laundering, how drug money was diverted to Clinton's campaign coffers, and Vince Foster's direct involvement. He also knew that Foster and Hillary had been lovers—another major bombshell.

Everything came to a head shortly before Vince Foster's murder. "Gary Parks said he knew his father was in contact with Foster in the days before Foster's death. Parks said his family has phone records showing at least twelve calls made by Parks to the White House in the months before Foster's death, at least four of which went directly to the counsel's office."[710]

What were they discussing? One of the reasons Parks had been dialing Foster was "to demand payment for services rendered during the campaign."[711]

The sum was quite significant. "It has been said that Bill Clinton owed Jerry Parks $81,000 for 'security services rendered' during the campaign."[712]

As you'll see, financial matters were a secondary concern to Foster and Parks. Of vital, urgent, almost histrionic importance were the contents of Jerry Parks' files—and a certain person was going crazy about them. "About two weeks before his death, Vince Foster called Parks demanding the return of the information Parks had gathered on Clinton over the years. The matter was so sensitive that Foster used pay phones within the [Beltway]. He said Hillary was becoming frantic that Parks still had the documents and logs in his possession."[713]

Foster went on to explain that "Hillary had worked herself into a state about 'the files,' worried that there might be something in there that could cause real damage to Bill or herself."[714]

You better believe there was information that could hurt them. In addition to Mena and the dirty money which made its way into their campaign, "Parks had accumulated very thick files complete with photographs detailing the president's pattern of womanizing . . . Jerry Parks had compiled dossiers on many women, some as young as 17 years old. It was also rumored that he had helped Larry Nichols' lawyer Gary Johnson install the surveillance camera in the Quapaw Towers [home of Gennifer Flowers and Dan Lasater]."[715]

At this point we now know that Hillary Clinton had *direct knowledge* of Jerry Parks' files, and this information was so sensitive that it could destroy Bill and Hillary's political careers. Parks was murdered because of what he possessed. The only other person who was hyper-paranoid about the files was Vince Foster, and he was murdered on July 20, 1993. So who remained to order the hit on Jerry Parks? Answer: Hillary Clinton!

During the final week of his life, the files were again discussed, whereupon "Jerry told Vince Foster that there was indeed 'plenty to hurt both of them [the Clintons]. But you can't give her those files; that was the agreement.'"[716]

Then, according to Mrs. Parks, "the night before Foster met his demise on that fateful July 20, Foster had again telephoned her husband from a pay phone somewhere in Washington, probably on his way home to Georgetown from the White House. She related that the two men engaged in a heated exchange in which Foster spoke of a plan to meet Hillary Clinton at a location referred to as 'the flat' in order to turn over confidential files on Clinton still in Parks' possession."[717]

This time it was a heated exchange. Vince said that he had made up his mind. He was going to hand over the files and wanted to be sure that he had the complete set. "You're not going to use those files!" said Jerry, angrily. Foster tried to soothe him. He said he was going to meet Hillary at 'the flat' and he was going to give her the files.

"You can't do that," said Parks. "My name's all over this stuff. You can't give Hillary those files. You can't! Remember what she did, what you told me she did. She's capable of doing anything!"[718]

Hillary Clinton certainly is capable of doing anything because both Vince Foster and Jerry Parks were murdered within months of each other. What's most alarming is that Vince Foster apparently told Jerry Parks about something very "unpleasant" that Hillary once did. What the precise act was, we may never know; but both men exhibited a knowledge and fear of Hillary's capabilities and the lengths to which she would go if threatened in any way. Both men died violent deaths.

Another indicator of how aware Hillary Clinton was of Jerry Parks' murder came from Linda Tripp during grand jury testimony. "Prodded by the juror, Tripp returned to the subject of Jerry Parks' death. The 'flurry of activity,' the closed-door meetings, and the 'hush-hush' atmosphere in the White House all struck her as ominous and frightening. 'Maybe you had to be there,' said Tripp. 'The news of Parks' death was something they wanted to get out in front of. There was talk that this would be another body to add to the list of forty bodies or something that were associated with the Clinton administration at that time. I didn't know what that meant. I have since come to see such a list.'"[719]

The Clinton Body Count is real, and Jerry Parks' murder is proof positive. Linda Tripp continued speaking about Jerry Parks and Vince Foster. "He [Parks] had been killed. I didn't even at this point remember how, but it was the reaction at the White House that caused me concern, as did Vince Foster's 'suicide.' None of the behavior following Vince Foster's suicide computed to be just people mourning Mr. Foster. It was far more ominous than that, and it was extremely questionable behavior on the parts of those who were immediately involved in the aftermath of his death."[720]

Before moving on, there is one final point we need to address in regard to the phone calls between Parks and Foster. Specifically, Foster mentioned meeting Hillary at their secret flat or apartment, which has led many to believe that she was present for the murder, especially since blond hairs were found on his clothing, as well as a semen stain in his underwear. But this meeting did not take place. Foster "could not have met with Hillary Clinton because she was concluding a private trip to Santa Barbara, California—although Foster could mistakenly have believed he had a rendezvous with the First Lady. Instead of returning to Washington, Mrs. Clinton flew from California to Arkansas to visit her sick father, touching down in Little Rock at 7:40 pm local time."[721]

Therefore, the semen stain remains a mystery to this day. Was it simply an involuntary ejaculatory release upon death, or was it caused by something else?

Finally, to prove what a threat Parks' files were to Hillary, all anyone has to do is examine the actions taken by law enforcement agencies following his murder. After being mowed down Mob-style in the exact city where Bill Clinton served five terms as governor, "teams of FBI agents ransacked the Parks' house. They removed all office files, film negatives, tape recordings, and floppy discs."[722]

Further, if Jerry Parks was simply a nobody gumshoe head of a security agency, then why—on the day after he was assassinated—was his home teeming with federal agents... "men flashing credentials from the FBI, the Secret Service, the IRS, and she [Mrs. Parks] thought, the CIA? Although the CIA made no sense. Nothing made any sense. The federal government had no jurisdiction over a homicide case, and to this day the FBI denies that it ever set foot in her house. But the FBI was there, she insisted, with portable X-ray machines and other fancy devices. An IRS computer expert was flown in from Miami to go through Jerry's computers."[723]

Ponder this point for a moment. Considering how many people are killed each year in the United States, how often does the FBI show up; the Secret Service, or the IRS? The IRS for crying out loud! To further illustrate how far up the food chain this murder went, after Jerry Parks' computer was purged and all his taped telephone conversations confiscated, Mrs. Parks asked local Little Rock police officers when the materials would be returned. Their response? "They told [her] there's nothing they can do about the case as long as Bill Clinton is in office."[724]

Now let the debunkers and apologists explain away the Clinton Body Count.

CHAPTER FOUR   149

Hillary Clinton is shown with Jerry Parks.

OKLAHOMA CITY, OK: The north side of the Albert P. Murrah Federal Building in Oklahoma City shows the devastation supposedly caused by a fuel-and-fertilizer truck bomb that was detonated early April 19, 1993, in front of the building. The blast, the worst terror attack on U.S. soil until Sept. 11, killed 168 people and injured more than 500. Timothy McVeigh, convicted on first-degree murder charges for the bombing, was sentenced to death in 1997 and later executed.

BOB DAEMMRICH/AFP/GETTY IMAGES

CHAPTER FIVE

The Oklahoma City Bombing

BOMBS INSIDE THE ALFRED P. MURRAH BUILDING

In the hours following a quasi-botched bombing of the Alfred P. Murrah Building in Oklahoma City on April 19, 1995, KFOR-TV reported that Governor Frank Keating told President Bill Clinton that "right now they are saying this is the work of a very sophisticated group. This is a very sophisticated device. It has to have been done by an explosives expert."[725]

Shortly thereafter, as 168 people lay dead with countless others injured, the official story quickly changed. No longer was the explosion sophisticated, nor was it credited to experts.

Instead, two rank amateurs—Timothy McVeigh and Terry Nichols—supposedly using nothing more than a crudely constructed ANFO bomb (ammonium nitrate and fuel oil) were blamed for the incident.

As you'll see, the notion that a fertilizer bomb partially destroyed the Murrah Building is so preposterous that even a child would be hard-pressed to believe this fairy tale. Rather—and this point is of extreme importance—a series of bombs had been strategically placed inside the Murrah Building prior to April 19th, and they were what caused the massive damage. Further, government forces—including the FBI and ATF—had *complete foreknowledge* of this act, yet did nothing to prevent it (if not having a direct hand in initiating it in the first place).

Momentarily, I will provide a brief overview of the government's foreknowledge and involvement in the OKC bombing, culminating in an extensive analysis of the actual culprits (not a scapegoat named Timothy McVeigh who had peripheral contact with the real killers at Elohim City and was set up to take a Lee Harvey Oswald fall after the event took place). Once you finish this chapter, it will be undeniably apparent that similar to so many other incidents associated with the Clintons (Vince Foster's murder, etc), the American public has been snowed by a mountain of lies which covers the much darker underbelly of a governmental organized crime syndicate.

To begin, let's pose a question. How often do you see bomb squad trucks parked along the streets of your town or city? I'm sure most people would respond: not often, if ever. In addition, how often do you see these same bomb trucks parked only a block or two away from a building that subsequently gets bombed only minutes later? If you were told of such an occurrence, I'm sure most reasonable people would conclude that the bomb trucks had an indication that the nearby building was going to be hit, and the reason they were located in the vicinity was in preparation for the coming event. Of course, why the building in question was being bombed is a different matter entirely.

At any rate, guess what was parked only blocks away from the Alfred P. Murrah Building only moments before it was targeted. Bomb squad trucks!

There was no question that there had been a bomb squad truck in downtown Oklahoma City before the blast.

"I was coming down for a charity board meeting that I had at 7:30 in the Oklahoma Tower," said Daniel J. Adomitis, an Oklahoma lawyer. "There was a fairly large truck with a trailer behind it. It had a shield on the side of the door that said 'bomb disposal' or 'bomb squad' below it."[726]

Another woman, Renee Cooper, said that "she saw a bomb squad in front of the courthouse. There were six or seven men. It made her a little uneasy."[727]

When asked how she arrived at this conclusion, Ms. Cooper replied, "They had 'bomb squad' written across their jackets in huge letters."[728]

CHAPTER FIVE

These sightings were confirmed by others. "J.D. Reed, an employee with the Oklahoma County Assessor's office, also saw the bomb squad truck parked on the east side of Hudson Street in front of the county courthouse on April 19 prior to the bombing."[729]

Likewise, "Norma Joslin, a 30-year employee of the Oklahoma County Board of Elections, stated that she saw the bomb squad truck parked on the east side of Hudson Street in front of the county courthouse. She says she commented to a co-worker on the unusual nature of this sighting."[730]

Numerous people witnessed this bomb squad near the courthouse, and commented on how out of the ordinary it was. In other words, bomb squads weren't parked all around Oklahoma City on a daily, weekly, or yearly basis. These guys were there for a specific purpose. Although the FBI initially tried persuading witnesses that no such units were in the vicinity, "the Sheriff's Department finally admitted, after months of adamant denials by Sheriff J. D. Sharp, that the bomb disposal vehicle had indeed been in downtown Oklahoma City that morning."[731]

This disclosure is crucial, for now we're certain that the government was not only lying about the bomb squad's presence, but they were prepared for a significant blast that morning in Oklahoma City.

Another specific instance where the government deceived the public about their foreknowledge was the fact that not a single ATF agent lost their life in the bombing. Edye Smith, whose children were killed that day, put the matter into perspective during a live CNN interview:

"Where the hell was the ATF? I want to know. All 15 or 17 of their employees survived, and they were on the ninth floor. They were the target of this explosion, and where were they? Did they have a warning sign? Did they think it might be a bad day to go into the office? They had an option not to go to work that day, and my kids didn't. They didn't get an option. Nobody else in the building got that option. And we're just asking questions. We're not making accusations. We just want to know. And they're telling us: 'Keep your mouth shut. Don't talk about it.'"[732]

Ms. Smith's point was valid, because if we're to believe the government myth, militia member Timothy McVeigh specifically homed in on the Murrah building because of ATF atrocities at Waco two years earlier. But guess what. Kids in a day care center were killed, as were state workers and other innocent men and women. But the purported target—ATF—did not have a single casualty that day because not a single employee was present when bombs inside the building were detonated. Even though two of them may have reported to work earlier, every single ATF agent was conveniently out of the office at the time of the blast. Every one!

Realizing they had a public relations nightmare on their hands —one that left them with egg on their face—the ATF scrambled to arrive at a cover story. Stated differently, they started lying again, just as they had at Waco. "The ATF claimed that Alex McCauley, the resident in charge, was in an elevator when the bomb went off. He survived a free fall from the eighth to the third floor."[733]

Let's get this straight. An ATF agent took a plunge five floors down an elevator shaft—at freefall speed—that's fifty feet, and he survived? Will miracles never cease? Hundreds of other victims were crushed, suffocated, or buried in a mountain of debris; but incredibly, the supposed sole ATF worker comes out unscathed after dropping from what would be the equivalent of a five story building.

There's only one drawback to this story: it's another lie. Engineer Duane James from "the Midwestern Elevator Company, the firm that had actually searched the elevators for survivors,"[734] stated, "We found that five of the six elevators were frozen between floors, and a sixth had stopped near floor level. We had to go in through the ceilings of the elevators to check for people. All were empty."[735]

James continued, "Agent Alex McCauley could not possibly have broken out before the team arrived, not unless he had a blowtorch with him. The doors were all frozen shut. It took several of our men over twelve hours just to get the one elevator opened."[736]

CHAPTER FIVE 155

McCauley's story was an unadulterated lie. "None of the elevators had been in free fall. That's pure fantasy. Modern elevators have counterbalances and can't free fall unless you cut the cables, and none were. There are a series of backup safety switches that will lock an elevator in place if it increases in speed more than ten percent. The Midwestern Elevator Company took extensive photographs to document the inspection. These records were later received by ABC's *20/20* program. The pictures confirmed that all the safety cables were intact."[737]

Try to imagine the evil sickness of this gross deception. The ATF actually concocted a story where one of their agents supposedly free fell fifty feet and survived, then used superhuman strength to escape from an elevator that took professionals twelve hours to open—all to seemingly prove that the ATF hadn't been tipped-off beforehand. But it was all a grotesque lie.

There's additional proof of ATF and FBI foreknowledge of this heinous act where 168 innocent people—including children in a day care center—were murdered. One agent, "his face hidden behind a shadow for fear of ATF reprisal, asserted that he was told by an ATF agent that, 'we were tipped off by our pagers not to come to work that day.' His employer, who overheard the conversation, willingly confirmed this controversial claim."[738]

ATF agents weren't the only ones given a heads up that an attack was about to take place. Investigators from ABC's *20/20* "provided substantial proof that local fire department officials were instructed by the FBI five days before the blast that there were some people coming through town they should be on the lookout for."[739]

It seems quite a number of people, from the ATF, FBI, bomb squad, and emergency services knew that a dramatic event was about to take place. But no one bothered to tell the innocent people that went to work that morning and eventually got killed or maimed. Be assured, the government knew in advance. "In perhaps the most startling revelation, the *20/20* investigation uncovered proof that the Executive Secretariat Office at the Justice Department received a call 24 minutes before the explosion announcing that, 'the Oklahoma federal building has been bombed.' Unfortunately, in an unforgivable sin of omission, authorities failed to notify anyone of this strange call, much less demand the building in question be evacuated."[740]

On the contrary, all those inside were left to be potentially killed or injured.

If you're beginning to notice a pattern of lies, hold on because you haven't seen anything yet. The next myth to be exploded is the infamous 'Ryder truck' bomb which reportedly brought down the Murrah Building. More specifically, the bomb was supposed to have been made of "4,800 pounds of ammonium nitrate mixed with fuel oil to create a combustible 'slurry' known as ANFO."[741]

Actually, even this description isn't accurate because the government's story kept changing over time. "The FBI reported that the bombing of the Murrah Federal Building was caused by a single 1,200 pound bomb made of ammonium nitrate (AN) and fuel oil (FO), contained inside 55-gallon barrels and exploded within a 20-foot Ryder rental truck parked in front of the Murrah Building."[742742]

But wait; the government realized that anyone with even the slightest knowledge of physics would slice their story to smithereens. Why? Because, essentially, the Ryder/ANFO device was what explosives experts call an open-air bomb. In other words, rather than being physically affixed to the building itself (such as to a foundation beam which supported the building and is crucial to it remaining intact), the supposed bomb was sitting in a truck on the street, away from the structure. Common sense tells us that the farther away the bomb is from its target, the less impact it will have. As you'll see later, the expert of all explosives experts stated that the most destruction this ANFO bomb could have caused was to break a few windows in the Murrah Building. That's it.

The government understood the type of problem they had on their hands, so "the story later changed to a 4,800-pound ANFO bomb. Then during the trial of Timothy McVeigh, the story changed again to a 4,800 pound mixture of ammonium nitrate

(AN) and nitromethane (NM), a high performance racing fuel."[743]

The government's conspiracy theory soon reached the point of being laughable. "It would take weeks to build a 4,800-pound truck bomb this way, and it would not solve the technical challenge of achieving simultaneous detonation. Yet the prosecution insists that McVeigh and Nichols built the bomb in one day, on April 18, 1995, and then executed the flawless detonation of the biggest ANFO [or ANNM—Ed.] bomb in the history of U.S. terrorism."[744]

The problem of detonation mentioned above is particularly important because we're led to believe that McVeigh and Nichols had all these huge vats filled with ANFO [note: 4,800 pounds of this substance would equal over 100 five-gallon water jugs], and they needed them to be all wired together to spark (i.e. explode) at the exact same time to be effective. It takes a great amount of technical expertise to pull off such a feat; much more than these two bozos possessed. "When Timothy McVeigh and Terry Nichols tried to blow up a milk jug with a small fertilizer bomb in October 1994, the experiment was a fiasco. 'The blasting cap just sprayed the ammonium nitrate everywhere. It didn't work,' said Michael Fortier at McVeigh's trial."[745]

These guys couldn't blow up a damn milk bottle! Plus, an open-air bomb wouldn't have destroyed the Murrah Building. "The FBI had no scientific basis for concluding that the Murrah Building was blown up by an ammonium nitrate fertilizer bomb."[746]

Again, outright lies were fed to the American public. "The [FBI] labs guessed that the explosive charge was placed in 50-gallon white plastic barrels without conducting the requisite tests."[747]

Moreover, "they said that the detonator appeared to be a Primadet Delay system, but no trace of this was found at the crime scene."[748]

Isn't this lack of, or manipulation of, evidence starting to sound eerily like the Vince Foster case? "The Inspector General's report found that the FBI crime labs had repeatedly reached conclusions that incriminated the defendants without a scientific basis."[749]

Upon further reading we will establish one rock solid fact: an

ANFO bomb was physically incapable of causing the widespread damage that we witnessed in Oklahoma City, while McVeigh and Nichols didn't possess the technical expertise (or logistical capabilities—try to imagine how monumental the task of moving nearly 5,000 pounds of ANFO would be) to even build a bomb.

The actual destruction to the Alfred P. Murrah Federal Building was caused by bombs *inside* the building. The following information completely and utterly destroys the government's single bomb ANFO/ANNM fable. "After the rescue efforts had begun, there were reports of other bombs being found within the Murrah Building. The building was evacuated at least twice due to these reports."[750]

In the moments following this calamity, the sooner rescue workers were able to locate the victims the higher the probability was that they could be saved. Yet that morning in Oklahoma City, their efforts were halted at least two different times so that bomb squads could enter and remove unexploded bombs! The following passage is damning beyond words:

> At one point, Toria Tolley with CNN reported: "There is still a danger of another huge explosion. Police have confirmed two more bombs have been discovered in the building. Authorities say one of the bombs has been found and discarded. A bomb squad is reportedly dealing with the other one at this time."

Later KWTW reported: a third explosive device, another bomb—we don't know if it's three or four—but perhaps another bomb has been found inside that federal building. They are moving everyone back once again. This would be the fourth time that this has happened.[751]

I've seen the above raw footage with my own eyes, and the evidence is conclusive. The initial newscasts emanating from local OKC TV stations show bomb squads carrying unexploded bombs *out of* the Murrah Building. Such a disclosure completely flies in the face of what the government told us happened. According to their fairy tales, one ANFO/ANNM bomb outside the building caused all the damage; nothing else. Yet what follow are direct transmissions from OKC law enforcement officials.

> The highway patrol dispatcher logs clearly show that there were two bombs found in the Murrah Building after the blast. The following entries can be found: 10:29 am. There is another bomb on the south side of the building. Need to get away as far as possible ... evacuate the area of the building immediately. 10:37 am. OC Fire Dept. confirms they did find a second device in the building. [752]

They weren't the only sources for the reality of multiple bombs inside the building. "A DOD [Department of Defense] Atlantic Command memo from Norfolk, Virginia dated April 20, 1995 also shows two additional explosives were found."[753]

The evidence of bombs in the building is so overwhelming that it can no longer be denied. "Joe Harp is a retired CIA operative who now lives in Texas and told the following story. On the day of the bombing, he was in the Murrah Building at about 11:00 am and observed members of 'the fire department EOD' [Explosive Ordnance Disposal] removing two devices and placing them in the bomb disposal unit. He described the devices as military olive-drab in color and the size of round five-gallon drums. He also stated that, upon his arrival, he knew that the explosive device that caused the damage to the building was not an ANFO bomb because he could smell sulfur in the air that reminded him of the gas-enhanced 'Daisy Cutter' bombs that were used when he was in Vietnam."[754]

Not only did these devices cause the *real* damage to the Murrah Building, but those that were unexploded and had to be removed greatly hindered rescue efforts, indirectly causing more victims to perish. Following the blast, Dr. Tom Coniglione directly announced, "At the present time, the medical teams downtown are unable to get into the wreckage to retrieve more of the injured because of the presence of other bombs in the area. I've been told by the police department that just as soon as those bombs are defused, they will permit the medical teams to enter."[755]

During the earliest news telecasts, acclaimed terror authority Dr. Randall Heather noted, "We got lucky today, if you consider anything about this tragedy lucky. It's actually a great stroke of luck that we've got undefused [sic] bombs."[756]

Similarly, "at approximately 11:31 EST, on the day of the bombing, KFOR television broadcast the following announcement: 'The FBI has confirmed there is another bomb in the federal building. It's in the east side of the building. We're not sure what floor, what level, but there is definitely danger of a second explosion.'"[757]

Why didn't the federal government or the corporate media disclose this information on a wide-scale basis? Why the cover-up? Bottom line: "Although given little coverage by the mainstream press, eyewitness testimony and other supporting evidence show that undetonated charges were located and defused once rescue efforts were under way."[758]

Experts confirm that the official story regarding OKC was a bold-faced lie. First, Dr. Sam Cohen, who worked on the Manhattan Project and spent four decades in the nuclear weaponry field, snubbed his nose at the government's ANFO theory. "I believe that the demolition charges in the building were placed inside at certain key concrete columns and did the primary damage to the Murrah Federal Building. It would have been absolutely impossible and against the laws of nature for a truck full of fertilizer and fuel oil—no matter how much was used—to bring the building down."[759]

These are mighty powerful words; but oh so true. An open-air bomb can't create that much damage. "A series of Armament Directorate tests were conducted by Wright Laboratory at Eglin Air Force Base in Florida against simulated conventional urban buildings. This study was conducted to demonstrate the capability of explosive devices against cast-in-place concrete structures with steel reinforcement bars. The report states that "air blast alone was singularly ineffective in causing major damage to the Eglin test structure."[760]

Put more simply, open-air bombs don't destroy solidly built structures. To level them, you need explosives placed directly on the foundational support columns.

Others have confirmed this information. "In the spring of 1997, explosives experts at Eglin Air Force Base's Wright Laboratory Armament Directorate released a study on the effects of explosives against a reinforced concrete building similar to the Federal Building. The Air Force's test closely matched the conditions under which the government contends the Murrah Building was destroyed. [David] Hoffman quotes from the report: It must be concluded that the damage at the Murrah Federal Building is not the result of the truck-bomb itself, but rather due to other factors such as locally placed charges within the building itself."[761]

Another gentleman who invested considerable time studying this event was Brigadier General Ben Partin, the expert's expert on military explosives and weaponry. As this tragic event unfolded, Partin commented, "When I first saw pictures of the truck-bomb's asymmetrical damage to the Federal Building, my immediate reaction was that the pattern of damage would have been technically impossible without supplementing demolition charges at some of the reinforcing concrete column bases."[762]

According to Partin, "to produce the resulting damage pattern in the building, there would have to have been an effort with demolition charges at column bases to complement or supplement the truck bomb damage."[763]

The government has lied since day one. "According to [Partin's] detailed analysis, it would be physically impossible for an ANFO bomb to have destroyed the many steel-reinforced concrete columns which were situated far from the [truck bomb]."[764]

Partin essentially relied on simple logic. If an open-air bomb is detonated, those structures closest to the explosion should suffer the most damage, while those farther away would be affected to a lesser extent. But in Oklahoma City, the laws of nature didn't apply. "To substantiate his assertions, the military expert notes that building columns B-4 and B-5, which were in direct proximity to the blast, remained standing, while column A-7, which stood some 60 feet from the Ryder truck, was mysteriously demolished. 'The much closer columns are still standing, while the much larger column A-7 is down. These facts are sufficient reason to know that columns B-3 and A-7 had demolition charges on them,' he states confidently."[765]

Others have concurred with this opinion.

- Army veteran Gary McClenny, in a May 16, 1995 letter to FBI Director Louis Freeh: "Ammonium nitrate is a poor choice for breaching reinforced concrete."[766]
- Demolitions expert Sam Groning "recalls setting off 16,000 pounds of ANFO and alleges he was standing upright a mere 300 yards from the blast site."[767] That's four times the size of McVeigh's supposed bomb, and it couldn't even knock a man off his feet.
- An August 1996 FEMA study concluded that "4,800 pounds of ANFO would have been virtually unable to have caused the so-called thirty-foot crater in OKC."[768]
- A leaked Pentagon study reported that "the destruction of the federal building last April was caused by five separate bombs."[769]
- The 1997 Eglin Blast Effects study "could not ascribe the damage that occurred on April 19, 1995 to a single truck bomb containing 4,800 pounds of ANFO and instead suggested that other factors such as locally placed charges within the building itself may have been responsible."[770]
- Neutron bomb inventor Samuel Cohen asserted, "It seems to me that the evidence has got-

ten much stronger in favor of internal charges, while the ammonium nitrate bomb theory has fallen apart."[771]

- Author David Hoffman "cites reports of physical evidence such as more damage being done to the roof [of the Alfred P. Murrah Building] than relatively close to the truck, [and] elevator doors blown away from the shafts and toward the truck]."[772]
- U.S. Government Technical Manual No. 9-1910 contained the following information. "ANFO couldn't possibly produce a shock wave capable of mangling the building's concrete supports."[773]
- Dr. Charles Mankin of the University of Oklahoma Geological survey found "there were two separate explosions based on his analysis of seismographic data from two facilities. Seismographs show two distinct 'spikes' roughly ten seconds apart."[774]

The above individuals are authorities and/or experts in their fields, and all have given credence "to the existence of additional (and deadlier) explosives inside the building."[775]

Plus, remember our analysis of the original news reports which were carried by the local Oklahoma City media. "KFOR television broadcast that as many as two explosive charges had been located that were far more lethal than the *original* charge that nearly toppled the Murrah Building."[776]

Nationwide media sources—at least initially—also corroborated the multiple bomb story. "As reported widely on CNN and TV stations across the nation, up to four primed bombs were found inside what remained of the Murrah Federal Building on April 19, 1995."[777]

Local authorities are also in agreement. "Radio logs and other documentary materials provide transcripts of OKC police and fire department personnel discussing the removal of additional explosives. Reports of up to four bombs have surfaced."⁷⁷⁸

The preponderance of evidence is 100% undeniable. "Highly powerful non-ANFO explosive devices were detonated inside the building."⁷⁷⁹

In this sense, "If ANFO is physically incapable of causing the level of damage sustained by the Murrah Building, and if evidence shows that more than one explosion occurred on April 19, 1995, one must at least consider the existence of a more far-reaching conspiracy than the one sanctified by the mainstream media."⁷⁸⁰

Last but not least, there is a huge amount of "evidence which seems to indicate that the federal government possessed prior knowledge of an imminent terrorist strike on the Murrah Building."⁷⁸¹

The above information changes the entire scenario in regard to OKC. First of all, why wouldn't the federal government tell us about additional bombs, and that ANFO could not have leveled the Murrah Building?

The answer is simple: they had two scapegoats—Timothy McVeigh and Terry Nichols—and an agenda which they were pursuing. More importantly, they had direct knowledge that this event was going to occur, and they allowed it to take place.

As you will see in the following section, the government's foreknowledge of the OKC bombing was so vast that there should have been extensive arrests within the FBI, ATF, Clinton White House, CIA, and the Oklahoma state legislature.

One of the primary sources of direct, firsthand knowledge was ATF informant Carol Howe, who "had infiltrated Elohim City and stumbled on a conspiracy to bomb federal buildings in the state of Oklahoma. The plot was led by Dennis Mahon and Andreas Strassmeir. Furthermore, the main gist of this had been passed on to the U.S. government before the Oklahoma bombing."⁷⁸²

Although more details will be provided shortly, the main organizational point for this attack was a compound in rural Oklahoma called Elohim City, which had been highly infiltrated by factions of the federal government:

> By Christmas [1994] the plot was taking shape. Strassmeir and Mahon, the ringleaders, had picked three possible targets for attack in the state of Oklahoma: the IRS, plus federal buildings in Tulsa, and the "federal building" in Oklahoma City. Carol [Howe] has stated under oath that she reported these threats to her ATF case officer.[783]

Howe's assertions were later verified by government documents.

> An April 21 [1995] FBI memo confirms that the Bureau was fully aware of Carol's clandestine intelligence within two days of the bombing. 'Mehaun [Mahon] has talked with Carol about targeting federal installations for destruction through bombings, such as the IRS Building, the Tulsa Federal Building, and the Oklahoma City Federal Building. Strassmeyer (sic) has talked frequently about direct action against the U.S. Government. He is trained in weaponry and has discussed assassinations, bombings and mass shootings.[784]

This memo is the smoking gun of the Oklahoma City bombing.

There were individuals within the government and media who became aware of this information and refused to remain silent about it. One was retired Marine Lieutenant Colonel Roger Charles who was fired from ABC News for speaking out in protest. The reason? He was told "this story would bring the country down."[785]

Indeed, there is verifiable proof that the U.S. government was fully aware of a mass bombing—prior to it occurring with their own informants on the inside—and they didn't do a damn thing to prevent it. 168 innocent citizens, including children in a day care center, were slaughtered in cold blood.

Their guilt is appallingly evident.

"Two days after the Oklahoma bombing Carol Howe reminded the FBI that Strassmeir was a terrorist instigator who had talked frequently about direct action against the U.S. government. . . . The FBI record of her debriefing, dated April 21, 1995, goes on to say that Strassmeir had taken three trips to Oklahoma City in November 1994, December 1994, and February 1995. It also mentions the fact that Strassmeir's friend Dennis Mahon had threatened to blow up the Oklahoma Federal Building, yet the FBI saw no reason to interview Strassmeir."[786]

If that's not bad enough, let's push the envelope all the way. Not only did the U.S. government have informants within Elohim City, they also had their own agents, including Andreas Strassmeir! He was the ringleader, and he was the man who organized the OKC bombing. It wasn't Timothy McVeigh. He was simply another Lee Harvey Oswald patsy.

As you'll see in the following section, there is even substantial proof that Strassmeir and McVeigh were hanging out together prior to the OKC attack: "McVeigh was seen with Strassmeir and Michael Brescia eleven days before the bombing. The three men were at a strip club called Lady Godiva's. We know that the date was April 8 [1995] because [of] the security cameras."[787]

There is also evidence that McVeigh met with officials from the government.

According to investigative researcher David Hall: "On the night before the bombing, several witnesses saw McVeigh meet with ATF agent Alex McCauley and two other individuals of Middle Eastern descent in an Oklahoma City McDonald's at approximately 9:30."[788]

[Yes, this is the same Alex McCauley who purportedly fell five stories in an elevator, then broke out through the steel doors and emerged unharmed. Totally absurd.]

Late in 1994, a federal agent revealed that the government had put out the word that Strassmeir was classified as "hands off."

In a conversation with the publisher of *The John Doe Times*,

Mike Vanderboegh, the agent said: "'We've gone as far as we can with this; we've been told to back off. Maybe you guys can do something with it.' Then he told [Vanderboegh] that Strassmeir had been the government-sponsored snitch inside the Oklahoma bombing."[789]

THE ELOHIM CITY CONNECTION

INTRODUCTION

According to the federal government, they had no idea whatsoever that the Alfred P. Murrah Building was going to be bombed on April 19, 1995. And, to convince the American public, Attorney General Janet Reno swore that there would be no stone unturned in their investigation. So, 2,000+ federal agents were placed on the case; and according to them, 20,000 people would eventually be interviewed.

In addition, the investigators checked 43,000 tips, journeyed from Arizona to Las Vegas, and from upstate Michigan to the Philippines in search of answers. In all, they would generate over one billion documents and spend over one million investigative hours on this case.

And what, ultimately, did the government conclude after this exhaustive investigation? Answer: that there was no evidence of anyone involved in the OKC bombing other than Timothy McVeigh and Terry Nichols.

As I will prove, though, the government—including the FBI, ATF, Department of Justice, and CIA, among others—lied through their teeth about having no foreknowledge of, or involvement in, the Alfred P. Murrah bombing on April 19, 1995.

Specifically, events at a 400-acre compound called Elohim City hold the key to OKC, and elements within our federal government were 100 percent certain that the horrific events of that day would take place.

Regrettably, of the 2,000 federal agents, 20,000 people interviewed, and one million investigative man-hours spent on this case, not one agent was dispatched to Elohim City. In fact, Associated Press writer Paul Query quoted an unnamed law enforcement official who had this to say on the subject: "Elohim City is not a current subject of interest."

Elohim City is not only ground zero for one of the gravest miscarriages of justice in this country's history; it is also one of the federal government's biggest sources of fear, for it reveals in painstaking detail how intimately and directly involved they were in the bombing of the Alfred P. Murrah Building.

ANDREAS STRASSMEIR

To substantiate my introductory claims, I will systematically and methodically show how all roads led to Elohim City. To do so, I'm going to follow, in chronological order, the movements of a man named Andreas Strassmeir, as well as a fascinating cast of characters surrounding him.

To begin, we need to introduce Mr. Strassmeir, who was a German national before immigrating to the United States for a lengthy stay in 1991, where he eventually became the head of security at Elohim City.

Strassmeir was the son of Gunter Strassmeir, who was the architect of German reunification and a top aide to German chancellor and Bilderberg luminary Helmut Kohl. In addition, Strassmeir's grandfather was a founding member of the Nazi party (which, immediately after WWII, had direct ties to American intelligence via Project Paperclip), while the Strassmeir name is one of the most respected and influential in Germany.

In all, the Strassmeir family was connected to the power elite in every sense.

Strassmeir himself spent seven years in the German army as a Bundeswehr officer, where he served with the Panzer Grenadiers, which is an elite intelligence unit. And, in case you're wondering, Strassmeir's area of expertise was none other than disinformation. This point is extremely important, as we'll see later, because even though Strassmeir is portrayed as an ardent neo-Nazi, he spoke fluent Hebrew (Israel's state language), while *The London Times* reported that he had a Jewish girlfriend who served in the Israeli Army.

Is this what we would expect from a notorious "Jew-hater"?

Moving along, even though Strassmeir migrated to the United States in 1991, his first visit here was on April 7, 1989 when he flew to Washington, D.C. What makes his arrival peculiar is that in the Immigration and Naturalization Services (INS) computers, Strassmeir was given a special status of "AO." Now even though determining what this status means has been difficult for many researchers, his "AO" reference was completely scrubbed from computer files a few years later.

Why?

KIRK LYONS

To "officially" bring Strassmeir to America, an attorney named Kirk Lyons entered the picture.

Who is he?

Michael Collins Piper, author of *Final Judgment* and a veteran reporter for *American Free Press*, wrote in an unpublished article that, "For many years Kirk Lyons functioned in some way as a federal undercover agent and/or informant in a movement in which he put himself forward as a legal advocate and spokesman for its cause."

Piper went on to conclude that Lyons was undeniably, above all else, Strassmeir's "handler."

Lyons even visited Strassmeir's parents at their plush Berlin residence in 1991.

In fact, Lyons was the person who orchestrated Strassmeir's relocation to America.

He also obtained for him a driver's license by providing Strassmeir with an address in Knoxville, Tennessee; and he is quoted as saying, "I'm the reason that Andy was at Elohim City. I put him there. So if there was a plan, I guess I'm part of it." Not only did Lyons introduce Strassmeir to everyone at Elohim City, on April

18, 1995—one day before the OKC bombing—Lyons' law firm received a 15-minute phone call from a very important person in this scenario—Timothy McVeigh.

VINCENT PETRUSKIE

Once Strassmeir arrived on our shores in 1991, he quickly gravitated toward, of all things, the Civil War reenactment crowd. Why does this seemingly innocuous bit of trivia merit mention? Because historically, this group has been infiltrated by a variety of CIA splinter groups that used it as a front for illegal gun-smuggling. More importantly, though, *The London Times* reported that when Strassmeir first arrived in the United States, he was befriended by retired Army officers, CIA veterans, and Civil War reenactment history buffs. These men were part of a network that is very powerful in this country, and one that stretches into the Pentagon and other federal agencies.

One of these men was Vincent Petruskie, who was a special agent for the Air Force Office of Special Investigation (OSI) from 1954-1975, and who also knew Strassmeir's father in Berlin. Petruskie was also a foreign intelligence officer in Vietnam, a member of the 1131st U.S. Air Force Special Activities Squadron, a Special Projects Officer in the Special Activities Branch of the counter-intelligence division in Washington, D.C., and was also reactivated during the Gulf War to fulfill a "sensitive assignment."

Needless to say, Petruskie was connected to deep intelligence sources for decades, and interacted with a cabal of ex-military men and former & current CIA employees who were involved in gun running, mercenary actions, espionage, drug trafficking, blackmail & subversion, and money laundering. These were off-record, black budget operatives, and Vincent Petruskie made a career out of soliciting and deal-making with these shadowy figures.

So, when Andreas Strassmeir arrived in America and needed a place to stay, who opened their doors to him? None other than Vincent Petruskie of Petruskie Associates in Manassas, Virginia; a man who was making at the time $1.6 million/year by working out of his house. How did Strassmeir know Petruskie? In his own words, Strassmeir described his ally as, "a former CIA guy my father had known." But Petruskie's friendship didn't end at mere lodging. In addition, he tried to get Strassmeir a job at the DEA, the Treasury Department, with INS, and also the Department of Justice.

Even more bizarre is the story of when Andreas Strassmeir's station wagon was impounded by the Oklahoma Highway Patrol after he was pulled over for driving without tags or a valid license. Kenny Peace, a tow-truck driver from Muldrow, Oklahoma who yanked the vehicle, said that immediately after this event he started getting a flurry of calls from a Houston attorney, a general or major at Fort Bragg, North Carolina (quite possibly Petruskie), the Highway Patrol's district office, the State Department, and the Governor's office—all telling him to immediately release the vehicle. They also said that Andreas Strassmeir had full diplomatic immunity even though his visa had expired.

Furthermore, the contents of Strassmeir's briefcase held a copy of *The Terrorist's Handbook* (including how to build ANFO bombs & detonators with delayed fuses), job applications for the INS & DEA, foreign bank statements which showed he was by no means an impoverished pauper, and suspected government classified documents in both English and German. But most bizarre were the classified papers detailing negotiations by Strassmeir on behalf of Petruskie Associates to buy 747s from Germany's Lufthansa Airlines to begin a transport business out of Costa Rica! Now think about this incredible statement. Considering that Petruskie was involved with a shadow-group of black-budget operatives at the height of the crack cocaine craze, what do you think these airliners flying out of South America were going to be used for?

TEXAS LIGHT INFANTRY BRIGADE

After Strassmeir's early adventures with Vincent Petruskie, he aligned himself with a citizen's militia called the Texas Light Infantry Brigade (TLIB). The only problem was: the members of this group quickly became suspicious of Strassmeir's motives and loyalty, so they followed him late one night to a federal building. There, they saw Strassmeir approach an electric lock on the door, upon which he punched in the code on an electronic keypad. And just like that, Strassmeir gained access to the building. What makes this scenario relevant is that the federal building conveniently housed an office of the ATF. Anyway, after witnessing this transgression, the TLIB gave Strassmeir his walking papers for being a suspected undercover agent.

GERMAN INTELLIGENCE

Who was Andreas Strassmeir? On July 14, 1996, *The McCurtain Gazette* reported that, according to a highly placed source at the FBI's intelligence division, he was a paid ATF informant or asset sent to infiltrate Elohim City. This sentiment was echoed by Timothy McVeigh's lawyer, Stephen Jones, during a 1998 interview on KTOK radio in Oklahoma City. Jones said Strassmeir was a German national recruited by Louis Freeh to do deep undercover and intelligence operations for the FBI in the United States. He also said that he discussed Strassmeir's FBI alliance to the German government with U.S. prosecutor Beth Wilkinson. There is also FBI form 302 which has been unearthed stating that Strassmeir was a CIA asset on loan from the German government. Now, as you've noticed, three different agencies have been mentioned—the FBI, ATF, and CIA—in relation to who Strassmeir was working for. And until our government is more forthcoming with information, we can't be certain of any details other than he was a shared asset on loan to the U.S. government.

ELOHIM CITY

After being outed by the Texas Light Infantry Brigade, Strassmeir, under the tutelage of attorney Kirk Lyons, migrated to a 400-acre compound in rural Oklahoma (near Muldrow) named Elohim City. This enclave became, according to *Time* magazine, "the who's who of the radical right" because it housed members of the Aryan Republican Army; the Covenant, Sword, and Arm of the Lord; the

National Alliance; KKK; Aryan Nation; as well as many other militia and/or neo-Nazi style groups.

The Elohim City crowd was also prone to violence, as was revealed by U.S. Assistant Attorney Steven N. Snyder of Fort Smith, Arkansas, who said that a plot was hatched as far back as 1983 to blow up the Alfred P. Murrah Building. The primary movers in this conspiracy were Richard Wayne Snell, James Ellison, and Kerry Noble, who wanted to use plastic explosives and rocket launchers to topple the building. The authorities took this plot seriously enough to raid Elohim City in 1985, where they arrested Covenant founder James Ellison.

Kerry Noble, former Covenant member, said of Elohim City, "It has the potential, down the road, of being the most dangerous group in the country."

Yet, despite its notoriety, it was never again raided from 1985 until the OKC bombing in 1995. The big question is: why? Even an FBI report called *Project Megiddo* addressed the phenomenon surrounding Elohim City-style compounds when they said right-wing Christian terrorists posed the gravest danger to our country, and would be the most likely to incite violence in the months and years ahead.

ROBERT MILLAR

To understand the mind-boggling sense of immunity that was given to Elohim City, we need to look at Robert Millar, who founded this community in 1973. Despite his status as a spiritual leader of the militant right, senior FBI agent Peter Rickel testified on June 31, 1997 that, "Millar was in regular contact with the agency in the years before the bombing." Millar actually confirmed these words on July 1, 1997 when he told the *Tulsa World* newspaper that he repeatedly shared information with the FBI, DEA, and other law enforcement officials.

This is why *The McCurtain Daily Gazette* reported on July 1, 1997 that, "Millar's position as a mole for the FBI could explain why the compound has never been raided. Despite its use as a hideout for gun-runners, drug dealers, bank robbers and suspected members of the conspiracy that bombed the Alfred P. Murrah federal building in Oklahoma City, Elohim City has enjoyed a reputation as a place where fugitives can live without fear of arrest."

ELOHIM INFORMANTS

Robert Millar wasn't the only individual at Elohim City who was speaking with the authorities. There were plenty of others, including:

• **James Ellison**, former Covenant, Sword, & Arm of the Lord member who was married to Millar's grand-daughter and who testified against the Order.

• **Peter Langan**, the son of a retired U.S. Marine intelligence officer and leader of the Aryan Republican Army. After being arrested for robbing a Georgia Pizza Hut, the U.S. Secret Service intervened and had him released.

• **Gary Hunt**, paid informant of the ATF who was videotaped in the company of two other ATF agents at the Grand Continental Hotel in OKC a full week before the bombing. He was also videotaped, along with a companion, on April 19, 1995 by a OKC television station right after the bombing. Both men were carrying transmitters and walking rapidly from the Alfred P. Murrah Building. Hunt was even videotaped as a pall bearer at the funeral of an ATF agent.

• **"Christian Identity**," a group financed by the FBI to serve as *agents provocateurs* to incite violence and terrorism within the United States.

ELOHIM CRIMINAL ACTIVITY

As mentioned earlier, Elohim City was a sin city of sorts which harbored fugitives and criminals of all varieties. Of note were:

• **Michael Langon**, known as "Commander Pedro," who commandeered 22 different bank robberies in seven states which netted over $250,000.

CHAPTER FIVE

This spree extended over two years, and explosives were used in many of the heists. Oddly, even though Langon was wanted in six states, there wasn't even one crime scene arrest or fatality at any of the robberies, and never did the robbers encounter any bank guards or law enforcement officials.

- **Michael Brescia**, one of the actual bomb-planters inside the Alfred P. Murrah Building, was arrested on January 30, 1997 in Philadelphia for his participation in a number of bank robberies. He moved to Elohim City in 1994 and was a roommate of Andreas Strassmeir. Brescia has also been identified as John Doe # 2 by Dennis Mahon, ATF informant Carol Howe, and Timothy McVeigh's acquaintance/girlfriend, Catina Lawson.
- **Richard Guthrie**, the son of CIA parents and a Navy veteran, was also arrested for bank robbery, but not before frequently visiting Tim McVeigh in Arizona.
- Other shady characters included **Michael Fortier**, who Robert Millar admitted (to KOKH-TV) had lived at Elohim City shortly before the bombing.
- Then there is **Dennis Mahon**, who got his start in the Order, which was founded by Robert Matthews. He then went on to become third in line at the White Aryan Resistance (WAR). Mahon also served as a former Imperial Dragon of the Oklahoma KKK, and was described by Andreas Strassmeir as a "good friend." Equally important, Mahon admitted to meeting Timothy McVeigh several times, and said that Michael Brescia was "up to his ass" in the Oklahoma City bombing.

Are you starting to see a great deal of interconnectedness taking place here?

TIMOTHY MCVEIGH

Lo and behold, if you've been wondering how Timothy McVeigh fits into this picture, we'll start adding a few of his pieces to the puzzle. For starters, there are some "official" disinformation sources that say McVeigh had never even visited Elohim City. But we now know that McVeigh and Terry Nichols drove, on October 12, 1993 from Fayetteville, Arkansas to Elohim City to meet with Andreas Strassmeir. Also in attendance were bank robbers Richard Guthrie and Peter "Commander Pedro" Langon.

We can also connect McVeigh to the Elohim City coterie via:

- A hotel receipt dated September 13, 1994;
- A speeding ticket he received in 1993 a few miles from the compound;
- Phone records—McVeigh called Strassmeir at Elohim City on April 5, 1995 a few minutes after reserving a Ryder truck;
- Prisoner interviews;
- His participation in military maneuvers directed by Strassmeir at Elohim City on September 12, 1994;
- Informant reports—Carol Howe, who we will get to a little later, directly linked McVeigh (using the name "Tim Tuttle") to Strassmeir, Dennis Mahon, and Pete Ward at Elohim City.

With this information in mind, I can categorically conclude that Timothy McVeigh was at Elohim City in the months and years before the Oklahoma City bombing.

On the other hand, to further link McVeigh to the Elohim City criminal element, FBI documents show that they strongly suspected McVeigh of participating in a December, 1994 Ohio bank robbery with some Aryan Nation members, including Michael Brescia. This seems to make sense, because McVeigh's sister testified later that he wanted her to launder some money for him in

CHAPTER FIVE

December, 1994. This would also at least partially explain how McVeigh, with no job and a sporadic work record, would have the money to travel around the country and buy cases of *The Turner Diaries* which he sold at rented gun-show tables.

More proof of McVeigh's Elohim City links come from a highly documented April 8, 1995 event (merely a week-and-a-half prior to the OKC bombing) where McVeigh, Strassmeir, and Michael Brescia were videotaped by security cameras at Lady Godiva's strip joint in Tulsa, Oklahoma.

Their visit was verified by the *Fifth Estate*, Canada's version of *60 Minutes*. Of special note is McVeigh bragging to one of the dancers, "On April 19, 1995 you'll remember me for the rest of your life."

But to truly understand McVeigh's role in the OKC bombing, we need to dig a little deeper. David Paul Hammer, who spent 23 months with McVeigh on death row in Terre Haute, Indiana, says that McVeigh told him about meeting with three shadowy men with close ties to the U.S. military shortly after he left the Army. McVeigh also added that these men only went by code names, and that one of the meetings (with someone known only as "the Major") took place at Camp McCall, which was on the grounds of Fort Bragg, North Carolina.

Could this once again be Vincent Petruskie?

At this meeting with "the Major," McVeigh was told that he was passed over for a spot in the elite Army Special Forces so that he could be recruited into a black budget Department of Defense project where he would gather intelligence for the government on members of the radical right, including specifically the Aryans, KKK, and militias. Does this sound at all like the groups that inhabited Elohim City? In effect, then, McVeigh would become a pseudo-agent for the United States government.

I realize that such a scenario sounds fantastic, but in a letter that was read in 1995 before a grand jury, Timothy McVeigh's sister said that he thought he was going into a Special Forces covert tactical unit to fight against evil-doers.

Author David Hoffman confirms this sentiment in his book *The Oklahoma City Bombing and the Politics of Terror*:

> McVeigh wrote his sister Jennifer while he was still in the Army telling her that he had been picked for a highly specialized Special Forces Covert Tactical Unit (CTU) that was involved in illegal activities. The letter was introduced to the federal grand jury. According to former grand juror Hoppy Heidelberg, these illegal activities included "protecting drug shipments, eliminating the competition, and population control.

The AP also reported that the government had been closely monitoring those who came to show their support for the Branch Davidians prior to the Waco siege. McVeigh, of course, was in attendance, handing out anti-New World Order literature.

Could it be that McVeigh had been sheep-dipped in the exact same manner as Lee Harvey Oswald prior to the JFK assassination? To those who've studied this subject, we know that Guy Banister and E. Howard Hunt made sure that Oswald was photographed handing out pro-Castro leaflets in New Orleans, and they even got him on a local radio show to secure the connection. Could McVeigh also have been reinvented as a "racist revolutionary" who would play a *Manchurian Candidate* role in some later black-op project?

Before ruling out the possibility, let's return to another quote from David Hoffman's book:

> In an illuminating series of phone calls to Representative Charles Key, an anonymous source stated that McVeigh was present at several meetings with ATF and DEA agents in the days immediately preceding the bombing. The meetings took place in Oklahoma City at different locations. The ostensible purpose of these meetings was to pro-

vide McVeigh with further instructions, and to facilitate a payoff. David Hall of KPOC-TV uncovered information that McVeigh had met with local ATF agent Alex McCauley in a McDonalds the night before the bombing. The ATF agent was seen handing McVeigh an envelope.

Adding another element to the espionage angle is James Nichols, who in his book *Freedom's End* claims that McVeigh was met in prison by the notorious MK-ULTRA mind-bender Dr. Jolyon West, who not only pronounced Jack Ruby "insane" after killing Lee Harvey Oswald, but also handled Sirhan Sirhan following the Robert F. Kennedy assassination. Moreover, McVeigh also stated that he thought he'd been implanted with a computer microchip while serving in the Army, and many have declared that he was under the influence of mind-control drugs during his incarceration after the bombing.

A further insight into McVeigh's personality was provided by a woman named Lynda Haner-Mele, who worked with McVeigh at Burns Security in early 1992.

> Tim wasn't the type of person who could initiate action. He was very good if you said, "Tim, watch this door—don't let anyone through." The Tim I knew couldn't have masterminded something like the OKC bombing. It would have had to have been someone who said, "Tim, this is what you do. You drive the truck."

All of this leads us once again back to Andreas Strassmeir, who admitted that he met Timothy McVeigh in the late spring of 1993 at a Tulsa gun show, and that he was in possession of McVeigh's Desert Storm military uniforms.

Furthermore, ATF infiltrator-agent Carol Howe has unequivocally stated that Andreas Strassmeir was the OKC mastermind and prime instigator of the bombing; and McVeigh was merely his protégé. She also said that Strassmeir exerted "extraordinary influence over McVeigh."

CAROL HOWE

Anyone familiar with the deep dirty secrets of the OKC bombing intuits that Carol Howe's role as an informant, along with her subsequent testimony, are the incriminating smoking guns that completely shred the government's credibility. For starters, official sources denied that Howe was even employed by them. But now, many years later, we know for a fact that Ms. Howe's Confidential Informant number was: 53270-183 (or, for short, CI-183).

After being caught in this lie, the government said that Howe was dropped from their employ in June, 1995, after the OKC bombing. But an ATF report dated January 31, 1996 stated, "It is required that CI 53270-183 be retained as an active informant." Plus, under cross-examination, Howe's superior, Karen Finley, admitted that she was an active informant until December 18, 1996.

We have further proof of Howe's status as an informant via internal ATF documents, specifically Karen Finley's preliminary report, which had an ATF Investigation Number of 53270-94-0124-B, and was recorded on form # 3270.2. This form was signed by not only Finley, but also David E. Roberts (Resident in charge of the Tulsa field office) and Tommy Wittman; and was forwarded to Lester D. Martz, Special Agent in charge of the Dallas Field Division of the ATF.

In this report, Howe's work was described as "sensitive" and "significant" according to ATF official Robert Sanders.

Furthermore, on Feb. 22, 1995, Ken Stafford, an Oklahoma State Patrol pilot, told Karen Finley that the FBI had an informant inside Elohim City in addition to Howe. In true spy-versus-spy fashion, though, the ATF and FBI agents did not know of the other's existence or identity.

Now that we have proof that Carol Howe was an ATF informant, what type of information did she feed to this agency? To answer this question, we'll start with ATF Special Agent Karen Finley's testimony on April 24, 1997:

> **Question**: Ms. Howe told you about Mr. Strassmeir's threats to blow up federal buildings, didn't she?
> **Finley**: In general, yes.
> **Question**: That was before the OKC bombing?
> **Finley**: Yes.
> **Question**: Now, Ms. Howe actually took some of these people from Elohim City at your direction to Oklahoma City, didn't she?
> **Finley**: She went with them. She probably didn't drive.
> **Question**: This trip to OKC by Elohim City residents occurred before the bombings, actually by a few weeks, didn't it?
> **Finley**: No, it would be months . . . fall of '94.
> **Question**: Are you sure? So, it wasn't the third week of February?
> **Finley**: Oh, I'm sorry; we did send her back.
> **Question**: The very next day, you asked Ms. Howe to take you to Oklahoma City and show you the places they visited, didn't you?
> **Finley**: I don't know if it was the next day, but yes, I took her to OKC and asked her the places.

With this incriminating testimony in mind, let's cut to the chase. To begin, in the months prior to the OKC bombing, Carol Howe submitted over 70 reports to Karen Finley, her ATF control officer. She was also polygraphed at least a dozen times to check her reliability, and each time she passed with flying colors. Also, ATF reports described Howe as a "key" witness, along with being "stable and capable."

Why, then, wouldn't the ATF want Ms. Howe's testimony to be

heard? As we have already seen, it all boils down to foreknowledge and direct complicity. Howe told her superiors in no uncertain terms that Andreas Strassmeir and Dennis Mahon were the primary instigators of the OKC bombing. She also told the ATF that Strassmeir teamed up with a KKK leader from Tulsa—Dennis Mahon—to bomb the Alfred P. Murrah Building in Oklahoma.

She also reported that Strassmeir and Mahon made three trips to OKC to case various locales—one in November, 1994; the next in December, 1994; and finally in February, 1995. Howe even accompanied them on one of these trips. Plus, these assertions were corroborated by Karen Finley—under oath—on April 24, 1997. Finley even accompanied Howe to OKC to see the exact areas that Strassmeir and Mahon cased.

Is it clear what is being presented here? The ATF knew that Strassmeir and other Aryan Republican Army members had discussed blowing up federal buildings in OKC. They knew that the Alfred P. Murrah Building was a target, just like it was in 1983 when other Elohim City residents plotted to destroy it. They knew that Timothy McVeigh and others had spoken of bombing the APM Building because Carol Howe notified her superiors of this fact. Even Robert Millar, Elohim City founder, called for a preemptive strike against the government several months before April 19th.

If you're still not convinced, during Carol Howe's trial, ATF Agent Karen Finley testified that the FBI, as well as her agency, "had the information in advance of the bombing of the Murrah Building." She also admitted that Howe warned them of bomb threats against federal buildings before April 19, 1995. In addition, during her own trial, Carol Howe was asked by her lawyer, Clark Brewster, if she thought she had provided sufficient information for the ATF to conduct an investigation that would have confirmed the bombing of the Alfred P. Murrah Building would take place. Howe answered yes. She is also quoted as saying, "It is the indisputable truth that the government had 'detailed prior knowledge' of the plot to bomb the building, but somehow failed to stop it."

Ms. Howe's words are confirmed by an event which took place

on February 7, 1995 when Karen Finley and other ATF agents flew with Oklahoma State Patrol pilot Ken Stafford over Elohim City to photograph and videotape the complex to gather intelligence for a possible raid to arrest Strassmeir and others. They were specifically targeting Strassmeir because Howe told ATF officials that he kept declaring, "It's time to go to war," and "It's time to start bombing federal buildings."

This type of inflammatory rhetoric alarmed the authorities to such an extent that an arrest/raid was scheduled for February, 1995. But, in that same month, this invasion of Elohim City was scrubbed after senior members of the ATF, FBI, and U.S. Attorney's Office met.

The ramifications of this decision cannot be overemphasized, as former Oklahoma State Representative Charles Key stated to *World Net Daily* on May 22, 2001: "It's fair to speculate that the FBI got the ATF to call the raid off, or told them to, or someone with higher authority did." He added, "If they had not called that raid off, it alone may have stopped the bombing of the Murrah Building."

It should also be noted that the Immigration and Naturalization Service (INS) cancelled the FBI's notice to detain Andreas Strassmeir, and that the State Department wouldn't assist in getting Germany's cooperation to question Strassmeir after the bombing. Lastly, even though Carol Howe—who provided mountains of information to the ATF, urged them to raid the Elohim City bunker, and who was taken to the basement of the old Pepco Building in downtown Oklahoma City for debriefing only hours after the bombing—was prohibited from testifying at Timothy McVeigh's trial. The reason? Judge Richard Matsch said that her testimony might "confuse" the jurors.

FOREKNOWLEDGE AT ELOHIM CITY

The most pressing question at this point is: why would those at the highest levels of government—all the way up to the Department of Justice—call off this raid? According to Robert Sanders, a top ATF official, Elohim City was under intense scrutiny by federal agencies at the top levels of management. The reports given to these individuals about the activities at Elohim City include: illegal explosives and firearms, illegal immigration, planned terrorism, a history of violence, and incendiary rhetoric. Worse, this information went to the FBI, ATF, Treasury, Department of Justice, National Security Council, and even Bill Clinton's White House.

Plus, most everyone included in this sordid Elohim City saga was either: an operative, spook, or informant, including: Andreas Strassmeir, Kirk Lyons, Vincent Petruskie, Robert Millar, James Ellison, Peter Langan, Gary Hunt, Timothy McVeigh, and Carol Howe.

The foreknowledge of an April 19 bombing was so widespread that Richard Wayne Snell, a member of James Ellison's Covenant, Sword, & Arm of the Lord, bragged about this catastrophe on the day of his execution—coincidentally on April 19, 1995. Arkansas prison official Alan Ables said of Snell: "He repeatedly predicted that there would be a bombing or explosion on the day of his death." When his prophetic words about the OKC bombing came true, he knowingly chuckled and laughed before being put to death.

Similarly, Chevie Kehoe, another bank robber associated with the Elohim City crowd, showed-up at a Spokane motel about 45 minutes before the bombing to watch the event on CNN. The hotel manager told *The Spokane Review* that Kehoe had been talking about it for days. "It's about time," he eventually proclaimed with manic excitement.

Also, as a side-note, Elohim City founder Robert Millar admitted that Kehoe and his brother had lived at the compound.

Could it be that the entire OKC bombing was a covert government cover-up? Considering all those on the 'inside' who were funneling data to the authorities, plus the totally hands-off, immune status that these men enjoyed, what else can we conclude? Was a cabal within our federal government actually scapegoating those at Elohim City by enticing them into committing illegal acts, or a conspiracy to do so; all the while as they were being egged-on by paid provocateurs?

The McCurtain Gazette reported (July, 1996) the ominous words of a former government undercover agent who said, "It is typical for agencies such as the CIA, FBI & ATF to place multiple moles inside a place like Elohim City and play one resource off the other, without either one knowing the other's identity."

Mike Vanderboegh, editor of *The John Doe Times*, echoed this sentiment on July 4, 1997:

> Not even in czarist Russia did the secret police send paid provocateurs to provoke the other paid provocateurs. Elohim City can thus be seen in its true light—not as an operation infiltrated and suborned by infiltrators—but rather as a wholly-owned subsidiary of the FBI/ATF.

STRASSMEIR'S IMMUNITY

Not surprisingly, all of the above information brings us back to Andreas Strassmeir. Karen Finley, Carol Howe's superior, said in an ATF report on November 29, 1994: "His [Strassmeir's] plans were to forcibly act to destroy the U.S. government with direct actions and operations such as assassinations, bombings, and mass shootings." She also informed her superiors that Strassmeir was a huge weapons dealer, and his status as of December, 1994 was that of an illegal alien.

Dennis Mahon, a co-conspirator in the bombing, had this to say of the situation: "If a person wanted to know about the bombing, then they should talk with Andy Strassmeir because he knows everything."

Similarly, *Media Bypass* reported in September, 1996 that high-level FBI sources said, "ATF computer indices reflect substantial intelligence-gathering activities in which Strassmeir participated." They continued, "Either Andy is their snitch or he is under investigation and has been for a long time. And considering the fact that it was Strassmeir that McVeigh made the call to . . . well, why do you suppose he wasn't interviewed right after that became known? Could it be that Andy's being protected?"

Ultimately, we have to ask ourselves, who did Strassmeir work for? Quite telling is the fact that when Timothy McVeigh's attorneys wanted Strassmeir's files, they had to ask the CIA for them! Also, it is now known that FBI Director Louis Freeh was aware of Strassmeir and had been monitoring his activities, and that he was a subject of interest to the State Department's Counter-terrorism Division of Diplomatic Protective Services.

More incredibly, a BOLO (Be On Look Out) alert was issued on Strassmeir in the weeks preceding the bombing by Tulsa ATF agents who were seeking his arrest. Yet, even though Strassmeir and Mahon were subjects of investigations in the days after the OKC bombing, they were subsequently dropped from any follow-ups. Why? Is this a case of one hand not knowing what the other was doing, or something more sinister? After all, if Strassmeir was arrested and started to sing, guess where everything would lead: directly to our federal government, and possibly beyond.

British journalist Ambrose Evans-Pritchard described the scenario as such: "The plot was hatched at Elohim City in the fall of 1994 under the guidance of Dennis Mahon and Andreas Strassmeir, two men who were clearly enjoying the protection of the FBI. McVeigh was undoubtedly part of the movement, and the bombing was probably part of a sting operation that went disastrously wrong."

Still, despite the incriminating evidence pointing to his involvement in the OKC bombing, in May of 1995, an Oklahoma news service took film footage of Andreas Strassmeir still residing at Elohim City!

Another clip shows him together with Michael Brescia. They were still living there, even after Carol Howe, during her debriefing by the FBI on April 20, 1995, identified Strassmeir as one of the primary perpetrators.

Even a member of the mainstream media—Roger Charles—a former *20/20* producer, told *Soldier of Fortune* magazine in July,

2001 that there was "compelling evidence that Strassmeir had access to prior knowledge regarding the bombing." He also noted that in subsequent interviews, Strassmeir said that:
1) Two yellow trucks were connected to the bombing, not just one;
2) Federal authorities put tracking devices on the trucks as they approached OKC that day.

The biggest question now is: where did Strassmeir get his information, and why wasn't he immediately arrested as a suspect? Instead, Strassmeir remained in the U.S. until January, 1996, whereupon he was whisked out of the country. And guess who facilitated this departure. First in line was the infamous attorney Kirk Lyons, while the actual dirty work was performed by Germany's elite counter-terrorism group, the GSG-9.

ANDREAS STRASSMEIR IN HIS OWN WORDS

After Andreas Strassmeir fled the country in early 1996, he began speaking out in various interviews. Here are a few of his more revealing quotes. While reading them, ask yourself: was Strassmeir a simple neo-Nazi klutz, or was he elaborating as someone with deep knowledge from inside the intelligence world?

> Quote 1: "It's obvious that it [OKC] was a government op that went wrong, isn't it? The ATF had something going with McVeigh. They were watching him. Of course they were."
>
> Quote 2: "McVeigh knew he was delivering a bomb, but he had no idea what was in the truck. He just wanted to shake things up a little; ya know, make a gesture."
>
> Again, we need to ask: Where was Strassmeir getting his information?
>
> Quote 3: When asked by British journalist Ambrose Evans-Pritchard if an informant could ever

speak out about Oklahoma City, Strassmeir replied, "How can he? What happens if it [the bombing] was a sting operation from the very beginning?" He continued, "What happens if it comes out that the plant was a provocateur? What then? Of course the informant can't come forward. He's scared stiff right now."

When Pritchard was asked if he thought Strassmeir was referring to himself as the plant, he responded, "Of course. There's no doubt that is exactly what he meant to convey. He was stating it as plainly as he could without admitting criminal culpability. . . ."

THE ANTI-DEFAMATION LEAGUE

At this stage, we need to ask once again: were Timothy McVeigh and Terry Nichols nutty bombers who acted alone to plan, coordinate, orchestrate, execute, and cover up the OKC bombing? As we've seen, an overwhelming amount of evidence proves that not only were others involved in this cataclysmic event, but various federal agencies had infiltrated and monitored many of the groups which gravitated to Elohim City. In fact, CNN reported in June, 1995 that two years before the bombing, McVeigh was already being surveilled by undercover agents at an Arizona gun show. Then, on June 3, 1995, *The Washington Post* stated that it was actually a McVeigh associate who tipped off the FBI that he was involved in the bombing. This point is crucial, because it irrefutably contradicts the official story that McVeigh only became known to them after he was arrested by a vigilant police officer during a traffic stop following the bombing.

Now, considering that McVeigh associated with known "hate groups," and their involvement in the OKC bombing is undeniable, why would organizations such as the Anti-Defamation League (ADL) and Morris Dees' Southern Poverty Law Center do everything imaginable to deflect blame AWAY from known Aryans, KKKers, and racists? In other words, why were they so vocifer-

CHAPTER FIVE

ously supporting the lone-nut theory when there was an unabashedly militant Nazi enclave at Elohim City? Wouldn't you think groups such as the ADL and SPLC would want to nail them to the wall at once?

The ADL's behavior can only be explained when we realize that this agent of the B'nai B'rith—which has secret files on over 10,000 American citizens and over 600 different organizations, while regularly sharing data with the Mossad and CIA—is hiding something. And what, pray tell, could they want to keep from public scrutiny? Quite simply, the ADL was directly involved in tailing Timothy McVeigh in the weeks and years preceding the bombing.

One of the most noted authorities on this subject is Michael Collins Piper, author of *Final Judgment* and *The New Jerusalem*. In an interview with Tom Valentine of *Radio Free America*, Piper stated very directly, "Although a lot of people like to talk about government foreknowledge of the OKC bombing plot, the fact is that much of that government knowledge actually came to the FBI and BATF, and probably even the CIA, from ADL informants active in the 'right wing.'"

A perfect example of how intricately the ADL had become entwined with McVeigh came about through the most unlikely of scenarios. On April 21, 1995, two days after the OKC bombing, *The Washington Post* ran a story about McVeigh in which they claimed he had placed a series of ads in *The Spotlight*, a populist newspaper that Piper wrote for. The source for this tip was none other than the ADL, and the article said that the ad was placed by McVeigh using the alias "T.Tuttle." In addition, it also named the dates upon which these ads ran, what he was selling (they mistakenly said rocket launchers when in fact they were flare guns), and that he'd also placed calls on a *Spotlight* phone card under the name "Darryl Bridges."

Now please remember, this article ran only two days after the bombing. Anyway, after Piper read this reference to the publication by which he was employed, he and others began a painstaking process to see if these assertions were true. It should be noted that

The Spotlight wasn't computerized, so the employees had to engage in a laborious, time-consuming search to even find the ads in question, let alone verify them. They couldn't simply punch a few keys and have it instantly pop up on their computer screens. Thus, they had to dig through file cabinet after file cabinet to locate these "T. Tuttle" ads.

Mysteriously, though, the ADL had no difficulty in forwarding this information to *The Washington Post*. How could this be, especially when McVeigh didn't even use his real name? The odds of stumbling upon such a find are astronomical. Or, could it be attributed to the ADL's highly sophisticated data bases with all its intelligence apparatus? Or, could it be that this information was already at their fingertips because they had been trailing McVeigh for quite some time?

But wait, the peculiarities get even more bizarre. . . .

For starters, the dates upon which the ADL told *The Washington Post* that "T.Tuttle's" ads ran in *The Spotlight* were wrong! McVeigh had originally contracted for the first of four ads to run the week beginning August 9, 1993.

But due to some type of production problem at the newspaper, the first ad didn't actually run until the following week—August 16, 1993.

Something seems to be awry, so let's be very clear about this. How could the ADL have known so much about these specific ads when McVeigh was using an alias, and *The Spotlight* records weren't even computerized? Plus, this was only two days after the bombing. So, if we figure in contact time, writing time, pre-production set-up time, printing time, and distribution time, the data had to have come to the ADL immediately. This seems impossible unless they had someone very close to McVeigh.

Michael Collins Piper even went so far as to say of this high-level connection: "Do you know how the ADL knew that McVeigh had advertised in *The Spotlight*? The ADL had a guy in McVeigh's inner circle, close to McVeigh."

The real clincher, though, resulted from a very peculiar reaction by *The Washington Post* and the ADL.

Upon realizing that the information they had run in their morning edition about the dates of McVeigh's ads was off by a week, and that such a disclosure would undeniably blow their cover, the *Post* completely scrubbed all references to the *Spotlight* ad and "T.Tuttle" in their afternoon edition.

Worse, they even erased all references to this advertisement in their microfiche records.

Strange behavior? You better believe it.

COVER-UP

Despite the preponderance of evidence presented in this section, Joseph Hartzler, the chief prosecutor at Timothy McVeigh's trial, said, "At no time did the FBI consider Andreas Strassmeir a subject of the OKC bombing investigation."

Regrettably for Mr. Hartzler, we now know this statement is untrue, because on April 27, 1995, FBI Special Agent Hudspeth made a background check on Andreas Strassmeir to German police intelligence.

This report was eventually returned to the State Department's Counter-terrorism Division, Office of Deputy Secretary of State Strobe Talbott.

[As we learned in Volume One of this trilogy, Talbott has been directly linked to Bill Clinton since the late 1960s.—Ed]

Incredibly, in light of all the direct evidence linking Strassmeir to the OKC bombing, the FBI didn't interview him until April 30, 1996, and this wasn't done in person, but via telephone. Such a blatant miscarriage of justice is even more damning when we consider that Strassmeir remained in the United States for eight months after the bombing, and didn't depart for Germany until January, 1996.

During these crucial eight months when Strassmeir remained in the U.S., our government had time to review over 70 reports filed by informant Carol Howe, along with 38 audio cassette tapes and two videotapes. The source of these figures was none other than ATF official Robert Sanders.

And what, you may inquire, was contained in Ms. Howe's recordings and reports? Well, the information pertained to the identity of the Elohim City residents, those who visited the compound, their organizational structure, family trees, telephone numbers, license plate numbers, explosives, guns, and even their tattoos.

Yet Elohim City was never raided . . . not once, even though the ATF and FBI knew that Dennis Mahon had been setting off 500-pound ANFO bombs in the months before April 19, 1995. Why didn't our government even question Mahon about his role in the OKC bombing? It's incredible.

In addition, a newly released FBI document which was obtained by Timothy McVeigh's attorney states, "There was evidence withheld by the government that another person could well have been the mastermind behind the bombing." Do you think they could have been referring to Andreas Strassmeir, or somebody even higher than him?

We also know that other relevant information was covered up after the bombing, because on May 10, 2001, the Department of Justice turned over 4,000 previously undisclosed FBI investigative papers. Furthermore, Chairman Dan Burton's House Government Reform Committee uncovered the whereabouts of numerous confiscated videotapes and photographs that most certainly would have refuted the official version of events.

These very same videos have also been cited by the Oklahoma Bombing Investigation Committee (OKBIC), yet the Department of Justice absolutely refuses to release them, even under the Freedom of Information Act.

At this point I could go on and on with a litany of examples which prove that a cabal within our federal government was directly involved in the OKC bombing, and that they subsequently covered up their actions; but instead I'll simply ask one question that harks back to the opening section of this speech: Do you feel that no stone went unturned in Attorney General Janet Reno's investigation?

If your answer is no, then even though the FBI, ATF, and CIA were undeniably complicit in the OKC cover-up, the ultimate responsibility leads directly to the doorstep of Janet Reno, former President Bill Clinton, and Ms. Jamie Gorelick, who was also instrumental in covering up the TWA Flight 800 disaster and 9-11. Militia members at Elohim City were not the ultimate driving force behind the Oklahoma City bombing disaster on April 19, 1995; they were simply a pretext used to cover for much more sinister forces directly inside our own federal government.

BRIGADIER GENERAL BENTON K. PARTIN SPEAKS OUT

On December 12, 2004 Lisa Guliani and I interviewed Ben Partin, who served thirty-one years of active duty in the United States Air Force, where he became known as the premier expert on weapons systems. He was also "responsible for the design and testing of almost every non-nuclear weapon device used in the Air Force."[790]

During the course of this discussion, Partin spoke out on many subjects, including the infamous bomb which was purportedly used to partially topple the Alfred P. Murrah Building.

Partin stated that the amount of ammonium nitrate and fuel oil, commonly known as ANFO, that McVeigh and Nichols supposedly used could not have brought down the building the way the government said it did. Damage to the building was very asymmetrical, it was not adjacent to the Ryder truck (where one would expect it to be), and the columns collapsed in a way that were technical impossibilities in regard to an ANFO bomb. What we should have seen with this sort of device would be a fairly symmetrical pattern because the building itself was symmetrical, yet the damage was not symmetrically consistent with the structure or the resulting crater.

When asked to compare the explosive strength of an open-air bomb to a direct impact bomb, Partin replied, "With an open-air bomb, your blast wave is moving through the air, and the only damage you can have is the damage propagated through air. The damage falls off inversely proportional to the cube of the distance. Now when you have the explosive right up against a concrete column, it doesn't take that much explosive to destroy the column." In laymen's terms, the farther away from a target an open-air bomb is, the less damage will occur. Therefore, the ANFO/Ryder truck bomb wouldn't be nearly as effective as an explosive placed directly against a building's column.

Partin continued his analysis of why an ANFO bomb could not have toppled the Alfred P. Murrah Building. "If it would have been in the ballpark to get an explosion out of it, it would not have been able to do the job that they claim it did. It's technically impossible. Even if it had been perfectly mixed and put there in pristine condition, within the exact proportion, it still would not have done what happened to the Murrah Building."

At this point, Lisa Guliani broached a subject which boggles the mind in terms of improbability. She explained how in the 25 years prior to the OKC bombing, the public hadn't heard anything about ANFO bombs. But in early 1994, the BATF and Army Corps of Engineers began conducting ANFO tests at White Plains Missile Range in New Mexico under the code name Dipole Might. Curiously, one of the people involved in that testing was agent Harry Everhart, who also happened to show up on the scene at the OKC bombing.

Here is where circumstances become more than coincidental. Harry Everhart, who performed the ANFO tests in New Mexico, "is an employee of the Bureau of Alcohol, Tobacco, and Firearms [and is] an accomplished ATF expert in ANFO truck bombs."[791][791]

Now remember, until OKC, ANFO hadn't been used as a weapon in any public acts of destruction for twenty-five years. Then, the year prior to OKC, Everhart started doing tests using this exact substance at a government military base.

So, who "was actually one of the first federal law officers to report the details of the bombing to his superiors from the scene in front of the Murrah Building, within minutes of the blast"?[792]

It was Harry Everhart! In fact, "the ANFO story was born only

CHAPTER FIVE

ten minutes after the blast when a high-ranking ATF official by the name of Harry Everhart witnessed the blast from nearby and called the ATF office in Dallas to excitedly announce, 'Someone had just blown up the federal building in OKC with a truckload of ANFO.'"[793]

First, try to calculate the odds that of all the places on the planet earth where ATF agent Harry Everhart could have been—he being the only man in the country to do official testing on ANFO bombs—that he was precisely in the exact same spot where an ANFO bomb went off—the first time in twenty-five years! The possibility of this happening by chance is so far beyond any stretch of the imagination that it's incalculable.

Secondly, how could Everhart have "known" so quickly the source of this explosion? "Some reports and investigators who have looked objectively at the bombing now argue that neither Everhart nor anyone else could have correctly deduced in such a short time exactly what caused the explosion."[794]

Anyway, General Partin said the story that the OKC bombing was performed by one guy—Timothy McVeigh—was phony. Rather, he said McVeigh was a patsy because the Randy Weaver case in Ruby Ridge was blamed on a religious-style militia. Then Waco was blamed on militias. Subsequently, Ruby Ridge and Waco really generated the militia movement in this country. Why? Because people saw the government doing things that were unconstitutional.

Finally, Partin was asked: "If we could rebuild the Alfred P. Murrah Building and put a Ryder truck exactly where it was on the morning of April 19, 1995, fill it with 4,800 pounds of ANFO, then set it off, how much damage would it actually cause?"

Partin didn't miss a beat. "You would have taken out some of the flooring on the first floor, and probably a little bit up to the third floor, and that's about it." He then went on to explain how the 1993 WTC truck bombing took out the flooring two floors up and three floors down around only one column. That's it. Plus, the Murrah Building was more flimsily constructed than the World Trade Center towers (which were two of the strongest buildings ever erected), while the bomb used there went off right next to a column—not an open-air bomb some distance away like at OKC.

Partin concluded by citing seismographic data which showed that there were additional explosions at the Murrah Building, corroborating what survivors inside the structure testified to later—that it felt like an earthquake when charges *inside the building* were being detonated. Then, moments later, there was another explosion from *outside* the building which sent glass flying inside the building. Thus, seismographic data coincides with the timing of bombs going off inside the building first, then from the Ryder truck outside second.

Because he had the courage to be truthful about OKC, General Partin was not called to testify at Timothy McVeigh's trial in Denver. In his own words, he said the reason why was "because there was too much of a government cover-up."

ADDENDUM TO DIPOLE MIGHT

Was the ATF in fact responsible, knowingly or unknowingly, for the explosion that destroyed the Murrah Building? Consider the following article which appeared in the June 5, 1995 issue of *Newsweek*:

> For the past year, the ATF and the Army Corps of Engineers have been blowing up car bombs at the White Sands Proving Ground in New Mexico. The project, codenamed Dipole Might, is designed to create a computer model to unravel terrorist car and truck bomb attacks. By coincidence, an ATF agent assigned to Dipole Might happened to be in Oklahoma City on April 19th, working at the Federal Courthouse, which stands across the street from the Murrah Building. He saw the devastation and called the ATF office in Dallas. The Murrah Building had just been hit by an 'ANFO' (ammo-

nium material) bomb of at least several thousand pounds, he reported. Within minutes, explosives agents trained under Dipole Might were dispatched to the scene. They identified the type and size of the bomb almost immediately.

Just how this agent (Harry Everhart) was able to immediately ascertain the building had been blown up by an ANFO bomb, when no forensic analysis had yet been conducted, is unclear. When Phil O'Halloran, a freelance journalist, attempted to ask the ATF Public Relations Bureau why a Dipole Might expert just happened to be in the courthouse at that moment, and how he could immediately have known the exact nature of the bomb, O'Halloran, rather than be given a rational explanation, was accused of attacking the agency and was promised a fax of agency views on right-wing conspiracists (which never arrived).[795]

(Coincidentally, Project Dipole Might was created via authorization of Bill Clinton's National Security Council.)

COLLATERAL DAMAGE

The most obvious question is: why would the government plant operatives inside Elohim City to plot an attack *against the government* . . . against itself? Such a notion seems convoluted beyond words. What would their motive be? Also, why would they have informants inside Elohim City who reported back to them (the government), then allow the plan to bomb a federal building move forward unimpeded? The idea makes less sense than the crazed characters did from *Alice in Wonderland*.

If one studies the history of state-sponsored terrorism, rather than accepting the spoon-fed lies delivered by official sources and their compliant lapdog press, an entirely different world will open before your eyes. In this sinister realm, we have a combination of Machiavellian amorality, Hegel's Dialectic, the end justifying the means, and a term which reportedly came out of Timothy McVeigh's mouth while he sat in prison: collateral damage. From the state's perspective, a few lives—even those of their own citizens—are worth sacrificing as collateral damage in light of a larger agenda. It's hard to imagine a sicker, more evil concept; but it exists, it is real, and it continues to this very day. We the people are pawns; innocent lambs to be slaughtered in a context which we're not even aware of.

So, why OKC; what were their motives?

ONE: "The dormant Anti-terrorism Bill was revived, inflated, and put on the fast track to passage."[796]

What essentially developed after the OKC bombing was pre-Patriot Act legislation which greatly enhanced the government's ability to surveil its citizens. "Before the April 19th bombing, two anti-terrorism bills were moldering in Congress. Since the bombing, they have been scrapped and new shiny versions, with the same repressive slants, have been pushed up before a Congress now rabid about taking out terrorists regardless of the facts, regardless of the cost to the Constitution."[797]

What we're talking about is Big Brother-style Big Government which laid the groundwork for post 9-11 legislation. "The overpowering trend involves more control of the citizenry, more Bill of Rights scrapping, more octopus-maneuvering, more taking over of local functions, more computerizing, more linking, [and] more corporate-government identity of interest and agenda."[798]

Even the terminology used in the mid-1990s was eerily similar to that which would be enacted only a few years later. Here's how it worked. George Bush Sr.'s people created the initial Big Brother legislature; Bill Clinton pushed through the prototype; and then George W. Bush finalized it after 9-11. The entire scenario is part-and-parcel of the Bush-Clinton-Bush cabal that we've witnessed since 1980. Following OKC, we saw "repressive anti-terrorism laws, Internet surveillance, crackdowns on politically suspect dissident groups, and the Clinton Administration's proposal to create a 'Homeland Defense Force' that will allow the U.S. military to police the citizenry."[799]

The most appalling aspect of this *1984* nightmare is that the entire bombing scenario was a fabrication. Timothy McVeigh didn't even remotely mastermind it. He was a fall guy. The U.S. government knew 100% that not only would OKC happen; they had operatives such as Andreas Strassmeir pushing the event to culmination. Plus, informants like Carol Howe filed continuing reports from the inside, letting the FBI and ATF know precisely what was taking place. OKC was step one in the modern era of Big Brother government which would eventually seize almost total control of this nation.

TWO: Motive number one was obviously the primary reason for the OKC bombing; but don't for a moment think that the Clintons didn't also have a personal stake in this matter. Stated differently, they saw a way to manipulate events for their own self-interest. As we pointed out earlier, a slew of Clinton scandals was boiling during their first term; many of which were about to be investigated at a federal level. But after OKC, the "focus of attention shifted from investigations into Whitewater, Waco, Ruby Ridge, Mena, ATF conduct, and the death of Vince Foster—all originally scheduled to begin congressional investigations four weeks after the bombing—to 'more pressing issues.'"[800]

The resulting media blitz superseded these trials, which were conveniently pushed to a back-burner. OKC, sadly enough, was but the first of many Clintonesque *Wag the Dog* uses of violence, war, and trauma to deflect attention away from their scandals.

THREE: The precise target in OKC also became an integral part of the equation to prevent an inquiry into the many Bush-Clinton crimes. "If the records from the Mena drug smuggling operation were moved to the Murrah Building from Little Rock (or duplicates kept there after originals were previously destroyed or disappeared), then it would prove very beneficial to those about to come under congressional investigation in the following months (May-June '95) to have those records destroyed, or seized and moved for later destruction."[801]

One has to ask: was the Alfred P. Murrah Building targeted because it housed documents which incriminated the Clintons and

Bushes? It's a distinct possibility.

FOUR: At the time of the OKC bombing, anti-government and militia movements had reached unprecedented levels in this country. Spearheaded by populist and anti-New World Order newspapers and a network of booksellers, these patriot groups began posing enough of a threat to those in Washington D.C. that they had to be taken seriously. But once Timothy McVeigh's face was plastered on television and magazines across the nation—garbed in a prison orange jumpsuit and scowling at the cameras—the militia movement was immediately and effectively destroyed. Timothy McVeigh—agent provocateur for the government—was their black eye. "A new 'Barbarian at the Gate' in the form of 'militias' was created by the media; giving citizens a 'domestic threat' to worry about."[802]

With crew-cut McVeigh sneering and referring to dead babies as collateral damage, the attack "provided the impetus for a state-sanctioned war against 'anti-government' dissent that has produced a chilling effect on certain forms of political activism in this country ever since."[803]

In effect, the "anti-American radical wild-eyed conspiracy theorist militia member" was born; and with the mainstream media, ADL, and Southern Poverty Law Center fueling the fire, those who sought honest government were branded enemies of the state.

Considering the above four motivating factors, it's safe to conclude that the Bush-Clinton cabal was successful in their endeavor to protect themselves and push forward an agenda by bombing the Alfred P. Murrah Building in Oklahoma City.

THE MURDER OF OFFICER TERRENCE YEAKEY

Throughout the course of this book, a host of corrupt law enforcement officials, intel operatives, and politicians has been exposed for their multitude of illegal activities, including drug trafficking, money laundering, murder, and state-sponsored terrorism. But there are among their ranks *honest* public servants who aren't bought off, compromised, blackmailed, or motivated by greed or career advancement. In other words, there are still plenty

CHAPTER FIVE

of good guys left.

But guess what happens to these virtuous individuals when they get in the way of those who belong to the Bush-Clinton cabal, the CIA, or the Dixie Mafia. They get brutally murdered in cold blood.

One of the most tragic examples ever was the case of Oklahoma police officer Terrence Yeakey. This man was one of the first on the scene after the Alfred P. Murrah Building was bombed by ordnance *inside* the structure. His efforts to save men, women, and children went beyond the heroic as he worked gruelingly for two days straight digging through the rubble to find survivors. "On May 11th the following year he was scheduled to receive the Medal of Valor from the Oklahoma City Police Department. He never got it. He was murdered on May 8, 1996, in the country, 2 ½ miles from El Reno."[804]

Officially, his death was ruled . . . hold your breath . . . a suicide. Yes, another suicide! How did Yeakey supposedly kill himself? This morbid portrait is even worse than the Vince Foster murder. According to public reports, "Terry slashed himself eleven times on both forearms before cutting his own throat twice near the jugular vein. Then, apparently seeking an even more private place to die, he crawled through another mile of rough terrain away from his car and climbed a fence before shooting himself in the head with a small caliber revolver. What appeared to be rope burns on his neck, handcuff bruises to his wrists, and muddy grass embedded in his slash wounds strongly indicated that he had some help in traversing the final distance."[805]

On the website *Officer.com*, a report stated, "All the autopsy evidence shows that Yeakey's wounds were consistent with a torture-execution. The fatal shot was fired from a pistol with a silencer, held in contact with Yeakey's skull, leaving a barrel imprint and very little powder residue. No pistol was found at the scene until the FBI arrived, over an hour after his body was found. Handcuff marks were on both wrists according to the funeral home director. By the time the body arrived at the funeral home, the wrist lacerations had been sewn up and mud and grass was inside—showing that Yeakey was dragged through the mud as he attempted to fight off his attackers."[806]

Yeakey's death was not a suicide; it was a political assassination. Why? Because Terrence Yeakey witnessed the aftermath of the explosions inside the Murrah Building, and it most certainly did not match up with the official story. On the morning of April 19th he called his wife, crying, "It's not true. It's not what they're saying. It didn't happen that way."[807]

What did Terrence Yeakey see inside that federal building? Obviously there were still unexploded bombs, plus the wreckage of those bombs that did not go off, including the twisted beams which could not have resulted from an open-air bomb out on the street. He and others saw what *really* happened. He "may have been the first to discover the sham."[808]

Yes, his wife "Tonia Yeakey revealed that her husband had been very upset by something that he had seen under the day care center on April 19th. He had wanted to go back and photograph it, but the officials would not let him onto the site again."[809]

Instead of covering up the truth, Yeakey continued to investigate this matter; his actions soon drawing notice from the authorities. On the day of his murder, Terry "was on his way to El Reno to check out something; but first he had to shake the FBI agents who were following him."[810]

He never made it home. Following his murder, "witnesses said that the inside [of his car] looked like someone had butchered a hog on the front seat."[811]

Could Yeakey have been fitting the final pieces to the puzzle, and then preparing to disclose his findings at the OKC Police Department award ceremony while receiving his Medal of Valor? Is that why three days prior to this ceremony, Yeakey was murdered in cold blood? The brutal, gangland-style hit is indicative of the Dixie Mafia's handiwork; and we need to consider that if they'll kill an officer of the law in such a hideous fashion, nobody is safe from their barbaric actions.

CHAPTER FIVE

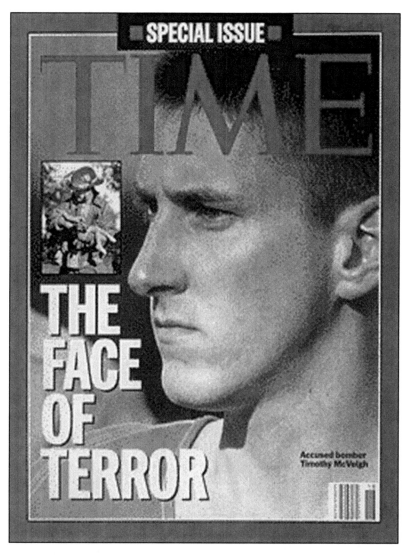

MASTERMIND OR PATSY? The *Time* magazine Oklahoma City "special issue" depicting the purported mastermind of the bombing of the Murrah building, Tim McVeigh, is shown above. McVeigh, it turns out, was more surprised than anyone when the small "send a message" bomb he thought he was carrying appeared to rip the entire face off of the OKC federal building. We now know McVeigh had contact with a wide array of ADL and FBI agents as well as an intriguing cast of characters including German intelligence operative Andreas Strassmeir.

A CHINESE PUZZLE: From 1994 to 1996, Johnny Huang, a Red Chinese national, made repeated visits to the Clinton White House to secure special favors in exchange for large amounts of cash destined for Bill and Hillary's personal coffers.

AFP/GETTY IMAGES

CHAPTER SIX

Chinagate & the Murder of Ron Brown

AMERICA BETRAYED

It was inevitable that a lifetime of crime, corruption, and deceit would eventually catch up with the Clintons. Oddly enough, none would have suspected that the biggest threat to topple their teetering house of cards would originate in the Asian world. The scandal became known as Chinagate, and from the earliest days of his political career, certain intelligence operatives had Bill Clinton's number. "Chinese spymasters would have seen Clinton as a good investment. In the patient style that typifies Chinese spycraft, they likely foresaw as early as 1977 that cultivating Clinton could open doors for them in the future."[812]

Of course some of these channels could be navigated legitimately; but if other tactics were necessary, "his wild sex life, alleged drug use, and corrupt business practices made him [Clinton] a perfect subject for blackmail."[813]

What we're talking about here is China's entrance onto the world stage as a global superpower. To accomplish such a feat, this sleeping giant needed a host nation to facilitate its ascent. In this sense, "the roots of the Red Chinese gaining a foothold into American politics can be traced to none other than Bill Clinton's Arkansas."[814] In return for having a red carpet rolled out for them, "Chinese agents helped secure the 1992 Democratic presidential nomination for Clinton with a multimillion dollar loan from an Arkansas bank under their influence."[815]

Both sides eventually won; Bill Clinton became president, while China has become the fastest growing economic machine on Earth via corporate America selling its soul (i.e., outsourcing), as well as the Chinese reaping the benefits of top-secret U.S. technology and military secrets. It was "a reckless exchange between the Clintons and associates of Chinese intelligence,"[816] and the Faustian deal did more damage to this nation than any of us will realize for quite some time. The results are horrifying:

- In 1997, Clinton allowed China to take over operation of the Panama Canal.
- Only a public outcry stopped Clinton in 1998 from leasing California's Long Beach Naval Yard to the Chinese firm Cosco.
- How did China catch up so fast? Easy. We sold them all the technology they needed—or handed it over for free. Neither neglect nor carelessness is to blame. Bill Clinton did it on purpose.
- As a globalist, Clinton promotes "multipolarity"—the doctrine that no country (such as the USA) should be allowed to gain decisive advantage over others.
- Defense contractors eager to sell technology to China poured millions of dollars into Clinton's campaign. In return, Clinton called off the dogs. Janet Reno and other officials responsible for counterintelligence stood down while Lockheed Martin, Hughes Electronics, Loral Space and Communications, and other U.S. companies helped China modernize its nuclear strike force.
- The Clinton machine received funding directly from known or suspected Chinese intelligence agents, among them James and Mochtar Riady, who own the Indonesian Lippo Group, John Huang, Charlie Trie . . . and others.

- While doing everything in his power to build up China's nuclear arsenal, Clinton aggressively downsized the U.S. military.
- [Clinton] ordered that America no longer have a "launch on warning" policy and replaced it with one that says America will retaliate only after it has been attacked. This nonsensical Clinton policy means that American cities and American military targets must first be destroyed before America retaliates.[817]

This list could obviously be continued, for the globalist Bush-Clinton cabal has bent over backwards to betray America by making China the next king of the hill. One simple example of this traitorous betrayal can be found in outsourcing and the world's largest retailer. Walk into any Wal-Mart and start looking at products on their shelves. Where are they made? Answer: China. America's once mighty manufacturing base has been eroded, and the market leader in buying these foreign products is Wal-Mart. Where is Wal-Mart located? In Bill Clinton's Arkansas; and they rose to power via his legislation and money from Arkansas kingmakers, Stephens, Inc.

Naturally, the situation is much more complex, and as you'll see, the Clintons were in the midst of Chinagate from their earliest days. Once Bill and Hillary's backstabbing of America became apparent, and potential legal action became a reality, the fallout was tragic.

- Two crucial witnesses, Commerce Secretary Ron Brown and Assistant Commerce Secretary Charles Meissner, perished together in a plane crash.
- At least eighteen other critical witnesses have fled the country.
- Another seven to nine witnesses have taken

the Fifth Amendment.
- Document tampering has been shameless. As the *New York Times* noted, "Much remains missing; Mr. Huang's Democratic National Committee (DNC) telephone logs, most of his outgoing correspondence, his travel records, details of visits to the White House and Clinton-Gore campaign headquarters.[818]

The reason Bill and Hillary became so entangled in this mess was simple: they needed money to keep their political machine running. As one author asked, "Who was the biggest contributor to the Clinton-Gore ticket in 1992? Not a corporation, not a labor union, not a Hollywood mogul, but Indonesian businessman James Riady and his wife, who gave $450,000 to elect Bill Clinton. During the final weeks of the campaign, the Riady family, its associates, and executives at Riady companies gave an additional $600,000 to the DNC and Democratic state parties."[819]

Taken one step further, the picture becomes even clearer. "The top contributors to the 1992 Clinton campaign were Chinese agents. In 1996, the leading Clinton donors were U.S. defense contractors doing business with Chinese missile manufacturers."[820]

With these huge amounts of tainted cash rolling in, investigative writers Edward Timperlake and William C. Triplett asked a question of vital importance in their book, *The Year of the Rat*: "Did the Clinton administration sell out America's national security to one of this country's leading and most dangerous adversaries merely to raise campaign cash? In the pages that follow, we will prove our answer, which is: yes."[821]

THE RIADY EMPIRE

To understand Chinagate, one must go back in time to one individual: Mochtar Riady. Who was he? "Mochtar Riady is an ethnic Chinese banker in Jakarta [who] started his financial empire with gun and drug running in the East Indies before World War II."[822]

Just like the CIA and a number of other secret societies throughout history, one of the themes common to many of the wealthy (illegal) elite is guns and drugs. The same applied to Mochtar Riady's empire: weapons and narcotics. These elements provide a common link to the intelligence world. Secondly, the CIA itself "has confirmed that the Riadys have long been connected to Chinese intelligence."[823]

In addition, although I won't delve into all the details, "the Riadys were in business with companies believed by many analysts to be a front for the Chinese intelligence services."[824]

Thirdly, "the Riady Empire, centered on its Lippo Group, is, as one financial analyst in Jakarta describes it, 'a carefully balanced house of cards.' *Newsweek* has noted, 'Moving cash around the globe in tangled webs of transactions has always been the Riady way.'"[825]

What does that description sound like to you? Of course: money laundering in the same vein as the CIA and BCCI.

So, the Riadys are directly linked to guns, drugs, Chinese intelligence, and money laundering. But that's only step one of this incredible tale. To increase his financial reach, Riady eyed the shiniest gem of all—America—and of all the people in the world to work with, who did Riady select? "He seeks the help of Jackson Stephens to act as his agent,"[826] — the Arkansas kingmaker who has been involved in every dirty deal imaginable. Stephens, as we've already learned, "brokered the arrival of BCCI to this country and steered their founder, Hassan Abedi, to Burt Lance [of the Jimmy Carter administration]."[827]

On top of everything else, we have uncovered yet again another tie to the most corrupt monetary institution of all time—BCCI. So, here is how the timeline unfolds which ties the Riadys to the Clintons in Arkansas. "In 1977 Mochtar Riady tried to buy the National Bank of Georgia. He failed, but one of the brokers in the deal was Jackson Stephens of Little Rock, Arkansas."[828]

Mochtar's son, James, subsequently became an intern for Stephens, Inc., and "through Jackson Stephens, James Riady met a rising politician, Arkansas Attorney General Bill Clinton."[829]

Afterward, James Riady "would say that he was sponsored by Bill Clinton."[830]

As Clinton's star was on the rise, so too was the young initiate. "In early 1984, James Riady and Jackson Stephens became co-owners of Arkansas's largest bank, the Worthen Bank."[831]

Who else was involved in this deal? "Other Worthen co-owners will eventually include BCCI investor Abdullah Taha Bakhish."[832]

Why should Worthen Bank ring a bell? Because in 1992, after the Gennifer Flowers fiasco blew up nationally and Bill Clinton's political campaign was in desperate need of funds, it was Worthen Bank which fronted him a two million dollar loan to resuscitate his drive for the presidency. Without it, his ship would have surely been sunk. But there was an equally crucial move which took place in the 1980s that tied the Riady family in with the Dixie Mafia and Stephens Inc. "1985 saw Mochtar and James Riady engineer the takeover of the First National Bank of Mena in a town of 5,400 with few major assets beyond a Contra supply base, drug running and money laundering operations."[833]

The Riady family were multi-millionaires who originated from the other side of the world. What are the odds that of all the banks in existence on this planet, they chose to buy one in a town with a population of 5,400 people? That's less people than attend some minor league baseball games. Do you think the fact that this bank was used to launder billions of dirty cocaine dollars had anything to do with their decision? After all, the Riadys made their fortune off guns and drugs—which fit in part-and-parcel with the Contra drug and gun operation in America! Funny how the world works, isn't it? Then they loan money to Bill Clinton so he can become president. As time passes, "Deals are worked on for Wal-Mart, Tyson Foods, and J.B. Hunt"[834] through the Riady-Arkansas connections.

Here is where things get interesting. During the mid-80s, Bill Clinton started to do business with the Riadys' Worthen Bank. Specifically, as governor, he deposited Arkansas state pension funds in this institution. Then problems arose. "In the first year

CHAPTER SIX

under Riady/Stephens management, the bank lost tens of millions of dollars in Arkansas state pension funds through a risky out-of-state investment."[835]

The loss was monumental. "Every penny of the $52 million that Worthen put at risk . . . was state pension fund money. And every penny of it was gone."[836]

Naturally, "the impending collapse put Bill Clinton in a political panic."[837]

If Governor Clinton had to confront the voters of Arkansas and tell them that he just blew $50+ million, his political boat would be sunk. But Clinton didn't have to worry because an Arkansas kingmaker came to his rescue. "The $52 million loss is covered by a Worthen check written by Jackson Stephens in the middle of the night . . . Clinton and Worthen escape a major scandal."[838]

One thing became perfectly clear: "the message was that they were not going to do anything to embarrass the Clinton administration."[839]

The Clinton-Riady relationship would endure for years. As mentioned, in 1992 when the Clinton camp was in desperate need of funds, he "turned to his chief moneyman, James Riady. In the middle of August, Clinton and Riady took a limousine ride together. Soon thereafter, a cascade of Riady money—nearly $600,000—made its way to the DNC."[840]

After being elected, the windfall continued. "The Clinton-Gore inauguration in mid-January 1993 was another opportunity for the Riadys to open their wallets. James Riady and John Huang each gave $100,000 to cover the cost of the inaugural parties."[841] The bond between them became so tight that it bordered on the macabre, if not downright sick. Take the Waco massacre for example.

> In Jakarta, James Riady likes to brag about where he was on the afternoon of April 19, 1993. On that day eighty members of the Branch Davidian religious cult were holed up in their compound outside of Waco, Texas, when it was shattered by a

tank-led assault. By the time the FBI and Treasury's Alcohol, Tobacco, and Firearms agents had completed their work, 17 American children had burned to death.

As might be expected, the White House was a busy place that afternoon, and the president was preoccupied. Clinton was not too distracted, however, to chat with his leading contributors—James Riady, John Huang, and Mark Grobmyer—in his little study off the Oval Office. Riady later told Indonesian diplomats that, during their chat, a television in the corner showed the Waco compound burning over and over as CNN repeated its coverage. Clinton even took time to show his visitors the White House Situation Room, then on full alert.[842]

There is a definite twisted sickness to the Clintons which defies description. White House entry logs confirm that Riady and his companions were in the presidential offices [West Wing] of the White House that day. How many other presidents, in the middle of such a tragedy, would have spent their time giving major donors a White House tour?"[843]

HUBBELL, HUANG, & HILLARY'S TREASON

As we proceed through this section, one may ask: the Clintons obviously received huge amounts of money from their Asian counterparts, but what did Riady & Company get in return? At this stage it appears to be a one-sided affair. But believe me, those behind Chinagate played the Arkansas connection like a fiddle. They paid; but the secrets they obtained in return were priceless.

The Chinese are patient, and as they integrated their way into the Clinton camp, they simply bided their time until a crack in the veneer appeared. That opening presented itself with one of Hillary's chief cronies—Webster Hubbell. As we know, Hubbell was an intimate at the Rose Law Firm, and a man who had his fingers in all sorts of dirty dealings. When the Clintons moved to Washington DC, they made Hubbell Associate Attorney General.

CHAPTER SIX

In essence, Hubbell ran the Justice Department while Janet Reno was merely their puppet on a string.

As with so many other Clinton associates, it didn't take long before Hubbell found himself in hot water, being charged or convicted of: defrauding law clients, the shady real estate con known as Castle Grande, overbilling clients, tax evasion, mail fraud, conspiracy, lying to regulators at the FDIC and RTC, defrauding the federal government, and cheating the City of Los Angeles out of $25,000 for bogus consultation work. But instead of selling Bill and Hillary down the river, Hubbell too became a fall guy and got bounced from office. His protection of Mrs. Clinton was so pronounced that even though "the Castle Grande indictment referred to the first lady more than 30 times [and] the charges implied that she had been as deeply involved in the illegal activities as Hubbell,"[844] he still wouldn't hang her out to dry. When White House official and Bill Clinton's former lover Marsha Scott asked Hubbell if he'd rat-out Hillary, he said with obvious resignation, "I would not do that. So I need to roll over one more time."[845]

Here is where James Riady enters the picture. He "often hired many of Bill Clinton's closest Arkansas cronies. Joseph Giroir and Webb Hubbell, both former law partners of Hillary Clinton, are or have been on the Riady payroll."[846]

Just two years into the Clinton presidency, Webb Hubbell was in serious trouble. By June, 1994 "he ran out of money. He was down to $6,780 in his checking account. Having resigned from Justice under a cloud, he had no job, his legal and other debts, including back taxes and penalties, were skyrocketing; and he was on his way to jail."[847]

To compound these problems, Hubbell saw what happened to so many others who became expendable to the Clintons, especially Vince Foster, who was murdered less than a year earlier. If there was any threat that someone would talk to the authorities, the axe quickly fell in a very real way. "It is no secret that the White House had been very worried about what Hubbell might reveal to Independent Counsel Kenneth Starr about Arkansas business deals and other matters. During this same summer of 1994 internal White House documents show that administration officials were 'monitoring' Hubbell's 'cooperation' with Starr."[848]

In other words, Hillary's secret police were on high alert.

At this point we see Beltway politics at their very worst. "Hubbell was broke. Whether he blackmailed the White House or the administration only feared he would do so, we don't know. But there's no question Clinton's team felt motivated to act."[849]

With chaos at their doorstep yet again, who appears on the scene as the fixer extraordinaire? Hillary Clinton. The two met, and "her visit with Hubbell on June 20 [1994] suggests she was in charge."[850]

Objective number one was to get the embroiled attorney general on his feet financially so that he wouldn't start singing to their adversaries. Being that the Clintons were constantly hounding everyone they knew for contributions, "to get money for Hubbell on such short notice would not have been easy. Foreign money was the White House's best opportunity."[851]

After their June 20 meeting, "there followed a busy week during which John Huang made at least five visits to the White House, usually in the company of James Riady."[852]

Matters of great importance must have been discussed because "on the following Monday, June 27, Hong Kong China, Ltd, a Riady-owned company, issued a check to Webster Hubbell for $100,000."[853]

Just like that, a sweet $100,000 was laid in Webster Hubbell's portly lap. But this wasn't "free money" by a long shot. In return, the Riadys placed a spy directly within the Clinton administration that had access to unheard of government secrets. "The Riadys would have extracted a price for their generosity. That price would have been [John] Huang's presidential appointment to the Commerce Department, where he could be a source of priceless military and economic intelligence."[854]

Obtaining such a post for Huang didn't come by accident. "The Clintons expended much effort, and the Riadys spent much cash,

CHAPTER SIX

to get John Huang his job at the Department of Commerce. The Clintons got value for their effort in the form of Lippo-financed payoffs to Webb Hubbell. The Riadys got value for their money in the form of economic intelligence forwarded to them—and, in all likelihood, through them to their associates in Chinese intelligence—by Huang."[855]

Take a moment and let this notion sink in. Putting John Huang in the Commerce Department "was the payoff to the Riadys. For services rendered in the 1992 campaign, and taking care of the Hubbell matter to the tune of at least $100,000 in 1994, they were able to insert their man into the heart of American politics and economic intelligence. Their agent, John Huang, was totally beholden to them. By luck or design, he was placed in a position where he would not be noticed but where he could collect American intelligence that would be immensely valuable to both the Riadys and their associates in Chinese intelligence."[856]

Unbelievably, matters get even more sinister. As you'll soon read, after Huang snagged highly-classified American secrets, there was one more step in the process. "Collecting was not enough; he [Huang] found a secure way—the Stephens office across the street—to transmit the information overseas."[857]

Jackson Stephens was aiding and abetting the Clintons and Riadys in their treasonous betrayal of the United States. Their acts were so heinous that House Rules Committee Chairman Gerald Soloman stated on June 11, 1997, "I have received reports from government sources that say there are electronic intercepts which provide evidence confirming that John Huang committed economic espionage and breached our national security by passing classified information to his former employer, the Lippo Group."[858]

Prior to looking at John Huang and an assortment of other Chinese infiltrators, let's be perfectly clear about who was behind this treasonous betrayal of the U.S. government. One, "the first lady had orchestrated Huang's appointment to Commerce. According to Commerce officials quoted by the highly regarded Jerry Seper of the *Washington Times,* Mrs. Clinton's involvement in the Huang appointment was common knowledge."[859]

Such a move wasn't easy, for Huang had to bypass the resistance of those career workers at Commerce who were rightfully suspicious of Huang's appointment. The reason Hillary masterminded this highly questionable move was simple: it was done to save her and Bill's hides by buying off Webster Hubbell so that he wouldn't sing to the feds. What we're talking about is treason, and "the weight of motivation, opportunity, and evidence points directly to Hillary Clinton's intervention."[860]

One person in the know was Nolanda Hill, Commerce Department Secretary Ron Brown's lover. In an interview with Brian Ross of ABC's *Primetime Live* she said, "Ron told me that the White House put him [Huang] there, and it was Ron's opinion that the White House meant Hillary in this instance."[861]

Hill continued, "He [Brown] believed that she [Hillary] was the person that made the call."[862]

Hillary's involvement with the Riady family was so extensive that it even reached into the Travelgate scandal. Do you recall that debacle from Book Two of this trilogy? A firm named World Wide Travel provided many of the airplane fares for Bill Clinton's 1992 presidential campaign to the tune of "$1 million in deferred billing."[863]

Hillary's chief Travelgate operative, David Watkins, boasted, "Were it not for World Wide Travel, the Arkansas governor may never have been in contention for the highest office in the land."[864]

In essence, without World Wide Travel—run by close Arkansas friends Harry and Linda Bloodworth-Thomasson—Clinton would never have been able to traverse the country during the primaries. Here's the catch: "A closer look at World Wide Travel's financial dealings reveals that their principal backer is none other than the Lippo Group's Worthen Bank"[865] which was run by the Riadys and Jackson Stephens!

Bankers and spies weren't the only ones to benefit from their years in "public service"; the Clintons too became extremely wealthy in the process. Hillary's "2005 Senate financial disclosure report revealed that she and her husband held joint Citibank deposit accounts containing between $5 million and $25 million, which produced between $50,000 and $100,000 in interest. In addition, she shared a Senate Qualified Blind Trust with her husband that was also worth between $5 million and $25 million."[866]

Politics has been *very very good* to the Clintons.

Ultimately, the above information brings us to deliberate acts of espionage that were waged against the U.S. government. The first man in our radar is Johnny Huang who—because of payoffs and bailouts for the Clintons—was appointed "assistant secretary of the Commerce Department [which] gave him secret clearance to attend classified CIA briefings."[867]

In addition, "evidently at the urging of the Riadys, Clinton made Huang vice chairman of the Democratic National Committee in 1995."[868]

That's not a bad return for bailing out Hubbell to the tune of $100,000.

The most pressing question at this juncture is: who was John Huang? As already mentioned, John Huang was employed by the Riadys; but not as a typical bean-counter or financial analyst. "Whatever Huang was doing, it wasn't traditional banking. His Lippo colleagues viewed him as James Riady's 'man in America' and a political 'fixer.'"[869]

What did he have his sights set on in the United States? "Huang's real job in the three or four years before he went to Commerce was overseeing the Riadys' political and financial investments in the Democratic Party in general; and Governor Bill Clinton in particular."[870]

The Clintons were their targets; with access to top-secret information their specific goal. John Huang was the conduit; a man who greased the wheels for the Riady family. After being appointed to his position within the Clinton cabinet, "Huang received an interim 'top secret' security clearance on the pretext that Commerce Secretary Ron Brown needed his services urgently. At that point Huang could see and hear American classified information up to the top secret level."[871]

The Riadys' influence was so brazen and arrogant that "Huang told the FBI that, in an early effort to cash in on his 'investment' in Clinton and Gore, Riady had wanted to place Huang in Clinton's National Security Council, but that was apparently too much for even the Clinton-Gore administration."[872]

So, Huang was planted in the Commerce Department, whereupon he received "thirty-seven briefings from the CIA, during which he was supplied with hundreds of classified CIA documents on subjects such as U.S.-China technology transfers [and] the Asian nuclear power industry."[873]

It seemed the freedom entitled to him was unlimited. "Huang also enjoyed unusual access to the White House, visiting at least sixty-seven times."[874]

What type of official documentation was Huang obtaining? "As a United States government official at the Commerce Department, Huang had access to four types of very valuable information: (1) CIA briefings, (2) CIA materials shared by others, (3) classified State Department cables on foreign economic and political matters, and (4) information that is confidential, even though not classified."[875]

Once Huang secured this data, something even stranger and more treacherous occurred. "*New York Times* columnist Bill Safire has described the Stephens, Inc. office at the Willard as a 'drop' for John Huang."[876]

Here is what would happen.

- Huang walked across the street to the Stephens office two or three times a week carrying a folder or small briefcase.
- He received overnight packages and faxes at the office.
- He sent faxes out of the office, used the copier, and made telephone calls from a small office set aside for visitors.[877]

It's beyond the realm of believability how treasonous this situation was. "Huang's activities could be explained in only one way: he was a spy. Whether he was helping out the Riadys or the Chinese government remains an open question."[878]

Because the Riadys paid off the Clintons, Bill and Hillary allowed them to insert a spy directly into their cabinet. Then John Huang would use the office of the family who put the First Couple in the White House—Arkansas's Stephens Inc. "From his telephone records, we know that Huang spoke frequently to a number of Stephens Inc. officials in Little Rock."[879]

Also, once he'd obtained U.S. government secrets, he'd immediately dispatch them to China via Stephens Inc. "On the morning of October 4, 1994, Huang was briefed for the first time by the CIA. Late that afternoon a fax was sent from the Stephens office to Lippo, Ltd. in Hong Kong."[880]

Here's the bottom line. "During a secret limousine ride, a foreign associate of Chinese military intelligence pledged $1 million in illegal campaign contributions to the Clinton-Gore ticket in 1992. His [Riady's] employee [John Huang] delivered on that promise, traveling around the United States with cash that has never been fully accounted for. In return for this largesse, the illegal donor [Riady] could place his employee in the United States government with 'top secret' access to American secrets about Communist China."[881]

If you're not convinced of the seriousness of this transgression to our national security, consider: "At least three of the documents that the CIA showed Huang had a special marking: MEM DISSEM. The significance of this marking, according to the CIA, is that 'unauthorized disclosure of the information contained in a MEM DISSEM could result in the death of an asset.' In other words, if the information leaked, the source of the information could be killed in retribution. The CIA does not exaggerate when it refers to these sources as extremely sensitive."[882]

Yet John Huang not only had access to this data, but "between March 15, 1993 and July 18, 1994 [he] entered the White House at least forty-seven times, according to Secret Service records. Nine of these visits was listed as with the president—most in the first family's quarters in the White House."[883]

John Huang was a spy, and the family he worked for—the Riadys—was directly tied to Chinese intelligence. In fact, one of Bill Clinton's primary fixers, Bruce Lindsey, "knew James Riady well. When Riady visited the White House, he used the telephone on Lindsey's desk to make outside calls."[884]

If such revelations don't fill you with unease, then maybe you should check your pulse because what we're discussing is flat-out treason and espionage. The Clintons sold out our country to compensate foreign assets who illegally contributed to their campaigns and saved them from political scandal. For such offenses, Bill and Hillary should have been arrested, tried, convicted, and sentenced to the fullest extent of the law.

Amazingly, the Clintons also attached themselves to a number of other shady Asians with links to organized crime, Red China, and numerous highly questionable activities. Below is a partial list of who Bill and Hillary mingled with; their Rogue's Gallery of Riady cronies, so to speak.

Chen Xitong (China): "It would be hard to find a more notorious and corrupt CCP official than Chen, or one with more blood on his hands from the June 1989 Tiananmen Square Massacre."[885]

When it came to the monsters giving orders, "Chen signed the martial law decrees justifying the use of tanks and flamethrowers against unarmed citizens."[886]

Yet Huang and James Riady were trying to get Chen a U.S. visa into this country.

Charlie Trie: "Pleaded guilty to minor campaign funding offenses [and] revealed to the FBI a much larger pattern of illegal campaign contributions to the Clinton-Gore ticket in 1996, including a substantial cash element."[887]

Guess who received this cold, hard cash. "On the morning of March 21, 1996, Trie dropped off hundreds of thousands of dollars to the president and first lady's favorite charity, the Presidential

CHAPTER SIX

Legal Defense Trust."[888]

This very same day, while Trie was making his rounds, he "opened an envelope and $460,000 in checks and money orders spilled out."[889]

Trie, who ended up residing in Little Rock, became so close to Mrs. Clinton that "they traveled together to Taiwan while Clinton was governor."[890]

What's so alarming is that Charlie Trie "belongs to a secret Chinese criminal society; he is a member of the 'Four Seas' triad gang"[891] and an agent for the PRC (People's Republic of China).

Np Lapseng: A "Macau criminal syndicate figure"[892] who was "in the business of exploiting Asian women for prostitution."[893]

He also "advises the Chinese government [and] according to the [Thompson] Committee, transferred $1.4 million to Charlie Trie to fund his contributions."[894]

There are several photos in circulation of this mobster-pimp with Bill and Hillary, plus Al Gore.

General Ji Shende: Head of Chinese military intelligence, "told Johnny Chung, according to Chung's own account: 'We like your president very much. We would like to see him reelected. I will give you 300,000 U.S. dollars. You can give it to the president and the Democrat Party.' Chung would funnel $100,000 of this stash into the DNC."[895]

Johnny Chung: This businessman made large donations to the Clintons. He "told prosecutors that he got his contribution money from Lieutenant Colonel Liu Chaoying. Lieutenant Colonel Liu is the daughter of General Liu, the most senior officer in the PLA [People's Liberation Army]."[896]

General Xu Huizi: Although the Clintons tried to conceal this news, one of China's most notorious killers visited Washington (and the Pentagon) in August 1994. What distinguishes this bloodthirsty man? "On the night of the Tiananmen Massacre, June 3-4, 1989, General Xu was, according to a U.S. army general, in 'tactical control' of the PLA troops in and around Beijing. At 4 pm on June 3, he gave the 'mount up and move out' order to the armored and mechanized units, thereby shouldering more responsibility for the deaths of his countrymen than any other officer in the PLA. Under his orders, children as young as three died from PLA gunfire."[897]

In all honesty, Xu doesn't sound much different from ATF and FBI agents that massacred women and children at Waco. To cover their hides, "the Clinton administration tried to keep Xu's visit a secret. For obvious reasons, it was not announced to the public. [But] upon his arrival, General Xu received a nineteen-gun salute from a U.S. military honor guard."[898]

These revelations bring an even darker, sicker perspective to how abhorrently immoral and soulless the Clintons are—all for the money they so desperately covet and for their own political advancement.

DEAD MAN WALKING

Ron Brown was killed because he refused to be another fall guy for the Clintons' crimes; and to protect himself he used his knowledge of Chinagate as leverage. Tragically for Brown, he failed to realize the ruthlessness and the ends to which Bill and Hillary would go to destroy those who'd choose to expose them. Although Brown died in a plane crash on April 3, 1996 ("just before 3:00 pm Croatia time, the Air Force CT-43A that bore him drifted 'inexplicably' off-course"[899]), his mistress Nolanda Hill said unabashedly, "I was there and am now convinced he was murdered."[900]

We've already seen the Dixie Mafia, Arkancides, and the Clinton Body Count at work; but would these bastards be so heartless as to actually sabotage an entire plane full of passengers merely to kill one man?

As you'll see, not only were the Clintons capable of such an act, they took the scenario one step further with Brown to ensure his death.

Prior to delving into this twisted murder case, we need to take another look at President Bill Clinton, who is, without a doubt, the absolute phoniest and most plastic public official to ever grace the American political stage. Following Ron Brown's funeral, Clinton was walking with Reverend Tony Campolo, trading stories about other black funerals they'd been to in the past. Of course this setting was supposed to be somber; Ron Brown had just died in a tragic "accident." But Clinton and the reverend were yukking it up, having a good time. Then, "as Clinton leaned back to laugh, he suddenly locked on to the camera and reflexively downshifted to a funeral gear, dropping his head in seeming sadness and wiping an imagined tear from his eye."[901]

This slug was such a fraud that he actually feigned crocodile tears for the news cameras.

But such superficiality was only one element of the weirdness which surrounded Ron Brown's murder. First, another significant figure killed in this Croatian plane crash was Assistant Secretary of Commerce "Charles F. Meissner, who was John Huang's immediate supervisor at Commerce."[902]

Just as important as who was on that plane was also who *wasn't*. The headlines read, "Enron Corp. Confirms *No* Enron Execs on Board Commerce Secretary Ron Brown's Missing Plane."[903]

So, the two individuals tied to the huge Chinagate scandal perished, while Ken Lay's Enron bigwigs were spared. How fitting. Bill and Hillary: pawns of big money, just like the Bush family.

Let's not mince words. There was nothing accidental about that downed aircraft or the people aboard it. "Plane crashes were a favorite method of assassination with the Dixie Mafia. . . . It was a perfect cover for murder because most of the evidence is destroyed or mutilated in a crash. Also, many people have an inability to accept the notion [that] murderers would kill so many innocent passengers to get one target. So the death of the target appears purely accidental."[904]

But Ron Brown was most certainly in the crosshairs that fateful day, not to mention the focus of a corruption investigation that had him dodging bullets on all fronts. Specifically, "Brown was the major target of an independent counsel probe headed by Daniel Pearson. Also, a conservative legal group, Judicial Watch, was investigating the possibly illegal ties to Brown and his Commerce

Department to DNC fundraising efforts."⁹⁰⁵

The troubles Brown faced were extremely serious, for "investigators were probing the possibility that Brown had been a frontman for the Clintons' now-famous backroom dealings with China—dealings in which it is alleged that the Clintons sold out U.S. security in exchange for Chinese campaign contributions."⁹⁰⁶

With the net widening, it became clear who would be the fall guy. "Subpoenas were flying in the probe, with the names of Brown and his son Michael listed among those scheduled to receive such subpoenas."⁹⁰⁷

If forced to take the stand, Brown would be presented with "evidence that he had taken money improperly or even illegally just before he took the post of Secretary of Commerce."⁹⁰⁸

Indeed, as chief investigator, "Pearson had already made allegations that Brown had accepted $700,000 in bribes from Vietnamese officials and that the Independent Counsel was only a few days away from issuing a criminal grand jury indictment against the Commerce Secretary."⁹⁰⁹

As this news came down the pike, the White House switched into panic mode. "President Clinton was said to be sweating bullets after learning of the extraordinary progress Pearson was making. Pearson had obtained subpoenas that showed his probe had widened to include Brown's ties to possibly illicit fundraising activities involving the Democratic National Committee and a DNC-affiliated group called the Asian Pacific Advisory Committee."⁹¹⁰

Soon, one thing became clear to Brown's girlfriend. From the Clintons' perspective, "Brown was damaged goods, and the White House was letting him know it. As [Nolanda] Hill saw it, the worse the damage, the better a bagman Brown would be. If his fundraising missions were ever exposed, the White House could lay it all off on a corrupt black man kept on the job only because of the White House's otherwise admirable sensitivity to racial issues."⁹¹¹

By now, hopefully you can peer behind the veil to ultimately see who was pulling the strings of not only this scandal, but also the cover-up. As Jim McDougal once assessed, "If you ever tried to discuss finances or anything but politics with Bill, his eyes would glaze over. Whatever one had to discuss, I discussed with Hillary."[912]

Similarly, "strong evidence suggests that Hillary was the mover and shaker behind Chinagate—just as she was in all of the Clintons' business affairs."[913]

Thus, with Ron Brown already in hot water over his own tangled business matters, Hillary made him her 'bagman' in the Chinagate affair. That way, he'd take the fall and they had plausible denial.

There was only one problem. Ron Brown wasn't going to be like the others before him who simply rolled over and played dead, especially after he heard some disturbing news about what was soon to transpire. Exploding, Brown sneered, "That f***ing bitch did it. She did it. We have both been named as co-targets."[914]

What was Brown ranting about? "The woman in question, the subject of Brown's wrath, was Attorney General Janet Reno. What she 'did' was call for an independent counsel, primarily to assess whether Brown had 'accepted things of value' from Hill in exchange for his influence."[915]

In other words, Janet Reno—who initially took her marching orders from a high-level operative for Hillary Clinton, Webb Hubbell—created an independent counsel to investigate Ron Brown's influence peddling. They were setting the wheels in motion to throw him under the bus. "But Brown had no intention of lying down and taking the rap for the Clintons. 'I'm too old to go to jail. I'm taking everyone with me,' Brown reportedly told associates during his final days."[916]

Those words marked Ron Brown's death sentence, for "in one White House scandal after another, all roads led to Hillary."[917]

The first lady had no intention of letting *anyone* drag them down, especially some "black man on the take." With Brown's threat lingering like a storm cloud, the plan for his murder was hatched.

Sensing that he better act quickly, "just two weeks before he died, Brown had a stormy meeting with Bill Clinton. Some say that the reckless words Brown spoke at that meeting sealed his doom."[918]

What type of dialogue occurred between them? "Brown demanded that Clinton get him off the hook. Brown apparently believed that Ken Starr was fixed, and he wanted Clinton to fix Daniel Pearson too."[919]

Ron Brown was correct in his assertion that Kenneth Starr was in the bag; a point which will become even clearer shortly in regard to Monica Lewinsky. Brown continued, telling "the president to call off the dogs, to shut down the independent counsel, to do whatever had to be done because he was not about to let Michael [his son] do jail time."[920]

According to Nolanda Hill, "I was absolutely convinced that Michael was looking at jail time."[921]

In this sense, not only had Brown gotten himself in a fix, but he'd also dragged his son into it too.

The stakes were now doubled. But the Clintons were one step ahead of Brown, for they'd been playing this game of intrigue a whole hell of a lot longer than he had. Realizing how greedy and hungry for power he was, "The White House enabled Brown's corruption and exploited it."[922]

Put differently, in Ron Brown they had another ready-made patsy. To raise money for the 1996 election, the Clintons sold out our country with deals to the Chinese. "Brown was the 'bagman' for many of them."[923]

This is when Brown realized that even though he was doing the Clintons' dirty work for them, *they* were the ones double-crossing him by initiating a special counsel. As a result, if Chinagate blew up, he'd be fingered, not them. So, at their meeting, Brown "went in and told Clinton he was going to blow the whistle on Asia and treason, just to get the independent counsel shut down."[924]

In essence, "he threatened the Clintons and their associates with exposure as leverage for his son's freedom."[925]

Brown laid all his cards on the table and "made it clear that he

CHAPTER SIX

was not going to take the fall for an administration rampant with corruption."[926]

The bottom line: Brown told Clinton, "Unless you get this Democrat independent counsel off my back, I may have to turn state's evidence. I may have to cooperate."[927]

Hillary would never in a million years stand for such a move, "and it was within the next two weeks that he [Brown] was sent to Bosnia. He did not know that he was scheduled to go there."[928]

In the meantime, the Clintons knew Ron Brown was a ticking time bomb. "When Brown did not get the response he wanted from Clinton, he resorted to his ultimate bargaining chip. If he had to, he told Clinton, he was prepared to reveal the president's treasonous dealings with China, almost none of which had yet to make the news."[929]

In addition, Brown added one final element to the equation. "He told the president he had 'lost control' of [Nolanda] Hill."[930]

Now there was more than one threat to expose the betrayal of their country.

What did President Clinton do? Obviously, the same thing he did practically every other time he got into trouble. He turned to his fixer. "The one person he would have told was his wife. He and Hillary could not have failed to recognize that if Brown went public on China, Clinton would certainly lose the election, probably the nomination, and quite possibly his freedom. The potential for disaster was real and imminent."[931]

Ron Brown "would not go down alone."[932]

Therefore, he was marked for death. To make the matter even dicier, "the president and his wife did not love Brown as Clinton avowed. Nor did they enjoy much, if any, of his friendship and warmth. No, the relationship, always cool, had turned cold. Brown feared the Clintons, feared to even call them, and they deeply distrusted him."[933]

Nolanda Hill confirmed this sentiment. "'Ron and Clinton did not like each other.' They never really did. In time, Brown's dislike would turn to fear. He would intuit it, if not fully understand, that the pathologies of Bill Clinton, and of Hillary as well, ran deeper than his own, and when the two combined, much deeper"[934] [i.e. they were capable of much more evil than he, especially when working in tandem].

So, the Clintons scheduled Ron Brown for another *fundraising trip*, "this time to the Balkans."[935]

His mistress immediately smelled a rat. "'This trip makes no sense,' Hill told him more than once. Brown did not disagree. The trip did not make sense from a fund-raising perspective."[936]

Like a dead man walking, "Brown begged not to go."[937]

Why? Despite being suspicious of their motives, Brown "was sick of being, in his own words, a motherf***ing tour guide for Hillary Clinton."[938] On top of that, "the trip was all too spontaneous and improvised. It bordered on chaotic."[939]

The Clintons wanted Ron Brown dead, and they wanted him dead quick. Brown, on the other hand, was so disconcerted about this venture that at a final White House meeting, "he found a minute alone with the president and asked him to send someone else to the Balkans. The president refused."[940]

Oddly enough, quite a number of "Enron execs would become frequent flyers on Brown trade missions. On the last one, with impressive clairvoyance, they chose to take their own plane."[941]

Do you think someone may have put a little bug in Kenneth Lay's ear and tipped him off beforehand? After all, he was notorious for doling out plenty of campaign funds.

Rightly so, Nolanda Hill also felt trepidatious about this flight. "Ron, there is something wrong with this,"[942] she told him, yet the murder mission of Ron Brown moved forward. At this stage, perhaps it is stating the obvious, but political assassinations do not take place in a vacuum (or by accident). Rather, someone needs to plan the job, set up accomplices, establish alibis, coordinate the cover-up, and have the motive and means to do so. As you'll see, all of these variables were present in the Ron Brown murder, especially a sense of urgency in eradicating him post-haste.

For starters, what would compel the Clintons to have their

Commerce Secretary eliminated? In simplest terms, Ron Brown got his hands dirty in a variety of underhanded deals, which gave rise to more than one investigation into his actions. In the meantime, he became the Clintons' "bagman" to collect "contributions" from the Asian spies listed earlier. When Nolanda Hill was asked by Federal District Judge Royce Lamberth in March 1998 if "it was Hillary's idea to use the trade mission to raise money,"[943] she responded in the affirmative; as did a fellow colleague at the Commerce Department "Sonya Stewart [who] also implicated Hillary Clinton in the trade mission scheme."[944]

Instead of rolling over for the Clintons, Brown threatened to expose the entire can of worms; treason, bribes, payoffs, espionage, and spying within the Commerce Department. Here is how serious it was. Ron Brown "knew the Riadys and the Lums and John Huang. He knew about the Chinese navy's attempt to secure a bridgehead in Long Beach. . . . He knew what money was involved and where it went, and he transported a whole lot of it, much of which was never recorded. Ron Brown, in fact, knew way too much at a time when the media knew about nothing. If there was any one man in America whose knowledge could undo the 'process' and sink Bill Clinton, it was Brown."[945]

At no time during his presidency did the Clintons face such an impending threat, and when "Ron Brown was murdered, some American of power must have commissioned that murder. That power would almost surely have derived from the higher reaches of the White House. The person wielding that power would have to have been calculating, cold-blooded, and authoritative. And the list of potential suspects is short. It inevitably, if uneasily, includes the Clintons."[946]

As one writer noted, "In early 1996, he [Ron Brown] posed a more immediate threat to the Clintons' precarious kingdom"[947] than any other member of their cabinet. If forced to become a fall guy, Ron Brown faced professional humiliation, extensive media scrutiny, and a possible jail sentence. He was a powder keg ready to explode.

So, guess who visited the Balkans a week and a half prior to Ron Brown's plane crash? "Hillary Clinton's visit to the cockpit of a CT-43A in Bosnia ten days before the crash was surely coincidental."[948]

Or was it? Think about this situation. Ron Brown threatened to bring everyone in the Clinton administration down, so of all the places on the globe, the first lady flies to the exact region of the planet where Ron Brown's plane slammed into a mountain under extremely questionable circumstances.

Let's follow the process logically. When Ron Brown was killed in Croatia, someone had to first establish the setting and give an okay. So, "Hillary's trip to the Balkans makes sense as a kind of 'strong signal' the Croatians would need before executing so harrowing a plan. There would be no need for conversation. That would be done through a broker, but a Croatian conspirator would want some powerful reassurance that the planned hit on Brown was authorized by the White House."[949]

Hillary herself couldn't kill Brown. They never do their own dirty work. So, "if Brown were murdered, the Croatians almost surely did the dirty work."[950]

But to get the ball rolling, "someone would have had to commission Brown's assassination. Someone else would likely have had to broker it. And a third party would have had to execute it. For so egregious and risky a venture, all parties would have had to have both the means and the motive."[951]

Hillary was the initiator; the CIA, the Chinese, or some other financial operative brokered the deal; and the Croatians executed the plan via an engineered plane crash. And the motive? Ron Brown "had too much insider dirt on the president and was too much of a potential liability to let live—what with the 1996 presidential campaign heating up."[952]

Now, prior to proving that Ron Brown was murdered, I'd like to move forward in time to an event I alluded to much earlier in this trilogy. Specifically, that the Monica Lewinsky affair was in fact welcomed and willingly offered to the American public by the Clintons and their protectors when news that Brown was deliberately killed became such a hot button issue in the black community that it threatened to blow sky high.

The first shots came from the Brown family itself. "In April 1998 Ron Brown's daughter told a New York talk radio audience that she believed that the Air Force investigation into her father's plane crash was slipshod and inadequate."[953]

Then, Brown's "business partner, Nolanda Hill, questioned whether or not it was an accident."[954]

Their doubts and suspicions became so abundant that "Tracey Brown revealed that the family had hired its own private pathologist to evaluate photographic evidence that her father was shot in the head."[955]

Shot in the head! Wasn't Ron Brown killed in a plane crash? Why would he have a bullet wound in his skull? These questions will all be answered shortly in our upcoming analysis, but for the time being, in the following rather lengthy passage I'd like to show how intense pressure from the black community became.

> "All we want is the kind of investigation that the president would allow if his dog were run over under mysterious circumstances," stated Wilbur Tatum, publisher of America's leading black newspaper, *The Amsterdam News*. "Why should we ask for less for Ron Brown than we would ask for a dog?" Staunch, hard-left Democrats such as Maxine Waters, NAACP President Kweisi Mfume, Al Sharpton, Jesse Jackson, and civil rights activist Dick Gregory all demanded answers to the mysteries of Ron Brown's death. Brown's daughter Tracey publicly questioned the integrity of the investigation. Maxine Waters, Chairwoman of the Congressional Black Caucus, wrote letters to President Clinton, Janet Reno, and the chairman of the Joint Chiefs of Staff expressing concerns about the apparent cover-up.

"We are not dreaming this up," Dick Gregory cried to a crowd of hundreds on Christmas Eve, 1997—the same day, coincidentally, that [Christopher] Ruddy confronted Bill Clinton in Washington's Union Station.

The protesters gathered outside Walter Reed Army Medical Center—main headquarters of the Armed Forces Institute of Pathology (AFIP). Gregory had cordoned off a building near the entrance to the hospital with yellow tape, calling the medical center a crime scene. He was promptly arrested and went on a hunger strike in jail.

It looked bad for the Clintons. The furor over Ron Brown's death was spilling over into the black media. Black Entertainment Television (BET) devoted a one-hour show to the controversy on December 11, 1997, featuring an interview with Christopher Ruddy. An Internet poll conducted during the show revealed that 75 percent of BET viewers believed that Ron Brown had been murdered. Ruddy subsequently appeared on CNBC's *Rivera Live*—with African-American talk jock Larry Elder filling in for Rivera—on January 30, 1998.

Ruddy told Howard Kurtz of the *Washington Post* on January 12, 1998 that the White House was "panicking." His appearances on BET and *Rivera Live* showed that "the Brown issue has gotten real legs," said Ruddy. "This story is not going to go away and they can't write it off as a conspiracy theory."[956]

Right here is a good place to stop. Imagine if the black community's outrage grew to such a fevered pitch that *white America* actually started to ask: could the Clintons have snuffed their own Commerce Secretary? If an even more far-reaching inquiry had developed and it was revealed that Bill and Hillary *did* kill one of their own cabinet members, not only would their presidency be over, but they would have likely been convicted and sentenced to prison for murder! A president and first lady jailed for their direct involvement in a political assassination would have been unprecedented, and a blow from which they'd never recover.

So, indeed, the White House was "panicked," they had motivation galore, and they had to act quickly to divert attention away from this issue. What did they come up with? Monica Lewinsky! Yes, the Clintons actually created, promoted, and initiated the Lewinsky scandal to get the media rolling on such a feeding frenzy that they'd immediately forget about the growing controversy surrounding the murder of Ron Brown.

Look at it this way. We've already established that Kenneth Starr was nothing more than a dupe who did everything in his power to cover up the Clinton crimes rather than expose them. In fact, when they heard Starr had been appointed as "independent" counsel, Bill and Hillary celebrated by throwing an impromptu party, complete with champagne.

Of course the Lewinsky fiasco was embarrassing to the president and first lady, but what would they prefer to endure: an awkward situation where the commander-in-chief had a pudgy young intern stimulate her vagina with a cigar and fellate Bubba in the Oval Office, or a full-blown murder trial? The answer is obvious. Monica Lewinsky was born out of Ron Brown's spilled blood. The Clintons weren't *ambushed* by the Monica Lewinsky story. They created her right from the start. They *wanted* the Lewinsky story to break. She was part of the plot all along—a deliberately initiated contingency plan if one was ever needed. Monica was Hillary's idea from day one, and horny old sexual predator Bill Clinton followed through on it. To them, Monica was nothing more than a hole—another scandal diverter if one was ever needed.

Before anyone knew it, Monica Lewinsky was in the headlines, on TV and radio, and talked about at water coolers all across the world. And as a result, "the Ron Brown scandal fizzled out like all Clinton scandals seem to do. The White House stonewalled, the

Justice Department dithered. The press looked the other way."[957]

Ironically enough, a man purporting to be a Clinton enemy was, in reality, nothing more than another power elite creation, ultimately emerging as a burgeoning Internet cover-up artist. "It turned out to be Matt Drudge who delivered the *coup de grace*. He broke the Monica Lewinsky story on January 17, 1998—five days after Ruddy's write-up in the *Washington Post*. Big Media jumped on the Lewinsky story with a zeal it had never shown for any other Clinton scandal. It was as if Ron Brown had never existed."[958]

Without a doubt, "the Monica tale had inundated the land and left every other news story gasping for breath."[959]

Ron Brown was dead . . . in more ways than one.

What about "leaders" in the black community like Jesse Jackson? What did they do? Well, Jesse "Me First" Jackson did what he always did in situations such as this one—he capitalized on it for his own benefit. "Jesse Jackson had a choice to make. He could either pick away at the administration on a story that had just lost its legs, or he could ride the rising tide of resentment in the black community and come to the besieged president's aid."[960]

Rather than demand an investigation into Ron Brown's murder, Jesse Jackson "chose to embrace the president once more. In an unintentionally comic saga, Jackson emerged as the president's spiritual advisor and, with the aid of his comely assistant Karin Stanford, comforted the president in the midst of his moral crisis. In August, after the president's grudging TV apology, Chelsea Clinton reportedly asked that Jackson come to the White House to counsel her and her mom."[961]

Please remember that this is the same Jesse Jackson that Bill Clinton called a "nigger" only a few years earlier. Also, Jackson's assistant in his role as "spiritual advisor"—Karin Stanford—was the same one that he was committing adultery with when Bill Clinton was having phone sex and intimate sexual relations with Monica Lewinsky.

Speaking of awkward, Jackson's comely assistant, the one photographed with him in the Oval Office when she was four months pregnant, had given birth to Jackson's now famous "love child." A $40,000 moving fee courtesy of Rainbow/PUSH and a $10,000 a month retainer would help keep the young Jackson child out of the news for more than a year.[962]

All in all, when the dust finally settled, Bill Clinton survived, Hillary Clinton survived, and Jesse Jackson survived. Ron Brown, on the other hand, was all but forgotten—killed by the Clintons and betrayed by his supposed brethren in the black community who turned their backs on him. Business as usual.

SPOOFING, SUICIDE, AND SURVIVORS

The day Ron Brown's plane crashed in Croatia, "a Swiss Air charter carrying Enron executives [was] one of five planes to land routinely on the airport's sole runway in the hour before Brown's plane was scheduled."[963]

A safe landing wasn't in the cards for Brown. "At 2:57 pm the plane's inertia carried the hundred thousand pound craft at 150 knots into the jagged hillside [of St. John's Peak]."[964]

What had happened? "For no firm reason that any official had been able to proffer, the CT-43A veered nine degrees off course in the last four minutes of the flight and crashed into a mountainside nearly two miles northeast of the airport."[965]

As news spread that Ron Brown's aircraft was down, other updates also began to filter in. "The weather at the time of the crash was widely reported to be terrible. One newsweekly called it 'the worst storm in ten years' with visibility 'just 100 yards.'"[966]

TV and magazines weren't the only ones to relay this information. "Hillary Clinton wrote in her syndicated column that the plane crashed 'in a violent rainstorm.'"[967]

Were these reports accurate, or was Hillary telling her umpteenth lie—one of so many that it's nearly impossible to keep track of them? After all, even if Dan Rather got it wrong, wasn't the White House able to obtain the best intelligence possible? Or was the American public being deliberately deceived? Decide for yourself. "An Air Force investigation concluded the weather was not a substantially contributing factor to the mishap."⁹⁶⁸

This crash report by the Air Force totaled twenty-two volumes. "Weather conditions broadcast by the control tower were basically good: winds were at 14 mph, with only a light to moderate rain."⁹⁶⁹

Further evidence rules out atmospheric conditions or aircraft malfunction.

> • As to the weather, despite the overheated claims of Ambassador Peter Galbraith, it remained good enough to allow the aircraft to land at Dubrovnik using an instrument approach.⁹⁷⁰
>
> • According to the Air Force report, "All aircraft systems were operating properly at the time."⁹⁷¹
>
> • The ground-based navigation aids were operating properly as well.⁹⁷²
>
> • The specific plane that Brown boarded was also in prime condition. "Defense Secretary William Perry had flown on the same plane only days earlier. So had Hillary and Chelsea a week or so before that."⁹⁷³
>
> • Five other planes landed safely at Dubrovnik in the hours before Brown's plane disappeared. One of these planes, which landed within an hour of the expected arrival of the Brown mission, carried the Croatian prime minister and the American ambassadors.⁹⁷⁴
>
> • None of these other planes "had experienced problems with the beacons."⁹⁷⁵

From what we can gather using the above information, the weather was fine, the plane was fine, the ground equipment was fine, and every other plane had no trouble landing. Yet the craft which Ron Brown flew in could not follow the beacons to Dubrovnik airport. Why? Consider: how could "two experienced pilots in a sturdy plane on a day with a light wind and tolerable

CHAPTER SIX

conditions miss an airport by nearly two miles when they were on course only twelve miles out?"[976]

The answer is found in a concept called *spoofing* "which is aviation vernacular for using a spurious navigational aid to trick a pilot to change course."[977]

As author Jack Cashill points out, this practice of "making a beacon," or "meaconing" was used by the British during WWII, as well as the Soviets, and also in Vietnam. Essentially, it is a "trick that deceived the pilots"[978] into not being able to home in on an electronic beacon that is transmitting a signal to their aircraft.

What follows is the best available scenario for what happened that day:

> [Air traffic controller] Niko Jerkuic does not report for work on the morning of April 3 [1996], but he has a busy day ahead of him. He is not looking forward to it. Just two days earlier, April 1, two large gentlemen from the Croatian intelligence service gave him an assignment he did not feel free to turn down. For reasons of national security, the agents needed to down a certain plane, and they needed his assistance. Electronics experts themselves, they would help as needed. To ease his resistance, they also offered Jerkuic a substantial sum of money if he was successful.
>
> The project is not technically difficult. Jerkuic has seen a lot in his forty-six years. He knows all about meaconing or "spoofing" as it is sometimes generically known. Since the 1940s, portable Non-Directional radio beacon (NDB) stations have been available to military and civilian operators and have proved especially useful in war torn areas like this one.
>
> The agents with whom he is working have brought along a gasoline driven generator, a tun-

able transmitter, and a temporary antenna, all loaded into the back of a pickup truck. Together, they drive to an isolated spot outside of Dubrovnik and only about three or four miles east-southeast of Kolocep Island, the site of the first beacon, the final approach fix.

Jerkuic sets the frequency of his portable beacon at 318 kilohertz to match that of the Kolocep beacon, the final approach fix, and encodes the KLP Morse code identifier. He cannot power it up, however, until all the earlier scheduled flights have landed.

Meanwhile, the doomed flight is cleared "direct to the KLP NDB." The pilots are told they are "number one for beacon approach" and assume they will get an approach clearance prior to KLP and will not have to enter "holding."

When the word comes from Dubrovnik tower that Brown's plane has checked in at 2:46 pm local time and the other planes have landed, Jerkuic shuts down the normal NDB and activates the "rogue" NDB. The automatic direction finder in the plane now points to Jerkuic's beacon near Dubrovnik.

At this distance, the needle shift is negligible. [The pilots] Davis and Shafer scarcely notice. Given its 318-kilometer frequency, Davis naturally assumes the radio signal to be coming from Kolocep and flies toward it. Remember, the Dubrovnik tower has no radar. At this stage, the radio signal is the pilots' only real guide to the world below the clouds.[979]

Thus, rather than heading toward the airport's runway, the pilots of Brown's plane are instead flying directly toward St. John's Peak because the rogue transmitter has altered their course. Before they know it—and before they can recover—bam, they're smashing

CHAPTER SIX

into a mountainside eight miles away. When all is said and done, "word of the crash comes over Jerkuic's radio, [then] he shuts down the temporary transmitter and reactivates the Kolocep beacon."[980]

Prior to examining what occurred once this plane crashed, we should first continue the story of Niko Jerkuic after "spoofing" Ron Brown's plane. What happened to him, you may wonder? On "Monday, April 5, the Associated Press was reporting that the man responsible for the Cilipi Airport's navigation system, maintenance chief Niko Jerkuic, had shot himself in the chest an hour after the bodies of Brown and the other Americans had been flown out of the airport on Saturday."[981]

He committed suicide one hour after the bodies were gone? Was that the motivating factor for this tragedy? Jerkuic felt so much remorse over the deaths that he killed himself? Well, actually, no. "The *New York Times* was reporting that a 'fatal romance' had left the forty-six-year-old bachelor despondent."[982]

Wait a second. Another suicide? Despondent? A gunshot wound? A man with very damning information about the murder of Ron Brown? Is this another Vince Foster scenario? These bastards only waited one hour after the bodies were gone to snuff Jerkuic. Plus, pathologists couldn't believe what they were hearing. "They had seen enough suicides to know that the chest was an unlikely place for an individual to deposit a fatal bullet."[983]

Put this picture into perspective. "Brown's plane may have been a victim of "spoofing"—aviation slang for what happens when a spurious navigation beacon is used to trick a pilot to change course."[984]

Who more than any other person could have exposed this nefarious scheme? "Airport maintenance chief Niko Jerkuic might have been able to shed some light on this and other questions. However, investigators never got a chance to grill him. He died of gunshot wounds three days after the crash. Officials ruled his death a suicide after a one-day investigation."[985]

Author and researcher Jack Cashill theorizes on how this event transpired. After Brown's plane is spoofed and Jerkuic returns home, he "answers the knock on his door and greets the two men who recruited him. He is still anxious, and they can see it. The Air Force investigators have arrived and will start interviewing airport personnel in two days. The Croatian agents cannot afford to let the Air Force talk to Jerkuic. 'We hate to do this,' says one agent as he casually shoots Jerkuic in the chest. They don't even try too hard to arrange a suicide scenario. They know who will be investigating."[986]

Just like that, Jerkuic is dead, and dead men tell no tales.

But even before Niko Jerkuic was murdered, an array of monkey business was taking place at the actual crash site. "According to official reports, there was only one survivor of the crash, a stewardess."[987]

Another version increased the number of living. Pathologist Lt. Colonel Steve Cogswell "concluded that the two flight attendants who'd been seated in a rear jumpseat were 'potential survivors.' He determined that there was enough unoccupied space for them (they were identified as Air Force Sergeants Shelley Kelley and Cheryl Turnage) to have survived the crash. In fact, Kelley actually survived for several hours, and was found alive by Croatian rescuers."[988]

Unfortunately, neither lived much longer. Kelley "died while being transported for medical assistance."[989]

Could there have been another survivor of the crash—a third party—Ron Brown?

More details emerged later at the memorial services. "The day of the funeral, a friend in a position to know had told [Nolanda] Hill 'for her own safety' that Brown had been found forty yards from the plane. 'It looked,' he said, 'like he was trying to get away.' Neither he nor Hill could have known about the hole in Ron Brown's head."[990]

A hole in Ron Brown's head?

What could that possibly be a reference to?

We'll analyze this situation in total, but before doing so, Jack Cashill again provides some magnificent insights into the murder

CHAPTER SIX

of Ron Brown. After his plane barreled into the mountainside, the Croatian agents in charge of the hands-on logistics:

> [M]ake their way to St. John's Peak and up the mountain, their passage concealed by the low hanging clouds. They smile when they see the plane. Damned if they didn't pull this job off. Better still, the bodies are scattered, and there are only a few black men among them. They pull out the photo of Brown and start checking. Brown is not hard to find. But what stuns the man is that he is farther from the plane than is anyone else. He appears to have crawled there. "Oh Christ," says the leader. He kneels down next to Brown and turns him over on his back. He is still not sure if Brown is dead or not. He pulls out his pistol and fires skillfully into the wound on top of Brown's head. In this part of the world, no one even blinks at the sound of gunfire.[991]

Some researchers have speculated that Brown was shot midflight, but such a scenario doesn't make sense because the gunman would have to accept dying in the subsequent plane crash, which is implausible.

Also, Brown couldn't have been shot prior to boarding the plane because we know he spoke with his mistress, and how would the administration explain their Commerce Department chief being carried off the craft dead?

What would be interesting is to see the Clintons' reaction when they learned that one of their idiotic agents actually shot Ron Brown in the head, thus foiling their "perfect plan" that this airplane crash was nothing more than an accident.

Now, with the added intrigue of a bullet hole in his skull, the accident suddenly turns into a political assassination.

What tangled webs they weave.

A LEAD SNOWSTORM

The news changed everything; and if I had to venture a guess, nobody in the Clinton camp had any idea that one of their operatives at the crime scene unloaded a shot into the head of Ron Brown. Once they did find out via frantically placed reports from the mortuary, they had to scramble just like they had when Vince Foster's dead body was discovered. But they couldn't completely cover up their incompetence because the *Pittsburgh Tribune-Review* reported that "Secretary of Commerce Ron Brown was found with an apparent gunshot wound to his head."[992]

If his plane crash was nothing more than a tragic accident, what was a bullet hole doing in the top of Brown's skull?

The anomaly was discovered shortly following Brown's sudden demise. At the "U.S. Army base at Dover, Delaware, three days after his death, Armed Forces Institute of Pathology photographer, U.S. Navy CPO Kathleen Janoski, noted a nearly perfectly circular hole in the top of Brown's head. It would measure just about 0.45 inches in diameter. 'Wow. That looks just like a bullet hole,' said Janoski."[993]

Her find was soon confirmed by others. Lt. Colonel Steve Cogswell declared, "I received a phone call from Air Force Colonel William Gormley, an assistant Armed Forces medical examiner with 25 years experience, who phoned from Dover and told me that there was 0.45 inch, inward beveling, perfectly circular hole in the top of Ron Brown's head.' Cogswell recalls the exchange that followed with Gormley. 'That sounds like a gunshot wound,' Cogswell shot back. 'Open him up. This man needs an autopsy. This whole thing stinks.'"[994]

Army Lt. Colonel David Hause had the same reaction. He "was working two tables away from the one at Dover Air Force Base where Brown was being examined when a commotion erupted and someone said, 'Gee, this looks like a gunshot wound.' Hause remembers saying, 'Sure enough, it looks like a gunshot wound to me, too.'"[995]

The consensus grew. "Gormley consulted with the other pathol-

CHAPTER SIX

ogists present, including Cmdr. Kilbane, and they all agreed it looked like 'an entrance gunshot wound.'"[996]

There were more. "A third pathologist, Air Force Major Thomas Patterson, also came forward. Although not present at the examination, he agreed the hole was 'suspicious and unusual' and worthy of an autopsy."[997]

At this point, considering the questionable circumstances and the victim's high profile status, the next step should have been obvious. "Standard procedures, especially for a cabinet officer, would have been a full autopsy. Dr. Cyril Wecht, who has done more than 13,000 autopsies, would later tell [Christopher] Ruddy there was more than enough evidence to suggest possible homicide in the Ron Brown death and that an autopsy should have been performed."[998]

This man had what "looked like a punched-out .45-caliber entrance hole"[999] in his skull. Moreover, it was a "wound which Air Force whistleblowers described as a possible bullet hole."[1000]

What does this gruesome detail mean? "A possible bullet wound on a dead member of the president's cabinet—or on any American, for that matter—demanded an autopsy and a serious homicide investigation. Brown got neither."[1001]

Incredibly, "Col. Gormley, the highest-ranking AFIP [Air Force Institute of Pathology] officer then at Dover, did not do the obvious. He did not call the FBI. He did not ask the Brown family to permit an autopsy. Nor did he take the opportunity to look for an exit wound or test for gunshot residue."[1002]

Nothing whatsoever was done; not a damn thing. As Air Force Lt. Colonel Steve Cogswell stated, "'When you got something that appears to be a homicide, that should bring everything to a screeching halt.' In the case of Ron Brown, nothing came to a screeching halt. No autopsy was ever performed on Brown."[1003]

Although another cover-up was in full swing, that didn't stop those with a conscience and a moral backbone from chronicling the Brown case. Kathleen Janoski "continued to take photos, more than two hundred in all, ignoring the pressure to hurry up and 'get the bodies out!' That pressure, as contract investigator Bob Veasey told her, came directly from the White House."[1004]

How curious. Despite numerous medical professionals publicly calling for an autopsy on Ron Brown due to circumstances pointing in the direction of a homicide, it was the White House that wanted the entire matter swept under the rug. Despite pressure not to do so, Brown's "wound was documented, photographed, and X-rayed in a medical examination at Dover AFB."[1005]

What did they show? Lt. Colonel Steve Cogswell exclaimed, "There it was. Even in a photo of the X-ray, they could see the 'lead snowstorm.'"[1006]

The 'lead snowstorm' he referred to was what appeared to be bullet fragments in Brown's skull which showed up on the X-ray. The reason Cogswell was forced to look at a *photo* of the X-ray was because "all the X-rays and photos of Brown's head are missing from the case file at the Armed Forces Institute of Pathology facility in Rockville, Maryland."[1007]

How many instances of missing evidence, lost documents, and obstruction of justice does it take before the American public realizes how absolutely corrupt the Clintons are? Let's examine what we've uncovered thus far:

- The circular hole struck the forensic photographer and attending pathologist as having the size and shape of a gunshot wound.
- Out of 35 passengers, only Brown received such a wound.
- Other pathologists on site at the Dover mortuary agreed the hole looked like a gunshot wound.
- When alerted to the hole, the pathologist, Col. William Gormley, did not check for an exit wound or test for gunshot residue.
- Members of the Brown family were not informed of the hole at the time. If they had been, they would have ordered an autopsy.

CHAPTER SIX

- When Cogswell strongly recommended a autopsy, Gormley ignored him.
- Apparent "metal fragments" on the original X-ray allegedly led AFIP to run multiple tests on its X-ray cassettes.
- Despite the absence of suspicion, the decision for an autopsy reached the White House.[1008]

The probability that someone had shot Ron Brown in the head became so strong that investigators even determined what type of device was used. Army Lt. Col. David Hause thought that the culprit was some type of "exotic weapon, like a captive-bolt gun. Designed to kill livestock, such a gun had been used by drug traffickers to kill an American DEA agent in Mexico in 1985 [Kiki Camarena]. In any case, Hause had told his AFIP interviewer that Secretary Brown's body should be exhumed and an autopsy performed by someone not associated with AFIP."[1009]

Regrettably, their actions were par for the course. "The Air Force chose to skip the 'Safety Board' phase of the investigation. With twelve years of experience at crash scenes, [Lt. Col.] Cogswell could not understand why. This was the first time in his experience that there was no Safety Board."[1010]

COVER-UP DU JOUR

As a lead-in to the cover-up of Ron Brown's murder, it should first be put forth that there were two other notable individuals murdered on the same day as Ron Brown who were very closely associated with him. The first was a colleague at the Commerce Department, his Assistant Secretary, Charles Meissner, who "massaged the system at Commerce so that [John Huang] could become a consultant lead to Commerce and receive a new top secret clearance."[1011]

Because he knew too much and would undoubtedly be subpoenaed if Chinagate ever broke, "Meissner died in the same plane crash that killed Ron Brown. In the winter of 1997, a United States official in a position to know [said] privately that Huang's association with Commerce created a 'climate of fear' among Commerce career employees—and that a lot of secrets died with Chuck Meissner."[1012]

In terms of the Clinton Body Count, that's called killing two for the price of one.

The dead possessed many secrets. "At Commerce, Brown kept a locked drawer filled with sensitive documents he had never turned over."[1013]

Immediately following his murder, Michael Brown—up to his neck in scandal, too—began a cover-up of his own. He told Nolanda Hill, "Any kind of documents that need to be shredded are being shredded as we speak."[1014]

Speaking of which, Nolanda Hill was the other woman in the know who had to be silenced. So, rather than snuffing her too, the Clintons resorted to the next best thing. "Ten days before her scheduled evidentiary hearing before Judge Lamberth, the Clinton Justice Department indicted Hill, as well as her business partner, Ken White, on fraud and tax evasion charges."[1015]

Yes, Hillary's pit bulls, the IRS, were once again at her beck and call.

At least Nolanda Hill didn't end up six feet under, which can't be said for Ron Brown's "co-worker, Barbara Wise, [who] was found locked in her office at the Department of Commerce, dead, bruised, partially nude and lying in a pool of blood."[1016]

Another Department of Commerce employee was dead, bringing the total to three. Why does Mrs. Wise's death matter? Because once again Chinagate enters the picture. Guess which office Barbara Wise was employed in.

A co-worker had found her [Wise] bruised and half-naked body on the fourth floor in Commerce's International Trade Administration office at 7:45 am. Wise had worked in this office for fourteen years. This was the same office in which John Huang, soon to become a household name, had also worked.[1017]

She worked side-by-side with the Chinese spy John Huang!

That's why she was killed. Plus, "Wise was reportedly very close to Ron Brown, according to *Insight* magazine managing editor Paul Rodriguez, who tracked this case closely. Apparently she had been under enormous pressure, emanating in part from within the Department of Commerce, not to cooperate with ongoing investigations on Capitol Hill. Nolanda Hill confirms Wise used to regularly brief Brown."[1018]

Here's what is strangest of all; a clear indicator of how worried the Clintons were about Chinagate. "About two hours after [Wise's] body was found . . . the President, Hillary, Chelsea Clinton, and producer Harry Thomasson boarded *Marine One* for Washington."[1019]

Why did they rush back to D.C.? Press secretary Mike McCurry explained (rather ineptly), "Mr. Clinton did not have some of the books he wanted to research for example to find poetry to read at the inaugural."[1020]

The President and his entire family "*unexpectedly* left Camp David in the Catoctin Mountains of central Maryland where Clinton and his extended family had enjoyed Thanksgiving to return to the White House."[1021]

For *poetry books*? Then, two hours later, they all returned to Camp David (except "Clinton carried a briefcase as he strolled to the waiting helicopter,"[1022] while he was "followed by an aide carrying a huge box of inaugural papers"[1023]).

Let me guess: Bill Clinton's briefcase and the file box of papers were all filled with . . . poetry for his speech. That's why they broke their vacation and raced back to D.C.—to get the collected works of Robert Frost and William Wadsworth Longfellow. Or, could it be something else? "The Clintons did have a history of removing files from offices under suspicion before the forces of justice could do the same. Undoubtedly, it was Hillary Clinton who had orchestrated the purge of Vince Foster's office after his death."[1024]

Now it looks like she did exactly the same thing after the untimely murder.

All of this information should have been released to the public on a wide-scale basis, investigated fully, and then acted upon to bring the guilty parties to justice. But yet again the Clintons and their handlers got away with murder. As you'll see, there were very definite forces at work to cover up the egregious killing of Ron Brown:

- "Deputy Secretary of State Strobe Talbott [Clinton's longtime Oxford friend and fixer] was reported to have made a strong request that the HRT TV team in Dubrovnik not film at the crash site. HRT is the acronym for Hrvatska Radiotelevizija, or Croatian Radio Television. Croatian officials readily complied."[1025] Imagine, a foreign government official telling another country's national press to black out a news event.
- There would be no Safety Board investigation . . . no ruminations about a rogue beacon, no questions about Niko Jerkuic, no interview with the crew of IFD 98 (the plane right behind Brown's), no autopsy, no valid X-rays, and no alerting the Brown family.[1026]
- How about this one? "Unverified reports state that there were traces of thermite on the bodies, a sign of an explosion. Clinton, probably for that reason and to forestall any further family requested autopsies, *ordered all bodies from the wreckage to be cremated.* This was according to a report by the National Vietnam POW Strike Force."[1027] Ultimately, the bodies weren't cremated; but if this report is true, it shows the lengths to which these individuals will go to cover up their crimes.
- "The Croatians, who are the first on the scene, report they have recovered the black boxes from the plane. Croatian, French and Russian TV all make similar reports in the days after the crash.

Even some U.S. officials say there were such devices aboard. Then the Pentagon suddenly says there were none."[1028] We now know this statement is an unmitigated lie for one specific reason. "Only a week before the crash, Hillary and Chelsea Clinton were on the same aircraft. We cannot believe that the Secret Service would allow the wife and daughter of the President of the United States to fly in any aircraft without such equipment on board if only to cover their own well tarnished asses in case of a crash."[1029]

Black boxes are the most fundamental of aircraft avionics. "Does the U.S. Air Force really believe the plane would not be equipped with such instrumentation?"[1030]

Here's the clincher. "An article in *Media Bypass* a few weeks after the crash quoted a Croatian official as saying, 'We have found the two black boxes at the crash site, one with the voice recording and the other which records all the aircraft's maneuvers!'"[1031]

• The builders of the plane's engines, Pratt & Whitney, wanted to send an investigator to the scene, a routine and expected procedure, but the Air Force, in a virtually unprecedented move, turned them back.[1032]

• In the fall of 1996, naval criminal investigator Jeanmarie Sentell made the following statement at the AFIP annex. "'Did you know the first set of Brown's head X-rays were destroyed?' she said conspiratorially. When [Kathleen] Janoski asked why, Sentell confided they showed a 'lead snowstorm.'"[1033]

As mentioned earlier, a lead snowstorm refers "to a pattern of metal fragments one might see after a gunshot wound. Sentell then offered another stunning tidbit: they took a second set of X-rays and made them deliberately less dense"[1034] so investigators couldn't see the lead snowstorm. Last but not least, "the AFIP would later admit all head X-rays were missing."[1035]

Famed coroner Cyril Wecht has said, though, that it is "very, very rare the times key X-rays actually disappeared."[1036] When the Clinton Body Count becomes part of the picture, however, such disappearances become commonplace occurrences.

- Commander Edward Kilbane, who signed Ron Brown's death report, made a "visit to the White House immediately after the crash."[1037] He has refused to comment publicly on why he visited the White House, with whom he met, or what was discussed.
- Colonel William Gormley admitted to *BET Tonight* cable television host Tavis Smiley that "he had chosen not to pursue an autopsy [on Ron Brown] based on discussions at the highest level in Commerce, at the Joint Chiefs of Staff, the Department of Defense, and the White House."[1038]

Such a revelation is proof positive that the cover-up extended to the highest reaches of our federal government, including Bill and Hillary Clinton. Gormley is also the same man who "did not look for an exit wound or test for gunshot residue."[1039]

- One of the individuals who pushed for the truth in this case, Lieutenant Colonel Steve Cogswell, "received written orders that he was not to comment in any way, shape, or form about matters involving Ron Brown's death."[1040]

In fact, "gag orders were imposed on all military personnel with knowledge of the Ron Brown case."[1041] These orders came straight from the AFIP (Air Force Institute of Pathology).

With gag orders in place, and then the deliberate creation of the scandal involving Monica Lewinsky, Ron Brown's murder would effectively be buried; but it should be included among many others in the Clinton Body Count files.

CHAPTER SIX 251

BROWN GOES DOWN: The death of Ron Brown is as strange as they come. And the timing was extremely fortuitous for Bill and Hillary Clinton. At the time of his death, Brown was being hounded by federal investigators to reveal financial shenanigans in which he was involved with Bill and Hillary. Insiders say he was preparing to cut a deal with investigators and give them all the dirt he had. His death conveniently ended a major threat to the Clintons.

SUPER SPYMASTER: An undated picture of William Casey, former director of the Central Intelligence Agency, who died in May of 1987 from what was determined officially to be a case of pneumonia. Casey resigned from the CIA in February of 1987. He is best known as the orchestrator of the "October Surprise" deal to delay release of American hostages held prisoner by the Iranian regime until after the battle between Carter and Reagan for the presidency, thus destroying Carter's chance for re-election. AFP/AFP/GETTY IMAGES

CHAPTER SEVEN

The Murder of Danny Casolaro

> *I am about to embark on a sweeping story that will unravel the 1990 world of evildoers who roam the Earth trafficking in weapons, drugs, and dirty money.*[1042]
> —From the notes of Danny Casolaro

Journalist Danny Casolaro was the initiator of a far-reaching concept known as *the Octopus* which, due to its immediate threat to the global organized crime syndicate (i.e. world government) caused him to be murdered on August 10, 1991. This Octopus was one of the inspirations for the book you are now reading, as I am bringing to the forefront much of the same material that Casolaro investigated but was never able to put into publishable form. The only real difference in our projects is that I've focused primarily on the Clinton and Bush crime syndicates, while Casolaro extended his scope in many other different directions.

Despite the variance with respect to our specific points of reference, Casolaro was the true innovator and groundbreaker, and when he began connecting the dots, many of the elitists in positions of power became especially uneasy. So, to set the stage for why Danny Casolaro was killed, we first need to understand precisely what the Octopus entailed.

Prior to his death, "Casolaro was working on a book aimed at exposing what he called 'the Octopus,' a group of less than a dozen shadowy figures whose machinations figured heavily, he claimed, in the Inslaw case, Iran-Contra, BCCI, and the October Surprise."[1043]

He added that the Octopus was "an international cabal whose services cover parochial political intrigue, espionage, the trade of weapons technologies—including bio-toxins—and also drug trafficking, money laundering, and murder."[1044]

From my perspective, the number of figures involved in the Octopus was far greater than a dozen, but the operatives mentioned in the prior sentences are certainly involved in this maze. Since Casolaro planned on writing an entire book on this subject, what would be most prudent at this point is to simply list the variables which he thought constituted the Octopus:

- MK Ultra
- George Bush and Operation Zapata
- Bay of Pigs
- JFK assassination
- Operation Phoenix (in Vietnam)
- Golden Triangle heroin trade
- Vietnam MIAs
- Operation 40 (CIA hit squad that murdered and overthrew or attempted to overthrow foreign leaders [e.g. Castro])
- Watergate and the ouster of Richard Nixon
- CIA-organized crime connection
- MI-5 British intelligence link to the CIA
- Shah of Iran
- BCCI
- Nugan Hand Bank
- October Surprise—Iranian arms deals
- Iran-Contra
- Oliver North guns/drugs
- Mena drug smuggling
- Inslaw—Promis software
- S&L scandal
- Pan Am 103 bombing
- Area 51
- Mossad spy network
- Wackenhut Corporation and Cabazon Indian Reservation
- Hughes Aircraft corruption
- Illuminati secret societies

CHAPTER SEVEN

I'm sure there were other elements included in Casolaro's Octopus, not to mention the names of many high-ranking luminaries. Regrettably, Casolaro never had the opportunity to write his magnum opus. Even more tragically, he was still in the research phase of this project and may have never even written *any* of it prior to his murder. But he did compile a voluminous amount of notes, and was well on his way to completing the research phase of his work. Clearly, the powers-that-be could not allow this exposé to be published. Others before him had presented individual pieces to the puzzle, but if Casolaro had laid the Octopus out in all its gruesome glory, political events in this country would have taken a different turn, especially for Bill and Hillary Clinton. As Casolaro followed each new lead like a coon hound on a scent, he eventually stumbled upon Mena and its connections to Iran-Contra, BCCI, and the Bush family. It's hard to imagine Bill Clinton winning the 1992 election had he been tied to Mena and the Octopus.

Casolaro's travels eventually took him to Martinsburg, West Virginia. The "FBI agent who was to have met with Casolaro the day he died [was] one Ted Gunderson,"[1045] who was the Senior Special Agent-in-Charge of the Los Angeles Bureau of the FBI. He also served as Special Agent-in-Charge of the Memphis and Dallas FBI; served on the Los Angeles Olympic Committee in 1984, and prior to his retirement in 1979 had over 700 persons under his command in Los Angeles and operated a $22 million annual budget. In other words, Gunderson was the real deal, and Casolaro was receiving what would be considered definitive insider information. In addition, on "Friday August 9 [1991] Casolaro met with a former Hughes Aircraft employee, William Turner, in the Sheraton parking lot at about 2:00 pm. Turner gave him some papers relating to alleged corruption at Hughes and at the Pentagon."[1046]

These were just some of the many agents, operatives, spooks, informants, reporters, and insiders he'd interviewed over the past several years, and due to the nature of his research, the heat was being turned up very high.

A volley of threats subsequently followed, and Casolaro knew his life was in danger. A few days prior to his murder, the journalist told his brother, "I have been getting some very threatening phone calls. If anything happens to me, don't believe it was accidental."[1047]

In addition, FBI special agent Thomas Gates testified before a House Judiciary Committee that Casolaro had told him an informant revealed, "If you continue this investigation, you will die."[1048]

Similarly, "a month before Casolaro died, a source with ties to the intelligence community warned him that he would be killed if he went through with his plans to visit a Washington, D.C. facility that was engaged in high-level corruption."[1049]

Lastly: Casolaro's housekeeper reported receiving several telephone calls on Friday, August 9 at Casolaro's house. At 9:00 am a male caller announced, "I will cut his body up and throw it to the sharks." An hour or so later another caller said simply, "Drop dead." . . . The following day, Saturday, August 10, she got a final call at 8:30 pm — approximately twelve hours after Casolaro's death. A man's voice said, "You son of a bitch, you're dead."[1050]

Danny Casolaro was indeed dead. "He drove to Martinsburg, West Virginia on Thursday, August 8 and checked into Room 517 of the Sheraton Hotel. Two days later, at 12:51 pm, hotel employees found his naked body in a bathtub full of bloody water. Time of death has been estimated at about 9:00 am. Both arms and wrists had been slashed a total of at least 12 times: one of the cuts went so deep that it severed a tendon."[1051]

The crime scene surrounding him was even grislier. "A shoelace was tied around the corpse's neck, and two plastic wastepaper basket liners floated in the tub, as if the victim had originally intended to suffocate himself."[1052] For some, the sight was overwhelming:

> There were three or four wounds on the right wrist and seven or eight on the left [sic]. There was blood splattered on the bathroom wall and floor. According to Ridgeway and Vaughn's *Village Voice* article, the scene was so gruesome that one of the housekeepers fainted when she saw it.[1053]

Incredibly, "police thought the case was a straightforward suicide."[1054] Suicide? Another suicide? The applicable factors, including the brutality of the attack on Casolaro's body, didn't add up to suicide. "According to friends and family, little in Casolaro's disposition or behavior could have led to suicide. The gashes in his wrists were too deep to be self-inflicted. The suicide note was unconvincing."[1055]

The deep, savage gashes in Casolaro's wrists were the first indicator that the official ruling was suspect. "Dr. James Starts of George Washington University reviewed the autopsy report and opined, 'One thing that was surprising to me is that I didn't see any hesitation marks. In suicides, you tend to find hesitation marks. People generally don't know the amount of pain they can tolerate, so they will hesitate and take, literally, a little slice. This man really cut deeply; down to the tendons. That's significant. That's unusual.'"[1056]

A police captain on the scene added, "The wrists were cut almost in a slashing or hacking motion."[1057]

Martinsburg paramedic Don Shirly agreed. "I've never seen such deep incisions on a suicide. I don't know how he didn't pass out from the pain after the first two slashes."[1058]

Yet we're supposed to believe that Casolaro gouged himself a dozen times in such a fashion—all the way down to his tendons? The human body can't tolerate such pain. It shuts down and goes into shock, rendering the person incapacitated. Casolaro didn't commit suicide. He was murdered, and the killers attacked his wrists with such viciousness that anyone could tell foul play was involved.

Take, for instance, the fact that "three of Casolaro's right hand fingernails looked as if they'd been chewed or bitten. There is no evidence Casolaro chewed his nails; and [John] Connolly [of *Spy* magazine] speculates that the nails might have been broken in a struggle."[1059]

Further, "both Danny's brothers and ex-wife [said] that Danny had always been afraid of needles and blood. This was corroborated by Olga, Danny's longtime housekeeper, who asserted that 'he's scared of his own blood.'"[1060]

Casolaro was so squeamish in the presence of blood "that he refused to allow samples to be drawn for medical purposes."[1061]

Lastly, "several of Casolaro's girlfriends [claimed] that the journalist was extremely uncomfortable about being seen naked, even during sexual activities—for Casolaro to kill himself in the nude seemed very out of character."[1062]

Remarkably, there was no criminal investigation, and the case was quickly covered up and declared a suicide. "Hotel management called the Martinsburg police, who brought along the local coroner, Sandra Brining, a registered nurse. Mrs. Brining ruled the death a suicide, took small blood and urine samples, and released the body to the Brown funeral home. Without authorization from officials or Casolaro's next of kin, the funeral home embalmed the body as a 'courtesy to the family.'"[1063]

Such an act—"the hasty, unauthorized and illegal embalming, seemed either extraordinarily inefficient or highly suspicious. West Virginia state law requires that next of kin be notified before a body can be embalmed."[1064]

Who authorized such a hasty cover-up of this sinister murder? According to Bill and Nancy Hamilton, creators of the Promis software, which became such an integral part of the Octopus, they had "been told by another one of their sources that a high-ranking DOJ official was present in the room when Casolaro was murdered. The DOJ employee had connections to the CIA."[1065]

The intrigue surrounding this case gets even more compelling. A former Department of Justice employee, Lois Battistoni, said that during a meeting with Norman E. Mixon of the DOJ and *San Francisco Chronicle* reporter George Williamson, it was revealed that "the Martinsburg (West Virginia) police called Sen. [Robert] Byrd's office after the alleged suicide. Sen. Robert C. Byrd is the senior senator from West Virginia. Battistoni says her understanding of the conversation is that the police were instructed to clean up the motel room through Byrd's office."[1066]

What's more, Casolaro's "research papers and notes . . . were nowhere in evidence at the murder scene."[1067]

Obviously the hit men knew enough to take whatever was present in his hotel room, never to be seen by prying eyes again. On top of that, evidence was actually removed from the scene. "The coroner's husband David [Brining], a fire department lieutenant, had the bathroom door removed less than a half-hour after the body was found."[1068]

First of all, why would someone from the fire department tamper with potentially criminal evidence? Isn't that the police department's jurisdiction? Plus, didn't anyone find it odd that he was married to the coroner, who made a rush judgment and destroyed potential evidence by illegally allowing the body to be embalmed? Why was this door removed? Was the lock broken, showing forced entry? Or was it kicked in, or did it hold bloody fingerprints? What other reason could there be to steal it from the scene? Finally, to illustrate how compromised these individuals were, "the coroner herself [Sandra Brining]—also an emergency room nurse—drained the bathtub without a filter,"[1069] destroying any remaining evidence, such as blood from an outside party, hair samples, etc.

At any rate, it's obvious that another murder/cover-up had occurred. The big question now is: does the killing of Danny Casolaro actually belong in the Clinton Body Count category? Technically, his death could more accurately be included in the Bush Body Count section; but as we've seen, the Clintons and Bushes have been working together—hand-in-hand on the same criminal team—for so long that their endeavors often overlap. Casolaro's death benefited both camps.

So, in this sense, let's examine the year of Casolaro's murder: 1991. What also occurred that same year? Bill Clinton declared his candidacy for the office of president. But Casolaro's investigation had led him to one specific topic which would have toppled both the Bush and Clinton crime families. Specifically, Casolaro was "en route to meeting an informant with evidence of CIA and NSA involvement in drug smuggling through Mena in support of American military operations in Central America."[1070]

Of course Bill Clinton was governor of Arkansas at the time while George Bush Sr. was vice president (and then later president) in charge of the entire operation.

Others have taken a different approach to this subject and said it wasn't a vast, far-reaching conspiracy at all that got Danny Casolaro murdered. Rather, his death resulted from his queries into one particular topic. "If Casolaro was murdered because of what he knew, Inslaw is the most probable cause. There is no evidence that his October Surprise theory, or his investigations into BCCI and the October Surprise, are likely to have uncovered information worth killing him for. Inslaw is a different matter. Here is a real crime, with real people who, if found guilty, would face real jail terms and stand to lose millions. It is possible that Casolaro, who was in close touch with Inslaw owners Bill and Nancy Hamilton, might have been too close to something conclusive which sealed his death warrant."[1071]

Inslaw, then, fingers such individuals as Attorney General Edwin Meese, Attorney General Dick Thornburgh, members of Israeli intelligence, Earl Brian, Attorney General William Barr, and Special Prosecutor Nicholas Bua. These are powerful men, and their dirty dealings were all interconnected with that which was taking place in Arkansas, including Mena, Park-O-Meter, and the ADFA.

Let me elaborate further, especially in regard to a key individual named Earl Brian. Who was he? It turns out that he was a close friend of the extremely corrupt Attorney General Edwin Meese, and he was the man who most benefited from the Promis software's theft. Why was Brian bequeathed such a golden goose? It seems "officials within the DOJ gave Brian Promis as a payoff for his assistance in transferring $40 million to the Iranians prior to the 1980 presidential campaign. The money along with future arms transfers were allegedly negotiated so the hostages then being held by Iran would not be released until after the election,

CHAPTER SEVEN

thus assuring a more likely win by Reagan over then-president Jimmy Carter."[1072]

The prime mover behind this sordid affair was former Wackenhut counsel and soon-to-be CIA Director William Casey, who "hired him [Brian] . . . to carry out the October Surprise deal."[1073]

Yet again, the tangled web of what has become known as "October Surprise" rears its ugly head, ultimately leading to Iran-Contra and vast drug imports into Mena. As we've already established in Book Two of this trilogy, Bill and Hillary's Arkansas was not only a hub for tons of cocaine, but also a manufacturing base where weapons were illegally modified for the Contras. Likewise, Casolaro was ready to expose the "efforts by a former CIA operative to use a California Indian reservation [Cabazon] as a front for supplying weapons to the Nicaraguan Contras."[1074]

In all, the continuation of an ongoing theme is represented in Casolaro's Octopus: guns and drugs, along with shady intel ops, dirty money, and the murder of those who wanted to expose them.

For whatever reason(s) Danny Casolaro was killed, his suspicious death is yet another example of how little emphasis is placed on the sanctity of human life by those in the political organized crime syndicate, especially when their power base is threatened. Although his efforts weren't as epic in nature as those of President John F. Kennedy, Danny Casolaro stepped on too many toes; and as a result, he too was murdered.

RISING STARR? Many people thought Kenneth Starr was a tough special counsel, going after the Clintons like a bulldog. But the truth is far different. During the investigation into the Vince Foster "suicide," Starr actually pressured two Arkansas state troopers to change their testimonies as to when they were notified of Foster's death to coincide with the bogus Clinton timeline. So what was Starr really doing?

AFP/GETTY IMAGES

CHAPTER EIGHT

The Clinton Body Count

110 + AND COUNTING

Thus far in this book we've outlined not only a continuing tendency on the part of the Clintons and their operatives to threaten those who've tried to expose their crimes and dirty deeds, but also the outright assassination of numerous individuals, including Jerry Parks and Ron Brown. Bill and Hillary Clinton have engaged in a systematic campaign of murder over three decades, and what follows is the most comprehensive Clinton Body Count ever compiled, with over 110 casualties now a part of it.

As one reads through each name and description below, please do a mental exercise. Try to imagine every politician who has ever stepped onto the public stage during the course of this country's history; and then compile a list of all those associated with them who have died under questionable circumstances. Start adding these deaths on a piece of paper and see if it comes anywhere near totaling 110. I can assure you that no other single political entity approaches that of the Clinton Body Count, the only notable exception being the Bush crime family, which we've already shown has worked hand-in-hand with the Clintons since the 1970s. In fact, some of the Body Count fatalities could legitimately be included on the Bush list since so many of their criminal activities overlapped (e.g. Waco, Mena, Iran-Contra, etc).

Also notice the viciousness and variance in these deaths. The odds that this many people closely associated with Bill and Hillary Clinton—most of whom posed a direct threat to them—could die in such a fashion is astronomical . . . off the charts. Consider that the 110 + deaths occurred by:

- Suicide
- Hanging
- Poisoning
- Car crashes
- Plane crashes
- Slit wrists
- Gunshot
- Stabbing
- Mob-style execution
- Pushed from window/building
- Decapitation
- Arson
- Run over by train
- Mutilation
- Drowning
- Bombing
- Beating and/or bludgeoning
- Other miscellaneous "accidents"

As Paula Jones warned in May 1999, "There are just too many of them that have come up dead or missing that have had some kind of dealings with the Clintons. There's a lot of people that have come up dead in Arkansas. If I turn up strangely dead, I didn't kill myself!"[1075]

Luckily for Jones, she became so high-profile that the Clintons weren't able to snuff her. Others weren't so fortunate. Similarly, in a September 1999 interview with CNBC's Chris Matthews, Gennifer Flowers said, "There is a Clinton death list."[1076]

When asked if she thought the president ordered these killings, she replied, "I believe that he did. And I believe that I wouldn't be sitting here talking with you today had I not become as high-profile as I did."[1077]

Likewise, Linda Tripp has referred to this "body count—a list of many people associated with Bill Clinton who had died under mysterious circumstances, such as plane crashes, mysterious illnesses, 'suicides,' and even outright murder."[1078]

Publisher Richard Mellon Scaife echoed a similar sentiment. "Listen, Clinton can order people done away with at his will. He's got the entire federal government behind him. God, there must be 60 people who have died mysteriously—including eight of Clinton's former bodyguards. There have been very mysterious deaths."[1079]

Another veteran of the Clinton wars put it in even stronger words: "The Arkansas State Police are nothing but a hit squad."[1080]

Of course, who could forget the Clintons' other source of mayhem—the Dixie Mafia, who had their own brand of execution? "Plane crashes were a favorite method of assassination with the Dixie Mafia. . . . It was the perfect cover for murder because most of the evidence is destroyed or mutilated in a crash."[1081]

Last but not least, although I haven't included it per se in the Clinton Body Count, one must figure in the following deaths:

- Waco massacre—86 dead
- OKC bombing—168 dead
- Ron Brown plane crash—35 dead
- TWA 800 cover-up—230 dead

On top of that, one can't discount Bill Clinton's convenient Wag the Dog-style bombings, skirmishes, and mini-wars whenever he got into hot water (e.g. Monica Lewinsky). As one writer observed, "the bombings helped to raise Clinton's poll numbers"[1082] and shifted attention away from his many scandals. The major problem was, innocent people were killed en masse, such as in the Sudan aspirin factory that they mistakenly bombed to divert attention away from his Oval Office shenanigans. Although Bill and Hillary had their own self-serving reasons for these attacks, we can't forget that there were corpses with actual blood seeping into the ground as a result.

If you glean anything at all from this book, please be aware that Bill and Hillary are cold-blooded killers, and they should be imprisoned for life (if not outright executed) for the crimes associated with their Clinton Body Count. To this date, they have absolutely not been held accountable for their crimes. They had motive (the self-preservation of their political careers), means (Dixie Mafia and the Arkansas State Police), resources (Mena drug money), protection (Arkansas court system and the D.C. power elite), as well as a pusillanimous corporate media that has covered up for them every step of the way.

ACTUAL CASES—READ 'EM AND WEEP

- Danny Casolaro: "A reporter investigating the Mena-BCCI-Contra-ADFA connections was found dead in the bathroom of his Sheraton Hotel room in Martinsburg, West Virginia with his wrists slashed [at least] ten times. Casolaro was studying the similarities between the Whitewater affair and the Inslaw scandal."[1083]

Casolaro "was on to all the secrets of the October Surprise, the BCCI banking scandal, the secret government Octopus, and the infamous Inslaw super secret software that super crook William Casey had stolen from the inventor (so that the CIA could sell it to banks and discover all the secret funds politicians had stashed in bank accounts across the world). Casolaro had confided to pals that he had the real stuff on Promis, the CIA's Octopus, Mena, and how Clinton had worked for Bush and Reagan and Casey, the NSC, and all those people hiding under the White House."[1084]

- Jonathan Moyle: "Found hanged by his own necktie inside a closet in his hotel room in Santiago, Chile while investigating the famous arms dealer, Carlos Cardoen."[1085]

It should be noted that Cardoen "brokered a deal between Dr. [Earl] Brian and a representative of Iraqi intelligence for the use of Promis."[1086]

As was shown in Book Two of this trilogy, Iran-Contra was intimately linked to drug trafficking in Mena, Arkansas.

CHAPTER EIGHT 267

- Jim McDougal: "Getting ready to talk about the activities at Mena, Jim had all the information on Mena."[1087]

Subsequently, "he was a key witness in Kenneth Starr's investigation"[1088] before being "injected with Lasix"[1089] while in prison.

- Johnny Lawhorn: After discovering Whitewater documents that incriminated Hillary Clinton, he "died in a one-car automobile crash."[1090]

- C. Victor Raiser II + Montgomery Raiser: "Killed in a plane crash near Anchorage, Alaska in July 1992. Victor Raiser was the former finance co-chairman of Bill Clinton's presidential campaign."[1091]

"Clinton's former press spokesperson once described Raiser as a 'major player' within the Clinton hierarchy and inner circle."[1092]

- Ed Willey: "Clinton's campaign chairman, died in November 1993 of allegedly self-inflicted gunshot wounds."[1093]

He was also the husband of Kathleen Willey, who on that same day accused Bill Clinton of sexually accosting her in the White House. In addition, "Willey was one of Clinton's fundraisers and supposedly was involved in transporting and/or collecting briefcases full of cash and some of the unusual underhanded methods of funding Clinton's campaign for the presidency."[1094]

- Herschel H. Friday: "A prominent Little Rock attorney who died in March 1994 [via an airplane explosion]. Friday was on Clinton's presidential campaign finance committee."[1095]

- Kathy Ferguson: Former wife of Larry Ferguson of "Troopergate" fame, she died of an allegedly self-inflicted gunshot wound in May 1994. She was very familiar with Clinton's trysts. "She also knew about conversations Larry Ferguson overheard while working for Clinton. One of these conversations was with David Hale."[1096] "She was also a close friend of Paula Corbin Jones, the woman who sued Clinton in federal court in Little Rock for sexual harassment."[1097]

Strangely, "Ferguson was right-handed and was shot behind her left ear. The medical personnel who originally examined the body claimed it was a homicide."[1098]

- Florence Martin: She "had worked with the CIA as a subcontractor for years. She had documents and paperwork, as well as the PIN number for Barry Seal's $1.645 billion account at Fuji Bank in the Cayman Islands. She was found dead in her home in Mabell, Texas in November 1994 with three gunshot wounds to the head."[1099]

- Mary "Caity" Mahoney, Aaron Goodrich, & Emory Evans: Mahoney was a "former White House intern who was murdered July, 1997 at a Starbucks coffee shop in Georgetown. The murder happened at the time she was to go public with her story of sexual harassment in the White House."[1100]

The grisly details are as follows. "Five bullets were pumped into her body in the back room of the Georgetown Starbucks. Two of her co-workers were also killed."[1101]

"Mahoney was murdered, shot once in the chest, once in the face and three times in the back of the head just three days after Clinton had warned Monica Lewinsky that it is illegal to threaten the President of the United States."[1102]

Speaking of which, Monica Lewinsky also enters the picture. "Following the discovery of Caitlin's body and those of her two fellow employees, word got around the Beltway that in her discussions with Vernon Jordan about a government job, she [Monica] is said to have told Jordan 'that she wants to cooperate because she doesn't want to end up like Caity!'"[1103]

Furthermore, "Monica Lewinsky was known to have frequented the Georgetown Starbucks and knew Mahoney."[1104]

- Vince Foster: "Former White House counselor and colleague of Hillary Clinton at Little Rock's Rose Law Firm. Died of a gunshot wound to the head. Ruled a suicide."[1105]

- Ron Brown: "Secretary of commerce and former DNC chairman. Reported to have died by impact in a plane crash. A pathologist close to the investigation reported that there was a hole in the top of Brown's skull resembling a gunshot wound. At the time of his death Brown was being investigated, and spoke publicly of his willingness to cut a deal with prosecutors."[1106]

- Paul Tulley: "Democratic National Committee political director found dead in his hotel room in Little Rock, September 1992. Described by Clinton as a 'dear friend and trusted advisor.'"[1107]
- Jerry Parks: "Head of Clinton's gubernatorial security team in Little Rock. Gunned down in his car at a deserted intersection outside Little Rock. Parks' son said his father was building a dossier on Clinton. He allegedly threatened to reveal this information. After he died the files were mysteriously removed from his house."[1108]
- James Bunch: "Died from a gunshot suicide. It was reported that he had a 'black book' which contained names of influential people who visited prostitutes in Texas and Arkansas."[1109]

Considering Bill Clinton's predilection for ladies of the night, there is every possibility that his name would have been contained in this book.

- John A. Wilson: "Was found dead in May, 1993 from an apparent hanging suicide. He was reported to have ties to Whitewater."[1110]
- Bill Shelton: "Arkansas State Trooper and fiancee of Kathy Ferguson. Critical of the suicide ruling of his fiancee, he was found dead in June, 1994 of a gunshot wound (also ruled a suicide) at the gravesite of his fiancee."[1111]

Shelton also said that Ferguson "definitely was not suicidal and that she was too beautiful and too vain about her appearance to shoot herself in the mouth. . . . His body was found a month later, also by a supposedly self-inflicted gunshot."[1112]

- Gandy Paugh: "Attorney for Clinton's friend Dan Lasater, he died by jumping out a window of a tall building in January, 1994. His client was a convicted drug distributor"[1113] and initially one of Bill Clinton's earliest high-stakes political donors.
- Suzanne Coleman: "Reportedly had an affair with Clinton when he was Arkansas Attorney General. She died of a gunshot wound to the back of the head. Ruled a suicide. She was also pregnant at the time of her death."[1114]

"She told friends she was seven months pregnant with Clinton's child. Seven days later, Susan Coleman and her unborn fetus were found dead."[1115]

- Paula Gruber: "Clinton's speech interpreter for the deaf from 1978 until her death on December 9, 1992. She died in a one car accident."[1116]

"Her body, according to Arkansas State Trooper reports, was 'thrown' 33 feet from the accident scene."[1117]

- Paul Wilcher: "Attorney investigating corruption at Mena airport with [Danny] Casolaro and the 1980 October Surprise. He was found dead on a toilet June 22, 1993 in his Washington, D.C. apartment. He delivered a report to Janet Reno three weeks before his death."[1118]

"Wilcher had also been investigating the Bureau of Alcohol, Tobacco and Firearms assault on the Waco, Texas Branch Davidians. Wilcher was also planning on producing a television documentary on his findings and had already made preliminary arrangements with a production company."[1119]

- Jon Parnell Walker: "Whitewater investigator for Resolution Trust Corporation. He jumped to his death from his Arlington, Virginia apartment balcony on August 15, 1993. He was investigating the Morgan Guaranty scandal"[1120] which involved Hillary Clinton and Jim McDougal, among others.

- Barbara Wise: "Commerce Department staffer who worked closely with Ron Brown and John Huang. She died November 29, 1996. Her bruised, nude body was found locked in her office at the Department of Commerce."[1121]

- Charles Meissner: "Assistant secretary of commerce who gave John Huang a special security clearance. He died shortly thereafter in a plane crash [along with Ron Brown]."[1122]

- Dr. Stanley Heard and Steve Dickson: "Died in a small plane crash. In addition to serving on Clinton's advisory council, he personally treated Clinton's mother, stepfather, and brother."[1123]

Dickson was Heard's attorney.

- Barry Seal: "Drug running pilot out of Mena, Arkansas. He was killed in a gangland-style slaying in [Baton Rouge] Louisiana."[1124]

Prior to his death, "Seal admitted that the money reaped through the [Mena] smuggling operations was laundered through the now defunct and totally discredited Bank of Credit and Commerce International (BCCI), and Clinton's Little Rock candy store, the Arkansas Development Finance Authority, headquartered in Little Rock. On February 19, 1986 Seal turned state's evidence against several other drug dealers operating in and out of Mena. The Drug Enforcement Administration released Seal to a halfway house where three assassins gunned him down with submachine guns. Clinton told [CIA operative] Terry Reed, 'Seal just got too damn big for his britches, and that scum basically deserved to die, in my opinion!'"[1125]

Stanley Huggins: "Investigated Madison Guaranty. His death was a purported suicide, and his report was never released."[1126]

Kevin Ives and Don Henry: "Known as 'the Boys on the Track' case. Reports say the boys stumbled upon the Mena, Arkansas airport drug operation. The initial report of death said they died due to falling asleep on the railroad tracks. Later reports claim the two boys had been slain before being placed on the tracks."[1127]

The following individuals had information on the Ives/Henry case:

- Keith Coney: Died when his motorcycle slammed into the back of a truck, July 1988. [Eyewitnesses stated that he was being pursued at the time of his "accident."]
- Keith McCaskle: Stabbed 113 times in November 1988.
- Gregory Collins: Died from a gunshot wound in January 1989.
- Jeff Rhodes: Was found shot, mutilated, and burned in a trash dump, April 1989.
- James Milan: Found decapitated. However, the coroner [Fahmy Malak] ruled his death was due to "natural causes."

- Jordan Kettleson: Found shot to death in the front seat of his pickup truck in June, 1990.
- Richard Winters: A suspect in the Ives/Henry deaths. He was killed in a set-up robbery in July, 1989.[1128]

The following Clinton bodyguards have died in freakish "mishaps"

- Major William S. Barkley, Jr.
- Captain Scott J. Reynolds
- Sergeant Brian Hanley
- Sergeant Tim Sabel
- Major General William Robertson
- Colonel William Densberger
- Colonel Robert Kelly
- Specialist Gary Rhodes
- Corporal Eric S. Fox
- Steve Willis—Waco
- Robert Williams—Waco
- Conway LeBleu—Waco
- Todd McKeehan—Waco[1129]

Continuing with "the Count":

- Judy Gibbs: "Former Penthouse pet and call girl, she reportedly counted Bill Clinton among her clients. Shortly after agreeing to help police in an investigation into Arkansas cocaine trafficking through the Mena airport with Clinton's obvious acquiescence, Gibbs was burned to death in a mysterious fire."[1130]
- William Colby: "In April 1996 the former Central Intelligence Agency chief who, at the time of his death, had recently become an editor of *Strate-*

CHAPTER EIGHT

gic Investment which was doing investigative reporting on the Vince Foster death. Colby's body was pulled from the waters of a Maryland river after being reported missing by his family. The investigating bodies expect everyone to believe that this 76-year-old former government workhorse left his kitchen, his computer and radio on, his door unlocked and half of a half-eaten meal.

They also expect us to believe that Colby just strolled out of his unlocked door to take a quick canoe ride down the white, rocky waters of the storm-swollen river adjacent to his residence. Authorities also claim that Colby "forgot" to wear his life preserver.

William Colby was about to write all about the CIA's "Operation Phoenix." Colby was head of the agency's Saigon division office during the Vietnam years and personally directed "Operation Phoenix." This was a sinister top-secret occult project that resulted in some 50,000 civilian men and women rounded up and taken to concentration camps, where they were brutally tortured and murdered."[1131] "When police entered his country home, they found both his radio and computer left on."[1132]

So, we're to believe that right in the middle of doing work on his computer and listening to music or a talk show, Colby darts from the house to paddle down the river to, in the vernacular of the Clinton Body Count, commit suicide? "An autopsy by a Maryland coroner found that Colby had died of drowning. The autopsy also claimed that the drowning was precipitated—get this—by a heart attack or stroke. Take your pick. But the coroner found no evidence of either."[1133]

Here is where things get really interesting. "Intelligence sources in MI-5 had claimed Colby was assassinated by U.S. government operatives."[1134]

Why would they have killed Colby? "The Clinton White House must have gone ballistic when they saw Colby's endorsement of [James Dale] Davidson's newsletter [*Strategic Investment*],"[1135] which showed, among many other things, "Clinton was linked to organized crime."[1136]

Lastly, a former government official "had little doubt that the hit [on Colby] was ordered at the highest levels."[1137]

Moreover, was Colby in a position to reveal Bill Clinton's background as a CIA snitch, and was this another reason to have him killed? "One former agency official would claim that the future president was a full-fledged 'asset,' that he was regularly 'debriefed,' and thus that he informed on his American friends in the peace movement in Britain. Similarly, he was said to have informed on [American] draft resisters in Sweden."[1138]

- Jim Wilhite: "An associate of Mack McLarty's who died in a 'skiing accident' although he was a very experienced man on the slopes. Wilhite died on December 21, 1992 in a one-person skiing accident. Strange how so many of the so-called Arkancides were 'one-person accidents' with no witnesses available."[1139]

- Dr. Ronald Rogers: Killed in a plane crash. The doctor "was en route to an interview in Washington with a reporter [where] he was going to reveal evidence of Clinton's well known cocaine use—courtesy of Mena airport."[1140]

The journalist in question was Ambrose Evans-Pritchard, and Rogers intended to "share some knowledge of a sensitive nature about personalities and transactions [in Arkansas]."[1141]

- Benjamin Franklin Talbot: "Millionaire businessman and Clinton political rival who died on September 5, 1988 in a mysterious automobile accident two days before he was to announce his campaign for governor—a real challenge to Bill Clinton."[1142]

- Lt. Colonel Mark Cwick: "As a member of the elite Marine Corps HMX-1 Unit, he was responsible for ferrying the President and other high-ranking officials around the Washington area. Police told the Associated Press that 'a car Cwick was trying to pass moved in front of him, and to avoid it, he swerved off the road into an embankment and hit some trees.'"[1143][1143]

- John F. Kennedy Jr., Carolyn Bessett, and Lauren Bessett: Anyone that doubts JFK Jr. was murdered must watch a documentary entitled *The Assassination of JFK, Jr.: Murder by Manchurian Candidate* by filmmaker and researcher John Hankey. In this video, it becomes 100% clear that Kennedy's plane didn't crash because of an accident, pilot incompetence, or some type of mechanical failure. It was sabotaged and deliberately downed. Why? Because he could have potentially been competition to Hillary Clinton for the Democratic Senate seat which opened up after Patrick Moynihan's retirement. We know that the possibility existed because "John F. Kennedy Jr. had approached [Judith] Hope earlier in the year [1999] and told her *he* was interested in running for Moynihan's seat in 2000."[1144]

This scenario is quite compelling because the only way Hillary could ever become president was by first landing a congressional job where she would gain experience and credibility. Without such tenure, she was merely an ex-president's wife; and a very disliked one at that. Thus, ever since these murmurs arose about a Kennedy candidacy, "She [Hillary] was always looking over her shoulder, a little worried that he might change his mind"[1145] and enter the race. Ultimately, she had no need to fret. "Scarcely a week after announcing her candidacy, Hillary was with Bill at Camp David when aides informed them that Hillary's only potential rival for the Senate nomination had vanished over the Atlantic. Days later, John Kennedy's Piper Saratoga was lifted from the bottom of the sea."[1146]

Another convenient occurrence. After all, two Kennedys had already been the victims of state-sanctioned assassinations; while Ted Kennedy wasn't even in the car when it plunged into the Chappaquiddick (Mary Jo Kopechne was driving). So what would stop the powers-that-be from killing a third Kennedy?

• Gary Johnson: "Arkansas lawyer badly beaten in 1992 after claiming to have videotapes of Clinton calling on Gennifer Flowers."[1147]

• Dennis Patrick: "Endured three attempts on his life after he discovered millions of dollars passing mysteriously through his account at the firm of Clinton supporter and friend Dan Lasater.[1148]

• Sandy Hume: "On Sunday, February 22, 1998 Sandy Hume, the twenty-eight-year-old son of journalist Britt Hume, was found dead in his Arlington, Virginia home of an apparent suicide. He was about to break a story confirming the White House's use of investigators to dig up dirt on critics and investigators."[1149]

- Larry Guerrin: "Killed in February, 1987 while investigating the Inslaw case."[1150]
- Alan Standorf: "An employee of the National Security Agency in electronic intelligence who leaked information to Danny Casolaro who was investigating Inslaw, BCCI, etc. Standorf's body was found in the backseat of a car at Washington National Airport on January 31, 1991.[1151]
- Dennis Eisman: "An attorney with information on Inslaw, Eisman was found shot to death on April 5, 1991."[1152]
- Ian Spiro, his wife, and three children: "Spiro had supporting documentation for grand jury proceedings on the Inslaw case. His wife and three kids were found murdered on November 1, 1992 in their home. They all died of gunshot wounds to the head. Ian's body was found several days later in a parked car in the [Anza-Borrego] Desert. Cause of death? The ingestion of cyanide. Declared a murder/suicide."[1153]
- Christine Mirzayan: "Clinton intern, died August 1, 1998. She was beaten to death with a heavy object near Georgetown University. What makes us think Bill's thugs did it? In the pre-trial publicity surrounding the Paula Jones lawsuit, *Newsweek's* Mike Isikoff dropped hints that a 'former White House staffer' with the initial 'M' was about to go public with her story of sexual harassment at 1600 Pennsylvania Avenue."[1154]
- Niko Jerkuic: "In charge of the radio beacon that guided *Air Force Two* into the mountain [carrying Ron Brown]. Committed 'suicide' shortly after the crash by shooting himself in the chest."[1155]
- Calvin Walraven: "Twenty-four years old, Walraven was a key witness in Jocelyn Elder's son's

drug case. Ten days after Elder's son was convicted of trafficking in cocaine, Walraven was found dead in his apartment, a gunshot blast to the head."[1156]

- Neil Moody: "Son of Vince Foster's widow's new husband. Died in a car crash. Neil Moody had discovered something very unsettling among his stepmother's private papers and was threatening to go public with it just prior to the beginning of the Democratic National Convention. He was alleged to have been talking to Bob Woodward of the *Washington Post* about a blockbuster story. Witnesses said they saw Neil Moody sitting in his car arguing with another person just prior to his old clunker car suddenly [speeding] off out of control and [hitting] a brick wall."[1157]

- Ron Miller: "Died October 12, 1997. He was the man who tape recorded Clinton fundraisers Gene and Nora Lum and turned those tapes (and other records) over to congressional oversight investigators. The Lums were sentenced to prison for campaign finance violations. Reportedly a healthy man, Ron suddenly took ill on October 3, 1997 and steadily worsened until his death four days later."[1158] Another account adds, "Less than four months after the Lums pleaded guilty, Ron Miller was rushed to a Norman, Oklahoma hospital after becoming ill at home. Doctors were never able to determine the cause of his affliction. Miller died days later. 'He went from being healthy to dying in a week,' J. Dell Gordon told the Associated Press, adding that Miller had just turned over 'boxes of material' to congressional investigators."[1159]

- Alan Whicher, Mickey Maroney, Donald Leonard, and Cynthia Campbell-Brown: Whicher "oversaw Clinton's Secret Service detail. In October

1995, Whicher was transferred to the Secret Service field office in the Murrah Building in Oklahoma City. Whatever warning was given to the BATF agents in that building (none of them came to work that day) did not reach Alan Whicher, who died in the bomb blast April 19, 1995."[1160]

All of these individuals "were Secret Service agents who had worked in the White House. All four were in the Murrah Building on April 19, 1995. Whicher, according to a caller on the G. Gordon Liddy show, was suspected of being the one who leaked the story to the press about Hillary throwing a lamp at [Bill Clinton]."[1161]

- Eric Butera: "An informant who came forward offering information regarding the murder of White House intern Mary Mahoney. He was promptly sent into a known crack house to make an undercover buy for the police and there was beaten to death by unknown assailants."[1162]

- Maynard Webb: "Owned a small aircraft repair business and stumbled on several aircraft whose tail numbers were being changed on a regular basis [just like they did at Mena]. Was about to go public when he walked head first into a spinning propeller."[1163]

- Lance Herndon: "Clinton appointee found bludgeoned to death in his bed. There has been the assertion that he may have been murdered because of his work on the White House database. He died in the period when the White House phone records disappeared."[1164]

- Russell Welch: "Arkansas drug investigator trying to prove highly placed men were involved in coke trafficking [at Mena]. Infected with military grade anthrax, he narrowly escapes death."[1165]

- Theodore Williams: "Brother of Betty Currie, Clinton's private secretary. Ted was run off the highway after being struck by a truck in December, 1997. He got out of his wrecked car, climbed up an embankment to the highway, and then another truck hit him, killing him instantly. This was just a month before Betty Currie was scheduled to testify about Bill Clinton's Oval Office doings."[1166]
- Dan Short: "Arkansas cocaine bank president. Missing. Took local bank into bankruptcy and told pals he laundered cash for the Arkansas coke cartel. The next day he and $71,000 were missing."[1167]
- Terrence Yeakey: Oklahoma City bombing rescue hero. "Official reports claim Yeakey slashed his wrists, one twice and the other three times, placed two slits in a vein at the bend of the elbow of one arm and four at the bend of the elbow of the other, and then stabbed himself with the knife in both sides of the throat, near the jugular vein. Then he walked one-and-a-half miles to where he shot himself in the side of the head."[1168]
- Shelly Kelley: "Stewardess and survivor [of Ron Brown plane crash]. Discovered only four hours after the crash with minor injuries . . . a very clean and precise three inch incision over the femoral artery is determined to be the cause [of her death], but an autopsy reveals the cut to have happened three hours after the airplane injuries."[1169]
- Admiral Mike Boorda: "Clinton's Chief of Naval Operations. Uncharacteristic suicide (gunshot to the chest) under suspicious circumstances just before a *Newsweek* interview."[1170]
- Carlos Ghigliotti: "Key expert witness in the Waco investigation who found compelling evidence that an FBI agent fired shots during the final

showdown at the Branch Davidian compound. Ghigliotti was an expert in analysis of infrared film technology who had worked for Representative Dan Burton's House Government Reform Committee. Ghigliotti's badly decomposed body was discovered April 29, 2000. In October 1999, Ghigliotti, a nationally recognized expert in thermal imagery and videotape, told Burton's committee that his analysis of tapes at Waco indicated that an FBI agent fired shots at the Branch Davidian Mount Carmel compound on April 19."[1171]

Moreover, "Ghigliotti intended to tell the Senate committee that government forces were shooting those trying to escape the fire. It would have been disastrous."[1172] In addition, Ghigliotti "had solid proof that the FBI was lying when they claimed they had not fired at the rear part of the framed building. 'Carlos had found the holy grail. He had proof the FBI was lying.'"[1173]

On top of that, Ghigliotti was willing to push the case into federal court. "He was finalizing his report to Congress, and he also had been advising attorneys waging a $100 million wrongful death suit against the government on behalf of the Davidians and their heirs."[1174] Ghigliotti was ruled to have died of natural causes.

- Charles Wilbourne Miller: "Vice president and board member of Alltel. Found shot to death with two guns. Multiple shots had been fired. Declared a suicide. Alltel is the successor to Jackson Stephens' Systematics, the company that provided the software for the White House's 'Big Brother' database system."[1175]

- John Millis: "Suicide. June 4, 2000. Had been highly critical of President Bill Clinton and former CIA Director John Deutch who had misused CIA computers at his home, thus compromising highly guarded files by exposing them to the Internet. Suicide occurred in a Fairfax County, Virginia motel."[1176]

- Colonel James Sabow: "A would-be whistleblower of drug running activity taking place on the naval base where he was stationed. Colonel James Sabow was found by his wife in the backyard of their home with his head blown off with a shotgun. The Navy ruled it a suicide."[1177]
- Douglas Adams: "Arkansas lawyer for swindled people (like those from Madison Guaranty, AFDC, etc). Found in Springfield, Missouri hospital parking lot with a gunshot wound to the head, January 7, 1997."[1178]
- Paul Olson: "Federal witness who was testifying to the FBI about political/federal drug corruption. Died in a plane crash. A bomb was suspected as the cause of the crash."[1179]
- Gordon Matteson: "May 1, 1997. Clinton associate. Shot in the head. Declared a suicide."[1180]
- Tony Moser: "Critic of the Arkansas Democratic Party political machine, he was killed as he crossed the street in Pine Bluff [Arkansas] ten days after being named a columnist for the *Democrat-Gazette* newspaper."[1181]
- Eric L. Henderson: "Shot to death while riding his bicycle in northeast Washington, D.C. He was a financial advisor to Ron Brown, and a close confidant to Brown and Nolanda Hill."[1182]
- Vicky Weaver: During the siege at Ruby Ridge, "Vicky Weaver died in the doorway of an Idaho cabin. Lon Horiuchi, an FBI HRT team member, launched the bullet that killed her."[1183]

CHAPTER EIGHT

Horiuchi was also in charge of one of the sniper teams at Waco which fired bullets into the Branch Davidian compound.

- Dr. Don Chumley: This physician "ran the Broadway Medical Clinic and was one of the first to arrive at the [Alfred P. Murrah] bombing site on April 19. They were sent [into] the underground parking garage where some people were trapped. Suddenly, three guys come running out of the basement yelling, 'There's a bomb! A bomb! It's gonna blow!' Chumley was killed five months later when his Cessna 210 crashed near Amarillo, Texas under mysterious circumstances."[1184] "Don Chumley evidently learned of the government's hastily planned cover-up surrounding the Oklahoma City bombing. Had he, like so many others, made the decision to go public?"[1185]

- Joey Gladden: Seven-year-veteran of the El Reno Federal Prison where Timothy McVeigh was sequestered. He wrote a book about corruption at El Reno. On January 14, 1996, three weeks before his death, he told his mother, "The federal government has power — you don't know the power. They could assassinate the president of the United States."[1186]

Three weeks later he was dead. "Gladden was found in his living room with a gunshot to his head."[1187]

- Mike Loudenslager: "In the weeks preceding the [OKC] bombing, this G.S.A. employee became increasingly aware that large amounts of ordnance and explosives were in the building and strongly urged a number of parents to take their children out of the Murrah Building. Because of his warnings, far fewer children were in the day-care center on that horrible Wednesday morning. Shortly after the bombing, Mike Loudenslager was actively helping in the rescue and recovery effort. A large number of those at the bomb site either saw or talked with him. During the course of the early rescue efforts, Loudenslager was seen and heard in a very heated confrontation with someone there.

To the absolute astonishment of a large number of police officers and rescue workers, it was later reported that G.S.A. employee Mike Loudenslager's body had been found inside the Murrah Building the following Sunday, still at his desk, a victim of the 9:02 am bombing! This, mind you, after he'd already been seen alive and well by numerous rescue workers at the bomb site after the bombing![1188]

- "Jack Colvert, Jackie Majors, and Buddy Youngblood—each of them had been at the Murrah Building that morning and each had also seen Mike Loudenslager alive and well after the bombing."[1189]
- Kenneth Trentadue and Richard Guthrie: Trentadue "supposedly committed suicide via a knotted or braided bed sheet, barely long enough to fit around his neck, in a suicide-proof [Oklahoma] prison cell."[1190]

The trustees who cleaned Mr. Trentadue's cell after his "suicide" found copious amounts of blood inside. This included bloody fingerprints which extended upward along the wall.

Being very skeptical as to a suicide, "family members removed the mortuary makeup and were shocked to find part of his skull crushed, his knuckles damaged, bruises, puncture-and-slash-wounds over a good portion of his body (including the sides of his feet), and his throat slashed. Boot heel marks were apparent around the right eye and his chest. All evidence points to the fact Kenneth Trentadue was subdued after a fight—brutally beaten, tortured and murdered."[1191]

Why was Trentadue killed? "A neo-Nazi bank robber named Richard Guthrie, one of the leading John Doe # 2 candidates—though never publicly identified as such—was found hanging in a prison cell in July, 1996. Kenneth Trentadue, a man who looked very much like Guthrie, right down to a snake-motif tattoo on one arm, appears to have been mistaken for him when he was picked up on a parole violation on the Mexican border in the summer of 1995."[1192]

Dennis Mahon [an influential member of the Elohim City gang] "believes Guthrie was murdered because he had threatened to reveal information about the proceeds of the loot [from a series of Midwest bank robberies]. Guthrie was found dead only a few hours after telling a reporter from the *Los Angeles Times* that he intended to write a tell-all book that would go a lot further into what [they] were really doing. He was also just days away from appearing before a grand jury."[1193]

- Frank Aller: Bill Clinton's former roommate at Oxford who purportedly committed suicide in 1971 by shooting "himself in the mouth."[1194] Coincidentally, this was at a time when Clinton "worked secretly with the CIA as an informer ratting out [his] fellow war resisters."[1195] The act of killing himself appeared to be peculiar for Aller, as "one of his professors who knew him well . . . stated that it seemed way out of character for this upbeat, intelligent young man to shoot himself."[1196] Could Aller have discovered Clinton's secret dual role as a CIA snitch?

- Ted Richardson: He was a "bombing and arson specialist for the Western District of Oklahoma"[1197] who sensed suspicious activity surrounding the Alfred P. Murrah bombing. He was described as "one of the few good guys, [with] a strong sense of conscience."[1198] Richardson supposedly committed suicide after the [Oklahoma City] grand jury was convened."[1199] His body was discovered in the following manner. "Richardson was found in a church parking lot with a shotgun wound to the chest. The medical examiner's report stated: 'no powder residue is apparent, either in the external aspect of the wound or in the shirt.' An interesting observation considering Richardson had allegedly pushed a shotgun up to his chest and pulled the trigger."[1200]
- Shawn Tea Ferrins: An exotic dancer at Lady Godiva's strip club, she spent time with Timothy McVeigh, Andreas Strassmeir, and Michael Brescia shortly before the OKC bombing and was aware that "McVeigh himself was being paid by the BATF, supported by the fact that he had $2,000 on him at the time of his arrest."[1201] Ferrins "was found dead in her apartment, aged 23, *shortly after* the existence of the [strip club surveillance] tape became known."[1202]
- John Hillier: "Video journalist and investigator. He helped to produce the documentaries *Circle of Power* and *The Clinton Chronicles*. He mysteriously died in a dentist's chair for no apparent reason."[1203]
- Aldo Frescoia: "A 57-year-old electronic surveillance expert working for the Secret Service. He had helped install [the White House] phone security system and could have overheard some inter-

esting conversations. In the spring of 1996, his airplane crashed."[1204]

- David Drye: A "plane crash, June 14 [1999], took the life of [Pat] Matrisciana's friend David Drye, a Concord, N.C. builder and well-known businessman."[1205] Pat Matrisciana created *The Clinton Chronicles*, one of the most damning videotapes ever compiled on the Clintons' crimes and affairs; a definite embarrassment to the administration. David Drye had funded the production of this documentary. Recalls Matrisciana, "The strange thing is that I was scheduled to fly with [Drye] to Washington and had to cancel out two hours before I was supposed to meet him in North Carolina. He made other plans and went on the plane. The plane crash was very suspicious, and it's under investigation. I can't help but wonder if that crash wasn't really for me. There have been so many accidents and unexplained deaths."[1206]

- Robert Bates: 39-year-old mechanic at the Mena airport who was willing to come forward with information about massive government drug dealing at this facility. "Allegedly drank himself to death on mouthwash."[1207] Mouthwash!

- Wallace Blaylock: His wife, Lenora Steinkamp, was caught on videotape in a compromising position with Bill Clinton. She had been a friend of the Clintons for decades. "In September, 1986 Steinkamp's husband, Wallace Blaylock, was found dead at their home"[1208] of a gunshot wound.

- Mike Samples: Murdered in June, 1995, he "was another grand jury witness for Don and Kevin [the Boys on the Tracks murders]. He was reported as knowing a great deal about the deaths of Ives and Henry. Sources say he had been involved with picking up drugs that were dropped out of planes at the Mena drop sites. He was shot to death in the head and was not found for some time."[1209]

- Woody Lemon: Died in a plane crash on May 16, 1998. "Lemon had the only copy of a report about explosive residue, the result of testing samples [which] had been taken from the Murrah building site and surrounding area. Lemon [as well as a man named Joe Harp] was on the scene in OK City shortly after the bombing. Harp said he saw olive drab canisters taken out of the building . . . Harp had signed an affidavit detailing his experiences and stating, in his opinion, the bomb(s) were not made of ANFO, but were mercury-fulminate based."[1210]

When this list is taken as a whole, one undeniable conclusion is reached. If we examine "the mortality rate in the Clinton campaign and administration, it exceeds what would ordinarily be expected from a study of the laws of statistical probability."[1211]

Imagine; 110+ deaths to those who posed an immediate threat to the subjects of this book. The Body Count is very real, and "many people have mysteriously died who knew about various aspects of the alleged corruption surrounding Bill and Hillary Clinton. There are those who believe that these people died because someone wanted to prevent them from telling their story."[1212]

When this list is viewed objectively, their suspicions certainly appear to be well founded.

CHAPTER EIGHT

MAJOR OBSTACLE GONE. Handsome and articulate, John F. Kennedy provided one of the few possible threats to a Hillary Clinton's bid for a Senate seat in New York. Some investigators now believe that his plane was professionally sabotaged and that Kennedy—an experienced pilot—was in fact murdered. Whatever the truth, one thing is certain: JFK Junior's death practically ensured Hillary's victory. AFP/GETTY IMAGES

BYE BYE? Hillary Clinton seemed shocked that a virtual unknown, Barack Obama, could have defeated her for the 2008 Democratic nomination for president of the United States. But don't count Hillary out. In 2012 she is almost guaranteed to make another run. And who knows: Maybe Obama will commit "Arkancide." One thing is for sure: The Clintons' political careers aren't over yet.

AFP/GETTY IMAGES

CHAPTER NINE

Presidential Pardons

FREE THE CRIMINALS

When a president and his wife have systematically engaged in drug trafficking, money laundering, embezzlement, kickbacks, mob-related activities, and murder; why would it surprise anyone that during the last days of their second term they engineered the largest release of criminals in the history of this country? Incredibly, "in the last hours of his presidency, Clinton had shocked America by insolently commuting thirty-six prison sentences and handing out 140 pardons to a collection of crooks, some of whom had been conspicuous in the Arkansas underworld. Brother Roger Clinton, himself a convicted drug dealer, was caught peddling some of the pardons."[1213]

As you will learn in this section, the crassness of such a brazen move enraged not only members of the Democratic Party, but even his closest allies. The Clintons are criminals. They interact with criminals. They side with criminals. And they free criminals. Imagine, "the granting of 177 presidential pardons and commutations of sentences on his last night in office. There was a libidinous crudeness to all of this.

It was a final self-indulgence, a total loss of control. Other presidents had granted last-minute pardons, had signed last-minute executive orders, had staged bathetic farewell tours—but the rapacious enormity of these conceits and absolutions seemed to recapitulate Clinton's most loathsome qualities."[1214]

These pardons weren't only self-indulgent; they were payoffs to a criminal class to which the Clintons belong. Shortly, you'll discover precisely who Bill and Hillary Clinton freed or gave a nod to, and I'm sure you'll be as appalled as were their counterparts. Jimmy Carter's former chief of staff, Hamilton Jordan, called Bill and Hillary 'The First Grifters' and said of their actions, "It is difficult for the average citizen to comprehend how outrageous Bill Clinton's pardons are to those of us who have worked in the White House."[1215]

Jordan's disgust revolves around the fact that a president—"under Article II, Section 2, of the United States Constitution"[1216]—can pardon or free *anyone*. "The power is absolute—even a serial killer could be pardoned—and utterly unreviewable. It cannot be rescinded by the next president . . . once granted, a pardon can never be taken away."[1217]

As with every other aspect of their lives, the Clintons abused their privileges and spat on the system with a reckless lack of concern. What they did extended well beyond the "schemes to rent out any bit of White House property that wasn't nailed down (i.e. sleepovers in the Lincoln Bedroom and rides aboard Air Force One for fat cat contributors)."[1218]

Instead, the Clinton pardons careened off the scale of what is acceptable in a democratic society. "The list of beneficiaries of Clinton's last-minute clemency only was as eclectic as one could imagine: small and big-time crooks, con men, bank robbers, terrorists, relatives, ex-girlfriends, a cross section of the Clinton cabinet, a former director of the CIA, perjurers, tax evaders, fugitive money lenders, Clinton campaign contributors, former members of Congress, and friends of Jesse Jackson."[1219]

Ponder this list. The Clintons side with criminals at every turn . . . at every opportunity. Birds of a feather flock together, and the Clintons naturally gravitate toward criminals. They freed drug dealers, mobsters, and robbers. Why? How can one person on earth justify that Bill and Hillary were—and still are—outright crooks? Their pardons were so inexcusable that "not since the opening of the gates of the Bastille have so many criminals been liberated on a single day."[1220]

To give you a better idea of what we're talking about, below is a sampling of the kind of scum that Bill and Hillary either pardoned or released, all leading to a crescendo with the king of all disgraces, Marc Rich. To get the ball rolling, Clinton pardoned "four Hasidic Jews on his last day in office. These four residents of New Square, a community made up primarily of Russian Jewish immigrants, have been convicted of defrauding the government of $40 million."[1221]

They're now free and clear. But if *you* try to get out of even paying a parking ticket, see what happens. Yet four crooks who bilked Uncle Sam out of $40 million got to skate, all with the approval of the Clintons. A Jewish woman described as a "communist bomb thrower" was also released. "Susan Rosenberg was a member of the Weather Underground, one of the most violent of the left-wing militias that disrupted the nation from the 1960s through the 1980s."[1222]

Then, of course, we have to factor in favoritism and cronyism. "Clinton pardoned three of his cabinet level appointees (Espy, Cisneros, and Deutch), one son of a cabinet member (Riley), one brother, and one of his alleged ex-girlfriends [Susan McDougal]."[1223]

Returning to the subject of terrorists, there were others as well on Bill Clinton's list of pardons. Yes, we're talking about real-life terrorists released during Clinton's final days. Specifically, he "freed a group of imprisoned Puerto Rican terrorists"[1224] known as the "Armed Forces of National Liberation [FALN]."[1225]

Who were they? "During the late 1970s and early 1980s the FALN was responsible for at least 130 bombings, resulting in the deaths of six people and many more injuries."[1226]

Worse, these terrorists were completely unremorseful, especially "the FALN's Adolfo Matos [who] made it clear that he and his colleagues were not ashamed of what they had done, saw no need to ask forgiveness, and fully intended to continue their personal war against the United States and innocent bystanders."[1227]

These men are unrepentant killers, Marxists, and separatists.

They are so dangerous that the "FBI's Assistant Director of National Security, Neil Gallagher, said that the people turned loose by Clinton 'are criminals, and they are terrorists, and they represent a threat to the United States.'"[1228]

But try to gauge how our commander-in-chief reacted. He "offered clemency to sixteen convicts who were members of the Puerto Rican terrorist group known as the FALN."[1229]

Police officers and national security representatives were outraged, but that's not the half of it. "President Clinton had not bothered to consult with relatives of the victims of FALN terrorism. In fact, the survivors of those murdered and those whose lives had otherwise been destroyed by the terrorists were not even informed that their attackers were being released."[1230]

So, why would Clinton make such a horrendous decision to release these America-hating terrorists? Simply, because it potentially benefited his wife, Hillary, who would "curry favor with New York's powerful Hispanic vote; another bloc crucial to her election [to the Senate]."[1231]

Amazingly, yet par for the course, was the fact that every decision they made revolved around an insatiable appetite for political advancement and personal power. "Clinton chose to help [FALN] in order to boost his wife's Senate campaign."[1232]

The situation was so obvious that "former U.S. attorney [Joseph] DiGenova remarked, 'Let me just say, categorically, the Puerto Rican terrorists were pardoned because they were a political benefit to the president's wife. Make no mistake about it. There is no justification for these pardons.'"[1233]

Some may wonder: after releasing Marxist, anti-American terrorists, how much worse could the pardons be? How about narcotics dealers? "Clinton commuted the sentences of twenty-one drug offenders"[1234] and was "tipped heavily in favor of persons who had used or distributed cocaine."[1235]

These included: cocaine traffickers, PCP manufacturers, LSD dealers, money launderers, those in association with the Cali cartel, and high-level drug kingpins. These men weren't college students who got busted for smoking a joint. They were major league dealers in illegal substances that poisoned our country. As I said earlier, Bill Clinton sides with criminals at every opportunity. It's his modus operandi.

Since we're on the subject of drugs, Bill Clinton allowed his brother Roger to get in on the pardoning act. Now remember, Roger not only snorted cocaine with his brother, the governor, but he was also a massive cocaine addict, a convicted drug dealer, a drug runner at Mena, and also a man who gave cocaine to underage teenage girls. This guy was as creepy, immoral, and untrustworthy as anyone in the Clinton inner circle, yet he was still allowed to capitalize on the president's final few days in office. "Witnesses emerged with cancelled checks, claiming that first brother Roger Clinton had shaken down a Texas family for $235,000 in exchange for a presidential pardon."[1236]

Corruption within the Clinton family was all inclusive, and Hillary's siblings weren't excluded from partaking in the pardon bounty. Hell, Hillary's brother took nepotism to even lower depths of depravity by finagling two pardons. "[Hugh] Rodham reportedly received a total of $434,000 for his 'work' on the Braswell and Vignali pardons."[1237]

Who were these two men? Get a load of this insanity. "Hugh Rodham persuaded President Clinton to pardon Carlos Anabel Vignali. All he was convicted of, after all, was shipping *half a ton* of cocaine to Minnesota. He got 15 years. Former U.S. Attorney Todd Jones called Vignali 'a major source of keeping a drug organization fed with dope.'"[1238]

Despite being a major drug dealer, Hillary's brother convinced Bill Clinton to set him free, but not before he greased a few wheels. "Vignali's father donated $150,000 to Los Angeles Democrats, and $10,000 to the national committee. More importantly, he paid Hugh Rodham $200,000 to get his son cleared. And it worked: Clinton commuted the drug dealer's sentence to time served."[1239]

That's Clinton justice—a mob boss buys his drug dealer son out of prison, while the Clintons and their pals all line their pockets.

Truly appalling.

But Hugh Rodham wasn't satisfied with one mere payoff. He had to get another one. "Hugh also got more than $200,000 for securing a pardon for Almon Glenn Braswell, who was sentenced to three years in jail for touting a phony cure for baldness, and peddling a remedy for prostrate problems, using photos of athletes like racer Richard Petty, football player Len Dawson, and Stan 'the Man' Musial, all of whom sued him. Braswell received a full pardon from Clinton."[1240]

Eventually, Braswell "was convicted of mail fraud and perjury."[1241]

In all, Roger Clinton and Hugh Rodham raked in a total of $669,000 via three presidential pardons; nearly $750,000! What was Hillary Clinton's reaction to "her brother [who] had arranged pardons for a notorious drug dealer and a swindler after the two men gave him $400,000 in payoffs?"[1242]

As usual, she lied through her teeth: "I did not know my brother was involved in any way in any of this."[1243]

She also added:

- "I did not have any involvement in the pardons that were granted."
- "I don't know anything other than what has now come out and I did not learn about that until recently."
- "I did not know any specific information."
- "I love my brother. I'm just extremely disappointed in this terrible misjudgment that he made."[1244]

It's amazing that Hillary can know every detail about every policy decision within their administration, but when it comes to the Clinton crimes and corruption, invariably *she knows nothing* and is forever in the dark. Plus, not once did she ever suggest that her brother should return the $400,000. She was merely disappointed.

CHAPTER NINE

But it goes even further than that, for her deceit is so transparent as to be laughable. "Both Hugh and Tony [Rodham] were basically living at the White House at the time. And of course Bill himself knew they were lobbying for the pardons. Is it at all conceivable that Bill Clinton said nothing to his wife about the pardons her brothers were promoting?"[1245]

Are you falling for Hillary's con game? We've already pointed out in painstaking detail that Mrs. Clinton was from the very beginning of their relationship the one in charge of management and detail. She ran the show and took care of business. It's a slap in the face for Hillary to say that she was unaware of these pardons. She's a liar that is nearly incapable of telling the truth. Figure it out for yourself. "When Hillary was running for the Senate, she went to considerable lengths to portray herself as an active, involved partner in her husband's presidency."[1246]

But when the going gets tough, she conveniently knows nothing. The audacity of her deceit is inexcusable.

Anyway, picture this scenario. "Is it credible that Bill didn't tell Hillary [about the pardons her brother arranged]? After his wife had been elected to the Senate, is it conceivable that Bill took an action that might directly have implicated her brothers in a blatant conflict-of-interest and influence-peddling scheme—and did so without consulting her?"[1247]

There is absolutely zero chance that Hillary didn't know what was occurring with these pardons. She had just been elected to the U.S. Senate.

Do you think there's a snowball's chance in hell she'd jeopardize everything by being unaware, especially in regard to such a brazen scheme as outlined above? Here is how one of Hugh Rodham's deals went down. "A $200,000 wire transfer from a G.B. Data Systems of Marina Del Ray, California, a company owned by Almon Glenn Braswell, [was sent] to the law firm in which Hugh Rodham was a partner."[1248]

When did it transpire? "The payoff was sent on January 22 [2001], the first business day after Bill Clinton pardoned Braswell, a quack and a convicted swindler."[1249]

When questioned about this matter, Hillary continued to lie to epic proportions.

> Question: The $400,000 your brother received had absolutely nothing to do with the president's decision to pardon these two men?
> Hillary: I believe that's the case. I absolutely believe that's the case. As far as I know, there was no connection whatsoever.[1250]

When someone lies to you, they assume you're stupid. Braswell wired $200,000 directly to Hugh Rodham's law firm, yet there's no monetary connection? Hillary's opinion of the American public must be so low that she thinks everyone is moronic enough to fall for her chicanery. The Clintons lie, and Hillary's the worst of all.

MARC RICH

Screams of protest came from nearly every conceivable quarter when President Bill Clinton pardoned Marc Rich, a man who "committed the largest tax fraud in the history of the United States."[1251]

Rich was one of the most corrupt, treasonous businessmen this nation has ever known; a dishonest scoundrel who:

> • "Struck lucrative oil deals with Iranian Ali Rezai" when that nation was referring to the United States as the 'Great Satan."
> • Began "trading with the Khomeini regime [after it] became a criminal offense" during President Jimmy Carter's oil ban.
> • "They continued dealing with Iran, paying for oil in weapons, automatic rifles, and rockets." [Marc Rich's tactics don't sound all that different than those of George Bush, Sr.]
> • After Americans were banned from doing

business with Libya and Colonel Muhamar Gaddafi due to their involvement in the Pan Am 103 bombing, Rich "bought Libyan crude oil through European third parties."
- He "propped up the Castro dictatorship in Cuba."
- Rich also "dealt in Soviet crude oil during the Cold War."
- He became "involved in a practice known as "daisy chaining," which are bogus trades that avoided regulations by relabeling old oil as new.
- He was "adept at 'calving,' an illegal practice in which a subsidiary based in the United States pays inflated prices for materials from another of its subsidiaries based elsewhere, thereby avoiding taxes."[1252]

I could continue, but in essence, Marc Rich was so excessively corrupt that he made Kenneth Lay and the Enron scandal look like a day in traffic court. Prosecutor Morris Weinberg commented that Marc Rich has "apparently made vast sums of money over the past twenty years by trading with virtually every enemy of the U.S."[1253]

In time, his practices were so extreme that "New York's elite southern district U.S. Attorney's Office eventually brought charges against Rich in a fifty-one count indictment, in part under RICO, the Racketeer Influenced and Corrupt Organization statutes."[1254]

The enormity of this case is mind-boggling. Rich was "accused of evading $48 million in taxes and 51 counts of tax fraud."[1255]

Realizing that he'd spend the rest of his life in prison, this worm-like, traitorous gangster did the only thing he could do to save his skin: he fled the country. "Rich was routinely described in the newspapers as a 'fugitive financier.' That seemed inadequate: this was no mere white-collar criminal. He evaded taxes, perhaps hundreds of millions in dollars in taxes. He traded oil, and perhaps arms, with America's enemies. He fled the country and renounced his citizenship. He was a grotesque, a caricature—sadly, inescapably, a Jewish caricature (particularly in his efforts to absolve his sins by slathering millions of dollars upon selected, often Israeli, charities)."[1256]

As was the case with many of the other *unpardonable* pardons, they were largely a Jewish phenomenon. Professor and psychiatrist Walter Reich of George Washington University said that the Marc Rich scandal "plays into the oldest and most damaging stereotypes and canards, and it is likely to give aid and comfort to the worst varieties of anti-Semitism . . . the canard of the Jewish connection with money and power that's easily evoked in the public imagination."[1257]

Despite the fact that Marc Rich was one of the most despicable human beings on the planet, who betrayed his country to the core, it was Jews whose voices spoke the loudest for his pardon. "One of those writing on behalf of Rich was Abraham Foxman, head of the Anti-Defamation League, which is supposed to fight anti-Semitism, not provide fodder for it."[1258]

Another was Israeli president "Ehud Barak, [who] was a significant actor in the pardon as well. He called the President three times to plead for Rich (who had contributed mightily to Barak's campaign fund)."[1259]

The individual most responsible for Rich's pardon, however, was his ex-wife, Denise Rich, who "had become a major Democratic donor just prior to his pardon, giving one million dollars to the Democratic Party and an enormous sum to the Clinton Library."[1260]

More specifically, the figures were: "Rich contributed $450,000 to the Clinton Library, $100,000 to Hillary Clinton's Senate campaign, and $1,000,000 to the Democratic Party."[1261]

Lastly, Denise Rich also gave "as a gift $7,000 worth of furniture to the Clintons."[1262]

Clearly, where the Clintons are involved, everything has a price. We see a direct financial benefit to Bill and Hillary from Marc Rich's ex-wife, especially to Hillary, who had just entered her first

Senate campaign. Please don't forget who this man is. "He was known as a financial gladiator, ruthless tycoon, and in the words of one trader, the 'prince of f***ing darkness.' It would have been impossible to write about such a person from the outside. His movements, companies, and dealings were all shrouded in secrecy."[1263]

In simpler words, Rich was a criminal and traitor; and when it came to his pardon, "law enforcement officials were outraged, particularly those who had been chasing Rich around the globe."[1264]

But why did the Clintons pardon "one of America's most notorious fugitives"?[1265]

It was greediness that extended, cancer-like, to the core of their sickened souls. The technique was simple. "Marc Rich found that the same 'honey trap' schemes the Soviets employed so effectively, making ample use of women, resonated well with Clinton's most publicized weakness."[1266]

In other words, could it have been nothing more than blackmail?

I'm not convinced that this simplistic explanation is the entire story. Rather, the criminal, deviant elite stick together. To make it *appear* as if the pardon was granted due to greed, Denise Rich flaunted a few generous contributions to the Clintons, knowing full well that almost nobody would look any further. But the money was merely a superficial distraction used to divert attention away from the crux issue—the globalist ruling elite are members of a select organized crime syndicate who watch out for one another.

Accepting this premise, even some insiders were appalled by Marc Rich's pardon. Rudolph Giuliani (definitely no saint himself) "was dumfounded. He said that it was 'impossible, the president would never pardon a fugitive, especially Marc Rich. It cannot have happened.' But it did."[1267]

An even more recognizable figure, Jimmy Carter, "broke the code of the presidential brotherhood by calling Clinton's pardon of Rich 'disgraceful.'"[1268]

He continued, "I think President Clinton made one of his most serious mistakes in the way he handled the pardon situation the last few hours he was in office."[1269]

Even Senator Robert Byrd (once a KKK member) "would claim to be disgusted by the President's last official actions in office. Byrd characterized them as 'malodorous.'"[1270]

Which, by and by, brings us back full circle to Hillary: what was her reaction to the Marc Rich pardon? Recall that Denise Rich gave $450,000 to the Clinton Library, and $100,000 directly to her senatorial campaign fund — sums she would have 100 percent been aware of (not to mention the $1,000,000+ donations to the Democratic Party). So, what was Hillary's response to this abhorrent abuse of power via a presidential pardon? On January 29, 2001 CNN reported that Hillary said, "I have no opinion. I had no opinion before. I had no opinion at the time. I have no opinion now. And, you know, I really don't have any opinion about it."[1271]

Amazing. Simply, incredibly amazing. A month later, Hillary would lie to such an extreme that it strains the time-space continuum. Denise Rich gave the Clintons over half a million dollars—even furniture—yet Hillary explained, "I never knew about Marc Rich at all. You know, people would hand me envelopes, I would just pass them along. I knew nothing about the Marc Rich pardon until after it happened."[1272]

There can be no more despicable, deceitful woman in our political world right now than Hillary Clinton. Her actions are sickening to the furthest degree of anything we can comprehend as human beings.

CHAPTER NINE 303

Marc Rich was one of the worst white collar criminals in American history, evading paying $48 million in taxes and being charged with 51 counts of tax fraud by fleeing the country. Yet Bill Clinton pardoned this man whose crimes made the Enron scandal look like nothing. Jimmy Carter called the pardon of Rich disgraceful. Why did Bill pardon Rich? Was Bill Clinton being blackmailed by Rich?

ELITE CONNECTION: Vernon E. Jordan Jr. (right), a close friend and unofficial advisor to former-President Bill Clinton, walks up the steps of the U.S. District Courthouse in Washington, D.C. Jordan testified before the grand jury that was then investigating the relationship between the president and former White House intern Monica Lewinsky. (Man at left is unidentified.) Interestingly, Jordan is a prominent member of the Bilderberg group. Soon after Jordan got Bill Clinton invited to the 1991 Bilderberg meeting, this unknown governor of a politically insignificant state was president of the United States. Coincidence?

JAMAL A. WILSON/AFP/GETTY IMAGES

CHAPTER TEN

Power Behind the Throne

HUMAN RECONSTRUCTION & REMOLDING SOCIETY

The most elemental, yet most complex, aspect of global politics is that all the insiders, handlers, and manipulators want everyday citizens to believe that there is no major plan for society; that events simply happen and unfold randomly. But anyone who is willing to do their research, accept the truth, and allow a paradigm shift to occur in their thinking will discover that politics isn't ruled by chance, but by a conspiratorial process involving a cabal of like-minded internationalists that are ultimately led by world bankers. In this sense, to the best of their ability, the controllers have made world events resemble professional wrestling—pre-planned, orchestrated for public consumption, and staged for maximum effect. Such a concept isn't *conspiracy theory*; it's simple reality whether you want to believe it or not.

Franklin Roosevelt once said, "In politics, nothing happens by accident. If it happens, you can bet it was planned that way."[1273]

Likewise, veteran newsman Bill Moyers observed, "There is a secret government in America. It operates with the explicit and implied authority of the highest officials, and in the name of America's interests it has inflicted great damage on the unsuspecting people of other countries and on our own fundamental principles."[1274]

Rather than expounding on the philosophy and history of conspiracies, why don't I instead lay out a specific example of how the world works? Everyone remembers the great Vietnam-like struggle between the Soviet Union and Afghanistan which eventually resulted in the purported downfall of communism and ended the Cold War. Conveniently, these *mujahideen* freedom fighters from Afghanistan had within their ranks a leader whose name would eventually become infamous two decades later: Osama bin Laden.

But bin Laden—the bogeyman, 9-11 fall guy, and Lee Harvey Oswald patsy—wasn't all that important at the time. Rather, the key event which was never admitted until years later was initiated by one of the premier luminaries of globalism: Zbigniew Brzezinski. This cofounder of the Trilateral Commission (along with David Rockefeller) has long held that whoever controls Eurasia will control the world. Therefore, since the Soviet Union's long arm still held sway over Afghanistan—creating a great deal of turmoil—something had to be done to shake things up.

If one obtained all their information from the mainstream media at the time (late 1979), they'd imagine that a war simply broke out between the Soviets and Afghanistan. Brzezinski and others, such as Professor Samuel Huntington (author of *The Clash of Civilizations*), had other ideas. In essence, this war was step one in what would ultimately lead to 9-11 and the war in Iraq. "Brzezinski wrote how the Soviet invasion precipitated a large-scale buildup of the U.S. military presence in the Persian Gulf and a commitment to the defense of the Persian Gulf."[1275]

This stance led to the mindset that "an attempt by any outside force to gain control of the Persian Gulf region will be regarded as an assault on the vital interests of the United States of America."[1276]

These are extremely heavy words, and their repercussions have been felt up to present times. Other factors weighed upon their ultimate decisions, such as a "power vacuum created by the Shah [of Iran's] fall (to Shia fundamentalist radicals in 1979), after the earlier British withdrawal from the Persian Gulf in 1971."[1277]

According to Brzezinski and his cohorts, if the Soviets or Muslims assumed control of this region, the balance of power would tip in their direction. So, Brzezinski made a "candid admission that he intended by meddling in Afghanistan in 1979 (*before* the Soviet invasion) precisely to induce a Soviet military invasion."[1278]

CHAPTER TEN

Said in simpler terms, Brzezinski began the Afghan war by deliberately luring the Soviets into it! Why would he initiate such a bold move? Easy: he wanted to tie "the Soviets down in a mountainous and unconquerable Afghanistan"[1279] and "induce Soviet responses that would eventually weaken the Soviet Union and hasten its dissolution."[1280]

Finally, what was at stake? "A potential economic prize: an enormous concentration of natural gas and oil reserves located in the region."[1281]

What took place is precisely what Brzezinski envisioned. The Soviet Union fell, and the United States eventually moved into Afghanistan and the Middle East (although the Iraqi war turned out to be an unmitigated disaster). So, would you call the above description a *conspiracy theory*? If so, then you're wrong, because instead it is reality . . . a reality you didn't hear about on the *CBS Evening News*, or read about in your history books. Nonetheless, it is still reality, and no amount of denial can change the fact that the world is governed by conspiracies which are conceived of by international bankers, corporate heads, intelligence agencies, secret societies, think tanks, and a handful of top tier government officials. [And just for the record, do you know why Afghanistan was such a cherished gem in this battle for Eurasia? Because it is "the world's major heroin source,"[1282] and we've all seen how important drugs are in the Bush-Clinton cartel.]

In no time, George Bush, Sr. and CIA Director William Casey engineered the October Surprise (which got Ronald Reagan elected), Iran and Iraq waged war against each other (each side fueled by CIA weaponry), Israel started selling guns to Iran (part of Iran-Contra), and cocaine was being flown into Bill and Hillary's Arkansas to finance the war in Central America. Then, when Iraq's Saddam Hussein fell out of favor with the globalists, Israel bombed the hell out of them in 1981, while Bush Sr. invaded in 1989. Meanwhile, very conveniently, Osama bin Laden (former Afghan mujahideen leader from Saudi Arabia), along with the CIA and Pakistan's ISI, created al-Qaeda; all of which led to 9-11, the CIA-led invasion of Afghanistan (to recapture the opium fields from their Taliban foes), and the U.S. overthrow of Saddam Hussein after getting quagmired in another Vietnam-like war (reminiscent of what Brzezinski got the Soviets into in Afghanistan). Funny how the world works, isn't it? Events came full circle, almost like it was planned that way. The bankers keep lending money to governments (especially the U.S.), while collecting billions in interest; defense contractors rake in dough hand-over-fist; Big Oil is turning record-breaking profits; the CIA's heroin sales are off the charts; and Samuel P. Huntington's *Clash of Civilizations* (Christians versus Muslims) is an awful reality. Best of all (at least from their perspective), taxpayers keep footing the bills while *our children* (not theirs) keep spilling blood on the battlefield. What more could the globalists ask for?

In the States, what do we see? People awakening to their *real* enemy—the globalist cartel fronted by the Bushes and Clintons? Hell no. It's the same divide-and-conquer Hegelian Dialectic that's been utilized for years: Democrats versus Republicans—both of whom bow to and work for the same masters. Or, as author Gary Allen wrote decades ago about the 1968 presidential election, "There really was not a dime's worth of difference between presidential candidates. Voters were given the choice between CFR world government advocate Nixon and CFR world government advocate Humphrey. Only the rhetoric was changed to fool the public."[1283]

It's no different today with the Bushes and Clintons. They're teammates, and they work hand-in-hand with one another. Bush-Clinton-Bush-Clinton = USA R.I.P.

As we have shown on numerous occasions, the Clintons have been well connected and protected from the earliest days of their political careers. Bill, of course, was the catalyst—the chosen one with an oratorial "gift." In the beginning, it was Dixie Mafia-Hot Springs wheeler-dealer "Uncle Raymond [Clinton's] financing of Bill's early campaigns for Congress, Attorney General, and Governor."[1284]

That got the ball rolling. With this foundation set and an acquaintance with figures in the criminal underworld, "Bill Clinton learned the way the system really worked beneath the public pretense. He imbibed it from his mother, his covetous stepfather, and his powerful, haughty uncle; that what went on under the table or in the back room was all right, necessary, smart. He discovered by experience that what he did in that tradition, even the dissolute, dishonest, and pathological, was acceptable, that he and his methods, the outward gloss and inner squalor, would prove successful and even discreetly admired by peers and patrons."[1285]

He became a criminal; but not one that existed solely on the seamier side of life. Rather, he became a *political* criminal, one that would eventually walk among some of the most traitorous members of the global organized crime syndicate known as the New World Order. By doing so, he courted and was accepted into this shadowy cartel, primarily to do their bidding and the dirty work they weren't willing to do (i.e. incriminate themselves). Sure, Bill and Hillary received some handsome financial rewards, but in essence they were the idiot dupes; the pawns who first got suckered into the system by engaging in illegal activities (example: Hillary's $100,000 cattle futures scam). Then, once they took the plunge and were incriminated (with threats of prison sentences hanging over their heads), the Clintons couldn't turn back. They now became the punching bag for every nefarious act imaginable. George Bush Sr. needed money for the CIA's Contra operation, so the Clintons got handcuffed with Mena and its cocaine nightmare. As circumstances got stickier, murders resulted. Soon they were involved in money laundering, kickbacks, embezzlement, tax evasion, and any other number of government illegalities.

But here's the way the game is played. Those atop the control pyramid—at the highest reaches of the upper echelon—don't engage directly in criminal acts. They don't deal drugs or kill people. They don't get their hands dirty. Rather, they have others crawl through the pig slop for them. As a result, their dupes take the heat while they continue to rake in the dough. Bill and Hillary were the idiot dupes who eventually became imprisoned in this deceitful, ugly world. Sure, they made a conscious decision to engage in these illegal activities; but look at the turmoil they've faced as a result. Look at how blackened their hearts became after they sold their souls to the CIA. Look at the bitterness, hatred, lies, and brushes with the law. They're prisoners of those who laugh all the way to the bank while they—minions of the power elite—grovel in the muck.

Don't get me wrong; I'm certainly not apologizing for the Clintons or trying to portray them as victims, because they're not. Rather, they're sick, vile, miserable human beings that, by all rights, should be spending the rest of their lives in prison. All I'm doing is explaining how the system operates, and how Bill and Hillary are nothing more than glamorized prostitutes for the global elite. As such, their roles required them to be the peons—those that crawled through the sewer and took the blame for every criminal act. That's the decision they made when signing their infamous prearranged marriage contract so many decades ago.

But even before their names were signed on the dotted line, Bill Clinton needed a fixer and handler, while Hillary desperately sought a vehicle to springboard her way to the top. Sure, she could have made it a certain distance on her own, but never to the pinnacle. In this light, "Hillary was so ambitious that she would have found it hard to respect a man with modest goals. Bill Clinton might be trying at times, but he brought excitement into her life."[1286]

But it's unlikely that Hillary could have realized what she was getting herself into. In her early 20s while still a college student, a future in politics with the White House as her ultimate goal must have seemed thrilling beyond words. What she got instead was enslavement to someone else's goals, not her own. Hillary has been forced to lead her life on their terms, and the eventual reality has infuriated her. That's why she's so filled with anger, and feels such a need for totalitarian control. The demands she makes are the equivalent of pure survival. When one sells their soul, they sell their life. Hillary's controllers own her; with prison and/or her

CHAPTER TEN

murder the penalty if she fails. In college, Hillary liked the *idea* of playing in the big leagues. Once she got there, the reality was an entirely different story.

Anyway, plans were made for the Clintons early on, and to accomplish their goals, the powers-that-be needed handlers to facilitate their meteoric rise to success. As you'll see throughout this chapter, we're talking about extremely high rollers. Along the way, Bill Clinton (and his strategically placed wife) saw "the grinning faces of Arkansas's oligarchs as they passed him cash. He counted its dividends in his unprecedented early financial backing by national benefactors like Goldman Sachs. He found it anew in the nodding, sometimes fawning response he received from the beginning from a national media taken by his polish and surface substance, so like their own. He relied on it in the dozens of pre-presidential auditions he performed and passed at Pamela Harriman's Georgetown townhouse and elsewhere for the Democratic Party arbiters. He enlisted it in the professional hucksters and hit men like George Stephanopoulos and James Carville who flocked to his side. He called on it in the Jackson Stephens, Worthen Bank line of credit that enabled him to outlast his less prepared, [less] corrupted opponents."[1287]

The road to 1600 Pennsylvania Avenue was paved in fool's gold, for not only didn't Bill and Hillary foresee what they had bartered their souls for, but they also came to spout a philosophy which is so anti-human, so non-free will, and so antithetical to the liberties which man should enjoy that it turned their evil hearts even blacker. Consider what Hillary has become:

- In a speech at the University of Texas at Austin [1993], Mrs. Clinton talked about her conception of the new "Politics of Meaning." In ominous tones she announced, "Let us be willing to remold society by redefining what it means to be a human being in the 20th century, moving into the new millennium."[1288]

- While in college, Hillary Rodham joined a student group called the Cultural Values Committee which stressed, "pluralism, mutual respect and understanding"[1289] all buzzwords for multiculturalism, political correctness, globalism, and a New World Order.
- In a bow to state-run collectivism, Hillary said in 1993, "We must stop thinking of the individual and start thinking about what is best for society."[1290] (George Orwell's Big Brother would have smiled approvingly.)
- During her famous 1969 Wellesley graduation speech, Hillary regurgitated a garish brand of *Brave New World* rhetoric. "We're not interested in social reconstruction; it's human reconstruction."[1291]
- At her 1993 Austin commencement speech, Hillary stated, "We are at a stage in history in which remolding society is one of the great challenges facing all of us in the West."[1292]
- When speaking of child-rearing, Hillary said of us (that means you and me), "They have to be shown how to do it. They have to be, in a sense, 're-parented' to be able to be a good parent."[1293]
- Again, Hillary's view of parenting is apparent (and you're not in the picture). "Decisions about motherhood and abortion, schooling, cosmetic surgery, treatment of venereal disease, or employment and others where the decision or lack of one will significantly reflect the child's future should not be made unilaterally by parents."[1294]

If you will, please re-read the above quotes, then ask yourself: after all you've read about Hillary Clinton during the course of these three books, do you want *her* remolding society, or defining what it means to be a human being? Would you want her to be the arbiter of deciding *your* values? In regard to doing what is best for society, to whose society is she referring—ours, or *hers*? Better yet, would you want her to reconstruct you as a human being, or the society in which you live? Lastly, how many would step forward to have Hillary Clinton and the state parent their children? Whether you accept it or not, Hillary Clinton and the globalists adore the state for, as Paul A. Gigot wrote in *The Wall Street Journal* on March 13, 1992, "She believes in—no, swears by, the virtues of government social work."[1295]

Reminiscent of Georg Wilhelm Friedrich Hegel, the state is their ideal, with big government as the centerpiece. Illusion can no longer be an excuse. Hillary Clinton wants to be Big Sister, with an even more ominous Big Brother behind the curtain pulling her strings.

MASONS, JESUITS & RHODES SCHOLARS

If anyone doesn't believe that the Bushes and Clintons have been teammates for decades, let's pull back the veil for a moment and catch a glimpse of the real George W. Bush and Hillary Clinton. Supposedly these two individuals are entrenched political rivals— even enemies—but such a characterization is nothing more than mainstream media chicanery and illusion. A perfect example of their symbiotic relationship took place only half-a-year after George W. took office. If you recall, during the Clintons' final days in office, their staff—with full nodding approval from Hillary— completely trashed the White House and *Air Force One*.

Most people would be outraged if the former occupants of their residence did tens of thousands of dollars worth of damage to their new house only days before they moved in. But not George W. Bush. Against advice from many aides, Bush didn't expose their childish acts; rather, he shielded them and covered up the entire matter. Then, "The new president invited Mrs. Clinton to ride with him on *Air Force One* to attend John Cardinal O'Connor's funeral in New York in July, 2001. In a curious act of solidarity between exclusive members of the presidential club, Bush and Clinton sat side-by-side for the entire flight. 'He sat next to her both ways,' Representative Vito Fossella told WABC Radio."[1296]

Did Bush chastise the former first lady or chew her out for doing so much damage to the White House? Hardly. The only thing other passengers saw was "Bush schmoozing Mrs. Clinton as the two sat together for hours."[1297] How cozy.

Do you get it? Hillary and Bush are on the same team as George Bush Sr. and Bill Clinton. Look at it this way. All four attended Yale University.

But while the Bushes were members of the ultra-secret Skull & Bones fraternity, Bill was cutting his teeth with Jesuits and the Cecil Rhodes-spawned Oxford Round Table (i.e. Rhodes Scholars). Although they have different names and approaches, they're still globalists nonetheless, with the same goals and the same world vision. That's why George W. and Hillary were so buddy-buddy on *Air Force One*, and why Bush the elder and Bill Clinton are so close —- they're all in bed together.

To further illustrate this point, let's go back in time to square one—to little Bubba's earliest days. "The seduction and indoctrination of Bill Clinton began as a boy, when he was first chosen by Masonic recruiters because of his blood and family ties to certain conspiratorial forces."[1298]

Yes indeed, Bill Clinton was a Mason. By his own admission he writes in *My Life*, "Besides music, my major extracurricular interest from ninth grade on was the Order of DeMolay, a boys' organization sponsored by the Masons."[1299]

He continued, "I enjoyed the camaraderie, memorizing all the parts of the rituals, moving up the offices to be master counselor of my local chapter, and going to state conventions."[1300]

Finally, he ties it all in to his lifelong aspirations and career. "I learned more about politics by participating in the state DeMolay election, though I never ran myself."[1301]

His mother validates these statements in her autobiography. "Bill seemed to do all right. He kept himself incredibly busy during his high school career. He was active in DeMolay."[1302]

CHAPTER TEN

These accounts aren't conspiracy theory; they came directly from the Clintons themselves. Strangely enough, years later Bill Clinton began something called the "Governor's School" during his gubernatorial career in Arkansas. In 1991, while welcoming new students, Clinton boasted, "The Governor's School is one of my proudest achievements."[1303]

But what was the Governor's School? According to author, radio show host, and filmmaker Texe Marrs, "the gifted teenage boys and girls—the cream of Arkansas high schoolers—had been recruited from across the state. They were made to feel special, elitist, superior to the common rabble outside the Governor's School. They were told they were the 'chosen ones' who would revolutionize the world and overturn despised traditional values."[1304]

Do such sentiments sound eerily similar to the elitist Skull & Bonesmen and Rhodes Scholars? Of course once Bill Clinton got a taste of the "initiated" life of Freemasonry, he didn't stop there. After graduating high school, he next spring-boarded to "Georgetown University, a Catholic Jesuit school where Clinton's Illuminati mentor was . . . Professor Carroll J. Quigley."[1305]

This academic legend, author of the pivotal book *Tragedy and Hope*, who died in 1977, was so influential to Clinton that when delivering his 1992 acceptance speech at the Democratic National Convention in New York City, Clinton declared, "As a teenager I heard John Kennedy's summons to citizenship. And then, as a student at Georgetown, *I heard that call clarified by a professor named Carroll Quigley.*"[1306]

Note: "Quigley was the only one of his tutors mentioned in Clinton's acceptance speech."[1307]

Clinton uttered these words for one reason. They were "addressed to the hidden men who intend to rule over us, the monied czars and potentates of the Secret Brotherhood."[1308]

What, you may wonder, did Carroll Quigley advocate? Try this passage on for size (all the while recalling Hillary Clinton's infamous plea for a *reconstruction of society*):

The individual's freedom and choice will be controlled within very narrow alternatives—by the fact that he will be numbered from birth . . . and followed as a number through his educational training—his required military or other public service—his tax contributions—his health and medical requirements—and his final retirement and death benefits.[1309]

From the cradle to the grave—a national ID card (or an implanted microchip) . . . universal socialist health care—increased taxation, and the state as a be-all and end-all of society. "Quigley was Bill Clinton's mentor."[1310]

Another Quigley dictum was as follows: "Anyone who believes in such things as traditional values, simple absolutes and national sovereignty represents 'a revolt of the ignorant against the informed and educated.' Such people are 'unbelievably ignorant and misinformed.'"[1311]

According to Quigley, if you don't believe as they do, you're an imbecile and enemy of the state. What type of society did he and others such as billionaire banker Cecil Rhodes envision? There would be "nothing less than a world system of financial control in private hands able to dominate the political system of each country and the economy of the world as a whole. This system will be controlled in a feudalistic fashion by the central banks of the world acting in concert."[1312]

Do you have nightmare visions of Orwell's Big Brother looming over each city glaring down angrily at his ant-like citizens? This dystopic vision was precisely the invective being sent when Bill Clinton referred to the professor during his acceptance speech. "Just the mention of Quigley's name sent a clear message to America—indeed the world's banking community. He was telling bankers everywhere that, if elected, he'd carry out the economic theories of the renowned economist and professor of history at the Foreign Service School of Georgetown University."[1313]

CHAPTER TEN

Carroll Quigley knew who the secret rulers were, and so do Bill and Hillary Clinton. As former British Prime Minister Benjamin Disraeli once warned, "The world is governed by very different personages from what is imagined by those who are not behind the scenes."[1314]

The professor's influence didn't end with his lectures at Georgetown. "Under Quigley's direction, Clinton became a Rhodes Scholar."[1315]

Get this: according to fellow student Harold Snider, "Dr. Quigley encouraged us both [he and Bill Clinton] to go to England to do graduate work. I know that he wrote letters of recommendation for both of us and was very proud and pleased that we both went on to study at Oxford. Dr. Quigley was our mentor and friend. He left an indelible impression on our lives."[1316]

Quigley wasn't the only influential public figure to guide Clinton's career toward Oxford. While working for Arkansas's most famous senator in Washington DC, "Bill had asked his boss, Senator Fulbright, to recommend him for the Rhodes scholarship. Fulbright himself had been a Rhodes Scholar many years earlier, and Bill still believes Fulbright's support was crucial to his acceptance for the honor."[1317]

The intricacies of this arrangement are important to know. Clinton "had been working for two years on the Senate Foreign Relations staff,"[1318] and Fulbright was the powerful chairman of this committee. It was Fulbright who "had encouraged Clinton to apply for the coveted scholarship and had intervened to help assure Clinton was named as one."[1319]

There is another interesting figure that entered the picture— one that would later be intricately connected to Bill and Hillary. When Senator Fulbright was running for reelection in Arkansas, "[Jim] McDougal assigned Clinton to the post of Fulbright's driver."[1320]

At the time, "McDougal was something of a political kingmaker in Arkansas,"[1321] and they were known to chat with Fulbright in the Senate dining room. Lastly, one other twist emerges which years later brought Hillary into the mix. Specifically, "two of the senior partners [at the Rose Law Firm], William Nash and J. Gaston Williamson, were Rhodes Scholars, and Gaston had served on the committee that had selected Bill for the Rhodes scholarship."[1322]

As we noted earlier, Rose was an extremely powerful law firm, and Hillary's employment (and later partnership there) was integral in helping her rise to power. Other partners were Vince Foster, Webb Hubbell, and William Kennedy III; all to later become a part of the Clinton cabinet, while their involvement in Mena and ADFA money laundering cannot be ignored or plausibly denied. In all, we see a sequence of events unfold with young Bill Clinton: via Senator Fulbright, Jim McDougal, Professor Quigley, and influential Rose Law Firm partners—all leading to his admission as a Rhodes Scholar at Oxford.

Obviously, some very powerful individuals wanted the budding politician to make his journey to England, but why does Clinton's entry into Oxford matter?

What follows is a brief overview of this institution's founder. "Cecil Rhodes, a close associate of the Rothschilds and other international bankers, made a vast fortune feverishly exploiting South Africa, [then] established the Rhodes fund to finance the education of bright young men who had the potential to help bring about a new world order."[1323]

At the same time, "Rhodes and his One World associates also established a secret society known as the Round Table Group. Some years later it evolved into the Royal Institute of International Affairs (RIIA) in the U.K. and the Council on Foreign Relations (CFR) in the U.S. Dr. Quigley makes it abundantly clear that the CFR is merely a branch of the RIIA."[1324]

These luminaries—bankers and international board members—are the ones who run the world, and "at Oxford, he [Bill Clinton] received special training in the One World ideology espoused by Rhodes."[1325]

Now do you see why it was so important to push Bill Clinton along his career path? Quite a number of extraordinary people had

CHAPTER TEN

a lot riding on him.

"At Oxford, Clinton and those Rhodes Scholars who would be his co-conspirators became confirmed collectivists."[1326]

This seemingly minor—even obscure—point is crucial because there are two distinctions in the world today:

1) Individuals versus collectivists
2) Nationalists versus globalists

Bill and Hillary are of the collectivist mindset which dictates that the state supersedes the individual: select elitists should mold and reconfigure society according to their "vision." Consider this example. When Hillary Clinton wrote her book, *It Takes a Village*, "the Village—HRC's cozy synonym for the state—moves in: 'the village must act in the place of parents, it accepts those responsibilities in all our names through the authority we vest in the government.'"[1327]

This simple passage embodies the spirit of collectivism—the state runs the show while individuals are reduced to insignificant, essentially powerless, parts of the whole.

Despite their Georgetown, Oxford, and Yale educations, Bill and Hillary still didn't completely "get it," especially after relocating to Arkansas, where Bill Clinton (a) made his name in a failed Senate run, (b) became Attorney General, then (c) was elected as one of the nation's youngest governors ever. But after a single term in office, the powers-that-be weren't happy that Bill and Hillary had ideas of their own and weren't bowing to their demands.

So, they booted him from office to teach him an important lesson. Without delving into all the reasons why they were displeased, when Bill Clinton ran for reelection in 1980, the Arkansas elite hastily threw a candidate into the ring—Frank White—who eventually dethroned Bill and Hillary. Barbara Purdue, a gun-for-hire political operative, said, "Most people think it was a normal campaign. It wasn't. It was really put together at the last minute, maybe ninety days before the election."[1328]

The high rollers had to give the Clintons a reality check, even if it required some vote-scamming to do so. At the time, Bill Clinton was Arkansas's golden boy—the chosen one. Prior to the election, "the polls had him far ahead as late as mid-October, and no one— not even [Frank] White—believed Clinton would lose."[1329]

But the fix was in, and the flamboyant young governor took a mighty fall—one that devastated him. "Clinton was shocked. So was his staff. His appointees and supporters were shocked. Even Frank White was shocked."[1330]

Admittedly, "the voters *liked* Clinton, and were shocked that he lost. They had wanted to teach the young man a lesson, not kick him out of office."[1331]

I partially agree with the preceding assessment, but not completely. It wasn't the voters who removed Bill Clinton from office to teach him a lesson; it was the Arkansas elite who were incensed that Bill and Hillary brought in their own cabinet members and didn't follow *their* dictates. The loss literally crushed Bill Clinton. "It was a death watch. 'Here was this young, star governor, and you could see the returns coming in and that he wasn't going to win,' [Mack] McLarty said."[1332]

The blow was so humiliating that "McLarty saw the glimmer of a teardrop on his cheek."[1333]

What made the defeat even more bitter was the fact that Arkansas had been notorious for stuffed ballot boxes and rigged elections. It is almost a certainty that Clinton was a victim of such a scam. "NBC declared him the winner, which was even more painful. Ted Kennedy called him to congratulate him."[1334]

But something happened, and reality ultimately dawned on the Clintons. "In simpler Arkansas terms, he'd just learned that the big boys run the state."[1335]

Here is where we get to the crux issue which transformed the Clintons, who had been selected at an early age for the fast track. Bill, particularly, was bestowed with a stellar education (Georgetown, Oxford, Yale), and then thrust into the limelight. Hillary was his handler, and she too quickly benefited with a $100,000 payoff (via her cattle futures trading). Bill was first attorney general; then governor. But there was a problem. They didn't give back to their controllers in return. The Clintons had their own ideas; and the only way they'd learn was via a crushing defeat.

The 1980 gubernatorial loss was *the most important event ever in Bill and Hillary's lives.* "'This was the moment when Bill lost his guts,' said a colleague from earlier campaigns. 'From there on, he'd do whatever necessary to get elected and stay elected. He made his deal with the devil.'"[1336]

That decision was the key to everything. I'm sure somewhere in the interim after his loss, some of the power brokers sat down with Bill and Hillary and said, 'Look, we recruited you into the CIA, gave you money, and made you governor. Now, do you want to drift away into obscurity, or play the game?' This pact with the dark side not only led to Bill Clinton's reelection, but also to cocaine trafficking with George Bush, Sr. at Mena, ADFA money laundering, embezzlement, Dixie Mafia murders, and a general life of evil and criminality. In addition, after his gubernatorial loss and ensuing deal with the occult-oriented globalists, Bill Clinton set out on a massive cocaine binge with his brother Roger, as well as rampant whore-mongering that was reckless beyond words. Obviously, the weight of his decision overwhelmed Clinton, and the way he dealt with it nearly killed him.

On the other hand, Hillary was reminded of one of her father's sayings. "Don't ever forget two things about the establishment: it hates change, and it will always protect its prerogatives."[1337]

Those in the upper echelon of power didn't select Bill and Hillary because they liked them. Things don't work that way. Instead, they wanted them to implement their policies and directives. It's that simple. Thus, with Hillary in control, the Clintons did a 180 degree turn and bowed to their financial masters. "Badly shaken by his 1980 upset and determined never to offend corporate power again, Clinton let the word go forth: the high and the mighty had a man they could trust in the governor's mansion in Little Rock."[1338]

After Clinton was reelected in 1982, "the high and mighty responded in appropriate fashion. Money flowed south from Wall Street, from the big securities firms, banks and investment houses: Merrill Lynch, Goldman, Sachs & Co., Drexel Burnham, Citicorp, Morgan Stanley, Prudential Bache."[1339]

The cold, bitter truth is apparent: by selling their souls and literally becoming enslaved to their overlords, buckets of cash were bestowed upon the Clintons. Charles Lewis, director of the Center for Public Integrity, laid it all out. "These people—the big law firms, the associations, the big corporate lobbyists—are the permanent ruling class here. And they are guys who always back both horses."[1340]

When the Clintons didn't respond correctly to the moneyed interests, they were defeated and set back a notch. The only way to bounce back was to sell out completely. Look at it this way. Hillary was supposedly a radical leftist, yet after their 1980 defeat, guess what happened. "'Hillary was always very, very comfortable as the Democrats went right,' an old friend would say. 'She had sold out corporate and yuppie as fast as any Washington lawyer.'"[1341]

After falling in 1980, the only thing Bill and Hillary believed in was self-preservation and climbing the political ladder (and even that ideal wasn't defined in their own terms, but by those who pulled their strings). "Principles" was merely a word that didn't matter a hill of beans in comparison to the deal that had been brokered. Idealistic concepts were a thing of the past; reality now involved illegal drug trafficking, dirty money, and killing those who got in the way of the controllers' objectives. The Clintons had joined the mob, and there was no turning back.

Naturally, many others have played a similar game, including the Bushes. Some won, while those who didn't pan out were knocked down a notch (or worse). If Bill and Hillary were to attain the White House, certain obstacles along the way had to be eliminated. One of them was a former golden boy, establishment superstar, and CFR insider named Gary Hart. In 1988, Hart threw his hat into the presidential ring by vying for the Democratic nom-

CHAPTER TEN 323

ination. There was a problem, however: George Bush, Sr.—after running the dirty tricks operations during Reagan's two terms in office—was slated to be the victor in 1988. That was his reward.

So, Hart had to—figuratively—be run out of town. That's where Donna Rice enters the picture. While Bill Clinton was still an unknown adulterous governor in Arkansas, Gary Hart was a well-known adulterous senator running for the presidency. In other words, Hart's Achilles heel would be used to facilitate his downfall. The hit man in this scenario—similar to Richard Nixon's downfall—was ultimate insider Katherine Graham's corrupt newspaper. "The *Washington Post* put the Hart campaign on notice that it had been given a private detective's report purporting to show the candidate's involvement with yet another woman in Washington."[1342]

This thinly veiled threat occurred *after* Hart was photographed with Donna Rice aboard the *Monkey Business* yacht, and it effectively sank his presidential ambitions once and for all. "Less than a month after he had declared as the clear favorite, and only three days after the *Monkey Business* exposé, Hart withdrew."[1343]

The result was twofold. One, it opened the way for George Bush, Sr. to roundly trounce Democratic milquetoast candidate Michael Dukakis in 1988; and two, it took the edge off of the adultery issue for candidates in the future. Of course political figures had committed adultery for decades (even centuries), but the press had always covered up for them, including John F. Kennedy and Lyndon Johnson. So Gary Hart was the first big one that emerged full-blown in the media. Now, if Bill Clinton had decided to run in 1988, he might have been Gary Harted out of the race. But being as it was, he and Hillary had four more years to put their ducks in a row and better prepare themselves for the onslaught. At the time, though, according to one aide, "What happened to Gary Hart scared the hell out of him [Clinton]. He just pulled back and shivered like it had been him, and of course with the women it could have been."[1344]

There was one other factor which doomed Gary Hart. Although a member of the Council on Foreign Relations, he dared to expose the conspirators and their dirty deeds, especially in regard to the JFK assassination, Iran-Contra, and the CIA.

As a freshman senator he had been a key member of the celebrated Church committee investigating CIA abuses and specifically the agency's incessant links to organized crime. He had gone on to serve on the new Senate Intelligence Oversight Committee, where he continued to be known for advocating further investigation and exposure of the alliance between the mob and the U.S. intelligence community. Hart would be a vocal critic of CIA covert operations in general. A leading opponent of the Nicaraguan Contra war, the senator had barely escaped what he and others believed to be an assassination plot in 1983 when he flew into Managua at the time of an extraordinary CIA-sponsored Contra air strike against the capital.[1345]

At that point, Hart already seemed to be a marked man. But circumstances got even worse. The following years, "From 1984 to 1987, Hart was repeatedly on record voicing his skepticism about the official version of the assassination of President John F. Kennedy and promising that if elected president in 1988 he would order the opening of all CIA and other government files in question, looking in particular at the possible role of organized crime figures Santo Trafficante, John Rosselli, and Sam Giancana in the Kennedy murder—the last two of which had been killed during the Church Committee inquiry. By the mid-1980s, Hart was increasingly outspoken in exposing the sleaze factor in the Reagan administration, including the wider influence of the mob in Washington. According to someone familiar with a written record of the remark, Trafficante had said of Gary Hart, 'We need to get rid of the son of a bitch.'"[1346]

Ironically, Gary Hart was involved in much of what he attempted to expose, with some of it leading directly to his own brazen, extramarital activities. There was "evidence that Hart's fall was not what it seemed at the time. According to U.S. Customs sources, one part of the setting of the episode [with Donna Rice] had long been suspected of a role in drug running. Some of those

CHAPTER TEN 325

involved in Hart's Miami-Bimini weekend turned out to have links to organized crime and cocaine trafficking and, in spiraling circles beyond, to crime bosses of the Jewish and Italian syndicates, who in turn possessed ties to the U.S. intelligence committee dating back to the Bay of Pigs and earlier."[1347]

Obviously, Hart had entered the danger zone, and his fall from grace was not accidental. "Hart had been under surveillance by unknown parties for days and perhaps weeks before the weekend of March 27-29"[1348] and there had been great "detail about Hart's movements and phone records over the preceding period, intimate knowledge that should have prompted journalistic suspicion."[1349]

Gary Hart certainly wasn't Mr. Innocent, but at the same time—due to his desire to expose certain government figures with dirty hands—he was tailed, surveilled, and ultimately set-up as an adulterous senator who got caught with his hand in the cookie jar. His loss was Bill and Hillary's gain (as well as George Bush Sr., who escaped being fingered yet again for his involvement in the JFK assassination and Iran-Contra).

VERNON JORDAN & THE BILDERBERGERS

Quite possibly the primary handler during Bill and Hillary's long political career was veteran Bilderberg member Vernon Jordan. Previously I've outlined quite a number of instances where Jordan made his presence known in the Clintons' lives by introducing them to certain influential individuals, or interceding to save them from another skirmish. In fact, for years "Jordan [was] known far and wide as 'Washington's biggest fixer.'"[1350]

Throughout this section you will see how time after time Jordan appears on the scene to guarantee that the Clintons will be able to overcome certain bumps in the road. The first occurred after Bill Clinton lost his gubernatorial campaign in 1980. Voters said that one of the reasons they were displeased with him is because his wife refused to take his name, and instead retained Rodham as her surname. In Arkansas, this was a big no-no; and despite protests, admonitions, and advice from others, Hillary adamantly refused to budge.

That is, until Vernon Jordan paid her a little visit in Little Rock. Unlike others who pled with Hillary or recounted all the reasons why she had to appease Arkansas voters, Jordan simply *told* her what to do, and not many people were able to accomplish such a task. "Early one morning she [Hillary] was cooking me and Bill grits, and I told her she had to start using her husband's name. She understood,"[1351] Jordan recalled. Hillary confirms this story in her memoir. This anecdotal tale may not seem like a big deal to some readers; but it was monumental because Hillary's resistance to the idea was completely nullified and rendered non-existent in light of Jordan's directive.

The next move involved a 1992 pre-election issue that would dog Bill Clinton for years into the future: his adulterous ways. Everyone realized that the media would inquire about his philandering, especially in light of the Gary Hart debacle. What many wanted was an admission on Clinton's part that he had in fact cheated on Hillary. A variety of options were debated in the Clinton camp, but a final decision wasn't made until Jordan gave his advice. "Clinton and Hillary left for dinner. When Clinton came back a few hours later, he told [Frank] Greer, 'Hell, I just had dinner with Vernon Jordan and Jordan said, screw 'em! Don't tell 'em anything!'"[1352]

His advice stuck, and soon their 'we've had difficulties' mantra was being repeated at every turn. No admissions, and no quarter—straight from Vernon Jordan.

Their strategy worked, and Bill and Hillary won the 1992 election over their teammate and fellow Mena cocaine trafficker, George Bush Sr. Once they achieved victory, the Clintons had to select a cabinet that would serve with them. Who do you suspect was an integral part of this process? While Bill and Hillary conveniently stayed out of the way in Little Rock, "the transition . . . was ostensibly run from Washington by Democratic lawyers Warren Christopher and Vernon Jordan."[1353]

This information is confirmed by another source, which like-

CHAPTER TEN

wise has the Clintons hidden away while the real power base handled the dirty work. "Much to the surprise of Democratic Party leaders, the Clintons decided not to move to Washington immediately. Instead, they would lay plans for the new administration from their home base in Little Rock, while Warren Christopher and Vernon Jordan, the official heads of the transition team, ran a small office in the nation's capital."[1354]

Naturally in the Clintons' helter-skelter world, problems arose; and when they did, Bill and Hillary habitually drifted into Vernon Jordan's orbit. After Vince Foster was murdered, the first couple traveled to Martha's Vineyard where "they spent time with old friends Vernon and Ann Jordan, William and Rose Styron, and *Washington Post* publisher Katharine Graham."[1355]

Also present was Jackie Onassis and Maurice Tempelsman. Of special note is the fact that Katharine Graham was present, for her newspaper did more to cover up Foster's murder than any other entity in the world.

Similarly, when Webster Hubbell found himself in hot water and had to resign in shame, two entities came to his rescue. One was James Riady, who funneled $100,000 to the former associate attorney general. "Another lucrative retainer for Hubbell had come from Revlon. It had been arranged by board member Vernon Jordan. In March 1994, just as Hubbell was resigning his post at Justice, White House Chief of Staff Mack McLarty made notes of people who should be contacted to help Hubbell find employment. Jordan's name was on the list. The following month, Jordan had personally escorted Hubbell to New York to be introduced to top officials of the international cosmetics firm. The retainer had netted Hubbell $62,775."[1356]

Vernon Jordan was 'the Man'—fixer, handler, and accomplice. His status was so visible that "it was the first time in history that a president of the United States publicly stated that his best friend was an African-American."[1357]

Curiously, very few Clinton researchers have made this vital link, especially to the highly influential Bilderberg group.

Before examining this shadowy organization, however, we first need to go back in time to an event which magnified Jordan's direct influence over the Clintons as their director of operations. The media circus was eventually boiled down to one word: MONICA, and the Clintons were certainly in a world of trouble. As we pointed out earlier, the entire Monica scandal was released for public consumption because of a growing furor in the black community over the murder of Ron Brown.

Without reiterating the entire Monica saga, I'll instead show how Jordan repeatedly injected himself into this affair. After being served subpoena papers, Monica immediately phoned Vernon Jordan, who "invited her over, calmed her down, and said he was going to find her a lawyer."[1358]

For starters, why would a lowly intern even have the phone number of one of the most powerful men in the world? The answer is simple: "Both [Bill] Clinton and [secretary Betty] Currie called him on Lewinsky's behalf, something they had never done for any former aide, much less a former intern."[1359]

Jordan also admitted that he "assisted her in trying to find employment in the private sector in New York City."[1360]

If their contact was merely limited to legal help and employment, it could be overlooked. But Jordan stepped so far over the line in terms of legality that he should have been imprisoned alongside the Clintons. On January 13, 1998, Monica Lewinsky met Linda Tripp at the Ritz-Carlton, where Tripp was wearing a wire for the FBI. During the course of their conversation, Monica (who did not know she was being monitored) admitted that "Vernon Jordan had told her, 'It doesn't matter what anybody says [about her affair with Bill Clinton], you just deny it. As long as you say it didn't happen, then it didn't happen.'"[1361]

Not surprisingly, Bill Clinton gave Monica almost the exact same advice. By tampering with this witness, "both Clinton and Jordan could be charged with subornation of perjury (i.e. encouraging someone else to commit perjury), and obstruction of justice. Each of these three charges: perjury, subornation of perjury, and obstruction of justice in a civil lawsuit, is considered a felony and is punishable by up to five or ten years in prison."[1362]

Obviously, Vernon Jordan—one of the "protected class"—was never jailed, nor were Bill and Hillary Clinton, even though they were instrumental in the murder of Ron Brown, which forced them to release the Monica monster in the first place. But the entire debacle was an orchestrated charade, as can be evidenced from the following passage. After the media popped with every sordid detail of Monica's affair with President Clinton, Hillary was purportedly forlorn, morose, and deep in the throes of depression (or so we were told). In reality, nothing could be further from the truth. Reminiscent of Bill Clinton laughing and joking at Ron Brown's funeral, then immediately shedding a crocodile tear when the cameras were turned on; Hillary used the same technique during her "days of darkness."

On the flight from Andrews Air Force Base to Martha's Vineyard, Hillary was in a jovial mood, laughing and joking with Chelsea all the way. However, the moment *Air Force One* touched down at Edgartown airport, where TV cameras were waiting to record the embattled first family, Hillary turned into a different person. When she emerged from the plane, she was wearing a pair of dark sunglasses and the grim-faced expression of the Wronged Woman.[1363]

The entire scenario was nothing more than a fake drama . . . a ruse . . . political theater . . . and who was waiting for Hillary? You guessed it. "At the foot of the ramp, she received a consoling bear hug from Vernon Jordan, who was both a FOH (Friend of Hillary) and a FOB (Friend of Bill). The towering, handsome Jordan was frequently photographed riding with Bill Clinton in the presidential golf cart, puffing on a cigar and laughing at the President's off-color jokes."[1364]

Vernon Jordan was their fixer; the man who designed, orchestrated, and coordinated the Monica Lewinsky affair to save Bill and Hillary's presidency.

Where did Jordan obtain such clout? Essentially, his status was derived from being a perennial member of the most influential organization on earth—the Bilderbergers. What precisely is this cabal that seems to wield such control over the political events of our world? "The Bilderbergers are a group of powerful men and women—many of them European royalty—who meet in secret each year to discuss the issues of the day. Many suspicious researchers claim they conspire to manufacture and manage world events."[1365]

Although the Bilderbergers "still have no official name, [they] have been identified with the Bilderberg Hotel in Oosterbeek, Holland, where it was first discovered by the public in 1954. Its meeting in February, 1957 on Saint Simons Island near Jekyll Island, Georgia, was the first on U.S. soil."[1366]

More historical background: "The official creation of this highly secret organization came about in the early 1950s following unofficial meetings between members of Europe's elite in the 1940s. They included European foreign ministers, Holland's Prince Bernhard, and Polish socialist Dr. Joseph Hieronim Reitinger."[1367]

Further, "the primary impetus for the Bilderberg meetings came from Dutch Prince Bernhard, [who] was a former member of the Nazi Schutzstaffel (SS) and an employee of Germany's I.G. Farben in Paris. In 1937 he married Princess Juliana of the Netherlands and became a major shareholder and officer in Dutch Shell Oil, along with Britain's Lord Victor Rothschild. After the Germans invaded Holland, the royal couple moved to London. It was here, after the war, that Rothschild and Reitinger encouraged Prince Bernhard to create the Bilderberg group."[1368]

Whenever one mentions the Rothschild family, you know you're now discussing the absolute highest corridors of power on the globe. The Rothschilds, more than any other entity, wield greater control over world politics and economics—via their international banking cartel—than most people can imagine. Also in attendance each year is another luminary. "Close at hand will always be David Rockefeller [former chairman of the Chase Manhattan Bank] representing his family and especially Standard Oil of

New Jersey, one of the largest corporate structures in existence."[1369]

When world events transpire, these families invariably have an unseen hand shaping them.

Whether one believes in such a *conspiratorial* view of our existence is one's prerogative; but nonetheless, there are many honest, hard-working journalists that have done enough research to determine that the Bilderbergers "are above government. They dictate terms and run the world the way the Bilderberg brain trust decides it should be."[1370]

They are, in essence, "a classic example of [Professor Carroll] Quigley's global establishment in action."[1371][1371]

One investigator has even gone so far as to say that the annual Bilderberg conference is "an international master planning conclave."[1372]

How, you may wonder, does any of this clandestine intrigue affect Bill and Hillary Clinton? Well, let's put the matter into perspective. In early 1991, how many people in this country had even *heard of* Bill or Hillary Clinton? Hardly anyone. Yet "how did this unknown governor of a small, mostly rural state suddenly vault to the top even though his past is clouded with *proven* allegations of adultery, military draft dodging, and other counts of moral turpitude? [Was] someone—or some group—lurking in the shadows pulling his strings?"[1373]

Indeed, this analysis is correct, for as we've outlined exhaustively throughout this trilogy, there have always been forces at work guiding the Clintons, even before being indoctrinated into the CIA during their college years. One of the most dramatic parallels is with the Bush family, especially George Sr., who has been a constant companion to Bill and Hillary. "Clinton always had more in common with Bush than he let on. Granted, he ran against Bush as an outsider. But where Bush was once a card-carrying member of the Council on Foreign Relations and the Trilateral Commission, Clinton notched these two plus the dreaded Bilderberg group."[1374]

Consider: Bill Clinton has ties to Freemasonry, the Dixie Mafia, the Hot Springs underworld, CIA, Jesuits, Rhodes Scholars, the Yale elite, CFR, and the Trilateral Commission. In addition, guess who else belonged to the Bilderbergers: his mentors, Senator William Fulbright and Vernon Jordan. Bill Clinton is, without a doubt, "strictly a made guy."[1375]

As I've said, an arrangement was made quite some time ago that the line of succession after Jimmy Carter would be: Bush-Clinton-Bush-Clinton (assuming that George Bush, Sr. ran the covert operations under Ronald Reagan). So yes, "Bush had been a longtime member of the Trilateral Commission, which has interlocking leadership with Bilderberg. Clinton had been a Trilateralist for seven years and was promoted to Bilderberg in 1991. Thus, the world shadow government owned both presidential candidates [1992] in a typical win-win race."[1376] [Note: the Trilateral Commission was founded by David Rockefeller and Zbigniew Brzezinski in 1973, and was instrumental in filling slots in Jimmy Carter's cabinet after his election in 1976.]

The Bush-Clinton lock is so strong that it even affected the 2000 election. At the 1999 Portugal meeting, "Bilderberg leaders expressed confidence in retaining control of the White House. They noted that the likely Republican nominee, Governor George W. Bush of Texas, was the son of former President and Trilateralist George H. W. Bush. 'His father has talked to him,' one said. But what about [his opponent] Vice President Al Gore, the likely Democratic nominee? '*His* father [Clinton] has talked to him,' the Bilderberg man repeated with a confident chuckle."[1377][1377]

Is it clear? George Bush Sr. paved the way for Bill Clinton, and Bill Clinton spoke with Al Gore and had him bow down to George W. Bush after the Florida vote-rigging escapade. Plus, we showed a little earlier how chummy George W. was with Hillary, so the Bush-Clinton-Bush-Clinton succession is rolling along according to schedule. George Bush Sr. deliberately created a climate where Bill Clinton could win (Read My Lips: No New Taxes), while his son is creating a similar climate in which Hillary can emerge victorious

CHAPTER TEN

(Iraq scandal, illegal immigration, gasoline price gouging, GOP sex scandals, etc). Of course the Bilderbergers have quite a lot to do with each of the above situations.

Anyway, in 1991 the stage was set to have Bill Clinton emerge as our nation's next leader. The only problem was: nobody had ever heard of him. Sure, he gave a bumbling speech at the 1988 Democratic National Convention and appeared shortly thereafter on *The Tonight Show* with Johnny Carson; but overall, he was an unknown entity. Yet the powers-that-be "arranged for him to attend the 1991 Bilderberg meeting in Europe and to become a presidential candidate. Within months Clinton became president."[1378]

Such a process did not occur by accident. Rather, "it was the Bilderbergers who, in 1991 at their secretive meeting in Baden Baden, Germany, put the final stamp of approval on Clinton's try for the Oval Office."[1379]

It also didn't hurt that Bill and Hillary Clinton, along with their Dixie Mafia cohorts, were George Bush's hands-on operatives monitoring the Mena drug running network in Arkansas, as well as the money laundering and wet work (i.e. killing those who got in the way). "Clinton's hidden mentors were apparently well pleased with his performance in the governor's mansion; following a close relationship with the CFR and Trilateral Commission—and a visit to the 1991 Bilderberg meeting in Baden Baden, Germany—Clinton got the insiders' nod as a Democratic presidential candidate in 1992. It is amazing what membership in such elitist One World clubs can do for one's political image and career!"[1380]

Bottom line: Bill Clinton got "in the Oval Office for the simple reason that the powers-that-be wanted him there."[1381]

The secrecy of his trip to 1991's Bilderberg meeting should be some indication as to how guarded these individuals are. Bill Clinton was set to "board a plane to Washington DC to catch a transatlantic flight to Germany. He was weighted down by two large suitcases and flanked by two husky, uniformed, state troopers, his bodyguards, who helped him board the plane, but did not accompany him on the flight. 'How odd,' onlookers remarked. No one could remember when Clinton had traveled abroad without his omnipresent Arkansas State Police bodyguards. He was traveling solo now because his agenda was *top secret*."[1382]

Let's draw to a momentary halt at this point and ask a question. We know the Bilderberg meetings are very hush-hush, so just anybody doesn't get asked to attend. So how did this unknown governor from Arkansas make the list? "The invitation was tendered by Vernon E. Jordan."[1383] Yet again, Vernon Jordan injected himself into the Clintons' lives; a move which ultimately led them to the White House.

Remarkably, the Arkansas and national press were not notified of Clinton's secretive trip to Germany, nor were they aware (at least at the time) of where he went *after* leaving the Bilderberg meeting. His office later reported, "The governor has left the Bilderberg Conference in Germany and gone to the Soviet Union, where he was invited to meet Ambassador John Matlock, Jr. in Moscow."[1384]

What do we have here: another secret jaunt to Russia, similar to the one he took while attending Oxford University? How did this trip come about? Not surprisingly, it was arranged by another globalist. "The invitation to visit Moscow was tendered by Mrs. Ester Coopersmith (a Washington DC philanthropist and former U.S. Representative to the United Nations during Jimmy Carter's administration)."[1385]

During his visit, Clinton "was introduced to Soviet Interior Minister Vadim Bakatin"[1386] who would later be "appointed to head the former Soviet Union's dreaded secret police [i.e. the KGB]."[1387]

Oddly, none of this information regarding the Bilderberg meeting or his conference with the future head of Russia's version of the CIA ever emerged in the American mainstream media.

Clinton eventually returned to Arkansas—still a virtually unknown governor from an obscure Southern state—yet less than a year-and-a-half later he would be elected as the 42nd president of the United States. The phenomenon was simply astounding; but once Bill and Hillary were in office, what type of legislation did the power elite push them into passing? The answer boils down to one acronym: NAFTA.

The North American Free Trade Agreement epitomizes what the globalists want our world to become—a planet where corporate trade reigns supreme with no borders, national sovereignty, or standardized currencies. In time, NAFTA would lead to GATT (General Agreement on Tariffs and Trade), CAFTA (Central American Free Trade Agreement), the North American Union (modeled after the EU), and the NAFTA superhighway. The groundwork for NAFTA was laid during the Bush administration, but its Senate passage would be precarious under a Republican president. The reason why is obvious. Democrats would protest that George Bush Sr. was only looking out for Big Business and trying to undermine the unions. So, to overcome this obstacle, the globalists placed a *Democrat* in the Oval Office who could schmooze the liberals and union leaders. Their ploy was successful; NAFTA passed in 1993.

To accomplish this feat, the Clintons and their internationalist pals weren't above fear-mongering and other subversive techniques. "The administration offered hush-hush CIA briefings for members of Congress on the dire consequences in Mexico and the rest of Latin America if the trade agreement was rejected."[1388]

I suppose those were the same arguments used for the Contra War a decade earlier: if America didn't step up to the plate, communism would sweep across the border and we'd fall like dominoes (a la communism in Vietnam).

When Bill Clinton ultimately signed the NAFTA bill on September 14, 1993, he made the following comments. Please take note of the final sentence. "In an imperfect world, we have something which will enable us to go forward together and create a future that is worthy of our children and grandchildren, worthy of the legacy of America, and consistent with what we did at the end of World War II. We have to do that again. We have to create a new world economy."[1389]

Did he mean a new world economy; or a *new world order?* George Bush Sr. used the exact same phrase—*New World Order*—

numerous times during his presidency, and now Bill Clinton followed suit. Afterward, Bilderberg Bill was supported by the three globalist puppets who preceded him: "Ex-presidents Ford, Carter, and Bush."[1390]

Gerald Ford had been a member of Allen Dulles' CIA cover-up Warren Commission, as well as a one-time Bilderberg attendee himself. Jimmy Carter was a paltry creation of David Rockefeller and Zbigniew Brzezinski, while his cabinet was teeming with Trilateral Commission members. Finally, George Bush Sr. was Mr. Insider: a Trilateral Commission and CFR member and former CIA director. All three of these stooges "conveyed an urgency for approval of the [NAFTA] treaty."[1391]

NAFTA turned out to be a disaster for the United States on so many levels that I can't even begin to broach the subject at this moment. Rather, let's move on to one last issue. Some people may see the connection of Bill Clinton to the other globalists listed above, but what if they said: at least Hillary's not a Bilderberger.

Well, if anyone made such a statement, they'd be flat out wrong because "Hillary Clinton attended in 1997, becoming the first American first lady to do so. Thereafter, talk steadily grew concerning her future role in politics."[1392] This information is confirmed by veteran Bilderberg researcher Jim Tucker, who wrote about Hillary's attendance at the Lake Lanier, Georgia conference. "Mrs. Clinton's presence was kept off even Bilderberg's own 'confidential, not for circulation' list of participants. But her presence was confirmed [to Tucker] at the Lake Lanier Islands, Ga. meeting site. In Washington, the White House reluctantly confirmed her presence, although the mainstream press obeyed orders not to report the fact."[1393]

So, Bill Clinton attended the 1991 Bilderberg conference, and in 1992 was elected president. In 1997, Hillary attended, and in 2000 she was elected to the U.S. Senate. These two are globalists through-and-through, and the Rothschild-Rockefeller-led Bilderbergers are the power behind their throne.

CHAPTER TEN

60 MINUTES & ROSS PEROT

Considering that Bill and Hillary were dually involved in drug trafficking, money laundering, murder, adultery, government scams, and a host of other illegal acts, they needed a willing accomplice to assist them in their ascent toward the White House. They found an ally to *aid and abet* them in the U.S. corporate media—the same corporate luminaries who attend the annual Bilderberg meetings. Without their explicit consent, the Clintons would have been exposed decades ago, and eventually imprisoned for their crimes.

One of those individuals closest to Bill Clinton was his fellow classmate, Strobe Talbott. "Strobe is an old schoolmate and personal friend of Bill Clinton. Not only are they both Rhodes Scholars and Oxford classmates, they lived together while being schooled in England."[1394]

Eventually, Talbot became editor-at-large for *Time* magazine, and performed an extremely valuable service for the Clintons while serving in this capacity. After Iran-Contra operative Terry Reed wrote a book entitled *Compromised* about illegal drug running at Mena, who came to the Clintons' rescue? Strobe Talbott at *Time* magazine, who "published a smear article on Reed, ironically called *Anatomy of a Smear*, alleging that the whole story was a fabrication."[1395]

Talbot also stepped in during Clinton's draft dodging fiasco, writing in *Time* that Clinton's avoidance of the draft "should be interpreted to show a young man beginning to wrestle with his conscience."[1396]

Conscience! Does Talbot consider rampant deceit, nepotism, and blatant acts of betrayal *conscience*? Because of his service to Clinton, Talbott was "rewarded with the position of Ambassador-at-large to the former Soviet Union."[1397]

Coincidentally, Talbott was one of Clinton's cohorts during his secretive Moscow trip while a student at Oxford. Over time, one hand simply washed the other.

Interestingly, a *Time* magazine representative is usually in attendance every year at the annual Bilderberg meetings, as is a top representative from Katharine Graham's *Washington Post*. Likewise, another media staple was also included on the annual Bilderberg list. "*U.S. News & World Report* is owned by a strong Clinton supporter, media mogul Mort Zuckerman, while the *U.S. News* editor was none other than David Gergen, who was tapped to be Clinton's chief advisor."[1398]

Now do you see why so many of Bill and Hillary's crimes have gone by the wayside in the corporate media? Many of the TV and print giants are carefully positioned in the Bilderberg's hip pocket—ready to strike at whistleblowers while protecting those who are already bought, sold, and controlled.

There is no more fitting way to illustrate this notion than when Bill Clinton was in boiling hot water over allegations that he had an ongoing, twelve-year affair with lounge singer Gennifer Flowers. Sinking in the New Hampshire primary polls, snickered at in the national media (when his promiscuous ways were even mentioned), and running out of campaign funds, the possibility that Clinton's ship was sunk looked very real. That was until *60 Minutes* stepped in and saved the day.

Prior to delving into the specifics of this interview, it should be noted that the press—especially in Arkansas—had a long history of shielding Bill Clinton's criminal acts from the public. Sure, they'd criticize him about superficial issues; but when it came to damning, major league scandals, they were strictly sub rosa. "Neither Little Rock newspaper wrote about the alleged affairs. Small stories about the [Larry Nichols] lawsuit were buried in the *Arkansas Gazette* and the *Arkansas Democrat*. Both newspapers immediately sent out teams of reporters to investigate the charges. They came back with denials from all the women named. Nothing was ever printed."[1399]

When it came to drugs, "to push the issue to even more fanciful levels, after it was discovered that in fact he had smoked marijuana, the future president claimed that he had not inhaled."[1400]

The Arkansas press guffawed at this Pinocchio absurdity, yet

CHAPTER TEN

they completely buried any reference to the billions of dollars of cocaine that were openly being shipped into Mena—right in their own backyard—despite the fact that investigators were presenting them with reams of evidence of this illegal activity.

After Bill Clinton bombed at the 1988 Democratic National Convention on national TV, Johnny Carson and NBC came to his rescue to resuscitate his image. Following the show, "Harry Thomasson and Linda Bloodsworth-Thomasson, the creators and producers of the CBS shows *Designing Women* and *Evening Shade*, threw a party for the Clintons."[1401]

Likewise, after "the supermarket tabloid *Star* appeared on the stands with a report that Clinton had extramarital affairs with five women . . . the story was buried by the New Hampshire newspapers."[1402]

Even Hillary has been spared the glaring eye of what should be a watchdog press. During her tenure as the crooked first lady of Arkansas, "Hillary has had three narrow escapes during her political career. Her dealings in commodities [$100,000 windfall profits], the Whitewater real estate deal, and her legal representation of the Madison Bank at the Rose Law Firm all might easily have ruined her, and dragged Bill down as well."[1403]

But they didn't because the corporate media merely scratched the surface, accepted the Clintons' smokescreen, and let it rest.

It's obvious: "the press willingly overlooked Clinton's lies;"[1404] deceit perpetrated by a husband and wife where "no distinction exists between truth and lies within this administration [which] is solely rooted in [the] Clintons' guilt-free automatic lying."[1405]

Thus far we've seen CBS, NBC, *The Washington Post*, *U.S. News & World Report*, the Arkansas press, and the New Hampshire media all directly involved in covering up Clinton scandals.

The *coup de grace*, though, arrived with *60 Minutes*. The show was broadcast immediately following the 1992 Super Bowl to ensure maximum coverage and was conceived to "save the candidate's political reputation."[1406]

The reason for this telecast was apparent. According to famed producer Don Hewitt, "the Clintons came to us because they were in big trouble in New Hampshire. They were about to lose right there and they needed some first aid. They needed some bandaging. What they needed was a paramedic. So they came to us and we did it."[1407]

Here is how rigged the entire affair was. "The Clinton campaign staffers allegedly wrote the questions for [interviewer] Steve Kroft and he was not allowed to ask follow-up questions or stray from the script."[1408]

Thus, "on Sunday morning, January 26 [1992], security guards sealed off the third floor of the Boston Ritz-Carlton, where the *60 Minutes* interview was taped."[1409]

While Bill Clinton "looked like a scared kid"[1410] during the softball questioning, it was again Hillary the handler who stepped in at every juncture to save the day. Even more importantly, Don Hewitt of CBS News performed some video magic. "Hewitt's television team blatantly ignored the veracity of Gennifer Flower's testimony and 'doctored' the Clinton interview. Hewitt states, 'It was strong medicine the way I edited it, but he was a very sick candidate.' He actually credits his own skillful editing for putting Clinton's affair with Flowers to rest."[1411]

Hewitt even went so far as to "boast eagerly in an interview that he had 'saved' the Clinton presidency."[1412]

I'm not sure about you, but when did it become the responsibility of Big Media to save a candidate's election bid? Isn't the press supposed to be an impartial, neutral watchdog rather than a partisan lapdog? Of course we now know that the corporate media was massaged from the beginning by those who had a vested interest in seeing the Clintons appear on a national stage and assume political office at the highest levels. "William F. Buckley Jr.'s column on June 9, 1993 quoted liberal journalist and author Mickey Kaus as saying, 'the press saved Clinton during the campaign.'"[1413]

Sadly, in the controlled media, when it comes to government drug trafficking, money laundering, and state-sponsored political murders, these "issues are never addressed, investigated, or disproved, yet the people telling the story are *always* attacked. It appears the media are sending a more sinister message: if you are a victim of, or a witness to, government corruption involving the Clintons, then you better keep quiet or you'll be defending yourself against an unrelenting character assassination launched by the mainstream media."[1414]

Yes, when it comes to down-and-dirty truth on the nightly news, Bill Plante of CBS News once pushed through the veil and admitted, "It is not possible for us in the mainstream media to spell out the fraud that way, lest the American people get the right idea. It gets far too close to the way everything works, and what it's really all about."[1415]

Fraud and the way things work constitute a bitter reality, as another incredible story from the 1992 presidential election illustrates. Could it be that "President Bill Clinton and Ross Perot struck a deal in 1991 that initiated the billionaire industrialist's candidacy as a third-party spoiler to help the then-Arkansas governor unseat incumbent President George Bush?"[1416]

Is it possible that "Bill Clinton and Ross Perot had come to an understanding between them, that the flaky billionaire Texan would enter the 1992 presidential race as a third-party candidate to impede any likelihood that President George Bush would win re-election at the polls?"[1417]

Lastly, did there exist a "secret deal that Perot was essentially forced to make in June of 1992"[1418] which compelled him to pull out of the race; then jump back in?

According to former Arkansas Development Finance Authority employee Larry Nichols, who spoke with Arkansas State Police trooper Larry Patterson, a behind-the-scenes relationship did exist between Clinton and Perot. According to Nichols, "Until I had just recently spoken with Patterson, I only suspected that Clinton and Perot were cozy with each other. I had heard talk about a relationship they had, but there was nothing I could nail down. Patterson put everything in perspective and it made a great sense to me. He told me that Clinton and Perot met or talked to each other on the phone or face to face at least 50 times, from late September '91 until just before the November election the following year. Clinton met Perot in Dallas, in Little Rock, and other locales. Their get-togethers were clandestine. So far as Patterson could tell, they were in each other's company by themselves, so that's why, he believed, the story never got out. Patterson can also vouch for the fact that Clinton spoke on the phone from his office in the governor's mansion to Perot in Dallas, and that after the '92 Democratic convention in New York, which made Clinton the party's nominee, they met and spoke much more frequently."[1419]

Was it possible that a Clinton-Perot conspiracy existed? This information is damning beyond belief and further evidence that the 1992 U.S. presidential election was utterly and completely rigged. "The proofs of Clinton's ties with Perot are unmistakable. Shortly before Clinton announced his candidacy for the presidency on October 3, 1991, attorney Lloyd Cutler, a longtime friend who became Clinton's White House chief counsel after the election, went to Dallas for a dinner meeting with Ross Perot."[1420]

The following year, Perot's own son-in-law, Clay Mulford, identified the people who attended Perot's campaign meetings in Dallas between April and June 1992. They included "Ed Rollins and Hamilton Jordan, the famed campaign strategists called in by Perot to pick up the pace of his race for the Oval Office."[1421]

As well "Lloyd Cutler was at one."[1422]

The same Lloyd Cutler mentioned a little earlier? As former Maryland campaign director Lawrence Way stated, "There's the proof that Clinton and Perot had a deal going. What was President Clinton's future chief counsel doing at a campaign gathering for the third-party candidate?"[1423]

Indeed, what *was* he doing at this meeting? There are further ties between the Clintons and Perot, this time with their wives. "There's no question about the occasional encounters Perot's wife Margo had with First Lady Hillary Clinton in and about Dallas Presbyterian Hospital, where a building bearing Mrs. Perot's name has been in existence for several years. That is where abortions are performed and where Mrs. Clinton, an ardent pro-abortion advocate, had encounters with Mrs. Perot—as well as at another Dallas locale that harbors one more of the first lady's favorite ventures, a Planned Parenthood chapter in which Perot's wife serves as one of its most prominent advisers."[1424]

Obviously, Perot's role as a spoiler in the 1992 presidential race was successful, and Bill and Hillary eventually waltzed into the White House. But their connection with Perot didn't end there. For starters, "Perot played a large hand in first lady Hillary Rodham Clinton's efforts to craft the ill-fated health reform bill, which turned Clinton's first year in office into a debacle. Perot's name appears prominently on the advisory board for Hillary's now defunct task force, according to papers furnished by the National Archives in Washington, DC. The papers are headed, "Clinton White House Health Care Interdepartmental Working Group."[1425]

A copy of Perot's association with this group can be found "in a paper headed, 'the Diebold Institute Commission'"[1426] which has the title "Health Care Interdepartmental Working Group" atop the document, and "H. Ross Perot, chairman, the Perot Group"[1427] in its body. Ross Perot was a member of this health care commission—it's in black and white.

Would you like another link between the Clintons and Perots? In 1993, Bill Clinton appointed staunchly pro-abortionist Ruth Bader Ginsberg to the U.S. Supreme Court. It seems, coincidentally enough, that Ginsberg's husband, Martin, "a Harvard Law School graduate and noted tax attorney"[1428] "had been for many years Ross Perot's personal tax attorney and financial advisor."[1429]

In fact, "much of Perot's success in amassing his reported $2.5 billion fortune is readily attributed by many sources to Ginsberg's financial wizardry."[1430]

How does this intriguing tidbit of information affect the Clintons? It seems to many in the know that "Ruth Ginsberg's name was offered to Clinton by Perot himself."[1431]

In closing, Ross Perot has made a name for himself over the years as a fierce crusader for the rescue of prisoners of war from

Vietnam, as well as an opponent of illegal drug trafficking by the U.S. government. Yet Terry Reed, who we've mentioned many times before in this trilogy, wrote a book entitled *Compromised* which chronicled the import of vast amounts of cocaine from South America through Mena, Arkansas during the Iran-Contra operation. "The enterprise was sanctioned by President George Bush, operated by the CIA, and supervised by then-Governor Clinton, whose state received ten percent of the profits from the proceeds."[1432]

According to Terry Reed, he sent the manuscript to Perot. But instead of acting upon it and exposing this information to a nationwide audience, "Reed later claimed that Perot sent his manuscript to Clinton, and he was certain of that because, he said, the White House sought to have the book's publication stopped."[1433]

Politics certainly makes strange bedfellows, doesn't it?

THE CFR, TRILATERAL COMMISSION & GREENSPAN

Beginning with President Jimmy Carter, every administration up to the current one has been teeming with members of the Trilateral Commission. In addition, each cabinet since the early 1900s has also been packed with representatives of the Council on Foreign Relations, an adjunct of Cecil Rhodes' Round Table and the RIIA. These CFR and Trilateral loyalists—some of whom have also attended Bilderberg meetings—are avowed globalists and One Worlders who have more allegiance to their internationalist masters than to the sovereignty of their own nation.

The Clintons are no exception to this rule. "Bill Clinton is a member of the Trilateral Commission, whose chairman is David Rockefeller. The Commission was established in 1973 by David Rockefeller and his chief foreign policy advisor, Polish-born Zbigniew Brzezinski. The Trilateral Commission was set up in recognition of the fact that existing organizations such as the United Nations were moving too slowly towards the creation of a New World Order."[1434]

As we've already seen, the Arkansas governor was a made man

CHAPTER TEN

long before he ever ran for the presidency. "Clinton's ascendancy escalated when he was elected to the very selective Trilateral Commission in September of 1988. The ambitious Georgetown graduate was made a member of the Council of Foreign Relations in July of 1989. But it was not until he attended his first Bilderberg conference in 1991 in Baden Baden, Germany that Bill Clinton's political fortunes took an upward lunge."[1435]

Why was this event so important to his career? Because "it was decided there at Baden Baden that Clinton, then the unknown governor of the rural backwaters of Arkansas, would be given all the money and media attention necessary for electoral success. Only a year and a few months later, William Jefferson Clinton was sworn in as President of the United States of America."[1436]

Some people not familiar with the founders of these groups may wonder: how do they affect my life? In his influential book, *The Technetronic Era*, Brzezinski advocates the "gradual appearance of a more controlled and directed society. Such a society would be dominated by an elite . . . unrestrained by the restraints of traditional values. This elite would not hesitate to achieve its political ends by using the latest modern techniques for influencing public opinion and keeping society under close surveillance and control."[1437]

Brzezinski's mentor stood in full support of these views. "It is obvious that [David] Rockefeller wholeheartedly approves of Brzezinski's future plans for America. Five years after Brzezinski wrote the above words Rockefeller chose him to put together the Trilateral Commission. Such responsibilities go only to the most trusted confidants who operate on the same ideological wavelengths."[1438]

Being that Bill Clinton was a member of this unholy trinity (TC, CFR, Bilderberg), upon election, guess what happened. "Seventeen of his top nineteen cabinet officials were members of either the Trilateral Commission or the Council on Foreign Relations."[1439]

This selection process extended beyond his direct cabinet, however, as "practically all the top positions in the new administration had been given to members of the Council on Foreign Relations and the Trilateral Commission."[1440]

Rather than referring to these individuals in vague terms, let's take this opportunity to specifically name the appointed handlers who were in charge of advancing the goals of Bilderberg luminaries David Rockefeller, Zbigniew Brzezinski, and Vernon Jordan. They included: Harold "Master of Disaster" Ickes, Lloyd Cutler, David Gergen, Bruce Lindsey, Roger Altman, Mack McLarty, Lloyd Bentsen, and Warren Christopher. Of note is the fact that Mack McLarty was later linked to David Rockefeller in promoting the North American Union (a mirror of the European Union). Also, incredibly, David Gergen was an old crony of the Nixon, Reagan and Bush administrations; while Ickes has well-established ties to organized crime.

The above men can best be described as intermediaries, implementers, or conduits between the elite power brokers and Bill and Hillary. They were all "on board" philosophically with the internationalist agenda, and were put in place to ensure that *proper* globalist policies and policy makers were implemented.

So, let's review this situation. Residing atop the control pyramid are individuals such as the Rothschilds and Rockefellers, then directly below them people like Zbigniew Brzezinski and Vernon Jordan. Of course factored into this equation must also be the international corporations, intelligence agencies, and those heading global think tanks and trade organizations. Once Bill and Hillary were "selected," the above-named handlers were dispatched to choose their cabinet, etc.

But one last variable must be mentioned—one that if excluded would be a dramatic omission. After Bill Clinton was elected, Federal Reserve Chairman "[Alan] Greenspan went to Little Rock"[1441] to ensure that the Clintons were onboard with what the people who *really* run the world were doing—the bankers. To put this matter into perspective, the following passage is a real eye opener as to who was in control:

If you believe Bob Woodward of *The Washington Post*, it wasn't

CHAPTER TEN

until January 7, 1993, just 13 days before his inauguration, that Bill Clinton found out who really calls the shots. In his 1994 book, *The Agenda*, Woodward described a January strategy meeting in Little Rock where the president-elect was advised that a credible deficit-reduction plan was required in order to placate the bond market. "Clinton's face turned red with anger and disbelief. 'You mean to tell me that the success of the program and my re-election hinges on the Federal Reserve and a bunch of f***ing bond traders?' he responded in a half whisper."[1442]

In all honesty, I tend to disagree with Woodward's assessment that Bill Clinton was caught by surprise when Alan Greenspan laid down the law. Bill and Hillary had learned their lesson long ago in Arkansas as to who their masters were. They weren't under any illusions as to who pulled the strings and who held onto the reins of power. They were well aware that four entities ran the United States of America:

1) The Federal Reserve
2) The Council on Foreign Relations
3) The CIA
4) The NSA

The president and Congress are mere implementers of decisions made well above them on the food chain. Bill Clinton, being a member of the CFR, TC, and a Bilderberg attendee, as well as a clandestine CIA operative, would be quite cognizant of this hierarchy. Likewise, Hillary is also a member of the CFR and a Bilderberg member. Idealism was no longer a concept in their vocabulary. Rather, they were pragmatic puppets enslaved by a contract which they could not escape (except via death or imprisonment).

I could continue in this vein, but a perfect illustration of the Clintons' subservience to the Fed can be seen in a photograph of Alan Greenspan seated—by invitation—alongside Hillary Clinton at her husband's first State of the Union address.

Bill did the talking but, as the Chinese proverb so sagely puts it, a picture is worth a thousand words! That picture of Hillary Clinton, the most powerful woman on Earth, and Alan Greenspan, the world's top representative of banking and finance, side-by-side, in unison, burned an indelible image in the minds of millions of knowledgeable and perceptive Americans and, indeed, in the minds of thousands of astute foreign observers.[1443] The president (past, present, and future) was simply a marionette dancing in tune to music orchestrated by money men at the Fed.

ROCKEFELLER CONNECTION

Earlier in this book I wrote about how Bill Clinton would visit Governor Winthrop Rockefeller's mansion during breaks from college. Obviously, not every kid coming home for Christmas break has an opportunity to mingle with their state's governor, especially when it's a Rockefeller. Yet for Bill Clinton, it seemed doors such as these were routinely opened for him.

Take, for example, the night he met with Jimmy Carter, who was running for president at the time. During the campaign, Clinton had somehow failed to connect with the candidate, so his pal (and Rockefeller crony) Mack McLarty phoned Carter.

> Clinton was delighted to learn that McLarty had set up a meeting between them. He and Hillary boarded a small commuter airplane the same evening and flew to Little Rock. Upon their arrival, McLarty telephoned Carter's aide, Frank Moore.
> "Governor Carter has already gone to bed," Moore told him.
> "Frank, they're *here*. What are we going to do?"
> "Well, let me call him. It's not *that* late."
> Whereupon Moore "got Carter out of bed—it was ten o'clock at night—and Bill and Hillary went by and visited Jimmy Carter," McLarty said with a grin.[1444]

CHAPTER TEN

When this event occurred, Bill Clinton was merely the attorney general-elect of the second most backwater state in the union, yet the mention of his name gets the next president of the United States out of bed—a man who was mentored and coddled by Zbigniew Brzezinski and David Rockefeller! Such clout is unheard of, yet Bill and Hillary were already commanding such a presence. Why?

One clue can be found in a point we alluded to in the opening pages of this trilogy. With "a law degree in hand, [Bill] Clinton returned to Arkansas, a state that had been totally controlled for decades by the Rockefeller banking family. Indeed, it was Arkansas Governor Winthrop Rockefeller . . . who helped guide young Bill's career."[1445]

What precisely does this passage mean? Without becoming too conspiratorial, why would the Rockefellers focus so much attention on the nobody son of an alcoholic, abusive stepfather and a promiscuous mother whose supposed *real* father was purportedly killed in an automobile accident before he was born? Of all the millions of children born in every state across the nation, why was *this* kid selected from the very start to be the "chosen one"? The Rockefellers ran Arkansas (via the Stephens family), and thus their presence was well established there. On the other hand, Bill Clinton's mother was a floozy whose cover story about being impregnated by serviceman Bill Blythe doesn't add up. Then Blythe is conveniently killed in a one-car crash which, when viewed objectively, doesn't pan out with the facts. Eventually, this kid who was born in Hope had *every door imaginable* opened for him—all the way to the White House. He became a Mason, met John F. Kennedy, attended three of the most prestigious colleges in the world (Georgetown, Oxford, Yale), then was lavished with money galore while beginning a meteoric career in politics. The Rockefellers in Arkansas, a promiscuous mother, and a conveniently dead "real" father—are you beginning to connect the dots?

The reader can take from this scenario what "he chooses," but the key point to consider is: why was Bill Clinton selected to be placed on such a fast track of political success, and why were so many advantages bestowed upon him? This is a kid who very well could have wound up selling used cars all his life in Hot Springs, Arkansas; but instead, the golden ring was laid in his hand at every turn, with some of the most powerful people on the planet assisting him. How can that happen? By chance? Remember the Franklin D. Roosevelt adage—nothing happens in politics by accident. It if occurs, it was planned that way.

I could continue with more of the same, but instead I'll simply provide a few other interesting stories which shed some light on the Rockefeller mystique and how it affects Bill and Hillary Clinton. The first involves Bill's longtime mistress, Gennifer Flowers. Incredibly, she also has more than one *direct* link to the Rockefellers. Flowers wrote of her childhood, "Daddy was an airplane pilot who owned several airports in Arkansas. Winthrop Rockefeller kept some of his planes at those airports, and Daddy knew him quite well. Winthrop Rockefeller owned Petit Jean Mountain, where his house was located—Daddy would sometimes go to Petit Jean for special parties."[1446]

Special parties? What this sentence means is that Gennifer Flowers' father was connected. You don't attend Rockefeller functions if you're not a member of the club. So, similar to Bill Clinton being connected via his mobster Uncle Raymond, Flowers was also 'in the loop' and had access to this powerful family. Stranger still, Flowers eventually worked for the governor. She says, "In the course of working for that campaign, I wound up meeting Winthrop Rockefeller, Jr., and he started asking me out."[1447]

Consider this scenario. Gennifer Flowers' father is connected, while Bill Clinton's uncle is in like Flynn with the Dixie Mafia. Along the way, Winthrop Rockefeller Jr. asks Gennifer Flowers out; then Bill Clinton, a bona fide mobster, carries on a twelve-year affair with Gennifer Flowers, who at that point is nothing more than a mob moll.

Finally, after Clinton and Flowers split, she winds up marrying Finis Shellnut, who was a drug runner/mule for Seth Ward and

Dan Lasater—two key figures in the Mena cocaine operation. Coincidence?

Anyway, after Bill Clinton attends Georgetown, Oxford, and Yale, he returns to Arkansas where he "already had a close relationship with the White House, having run Carter's campaign in Arkansas in 1976."[1448]

Such a sequence of events is quite astounding, because anyone that researches Jimmy Carter's career knows that he was groomed since the early 1970s by Zbigniew Brzezinski and David Rockefeller, and that nearly his entire cabinet was filled with Trilateral Commission members. Plus, Jimmy Carter lived in Georgia, while Bill Clinton's home state was Arkansas—not exactly next door neighbors. With these variables in mind, we have to ask: "How did Jimmy Carter come to pick Bill Clinton as his presidential Arkansas state campaign manager? He was in Washington, DC for four years (*when Jimmy Carter was not*), then he was in England for two years, and New Haven, Connecticut for two more years."[1449]

In other words, their paths never crossed, and Bill Clinton had virtually no experience running a political campaign (except as an aide to George McGovern in 1972). Yet here he is, fresh out of college, and boom, he's appointed as the state campaign manager in a national presidential election! With no experience? Unheard of.

Hillary herself is no stranger to the Rockefeller sphere of influence. After George Bush, Sr. rolled over in 1992, allowing the Clintons to win the 1992 presidential election, Hillary received the following correspondence:

"I still cannot believe you won," Marc Tucker wrote to Hillary a few days after the election. "But utter delight that you did pervades all circles in which I move. I met last Wednesday in David Rockefeller's office with him, John Sculley, Dave Barram, and David Haselkorn. It was a great celebration. Both John and David R. were more expansive than I have ever seen them—literally radiating happiness. My own view and theirs is that the country has seized its last chance."[1450]

This passage is truly extraordinary. David Rockefeller—the ultimate American kingmaker—celebrated the Clintons' victory, radiated happiness, and was more expansive than his aide had ever seen him. Such a reaction is mind-boggling. Why would Rockefeller be so joyful? Answer: because the Clintons were set to do his bidding. Shortly after Bill and Hillary entered the White House, Tucker—on behalf of the National Committee on Education and the Economy—sent them a "single-spaced eighteen-page letter [which] laid out what he called 'a very large leap forward in terms of how to implement the agenda on which you and we have all been working.'"[1451]

What type of information did this memo contain? Although space does not permit me to delve into it at length, in essence the NCEE plan "was corporate fascism—a partnership between government and big business—to create a planned economy."[1452]

I don't know about you, but that description sure as hell sounds like the New World Order to me, especially when Tucker said of their plan, "Radical changes in attitudes, values and beliefs are required to move any combination of these agendas."[1453]

Do you recall when Hillary spoke of reshaping society and restructuring human beings? Could this Rockefeller agenda be part of that plan?

The Clintons, ultimately, were—and still are—nothing more than puppets. "The Rockefellers have controlled every incumbent President of the United States since Woodrow Wilson. Bill Clinton is no exception."[1454]

The Clintons are part of the Rockefeller outer circle, and even when they vacationed during their tenure at the White House, the Rockefeller influence was ever present. In August, 1995 while getting away to Jackson Hole, Wyoming; guess where they stayed. They "lodged at the sprawling home of Democratic Senator John D. Rockefeller III of West Virginia."[1455]

Plus, when Hillary ran for the Senate in 2000, "her top aide was Chief of Staff Tamera Luzzatto, a savvy Senate insider who had fifteen years of experience working for Senator Jay Rockefeller as his legislative director and chief of staff."[1456]

CHAPTER TEN

DUFFERS? Clinton and Jordan at a golf outing in the early 1990s.

So, even when branching out on her own, a Rockefeller insider was still there to "handle" her.

CONCLUSION

No other book has ever presented the sordid details of Hillary Clinton's life as exhaustively and comprehensively as the *Hillary (And Bill)* trilogy you have just completed. During the course of this series, we've examined the Clintons' amoral sex lives, the widespread criminal activities they've been involved in, and what happens to those who try to expose them (the notorious Body Count). In addition, we've recounted in great detail how the Clintons have worked hand-in-hand with George Bush Sr. in a variety of different illegal endeavors; most damning, of course, being their smoking gun cocaine trafficking at Mena, Arkansas.

Considering what type of soulless individual Hillary Clinton is, and how extensively she's betrayed and sold-out our country, how could our nation possibly have survived if she had perpetuated the presidential succession of Bush-Clinton-Bush-Clinton which was been designed by shadowy figures atop the international power control system? Hillary Clinton = U.S.A. R.I.P.

About the Author

VICTOR THORN FOUNDED SISYPHUS PRESS in the fall of 2000, and is the author of eight books, as well as 10 other chapbooks. He has published the works of numerous writers in the alternative media, and has also produced four CD-ROMs and DVDs, one of which is a five-disc collection which covers the John F. Kennedy Assassination (*Evidence of Revision*). Thorn is also the editor of four anthologies, and his political articles have appeared in various newspapers and magazines around the country.

One of his books, *The New World Order Exposed*, was translated and published in Japan in 2006, while *9-11 on Trial* has been republished by Progressive Press (Joshua Tree, Ca.), and was released in France coinciding with the fifth anniversary of 9-11.

He was also co-host of *The Victor Thorn Show* on the Reality Radio Network from 2002-2003.

In February, 2004 he and Lisa Guliani began WING TV (World Independent News Group), which was a daily Internet television and radio talk show which was viewed in over 100 countries worldwide.

Thorn has also made hundreds of radio and television appearances (including *Coast-to-Coast AM*, *The Lionel Show* on WOR 710, and Frank Whalen's *Frankly Speaking* on RBN), and did a weekly one-hour news update on Alex Merklinger's *Mysteries of the Mind*, while also appearing weekly on Vyzygoth's *From the Grassy Knoll* radio show.

Lastly, Thorn has been an avid political activist who spoke at the OKC Bombing 10th anniversary, as well as before the America First Party. He has also protested in six different states, not to mention in New York City on several occasions, and in front of the White House in Washington, D.C.

The WING TV website can be found at:
www.wingtv.net

Endnotes

CHAPTER ONE:
THE BOYS ON THE TRACKS

Arkancide

1. John Austin, *Rkansides* (Bloomington, 1st Books, 2000), p. ix
2. Mara Leveritt, *The Boys on the Tracks* (New York: St. Martin's Press, 1999), p. 322

Dr. Fahmy Malak

3. Richard Poe, *Hillary's Secret War* (Nashville: WND Books, 2004), p. 121
4. Michael Kellett, *The Murder of Vince Foster* (Columbia: CLS Publishers, 1995), p. 186
5. Patrick Matrisciana, *The Clinton Chronicles Book*, (Hemet: Jeremiah Books, 1994), p. 90
6. Leveritt, p. 28
7. Ambrose Evans-Pritchard, *The Secret Life of Bill Clinton* (Washington: Regnery Publishing, 1997), p. 265
8. Leveritt, p. 49
9. Matrisciana, p. 91
10. Richard Odom, *Circle of Death* (Lafayette: Huntington House Publishers, 1995), p. 200
11. Leveritt, p. 49
12. Ibid.
13. Odom, p. 202
14. Matrisciana, p. 92
15. Odom, p. 202
16. Matrisciana, p. 92
17. Ibid., pp. 91-2
18. Evans-Pritchard, p. 267
19. Leveritt, p. 65
20. Matrisciana, p. 90
21. George Carpozi, *Clinton Confidential* (Columbia: CLS Publishing, 1995), p. 145
22. Evans-Pritchard, p. 267
23. Austin, p. 16
24. Carpozi, p. 145
25. Kellett, p. 186
26. Matrisciana, p. 91
27. Austin, p. ix
28. Evans-Pritchard, p. 266
29. Meredith Oakley, *On the Make* (Washington: Regnery Publishing, 1994), p. 435
30. Evans-Pritchard, p. 266
31. Austin, p. 15
32. Kellett, p. 186
33. Matrisciana, p. 103
34. Ibid.
35. Carpozi, p. 144
36. Ibid.
37. Oakley, p. 435
38. Floyd Brown, *Slick Willie* (Annapolis: Annapolis-Washington Book Publishers, 1993), p. 45
39. Matrisciana, p. 102
40. Leveritt, p. 30
41. Ibid.
42. Ibid., p. 188
43. Evans-Pritchard, p. 266
44. Ibid.
45. Matrisciana, p. 103
46. Leveritt, pp. 140-1
47. Ibid., p. 187
48. Ibid.
49. Ibid.
50. Ibid., p. 141
51. David Bresnahan, *Damage Control* (Salt Lake City: Camden Court Publishers, 1997), p. 78
52. Leveritt, p. 194
53. Oakley, p. 435
54. Leveritt, p. 115
55. Carpozi, p. 136
56. Oakley, p. 435
57. Leveritt, p. 115
58. Ibid., p. 116
59. Ibid.
60. Carpozi, p. 136
61. Ibid., p. 138
62. Ibid.
63. Ibid.
64. Ibid.
65. Ibid.
66. Ibid.
67. Ibid.
68. Ibid., p. 139
69. Ibid.
70. ibid.
71. Evans-Pritchard, p. 266
72. Leveritt, p. 118
73. Ibid.
74. Matrisciana, p. 102
75. Ibid.
76. Carpozi, p. 141
77. Ibid.
78. Ibid.
79. Kevin H. Watson, *The Clinton Record* (Bellevue: Merril Press, 1996), p. 34
80. Matrisciana, p. 102
81. Carpozi, p. 136
82. Leveritt, p. 120

83. Oakley, pp. 437-8

Dan Harmon

84. Matrisciana, p. 100
85. Leveritt, p. 122
86. Jean Duffey, *The Mena Connection is Made*, May 29, 1997, p. 1
87. Odom, p. 203
88. Leveritt, p. 82
89. Ibid., p. 206
90. Matrisciana, p. 99
91. Ibid., p. 93
92. Evans-Pritchard, p. 257
93. Ibid., p. 258
94. Ibid., p. 259
95. Ibid., pp. 262-3
96. Matrisciana, p. 97
97. Evans-Pritchard, p. 263
98. Ibid.
99. Roger Morris, *Partners in Power* (Washington: Regnery Publishing, 1996), p. 459
100. Odom, p. 201
101. Leveritt, p. 84
102. Ibid., p. 66
103. Evans-Pritchard, p. 255
104. Duffey, p. 2
105. Ibid.
106. Leveritt, p. 199
107. Odom, p. 201
108. Ibid.
109. Evans-Pritchard, p. 270
110. Odom, p. 202
111. Evans-Pritchard, p. 264
112. Matrisciana, p. 98
113. Odom, p. 203
114. Ibid., p. 201
115. Austin, p. 17
116. Poe, p. 122
117. Leveritt, p. 321
118. Christopher Ruddy, *Vincent Foster: The Ruddy Investigation* (Tulsa: United Publishing, 1996), p. 142
119. Kristina Borjesson, *Into the Buzzsaw* (Amherst: Prometheus Books, 2002), p. 178
120. Matrisciana, p. 101
121. Evans-Pritchard, p. 268
122. Ibid., p. 273
123. Ibid., p. 274

Dixie Mafia: Murder, Inc.

124. Matrisciana, p. 93
125. Odom, p. 204
126. Evans-Pritchard, p. 269
127. Matrisciana, p. 94
128. Austin, p. 16
129. Matrisciana, p. 95
130. Odom, p. 205
131. Evans-Pritchard, p. 269
132. Sam Smith, *Arkansas Connections*, p. 16
133. Matrisciana, p.95
134. Smith, p. 16
135. Odom, p. 205
136. Austin, p. 17
137. Matrisciana, p. 94
138. Ibid., p. 95
139. Ibid.
140. Odom, p. 206
141. Leveritt, p. 296
142. Evans-Pritchard, p. 269
143. Bresnahan, p. 80
144. Ibid.
145. Ibid., p. 77
146. Ibid., p. 78

CHAPTER TWO:
MASSACRE AT WACO

Hell on Earth

147. Elizabeth Drew, *On the Edge* (New York: Simon & Schuster, 1994), p. 131
148. Ambrose Evans-Pritchard, *The Secret Life of Bill Clinton* (Washington: Regnery Publishing, 1997), p. xiv
149. Ibid.
150. Evans-Pritchard, p. xv
151. James Tabor & Eugene Gallagher, *Why Waco* (Berkeley: University of California Press, 1995), p. 3
152. Rodney Stich, *Defrauding America* (Alamo: Diablo Western Press, 1994), p. 480
153. Ibid.
154. Deborah Stone & Christopher Manion, *Slick Willie II* (Annapolis: Annapolis-Washington Book Publishers, 1994), p. 6
155. Ibid., p. 7
156. R. W. Bradford, *It Came From Arkansas* (Port Townsend: Liberty Publishing, 1993), p. 131
157. Tabor, Gallagher, p. 3
158. David Southwell & Sean Twist, *Conspiracy Files* (New York: Gramercy Books, 2004), p. 173
159. Stone, Manion, p. 6
160. Ibid.
161. Ibid.
162. Evans-Pritchard, p. xv
163. Southwell, Twist, p. 174
164. Richard Odom, *Circle of Death* (Lafayette: Huntington House Publishers, 1995), p. 192
165. Ibid., p. 57
166. Tabor, Gallagher, p. 19
167. Ibid.
168. Bradford, p. 153

169. Ibid., p. 152
170. Odom, p. 193
171. Ibid.
172. Ibid., p. 171
173. Michael Kellett, *The Murder of Vince Foster* (Columbia: CLS Publishers, 1995), p. 189
174. Kenn Thomas, *Parapolitics* (Kempton: Illinois, Adventures Unlimited Press, 2006), p. 184
175. Michael Kellett, *Phantoms of the World Stage* (Columbia: Maryland, Evidence First Publishing, 2006), p. 343
176. Kellett, *The Murder of Vince Foster*, p. 190

Police State

177. Odom, p. 194
178. Stone, Manion, p. 7
179. Mack White, *Waco, Vince Foster, and the Secret War*, October 24, 2000, p. 3
180. Bradford, p. 149
181. Dick Reavis, *The Ashes of Waco* (Syracuse: Syracuse University Press, 1995), p. 69
182. Ibid., p. 70
183. Ibid., p. 69
184. Ibid.
185. Ibid.
186. Bradford, p. 131
187. Ibid., p. 149
188. Odom, p. 177
189. Ibid., pp. 177-8
190. Ibid., p. 178
191. Bradford, p. 131
192. Reavis, p. 71
193. Ibid.
194. Odom, p. 178
195. David Limbaugh, *Absolute Power* (Washington: Regnery Publishing, 2001), p. 19
196. Kellett, *Phantoms of the World Stage*, p. 346
197. Bradford, p. 127
198. Stone, Manion, p. 7
199. Stich, p. 480
200. Bradford, p. 128
201. Ibid.
202. Kellett, *Phantoms of the World Stage*, pp. 350-1
203. Ibid., p. 253
204. Stone, Manion, p. 10
205. Ibid.
206. Bradford, p. 127
207. Ibid.
208. Evans-Pritchard, p. xvi
209. Stich, p. 481
210. Bradford, p. 154
211. Ibid., p. 155
212. Stone, Manion, pp. 8-9
213. Ibid., p. 8
214. Odom, p. 49
215. Stone, Manion, p. 9
216. Ibid.
217. Ibid.
218. Tabor, Gallagher, p. 2
219. Stich, p. 482

Hillary Clinton: Baby Killer

220. Stone, Manion, p. 7
221. Odom, p. 192
222. Ibid., p. 188
223. Ibid., p. 176
224. Ibid., p. 189
225. Ibid.
226. Ibid.
227. Ibid.
228. Ibid., p. 191
229. Ibid.
230. News Commentary, *Did Hillary Clinton Order Waco Assault*, Winter, 2001, pp. 1-2
231. Ibid., p. 2
232. Ibid., p. 3
233. Ibid.
234. Ibid.
235. Ibid., p. 2
236. White, p. 6
237. APFN, *Hillary Directed Waco*, February 10, 2001, p. 1
238. Ibid.

FBI & Delta Forces

239. White, p. 3
240. Ibid., p. 6
241. Ibid., p. 3
242. Kellett, *Phantoms of the World Stage*, p. 352
243. Ibid, p. 261

Motive

244. White, p. 4
245. Ibid., pp. 4-5
246. Odom, p. 174
247. Ibid.
248. Ibid., p. 193
249. Limbaugh, p. 13

Waco: A New Revelation

250. MGA Films, *Waco: A New Revelation*, 1999 – documentary
251. Kellett, *Phantoms of the World Stage*, p. 311
252. Ibid., p. 267
253. Ibid., p. 313
254. Ibid., p. 342
255. Ibid., p. 347

256. Ibid., p. 268
257. Ibid., p. 304
258. Ibid.
259. Ibid., p. 333
260. Ibid., p. 297
261. Ibid., p. 266
262. Ibid.
263. Ibid., p. 75
264. Ibid., p. 74
265. Limbaugh, p. 33

CHAPTER THREE:
THE MURDER OF VINCE FOSTER

Consensus Reality & Mainstream Media Cowardice

266. John Austin, *Rkansides* (Bloomington, 1st Books, 2000), p. 117
267. James B. Stewart, *Blood Sport* (New York: Touchstone Books, 1996), pp. 35
268. Ambrose Evans-Pritchard, *The Secret Life of Bill Clinton* (Washington: Regnery Publishing, 1997), p. 113
269. Ibid., pp. 113-4
270. Ibid., p. 116
271. Michael Kellett, *The Murder of Vince Foster* (Columbia: CLS Publishers, 1995), p. 116
272. Deborah Stone & Christopher Manion, *Slick Willie II* (Annapolis: Annapolis-Washington Book Publishers, 1994), p. 65
273. Christopher Ruddy & Carl Limbacher, *Bitter Legacy* (NewsMax: West Palm Beach, 2001), p. 144
274. Ibid.
275. Richard Poe, *Hillary's Secret War* (Nashville: WND Books, 2004), p. 100

The Arkansas Group

276. Kellett, p. 94
277. Gary Aldrich, *Unlimited Access*, (Washington: Regnery Publishing, 1998), p. 75
278. Austin, p. 22
279. Christopher Ruddy, *Vincent Foster: The Ruddy Investigation* (Tulsa: United Publishing, 1996), p. 106
280. Evans-Pritchard, p. 223
281. Ibid.
282. Ibid.
283. Kellett, p. 94
284. Ibid.
285. David Brock, *The Seduction of Hillary Rodham* (New York: Free Press Paperbacks, 1996), p. 390
286. Ibid.
287. Ibid.
288. John Harris, *The Survivor* (New York: Random House, 2005), p. 72

289. Kenn Thomas & Jim Keith, *The Octopus* (Portland: Feral House, 1996), p. 137
290. Brock, p. 390
291. Thomas, Keith, p. 137
292. Sander Hicks, *From Vince Foster to Venezuela*, p. 2
293. Evans-Pritchard, p. 226
294. Ibid.
295. Kellett, p. 126
296. Ibid., p. 127
297. Ibid.
298. Evans-Pritchard, p. 115
299. Ibid.
300. Ibid.
301. Ibid.
302. Ibid.
303. Ibid., p. 116
304. Ibid., p. 114
305. Stewart, p. 33
306. Kellett, p. 176
307. Stone, Manion, pp. 66-7
308. Ibid., p. 67
309. Stewart, p. 33

The Real Murderer Revealed

310. Roger Morris, *Partners in Power* (Washington: Regnery Publishing, 1996), p. xxi
311. Brock, p. 395
312. Kellett, p. 88
313. Ibid., p. 91
314. Stone, Manion, p. 61
315. Martin Gross, *The Great Whitewater Fiasco* (New York: Ballantine Books, 1994), p. 188
316. Kellett, p. 93
317. Uri Dowbenko, *Bushwhacked* (Pray: Conspiracy Digest, 2003), p. 97
318. Ibid., p. 96
319. Ruddy, p. 8
320. Jim Norman, *Fostergate* (Media Bypass, August 1995), p. 1
321. Ibid.
322. Jim Quinn, *Quinn Interview with Jim Norman* (Pittsburgh: WRRK, December 7, 1995), p. 3
323. Ibid.
324. Ibid.
325. Ibid.
326. Ibid.
327. Ibid.
328. Ibid.
329. Rodney Stich, *Defrauding America* (Alamo: Diablo Western Press, 1994), p. 573
330. Ibid.
331. Craig Roberts, *The Medusa File* (Tulsa: Consolidated Press International, 1997), pp. 354
332. Norman, p. 4

ENDNOTES

333. Ibid.
334. Ibid.
335. Roberts, p. 354
336. Devon Jackson, *Conspiranoia* (New York: Plume, 2000), p. 279
337. Quinn, p. 3
338. Roberts, p. 355
339. Norman, p. 1
340. Ibid.
341. Roberts, p. 356
342. Ibid., pp. 356-7
343. Ibid., p. 357
344. Michael Collins Piper, *The Judas Goats* (Washington: American Free Press, 2006), p. 236
345. Kellett, p. 209
346. Roberts, p. 357
347. Ibid.
348. Ibid.
349. Ibid.

No Malice or Forethought

350. Richard Franklin, *101 Peculiarities Surrounding the Death of Vince Foster*, # 95
351. Ibid., # 97
352. Kellett, p. 10
353. Ibid., p. 11
354. Franklin, # 96
355. Kellett, pp. 11-12
356. Ibid., p. 9

Another Semen Stain

357. L.D. Brown, *Crossfire* (San Diego: Black Forest Press, 1999), p. 64
358. Ibid., p. 160
359. Michael Isikoff, *Uncovering Clinton* (New York: Crown Publishers, 1999), p. 132
360. George Carpozi, *Clinton Confidential* (Columbia: CLS Publishing, 1995), p. 666
361. Kellett, p. 30
362. Ibid., p. 31
363. Ibid.
364. Ibid., p. 30
365. Isikoff, p. 132
366. Poe, p. 92
367. Kellett, p. 30
368. Austin, p. 123
369. Michael Kellett, *Phantoms of the World Stage* (Columbia: Maryland, Evidence First Publishing, 2006), p. 388
370. Austin, p. 123
371. Ibid.
372. Michael Kellett, *Phantoms of the World Stage*, p. 389
373. Ibid.
374. Ruddy, p. 135
375. Ibid., p. 7
376. Ibid., p. 136
377. Kellett, *The Murder of Vince Foster*, p. 208
378. Ruddy, p. 136
379. Ibid., p. 5
380. Ibid., p. 136
381. Ibid., p. 137
382. Evans-Pritchard, p. 193
383. Ruddy, p. 137
384. Kellett, *The Murder of Vince Foster*, p. 96
385. Ruddy, p. 169
386. Gross, p. 190
387. Morris, p. xxi
388. Barbara Olson, *Hell to Pay* (Washington: Regnery Publishing, 1999), p. 265
389. Ibid., p. 266
390. Ibid.
391. Austin, p. 122
392. Paul Fick, *The Dysfunctional President* (New York: Citadel Press, 1995), p. 176
393. Stewart, p. 395
394. Gross, p. 191
395. Christopher Andersen, *American Evita* (New York: William Morrow, 2004), p. 131
396. Ibid., p. 132

Fort Marcy Park

397. Ruddy, p. 169
398. Kellett, *The Murder of Vince Foster*, p. 12
399. Ruddy, p. 169
400. Kellett, *The Murder of Vince Foster*, p. 12
401. Ruddy, p. 169
402. Evans-Pritchard, p. 185
403. Ibid., p. 165
404. Ibid.
405. Ibid.
406. Kellett, *The Murder of Vince Foster*, pp. 11-12
407. Ibid., p. 13
408. Ibid.
409. Ibid., p. 14
410. Ibid.

Hoaxed Suicide

411. Ruddy, p. 20
412. Poe, p. 97
413. Ibid.
414. Ibid.
415. Ruddy, p. vii
416. Ibid., p. ix
417. Kellett, *The Murder of Vince Foster*, p. 44
418. Poe, p. 96
419. Patrick Matrisciana, *The Clinton Chronicles Book*, (Hemet: Jeremiah Books, 1994), p. 117

420. Kellett, *The Murder of Vince Foster*, p. 31
421. Franklin, # 85
422. Ibid.
423. Richard Odom, *Circle of Death* (Lafayette: Huntington House Publishers, 1995), p. 39
424. Ibid., p. 40
425. Evans-Pritchard, p. 134
426. Ibid.
427. Odom, p. 40
428. Evans-Pritchard, p. 125
429. Ruddy, p. viii
430. Aldrich, p. 77
431. Evans-Pritchard, p. 124
432. Ruddy, p. 138
433. Kellett, *The Murder of Vince Foster*, p. 131
434. Ruddy, p. 20
435. Austin, p. 124
436. Kellett, *The Murder of Vince Foster*, p. 147
437. Austin, p. 131
438. Ibid.
439. Ibid.
440. Ruddy, p. 5
441. Kellett, *The Murder of Vince Foster*, p. 42
442. Ruddy, p. x
443. Kellett, *The Murder of Vince Foster*, p. 22
444. Deborah Stone & Christopher Manion, *Slick Willie II* (Annapolis: Annapolis-Washington Book Publishers, 1994), p. 80
445. Odom, p. 39
446. Matrisciana, p. 128
447. Evans-Pritchard, p. 226
448. Matrisciana, p. 128
449. Ibid.
450. Evans-Pritchard, p. 210
451. Ibid., pp. 210-11
452. Matrisciana, p. 111
453. Ibid.
454. Ibid.
455. Poe, p. 96
456. Ruddy, p. 11
457. Matrisciana, p. 112
458. Ruddy, p. 12
459. Evans-Pritchard, p. 127
460. Stone, Manion, p. 79
461. Matrisciana, p. 108
462. Kellett, *The Murder of Vince Foster*, p. 51
463. Ibid., p. 45
464. Odom, p. 38
465. Matrisciana, p. 108
466. Evans-Pritchard, p. 133
467. Ibid.
468. Ruddy, p. viii
469. Ibid., p. 3
470. Gross, p. 190
471. Ibid.
472. Austin, p. 132
473. Stone, Manion, p. 79
474. Ibid.
475. Evans-Pritchard, p. 207
476. Odom, p. 40
477. Evans-Pritchard, p. 133
478. Ibid.
479. Kellett, *The Murder of Vince Foster*, p. 19
480. Ibid., p. 37
481. Ruddy, p. 47
482. Ibid.
483. Ruddy, p. ix
484. Evans-Pritchard, p. 131
485. Kellett, *The Murder of Vince Foster*, p. 114
486. Ibid., p. 115
487. Ibid., p. 57
488. Ruddy, p. x
489. Ibid., p. ix
490. Matrisciana, p. 111
491. Gross, p. 191
492. Kellett, *The Murder of Vince Foster*, p. 117
493. Evans-Pritchard, p. 144
494. Ibid., p. 136
495. Kellett, *The Murder of Vince Foster*, p. 50
496. Matrisciana, p. 125
497. Evans-Pritchard, p. 145
498. Austin, p. 138
499. Evans-Pritchard, p. 140
500. Ibid., p. 143
501. Ibid.
502. Matrisciana, p. 125
503. Ibid., p. 126
504. Kellett, *The Murder of Vince Foster*, p. 47
505. Ibid., p. 155
506. Austin, p. 117
507. Stewart, p. 396
508. Odom, p. 35
509. Evans-Pritchard, p. 123
510. Kellett, *The Murder of Vince Foster*, p. 156
511. Ibid.
512. Ibid., p. 157
513. Odom, p. 43
514. Ibid
515. Evans-Pritchard, p. 124
516. Poe, p. 104
517. Kellett, *The Murder of Vince Foster*, p. 161
518. Ibid., p. 248
519. Ibid.
520. Carpozi, p. 585
521. Ibid.
522. Kellett, *The Murder of Vince Foster*, p. 161
523. Kellett, *Phantoms of the World Stage*, p. 393
524. Poe, p. 104
525. Carpozi, p. 587
526. Poe, p. 104
527. Ibid.
528. Franklin, # 79

ENDNOTES

529. Ibid.
530. Poe, p. 105
531. Ibid.
532. Ibid.
533. Carpozi, p. 587

Murder at the White House

534. Barbara Olson, *The Final Days* (Washington: Regnery Publishing, 2001), p. 47
535. Craig Roberts, *The Medusa File* (Tulsa: Consolidated Press International, 1997), p. 358

Hillary's "Plumbers" Break In

536. Edward Klein, *The Truth About Hillary* (New York: Sentinel, 2005), p. 23
537. Odom, p. 23
538. Kellett, *The Murder of Vince Foster*, p. 63
539. Ibid.
540. Ibid.
541. Jack Cashill, *Ron Brown's Body* (Nashville: WND Books, 2004), p. 220
542. Kevin Watson, *The Clinton Record* (Bellevue, Washington, Merril Press, 1996), p. 84
543. Olson, *Hell to Pay*, p. 267
544. Klein, p. 23
545. Elizabeth Drew, *On the Edge* (New York: Simon & Schuster, 1994), p. 385
546. Stone, Manion, p. 80
547. Ruddy, p. 138
548. Evans-Pritchard, *The Secret Life of Bill Clinton*, pp. 196-7
549. Ibid., p. 196
550. Franklin, # 100
551. Drew, p. 384
552. Brock, p. 395
553. Joyce Milton, *The First Partner* (New York: Perennial, 1999), p. 299
554. Kellett, *The Murder of Vince Foster*, p. 101
555. Ibid.
556. Norman, p. 6
557. Gross, p. 194
558. Aldrich, p. 77
559. Evans-Pritchard, p. 197
560. Ibid.
561. Milton, p. 297
562. Austin, p. 128
563. Ruddy, p. 23
564. Milton, p. 298
565. Brock, p. 391
566. Ruddy, p. 22
567. Odom, p. 49
568. Ruddy, p. 22
569. Drew, p. 257
570. Olson, *Hell to Pay*, p. 267
571. Kellett, *The Murder of Vince Foster*, p. 119
572. Ibid., p. 62
573. Austin, p. 129
574. Kellett, *The Murder of Vince Foster*, p. 100
575. Ibid., p. 98
576. Ibid., p. 99
577. Olson, *Hell to Pay*, p. 268
578. Ibid.
579. Watson, p. 84
580. Gross, p. 195

The Fake Suicide Note

581. Kellett, *The Murder of Vince Foster*, p. 77
582. Ibid.
583. Austin, p. 133
584. Stone, Manion, p. 71
585. Ibid., p. 72
586. Kellett, *The Murder of Vince Foster*, p. 169
587. Ibid.
588. Stone, Manion, p. 71
589. Ibid.
590. Ibid., p. 72
591. Ibid., p. 73
592. Ruddy, p. 3
593. Stone, Manion, p. 68
594. Ibid.
595. Ibid., p. 72
596. Andersen, p. 132
597. Kellett, *The Murder of Vince Foster*, p. 171
598. Ibid., pp. 171-2
599. Ibid., 172
600. Ibid., p. 173

The Starr-Fiske Cover-up

601. Richard Poe, *Hillary's Secret War* (Nashville: WND Books, 2004), p. 102
602. Ibid.
603. Christopher Ruddy & Carl Limbacher, *Bitter Legacy* (West Palm Beach, NewsMax, 2001), p. 66
604. Poe, p. 103
605. Ibid.
606. Ibid.
607. Ibid.
608. Ibid.
609. Ibid.
610. David Bresnahan, *Damage Control* (Salt Lake City: Camden Court Publishers, 1997), p. 141
611. Poe, p. 103
612. Ibid.
613. Ibid.
614. Poe, p. 102
615. Evans-Pritchard, p. 113
616. Franklin, # 81
617. Ruddy, Limbacher, *Bitter Legacy*, p. 67

618. Odom, p. x
619. Kellett, *The Murder of Vince Foster*, p. 207
620. Ibid.
621. Ibid.
622. Austin, p. 135
623. Ibid.
624. Ibid.
625. Jim Quinn, *Quinn Interview with Jim Norman* (Pittsburgh: WRRK, December 7, 1995), p. 1
626. Ibid., p. 2
627. Hicks, p. 6
628. Franklin, # 84
629. Kellett, *The Murder of Vince Foster*, p. 77
630. Evans-Pritchard, p. 192
631. Aldrich, p. 75
632. Evans-Pritchard, p. 128
633. Ibid.
634. Ibid., p. 139
635. Matrisciana, p. 131
636. Ibid.
637. Evans-Pritchard, p. 143
638. Ibid., p. 140
639. Kellett, *The Murder of Vince Foster*, p. 40
640. Matrisciana, p. 116
641. Ibid.
642. Evans-Pritchard, p. 125
643. Ibid., p. 141
644. Ibid.
645. Matrisciana, p. 113
646. Ibid.
647. Ibid., p. 127
648. Ibid.
649. Evans-Pritchard, pp. 127-8
650. Franklin, # 101
651. Evans-Pritchard, p. 216
652. Ibid.
653. Ibid., p. 214
654. Ibid., p. 215
655. Ibid.
656. Ibid.
657. Austin, p. 134
658. Ibid.
659. Ibid.

CHAPTER FOUR:
THE MURDER OF JERRY PARKS

660. Ambrose Evans-Pritchard, *The Secret Life of Bill Clinton* (Washington: Regnery Publishing, 1997), p. 245
661. Patrick Matrisciana, *The Clinton Chronicles Book*, (Hemet: Jeremiah Books, 1994), p. 67
662. John Austin, *Rkansides* (Bloomington, 1st Books, 2000), p. 146
663. Christopher Ruddy & Carl Limbacher, *Bitter Legacy* (West Palm Beach, NewsMax, 2001), p. 151
664. Evans-Pritchard, p. 234
665. George Carpozi, *Clinton Confidential* (Columbia: CLS Publishing, 1995), p. 466
666. Matrisciana, p. 143
667. Ibid., p. 68
668. Ambrose Evans-Pritchard, *Foster Hired Detectives to Spy on Clinton* (London: Sunday Telegraph, October 6, 1996), p. 3
669. Evans-Pritchard, *The Secret Life of Bill Clinton*, p. 233
670. Ibid.
671. Ibid.
672. Carpozi, p. 465
673. Ibid.
674. Evans-Pritchard, *Foster Hired Detectives to Spy on Clinton*, p. 3
675. Carpozi, p. 465
676. Ibid.
677. Evans-Pritchard, *Foster Hired Detectives to Spy on Clinton*, p. 3
678. Carpozi, p. 465
679. Matrisciana, p. 78
680. Ibid., p. 69
681. Ibid.
682. Carpozi, p. 466
683. Evans-Pritchard, *The Secret Life of Bill Clinton*, p. 236
684. Ibid., p. 237
685. Ruddy, Limbacher, p. 156
686. Matrisciana, p. 74
687. Evans-Pritchard, *The Secret Life of Bill Clinton*, p. 236
688. Matrisciana, p. 71
689. Ibid., pp. 70-1
690. Ibid., p. 72
691. Evans-Pritchard, *The Secret Life of Bill Clinton*, p. 239
692. Ibid.
693. Austin, p. 43
694. Ibid.
695. Ibid.
696. Evans-Pritchard, *The Secret Life of Bill Clinton*, p. 246
697. Evans-Pritchard, *Foster Hired Detectives to Spy on Clinton*, p. 1
698. Ibid.
699. Sam Smith, *Arkansas Connections*, p. 7
700. Evans-Pritchard, *Foster Hired Detectives to Spy on Clinton*, p. 2
701. Matrisciana, pp. 74-5
702. Evans-Pritchard, *The Secret Life of Bill Clinton*, p. 245
703. Ibid., p. 247
704. Ibid.
705. Ibid., p. 246
706. Ibid., p. 247

ENDNOTES

707. Ambrose Evans-Pritchard, *Phone Call Rings Clinton Alarm Bells* (London: Sunday Telegraph, October 6, 1996), p. 2
708. Evans-Pritchard, *Foster Hired Detectives to Spy on Clinton*, p. 1
709. Ruddy, Limbacher, p. 155
710. Ibid.
711. Austin, p. 145
712. Ibid.
713. Evans-Pritchard, *The Secret Life of Bill Clinton*, p. 247
714. Austin, p. 146
715. Evans-Pritchard, *The Secret Life of Bill Clinton*, p. 247
716. Austin, p. 146
717. Evans-Pritchard, *The Secret Life of Bill Clinton*, p. 248
718. Richard Poe, *Hillary's Secret War* (Nashville: WND Books, 2004), p. 93
719. Austin, p. 44
720. Evans-Pritchard, *Phone Call Rings Clinton Alarm Bells*, p. 2
721. Richard Franklin, *101 Peculiarities Surrounding the Death of Vince Foster*, # 99
722. Evans-Pritchard, *The Secret Life of Bill Clinton*, p. 249
723. Evans-Pritchard, *Foster Hired Detectives to Spy on Clinton*, p. 3

CHAPTER FIVE:
OKLAHOMA CITY BOMBING

Bombs Inside the Alfred P. Murrah Building

724. OKBIC, *Final Report* (Oklahoma City: OKBIC, 2001), p. 171
725. Ambrose Evans-Pritchard, *The Secret Life of Bill Clinton* (Washington: Regnery Publishing, 1997), pp. 16-7
726. Ibid., p. 17
727. Ibid.
728. OKBIC, p. 277
729. Ibid.
730. Evans-Pritchard, p. 17
731. Ibid., p. 12
732. Ibid., p. 13
733. Ibid.
734. Ibid.
735. Ibid.
736. Ibid., p. 14
737. Russ Kick, *You Are Being Lied To* (New York: The Disinformation Company, 2001), p. 142
738. Ibid.
739. Ibid.
740. Ibid., p. 139
741. OKBIC, p. 171
742. Ibid., p. 175
743. Evans-Pritchard, p. 67
744. Ibid.
745. Ibid., p. 6
746. Ibid., p. 7
747. Ibid.
748. Ibid.
749. OKBIC, p. 175
750. Ibid.
751. Ibid., p. 178
752. Ibid.
753. Ibid., p. 179
754. Ibid.
755. Kick, p. 140
756. Ibid.
757. Ibid.
758. OKBIC, p. 187
759. Ibid.
760. Michael Kellett, *Phantoms of the World Stage* (Columbia: Maryland, Evidence First Publishing, 2006), p. 160
761. Ibid., pp. 81-2
762. Kick, p. 139
763. Ibid.
764. Ibid.
765. Ibid., p. 140
766. Ibid.
767. Ibid.
768. Ibid.
769. Ibid.
770. Ibid.
771. Kellett, p. 161
772. Kick, p. 140
773. Ibid., p. 141
774. Ibid.
775. Ibid.
776. Ibid.
777. Ibid.
778. Ibid.
779. Ibid.
780. Ibid.
781. Evans-Pritchard, p. 37
782. Ibid., p. 60
783. Ibid., p. 66
784. Ibid., p. 72
785. Ibid., p. 77
786. Kellett, p. 83
787. Ibid., p. 84
788. Ibid., p. 35

Elohim City Connection

789. Victor Thorn, *The OKC Bombing-Elohim City Connection* (State College, Pennsylvania: Sisyphus Press, 2005), pp. 3-38

Brigadier General Benton K. Partin Speaks Out

790. Kellett, p. 81
791. Lawrence Myers, *Why Did Bill Clinton's National Security Council Fund ATF "Experiments" in Building Home Made ANFO Truck Bombs in 1994?* (Media Bypass, November 1996), p. 1
792. Ibid.
793. Pat Shannan, *OKC Bombshell Implicates Feds in Murrah Blast* (Washington: American Free Press, January 7, 2004), p. 1
794. Ibid.
795. David Hoffman, *National Security Council Link in Oklahoma Bombing?* (*Washington Weekly*, February 3, 1997), p. 1

Collateral Damage

796. Craig Roberts, *The Medusa File* (Tulsa: Consolidated Press International, 1997), pp. 375
797. Jon Rappoport, *Oklahoma City Bombing* (Los Angeles: Blue Press, 1995), pp. 46-7
798. Ibid., p. 46
799. Kick, p. 142
800. Roberts, p. 375
801. Ibid., p. 373
802. Ibid., p. 375
803. Kick, p. 142

The Murder of Officer Terrence Yeakey

804. Pat Shannan, *Who Killed Terrence Yeakey?* APFN, p. 1
805. Ibid., p. 2
806. Officer.com *Don't You Ever Forget Terrence Yeakey*, p. 1
807. Shannan, p. 1
808. Ibid.
809. Ibid., p. 4
810. Ibid., p. 2
811. Ibid.

CHAPTER SIX:
THE MURDER OF RON BROWN

America Betrayed

812. Richard Poe, *Hillary's Secret War* (Nashville: WND Books, 2004), p. 80
813. Ibid.
814. Bob Momenteller, *Deep Inside the Clintonian Reich* (Ether Zone, November 1, 1998), p. 1
815. Edward Timperlake & Edward Triplett, *Year of the Rat* (Washington: Regnery Publishing, 1998), p. 218
816. Ibid., p. 42
817. Poe, pp. 162-3
818. Timperlake, Triplett, pp. 3-4
819. Ibid., p. 7
820. Christopher Ruddy & Carl Limbacher, *Bitter Legacy* (West Palm Beach, NewsMax, 2001), p. 83
821. Timperlake, Triplett, p. 4

The Riady Empire

822. Momenteller, p. 1
823. Timperlake, Triplett, p. 183
824. Joyce Milton, *The First Partner* (New York: Perennial, 1999), p. 364
825. Timperlake, Triplett, p. 8
826. Momenteller, p. 1
827. Ibid.
828. Timperlake, Triplett, p. 9
829. Ibid.
830. Momenteller, p. 1
831. Timperlake, Triplett, p. 9
832. Momenteller, p. 2
833. Ibid.
834. Ibid.
835. Timperlake, Triplett, p. 10
836. James Adams, *What's Up in Jakarta?* (The American Spectator, September 1995), p. 3
837. Ibid.
838. Momenteller, p. 2
839. Adams, p. 4
840. Timperlake, Triplett, p. 12
841. Ibid., p. 13
842. Ibid., pp. 13-4
843. Michael Kellett, *Phantoms of the World Stage* (Columbia: Maryland, Evidence First Publishing, 2006), p. 285

Hubbell, Huang, and Hillary's Treason

844. Byron York, *Hillary's Web.* (New York: National Review, July 26, 1999), p. 2
845. Ibid.
846. Timperlanke, Triplett, p. 10
847. Ibid., p. 36
848. Ibid., p. 38
849. Ibid., p. 39
850. Ibid., p. 40
851. Ibid.
852. Milton, p. 365
853. Ibid.
854. Timperlake, Triplett, p. 40
855. Ibid., p. 43
856. Ibid., p. 60
857. Ibid.
858. Ibid., p. 43
859. Ibid., p. 41
860. Ibid., p. 33
861. Ibid.

ENDNOTES

862. Milton, p. 367
863. Momenteller, p. 3
864. Ibid.
865. Ibid.
866. Amanda Carpenter, *The Vast Right-Wing Conspiracy's Dossier on Hillary Clinton* (Washington: Regnery Publishing, 2006), p. 15
867. Poe, p. 80
868. Ibid.
869. Timperlake, Triplett, p. 28
870. Ibid., pp. 28-9
871. Ibid., p. 30
872. Ibid., p. 234
873. Milton, p. 365
874. Ibid., p. 366
875. Timperlake, Triplett, p. 49
876. Ibid., p. 56
877. Ibid.
878. Milton, p. 366
879. Timperlake, Triplett, p. 57
880. Ibid.
881. Ibid., p. 234
882. Ibid., p. 50
883. Ibid., p. 28
884. Ibid., p. 29
885. Ibid., p. 14
886. Ibid., p. 15
887. Ibid., p. 235
888. Ibid., p. 110
889. Ibid., p. 111
890. Ibid., p. 108
891. Ibid., p. 107
892. Ibid., p. 215
893. Ibid.
894. Rich Lowry, *Legacy* (Washington: Regnery Publishing, 2003), p. 141
895. Ibid.
896. Timperlake, Triplett, p. 187
897. Ibid., p. 154
898. Ibid.

Dead Man Walking

899. Jack Cashill, *Ron Brown's Body* (Nashville: WND Books, 2004), p. vii
900. Ibid., p. 210
901. Ibid., p. 206
902. Milton, p. 368
903. Cashill, p. vii
904. Christopher Ruddy, *Arkansas' Murderous Ways* (Newsmax: October 22, 1998), p. 3
905. Poe, p. 161
906. Ibid.
907. Ruddy, Limbacher, p. 134
908. Ibid.
909. John Austin, *Rkansides* (Bloomington, 1st Books, 2000), p. 51
910. George Carpozi, *Clinton Confidential* (Columbia: CLS Publishing, 1995), p. 657
911. Cashill, p. 155
912. Poe, p. 165
913. Ibid.
914. Cashill, p. 147
915. Ibid.
916. Poe, p. 164
917. Ibid.
918. Ibid., p. 165
919. Ibid.
920. Cashill, p. 185
921. Ibid., p. 184
922. Ibid., p. 257
923. Ibid.
924. Ibid., p. 283
925. Ibid., p. 257
926. Poe, p. 166
927. Ibid.
928. Ibid.
929. Cashill, p. 185
930. Ibid.
931. Ibid., pp. 185-6
932. Austin, p. 52
933. Cashill, p. x
934. Ibid., p. 66
935. Ibid., p. 187
936. Ibid.
937. Ibid. p. ix
938. Ibid.
939. Ibid.
940. Ibid., p. 188
941. Ibid., p. 124
942. Ibid., p. 189
943. Ibid., p. 168
944. Ibid., p. 169
945. Ibid., p. 182
946. Ibid., p. 289
947. Ibid., p. 288
948. Ibid., p. 289
949. Ibid.
950. Ibid., p. 283
951. Ibid.
952. Devon Jackson, *Conspiranoia* (New York: Plume, 2000), p. 273
953. Ruddy, Limbacher, p. 133
954. Ibid., p. 132
955. Ibid., p. 134
956. Poe, p. 170
957. Ibid., pp. 170-1
958. Ibid., p. 171
959. Cashill, p. 242
960. Ibid.
961. Ibid., p. 243
962. Ibid.

Spoofing, Suicide, and Survivors

963. Cashill, p. 191
964. Ibid., p. 194
965. Ibid., p. 257
966. Hugh Sprunt, *The Third Man*, March, 1998, p. 3
967. Poe, p. 160
968. Ruddy, Limbacher, p. 135
969. Poe, p. 160
970. Cashill, p. 258
971. Ibid.
972. Ibid.
973. Ibid., p. 199
974. Sprunt, p. 3
975. Austin, p. 62
976. Cashill, p. 259
977. Ruddy, Limbacher, p. 135
978. Cashill, p. 271
979. Ibid., pp. 271-2
980. Ibid., p. 272
981. Ibid., p. 205
982. Ibid., p. 206
983. Ibid.
984. Poe, p. 161
985. Ibid.
986. Cashill, p. 273
987. Sprunt, p. 4
988. Carpozi, p. 660
989. Ibid., p. 661
990. Cashill, p. 207
991. Ibid., p. 273

A Lead Snowstorm

992. Poe, p. 159
993. Cashill, p. x
994. Ibid., p. 205
995. Sprunt, p. 3
996. Cashill, p. 204
997. Ibid., p. 241
998. Sprunt, pp. 3-4
999. Poe, p. 168
1000. Ibid., p. 167
1001. Ibid.
1002. Cashill, p. 204
1003. Poe, p. 167
1004. Cashill, p. 204
1005. Poe, p. 168
1006. Cashill, p. 212
1007. Poe, p. 168
1008. Cashill, p. 261
1009. Ibid., p. 241
1010. Ibid., p. 205

Cover-up Du jour

1011. Timperlake, Triplett, p. 32
1012. Ibid.
1013. Cashill, p. 198
1014. Ibid.
1015. Ibid., p. 247
1016. Austin, p. 65
1017. Cashill, p. 218
1018. Ibid., p. 219
1019. Ibid.
1020. Ibid.
1021. Ibid.
1022. Ibid.
1023. Ibid.
1024. Ibid.
1025. Ibid., p. 198
1026. Ibid., p. 290
1027. Austin, p. 62
1028. Sprunt, p. 3
1029. Austin, p. 59
1030. Ibid.
1031. Ibid.
1032. Sprunt, p. 3
1033. Cashill, p. 211
1034. Ibid.
1035. Ibid., p. 262
1036. Ibid., p. 237
1037. Ibid., p. 262
1038. Ibid., p. 238
1039. Ibid., p. 239
1040. Austin, p. 64
1041. Poe, p. 169

CHAPTER SEVEN:
THE MURDER OF DANNY CASOLARO

1042. C.D. Stelzer, *Danny's Dead*, 1996, p. 12
1043. David MacMichael, *The Mysterious Death of Danny Casolaro* (Covert Action Information Bulletin, Winter 1991), p. 2
1044. Stelzer, p. 2
1045. MacMichael, p. 1
1046. Ibid., pp. 9-10
1047. John Connolly, *Dead Right*, Spy Magazine, January 1993, p. 2
1048. Ibid.
1049. Stelzer, p. 14
1050. MacMichael, p. 11
1051. Ibid., p. 2
1052. Kenn Thomas & Jim Keith, *The Octopus* (Portland: Feral House, 1996), p. 1
1053. Danny Casolaro – Wikipedia, p. 5
1054. Ibid.
1055. Thomas, Keith, p. 3

1056. Wikipedia, p. 9
1057. Connolly, p. 6
1058. Wikipedia, p. 9
1059. Ibid., p. 10
1060. Ibid., p. 9
1061. MacMichael, p. 3
1062. Wikipedia, p. 10
1063. MacMichael, p. 3
1064. Ibid.
1065. Stelzer, p. 15
1066. Ibid., p. 12
1067. Thomas, Keith, p. 114
1068. Ibid., pp. 114-5
1069. Ibid., p. 115
1070. Daniel Hopsicker, *Barry & the Boys* (Eugene: Mad Cow Press, 2001), p. 6
1071. MacMichael, pp. 11-12
1072. Stelzer, p. 8
1073. James Ridgeway and Doug Vaughan (New York: *The Village Voice*, October 15, 1991), part 13
1074. Connolly, p. 1

CHAPTER EIGHT:
THE CLINTON BODY COUNT

120+ and Counting

1075. John Austin, *Rkansides* (Bloomington, 1st Books, 2000), p. 24
1076. Christopher Ruddy & Carl Limbacher, *Bitter Legacy* (West Palm Beach, NewsMax, 2001), p. 127
1077. Ibid.
1078. Ibid., p. 143
1079. Richard Poe, *Hillary's Secret War* (Nashville: WND Books, 2004), p. 91
1080. Patrick Matrisciana, *The Clinton Chronicles Book*, (Hemet: Jeremiah Books, 1994), p. 159
1081. Ruddy, Limbacher, p. 149
1082. Christopher Hitchens, *No One Left to Lie To* (London: Verso, 1999), p. 101

Read 'em and Weep

1083. Richard Odom, *Circle of Death* (Lafayette: Huntington House Publishers, 1995), p. 208
1084. Clinton Circle of Death website, p. 3
1085. Al Martin, *The Conspirators* (Pray: Montana, National Liberty Press, 2001), p. 15
1086. James Ridgeway, *Software to Die For* (New York: The Village Voice, September 24, 1991), p. 5
1087. Austin, p. 38
1088. Emerson Review, *Clinton Body Count* (Frederic, MI, February 8, 2007), p. 2
1089. Austin, p. 29
1090. Ibid., p. 38
1091. Odom, p. 208
1092. Austin, p. 104
1093. Odom, p. 208
1094. Austin, p. 109
1095. Odom, p. 208
1096. Ibid., p. 209
1097. Ibid.
1098. Austin, p. 111
1099. Odom, p. 209
1100. Emerson Review, p. 2
1101. Austin, p. 22
1102. Ibid., p. 72
1103. Ibid.
1104. Ibid., p. 71
1105. Emerson Review, p. 2
1106. Ibid.
1107. Ibid.
1108. Ibid.
1109. Ibid.
1110. Ibid.
1111. Ibid.
1112. Michael Kellett, *Phantoms of the World Stage* (Columbia, Maryland: Evidence First Publishing, 2006), p. 43
1113. Emerson Review, p. 2
1114. Ibid.
1115. Austin, p. 23
1116. Emerson Review, p. 2
1117. Austin, p. 98
1118. Emerson Review, p. 2
1119. Austin, p. 106
1120. Emerson Review, p. 2
1121. Ibid.
1122. Ibid.
1123. Ibid.
1124. Ibid.
1125. Austin, p. 101
1126. Emerson Review, p. 2
1127. Ibid.
1128. Ibid.
1129. Ibid.
1130. Austin, p. 23
1131. Ibid., pp. 95-6
1132. Ruddy, Limbacher, p. 140
1133. Ibid., p. 141
1134. Ibid.
1135. Ibid., pp. 141-2
1136. Ibid., p. 140
1137. Ibid., p. 142
1138. Kellett, p. 96
1139. Austin, p. 99
1140. Ibid., p. 110
1141. Kellett, p. 35
1142. Austin, p. 113
1143. Ruddy, Limbacher, p. 128
1144. Christopher Andersen, *American Evita* (New York: William Morrow, 2004), p. 158

1145. Ibid., p. 159
1146. Ibid., p. 180
1147. R. Emmett Tyrrell, *Boy Clinton* (Washington: Regnery Publishing, 1996), p. 141
1148. Ibid.
1149. Clinton Circle of Death website, p. 2
1150. Ibid., p. 3
1151. Ibid.
1152. Ibid.
1153. Ibid., pp. 3-4
1154. Ibid., p. 4
1155. Ibid. pp. 5-6
1156. Ibid., p. 8
1157. Ibid.
1158. Ibid.
1159. Kellett, p. 33
1160. Clinton Circle of Death website, p. 11
1161. Kellett, p. 33
1162. Clinton Circle of Death website, p. 15
1163. Ibid.
1164. Ibid., p. 16
1165. Ibid., p. 17
1166. Ibid.
1167. Ibid.
1168. Mike Blair, *Oklahoma City Bombing Witnesses Are Dying Fast* (Washington: Spotlight, May 19, 1997), p. 1
1169. Dead People Connected with Bill Clinton, p. 3
1170. Ibid., p. 2
1171. Arkancide Clinton Body Count Website
1172. Kellett, p. 67
1173. Ibid.
1174. Ibid., p. 68
1175. Arkancide Clinton Body Count webside
1176. Ibid.
1177. Ibid.
1178. Dead People Connected with Bill Clinton, p. 2
1179. Ibid., p. 3
1180. What Really Happened website
1181. Ibid.
1182. Joseph Farah, *The Clinton Body Count* (World Net Daily, September 24, 1998), p. 2
1183. Walter Lee, *Vicky Weaver*, p. 1
1184. David Hoffman, *The Death of an Oklahoma Bombing Witness*, p. 1
1185. Kellett, p. 88
1186. *The Oklahoma Bombing: Witnesses Allege Government's Prior Knowledge and Complicity*, p. 9
1187. Kellett, p. 88
1188. Michael O'Camb, *Unresolved Deaths in Oklahoma*, December 10, 2000, pp. 1-2
1189. Ibid.
1190. Ibid., p. 3
1191. Ibid.
1192. Andrew Gumbel, *The Unsolved Mystery of the Oklahoma City Bombing*, Truthdig, February 21, 2006, p. 2

1193. Kellett, pp. 85-6
1194. Ibid., p. 252
1195. Ibid., p. 251
1196. Ibid.
1197. Ibid., p. 89
1198. Ibid.
1199. Ibid.
1200. Ibid., p. 90
1201. Ibid., p. 85
1202. Ibid.
1203. David Bresnahan, *Damage Control* (Salt Lake City: Camden Court Publishers, 1997), p. 203
1204. Kellett, pp. 32-3
1205. Downside Legacy Research website, February 6, 2001
1206. Ibid.
1207. Ibid.
1208. Ibid.
1209. Ibid.
1210. Ibid.
1211. Kenn Thomas, *Parapolitics* (Kempton, Illinois, Adventures Unlimited Press, 2006), p. 185
1212. Bresnahan, p. 17

CHAPTER NINE:
PRESIDENTIAL PARDONS

Free the Criminals

1213. Emmett Tyrrell & Mark Davis, *Madame Hillary* (Washington: Regnery Publishing, 2004), p. 95
1214. Joe Klein, *The Natural* (New York: Sentinel, 2005), p. 204
1215. Barbara Olson, *The Final Days* (Washington: Regnery Publishing, 2001), p. 193
1216. Ibid., p. 7
1217. Ibid.
1218. Carl Limbacher, *Hillary's Scheme* (New York: Crown Forum, 2003), p. 224
1219. Olson, p. 123
1220. Ibid., p. 10
1221. Thomas D. Kuiper, *I've Always Been a Yankees Fan* (Los Angeles: World Ahead Publishing, 2006), p. 47
1222. Olson, p. 21
1223. Ibid., p. 161
1224. Jerry Oppenheimer, *State of a Union* (New York: Harper Collins, 2000), p. 276
1225. Ibid.
1226. Joyce Milton, *The First Partner* (New York: Perennial, 1999), p. 420
1227. Olson, p. 17
1228. Ibid., p. 18
1229. Milton, p. 420
1230. Olson, p. 18

ENDNOTES

1231. Oppenheimer, p. 276
1232. Olson, p. 16
1233. Ibid., p. 19
1234. Ibid., p. 162
1235. Ibid., p. 150
1236. Limbacher, p. 60
1237. Olson, p. 154
1238. Dick Morris, *Rewriting History* (New York: Regan Books, 2004), p. 171
1239. Ibid.
1240. Ibid., p. 172
1241. Olson, p. 153
1242. Tyrrell, Davis, p. 95
1243. Kuiper, p. 46
1244. Morris, p. 172
1245. Ibid., p. 173
1246. Olson, p. 181
1247. Morris, p. 173
1248. Olson, p. 153
1249. Ibid.
1250. Ibid., p. 181

Marc Rich

1251. Olson, p. 131
1252. Ibid., pp. 130-1
1253. Ibid., p. 131
1254. Ibid.
1255. American Conservative Union, *Hillary Rodham Clinton* (Ottawa: Green Hill Pub., 2005), pp. 48-9
1256. Klein, p. 204
1257. Olson, p. 202
1258. Ibid.
1259. Klein, p. 205
1260. Tyrrell, Davis, p. 95
1261. Klein, p. 205
1262. Morris, p. 244
1263. Olson, p. 128
1264. Ibid., p. 141
1265. Ibid., p. 8
1266. Ibid., p. 140
1267. Ibid., p. 141
1268. Christopher Andersen, *American Evita* (New York: William Morrow, 2004), p. 206
1269. Olson, p. 169
1270. Andersen, p. 206
1271. Kuiper, p. 46
1272. Ibid.

CHAPTER TEN:
POWER BEHIND THE THRONE

Free the Criminals

1273. Jim Marrs, *Rule by Secrecy* (New York: Perennial, 2000), 14
1274. Jonathan Kwitny, *The Crimes of Patriots* (New York: W. W. Norton & Company, 1987), p. back cover
1275. Peter Dale Scott, *Drugs, Oil, and War* (Lanham, Maryland: Rowman & Littlefield Publishers, 2003), p. 30
1276. Ibid.
1277. Ibid.
1278. Ibid.
1279. Ibid.
1280. Ibid.
1281. Ibid.
1282. Ibid., p. 31
1283. Marrs, p. 38
1284. Roger Morris, *Partners in Power* (Washington: Regnery Publishing, 1996), p. xviii
1285. Ibid.
1286. Joyce Milton, *The First Partner* (New York: Perennial, 1999), p. 81
1287. Morris, pp. xviii-xix
1288. Texe Marrs, *Big Sister is Watching You* (Austin: Living Truth Publishers, 1993), p. 56
1289. Hillary Clinton, *Living History* (New York: Scribner, 2003), p. 19
1290. Thomas D. Kuiper, *I've Always Been a Yankees Fan* (Los Angeles: World Ahead Publishing, 2006), p. 121
1291. Ibid., p. 78
1292. Ibid., p. 119
1293. Charles Allen & Jonathan Portis, *The Comeback Kid* (New York: Birch Lane Press, 1992), p. 213
1294. Ibid., p. 214
1295. Ibid., p. 215

Masons, Jesuits, and Rhodes Scholars

1296. Carl Limbacher, *Hillary's Scheme* (New York: Crown Forum, 2003), p. 63
1297. Ibid.
1298. Texe Marrs, *Circle of Intrigue* (Austin: Living Truth Publishers, 1995), p. 183
1299. Bill Clinton, *My Life* (New York: Alfred P. Knopf, 2004), p. 44
1300. Ibid., p. 45
1301. Ibid.
1302. Virginia Clinton Kelly, *Leading With My Heart* (New York: Pocket Star Books, 1994), p. 158
1303. Des Griffin, *Descent into Slavery* (Clackamas, Oregon: Emissary Publications, 1980), p. 301
1304. Ibid.
1305. Texe Marrs, *Circle of Intrigue*, p. 183
1306. Ibid., p. 184
1307. Des Griffin, *Fourth Reich of the Rich* (Clackamas, Oregon: Emissary Publications, 1976), p. 111
1308. Texe Marrs, *Circle of Intrigue*, p. 184

1309. Texe Marrs, *Big Sister is Watching You*, p. 57
1310. Ibid.
1311. Griffin, *Descent into Slavery*, p. 292
1312. Griffin, *Fourth Reich of the Rich*, p. 119
1313. George Carpozi, *Clinton Confidential* (Columbia: CLS Publishing, 1995), p. 424
1314. Ibid.
1315. Griffin, *Fourth Reich of the Rich*, p. 115
1316. Robert E. Levin, *Bill Clinton: The Inside Story* (New York: S.P.I. Books, 1992), p. 49
1317. Ibid., p. 54
1318. James B. Stewart, *Blood Sport* (New York: Touchstone Books, 1996), p. 47
1319. Ibid.
1320. Ibid.
1321. Ibid., p. 49
1322. Hillary Clinton, p. 79
1323. Griffin, *Fourth Reich of the Rich*, p. 112
1324. Ibid.
1325. Ibid., p. 115
1326. R. Emmett Tyrrell, *Boy Clinton* (Washington: Regnery Publishing, 1996), p. 63
1327. Alexander Cockburn & Ken Silverstein, *Washington Babylon* (London: Verson, 1996), P. 275
1328. Meredith Oakley, *On the Make* (Washington: Regnery Publishing, 1994), p. 247
1329. Allen, Portis, p. 69
1330. Ibid.
1331. Dick Morris, *Rewriting History* (New York: Regan Books, 2004), pp. 80-1
1332. Oakley, p. 254
1333. Ibid., p. 255
1334. Ibid., p. 254
1335. Roger Morris, p. 276
1336. Ibid.
1337. Stewart, p. 212
1338. Cockburn, Silverstein, p. 251
1339. Ibid.
1340. Roger Morris, p. 4
1341. Ibid., pp. 280-1
1342. Ibid., p. 433
1343. Ibid.
1344. Ibid., p. 435
1345. Ibid., p. 433
1346. Ibid., pp. 433-4
1347. Ibid., p. 434
1348. Ibid.
1349. Ibid.

Vernon Jordan & the Bilderbergs

1350. Carpozi, p. 668
1351. Roger Morris, p. 277
1352. David Maraniss, *First in His Class* (New York: Touchstone Books, 1995), p. 461
1353. David Brock, *The Seduction of Hillary Rodham* (New York: Free Press Paperbacks, 1996), p. 295
1354. Milton, p. 248
1355. Christopher Andersen, *American Evita* (New York: William Morrow, 2004), pp. 134-5
1356. Michael Isikoff, *Uncovering Clinton* (New York: Crown Publishers, 1999), p. 275
1357. Jack Cashill, *Ron Brown's Body* (Nashville: WND Books, 2004), p. 100
1358. Jeffrey Toobin, *A Vast Conspiracy* (New York: Touchstone Books, 1999), p. 179
1359. Ibid., p. 177
1360. Wesley Hagood, *Presidential Sex* (New York: Citadel Press, 1995), p. 248
1361. Ibid., p. 250
1362. Ibid., p. 244
1363. Edward Klein, *The Truth About Hillary* (New York: Sentinel, 2005), p. 141
1364. Ibid.
1365. Jim Marrs, p. 39
1366. Ibid.
1367. Ibid., p. 40
1368. Ibid., pp. 40-1
1369. Carpozi, p. 429
1370. Ibid., p. 294
1371. Ibid., p. 428
1372. Ibid.
1373. Texe Marrs, *Circle of Intrigue*, p. 182
1374. Jonathan Vankin and Jon Whalen, *50 Greatest Conspiracies of All Time* (New York: Citadel Press, 1995), p. 320
1375. Ibid.
1376. Jim Tucker, *Bilderberg Diary* (Washington: American Free Press, 2005), p. 92
1377. Ibid., p. 152
1378. Griffin, *Descent into Slavery*, p. 293
1379. Texe Marrs, *Circle of Intrigue*, p. 184
1380. Griffin, *Fourth Reich of the Rich*, p. 116
1381. Ibid.
1382. Carpozi, p. 293
1383. Ibid., p. 295
1384. Ibid., p. 296
1385. Ibid.
1386. Ibid., p. 301
1387. Ibid.
1388. Elizabeth Drew, *On the Edge* (New York: Simon & Schuster, 1994), p. 341
1389. Paul Roer, *The Rants, Raves & Thoughts of Bill Clinton* (Brooklyn: On Your Own Publications, 2002), p. 115
1390. Drew, p. 299
1391. Ibid.
1392. Jim Marrs, p. 40
1393. Tucker, p. 139

60 Minutes & Ross Perot

1392. Terry Reed & John Cummings, *Compromised* (New York: S.P.I. Books, 1994), p. 511
1394. John Austin, *Rkansides* (Bloomington, 1st Books, 2000), p. 14
1395. Ibid.
1396. Patrick Matrisciana, *The Clinton Chronicles Book*, (Hemet: Jeremiah Books, 1994), p. 15
1397. Ibid.
1398. Allen, Portis, p. 187
1399. Paul Fick, *The Dysfunctional President* (New York: Citadel Press, 1995), p. 71
1400. Allen, Portis, p. 128
1401. Ibid., p. 179
1402. Dick Morris, p. 151
1403. Paul Fick, *The Dysfunctional President* (New York: Citadel Press, 1998), p. 71
1404. Fick (1995), pp. 70-1
1405. Austin, p. 83
1406. Milton, p. 223
1407. Austin, p. 83
1408. Allen, Portis, p. 190
1409. Milton, p. 222
1410. Matrisciana, p. 153
1411. Austin, p. 83
1412. Fick (1998), p. 70
1413. Matrisciana, p. 152
1414. Al Martin, *The Conspirators* (Pray, Montana: National Liberty Press, 2001), p. 309
1415. Carpozi, p. 571
1416. Ibid.
1417. Martin, p. 159
1418. Carpozi, p. 575
1419. Ibid., p. 576
1420. Ibid., p. 577
1421. Ibid.
1422. Ibid.
1423. Ibid., p. 580
1424. Ibid., p. 572
1425. Ibid., p. 573
1426. Ibid., p. 574
1427. Ibid., p. 579
1428. Ibid., p. 580
1429. Ibid.
1430. Ibid.
1431. Ibid., pp. 580-1
1432. Ibid., p. 581

The CFR, Trilateral Commission & Alan Greenspan

1443. Oakley, p. 161
1444. Texe Marrs, *Circle of Intrigue*, p. 184
1445. Gennifer Flowers, *Sleeping with the President* (New York: Anonymous Press, 1996), p. 26
1446. Ibid.
1447. Allen, Portis, p. 53
1448. In *Aaron's Own Opinion* website, December 3, 2005, p. 4
1449. Milton, p. 245
1450. Ibid.
1451. Ibid., p. 246
1452. Ibid.
1453. Texe Marrs, *Circle of Intrigue*, p. 59
1454. Ibid.
1455. Klein, p. 209

Bibliography

PRIMARY SOURCES

Aka, Dr. Charles K. *Bill Clinton: Man of the Public*. Bloomington, Indiana: 1st Books, 2002

Aldrich, Gary. *Unlimited Access: An FBI Agent Inside the Clinton White House*. Washington: Regnery Publishing, 1998

Allen, Charles F. and Portis, Jonathan. *The Comeback Kid: The Life and Career of Bill Clinton*. New York: Birch Lane Press, 1992

American Conservative Union. *Hillary Rodham Clinton: What Every American Should Know*. Ottawa, Illinois: Green Hill Publishers, 2005

Andersen, Christopher. *American Evita: Hillary Clinton's Path to Power*. New York: William Morrow, 2004

Andersen, Christopher. *Bill and Hillary: The Marriage*. New York: William Morrow, 1999

Austin, John. *Rkansides: The Legacy & Body Count of Bill Clinton*. Bloomington, Indiana: 1st Books, 2000

Birnbaum, Jeffrey H. *Madhouse: The Private Turmoil of Working for the President*. New York: Times Books, 1996

Blumenthal, Sidney. *The Clinton Wars*. New York: Plume, 2003

Bradford, R.W. *It Came From Arkansas: The Bill Clinton Story*. Port Townsend, WA: Liberty Publishing, 1993

Bresnahan, David M. *Damage Control: The Larry Nichols Story*. Salt Lake City: Camden Court Publishers, 1997

Brock, David. *The Seduction of Hillary Rodham*. New York: Free Press Paperbacks, 1996

Brown, Floyd G. *Slick Willie: Why America Cannot Trust Bill Clinton*. Annapolis: Annapolis-Washington Book Publishers, 1993

Brown, L.D. *Crossfire: Witness in the Clinton Investigation*. San Diego: Black Forest Press, 1999

Brummett, John. *High Wire: The Education of Bill Clinton*. New York: Hyperion, 1994

Carpenter, Amanda B. *The Vast Right-Wing Conspiracy's Dossier on Hillary Clinton*. Washington: Regnery Publishing, 2006

Carpozi, George. *Clinton Confidential: The Unauthorized Biography of Bill and Hillary Clinton*. Columbia, Maryland: CLS Publishing, 1995

Cashill, Jack. *Ron Brown's Body: How One Man's Death Saved the Clinton Presidency and Hillary's Future*. Nashville: WND Books, 2004

Clinton, Bill. *My Life*. New York: Alfred P. Knopf, 2004

Clinton, Hillary Rodham. *Living History*. New York: Scribner, 2003

Drew, Elizabeth. *On the Edge: The Clinton Presidency*. New York: Simon & Schuster, 1994

Evans-Pritchard, Ambrose. *The Secret Life of Bill Clinton: The Unreported Stories*. Washington: Regnery Publishing, 1997

Fick, Paul. *The Dysfunctional President: Inside the Mind of Bill Clinton*. New York: Citadel Press, 1995

Fick, Paul. *The Dysfunctional President: Understanding the Compulsions of Bill Clinton*. New York: Citadel Press, 1998

Flowers, Gennifer. *Sleeping with the President: My Intimate Years with Bill Clinton*. New York: Anonymous Press, 1996

Gross, Martin L. *The Great Whitewater Fiasco: An American Tale of Money, Power, and Politics*. New York: Ballantine Books, 1994

Harris, John F. *The Survivor: Bill Clinton in the White House*. New York: Random House, 2005

Hitchens, Christopher. *No One Left to Lie To: The Triangulations of William Jefferson Clinton*. London: Verso, 1999

Ingraham, Laura. *The Hillary Trap: Looking for Power in All the Wrong Places*. New York: Hyperion, 2000

Isikoff, Michael. *Uncovering Clinton: A Reporter's Story*. New York: Crown Publishers, 1999

Jackson, Candice E. *Their Lives: The Women Targeted by the Clinton Machine*. Los Angeles: World Ahead Publishing, 2005

Kellett, Michael. *The Murder of Vince Foster*. Columbia, Maryland: CLS Publishers, 1995

Kellett, Michael. *Phantoms of the World Stage*. Columbia, Maryland: Evidence First Publishing, 2006

Kelly, Virginia Clinton. *My Life: Leading with My Heart*. New York: Pocket Star Books, 1994

Klein, Edward. *The Truth About Hillary*. New

BIBLIOGRAPHY

York: Sentinel, 2005

Klein, Joe. *The Natural: The Misunderstood Presidency of Bill Clinton*. New York: Broadway Books, 2002

Kuiper, Thomas D. *I've Always Been a Yankees Fan: Hillary Clinton in Her Own Words*. Los Angeles: World Ahead Publishing, 2006

Limbacher, Carl. *Hillary's Scheme: Inside the Next Clinton's Ruthless Agenda to Take the White House*. New York: Crown Forum, 2003

Limbaugh, David. *Absolute Power: The Legacy of Corruption in the Clinton-Reno Justice Department*. Washington: Regnery Publishing, 2001

Levin, Robert E. *Bill Clinton: The Inside Story*. New York: S.P.I. Books, 1992

Lowry, Rich. *Legacy: Paying the Price for the Clinton Years*. Washington: Regnery Publishing, 2003

Maraniss, David. *First in His Class: The Biography of Bill Clinton*. New York: Touchstone Books, 1995

Matrisciana, Patrick. *The Clinton Chronicles Book*. Hemet, California: Jeremiah Books, 1994

McDougal, Jim and Wilkie, Curtis. *Arkansas Mischief: The Birth of a National Scandal*. New York: Henry Holt and Company, 1998

Milton, Joyce. *The First Partner: Hillary Rodham Clinton*. New York: Perennial, 1999

Morris, Dick. *Rewriting History*. New York: Regan Books, 2004

Morris, Roger. *Partners in Power: The Clintons and Their America*. Washington: Regnery Publishing, 1996

Moser, Edward P. *Willy Nilly: Bill Clinton Speaks Out*. Nashville: Caliban Books, 1994

Noonan, Peggy. *The Case Against Hillary Clinton*. New York: Harper Collins, 2000

Oakley, Meredith L. *On the Make: The Rise of Bill Clinton*. Washington: Regnery Publishing, 1994

Odom, Richard. *Circle of Death: Clinton's Climb to the Presidency*. Lafayette, Louisiana: Huntington House Publishers, 1995

O'Leary, Bradley S. *Top 200 Reasons Not to Vote for Bill Clinton*. Austin: Boru Publishing, 1996

Olson, Barbara. *Hell to Pay: The Unfolding Story of Hillary Rodham Clinton*. Washington: Regnery Publishing, 1999

Olson, Barbara. *The Final Days: The Last Desperate Abuses of Power by the Clinton White House*. Washington: Regnery Publishing, 2001

Oppenheimer, Jerry. *State of a Union: Inside the Complex Marriage of Bill and Hillary Clinton*. New York: Harper Collins, 2000

Patterson, Lt. Colonel Robert "Buzz". *Dereliction of Duty: The Eyewitness Account of How Bill Clinton Compromised America's National Security*. Washington: Regnery Publishing, 2003

Poe, Richard. *Hillary's Secret War: The Clinton Conspiracy to Muzzle Internet Journalists*. Nashville: WND Books, 2004

Reed, Terry and Cummings, John. *Compromised: Clinton, Bush and the CIA*. New York: S.P.I. Books, 1994

Roer, Paul. *The Rants, Raves & Thoughts of Bill Clinton*. Brooklyn: On Your Own Publications, 2002

Ruddy, Christopher. *Vincent Foster: The Ruddy Investigation*. Tulsa: United Publishing, 1996

Ruddy, Christopher and Limbacher, Carl. *Bitter Legacy: The Untold Story of the Clinton-Gore Years*. West Palm Beach: Newsmax, 2001

Sheehy, Gail. *Hillary's Choice*. New York: Random House, 1999

Stephanopoulos, George. *All Too Human: A Political Education*. Boston: Little Brown & Company, 1999

Stewart, James B. *Blood Sport: The President and his Adversaries*. New York: Touchstone Books, 1996

Stone, Deborah J. and Manion, Christopher. *Slick Willie II: Why America Still Can't Trust Bill Clinton*. Annapolis: Annapolis-Washington Book Publishers, 1994

Timperlake, Edward and Triplett, William C. *Year of the Rat: How Bill Clinton and Al Gore Compromised U.S. Security for Chinese Cash*. Washington: Regnery Publishing, 1998

Toobin, Jeffrey. *A Vast Conspiracy: The Real Story of the Sex Scandal That Nearly Brought Down a President*. New York: Touchstone Books, 1999

Tyrrell, R. Emmett. *Boy Clinton: The Political Biography*. Washington: Regnery Publishing, 1996

Tyrrell, R. Emmett and Davis, Mark W. *Madame Hillary: The Dark Road to the White House*. Washington: Regnery Publishing, 2004

Warner, Judith. *Hillary Clinton: The Inside Story.* New York: Signet, 1993

Watson, Kevin H. *The Clinton Record: Everything Bill & Hillary Want You to Forget.* Bellevue, Washington: Merril Press, 1996

Woodward, Bob. *The Agenda: Inside the Clinton White House.* New York: Simon & Schuster, 1994

SECONDARY SOURCES

Bainerman, Joel. *Inside the Covert Operations of the CIA & Israel's Mossad.* New York: S.P.I. Books, 1994

Beaty, Jonathan and Gwynne, S.C. *The Outlaw Bank: A Wild Ride into the Secret Heart of BCCI.* New York: Random House, 1993

Borjesson, Kristina. *Into the Buzzsaw: Leading Journalists Expose the Myth of a Free Press.* Amherst, New York: Prometheus Books, 2002

Cockburn, Alexander and Silverstein, Ken. *Washington Babylon.* London: Verso, 1996

Cockburn, Alexander and St. Clair, Jeffrey. *Whiteout: The CIA, Drugs, and the Press.* London: Verso, 1998

Coleman, Dr. John. *Socialism: The Road to Slavery.* Carson City, Nevada: Joseph Publishing Company, 1994

Cooley, John K. *Unholy Wars: Afghanistan, America and International Terrorism.* London: Pluto Press, 1999

Dowbenko, Uri. *Bushwhacked: Inside Stories of True Conspiracy.* Pray, Montana: Conspiracy Digest, 2003

Ehrenfeld, Dr. Rachel. *Evil Money: The Inside Story of Money Laundering & Corruption in Government, Banks & Business.* New York: S.P.I. Books, 1992

Farren, Mick. *CIA: Secrets of "The Company".* New York: Chrysalis Books Group, 2003

Findley, Representative Paul. *They Dare to Speak Out: People and Institutions Confront Israel's Lobby.* Westport, Connecticut: Lawrence Hill & Company, 1985

Griffin, Des. *Descent Into Slavery.* Clackamas, Oregon: Emissary Publications, 1980

Griffin, Des. *Fourth Reich of the Rich.* Clackamas, Oregon: Emissary Publications, 1976

Hagood, Wesley O. *Presidential Sex: From the Founding Fathers to Bill Clinton.* New York: Citadel Press, 1995

Hidell, Al and D'Arc, Joan. *The New Conspiracy Reader.* New York: Citadel Press, 2004

Hopsicker, Daniel. *Barry & the Boys: The CIA, the Mob and America's Secret History.* Eugene, Oregon: Mad Cow Press, 2001

Hopsicker, Daniel. *Welcome to Terrorland: Mohamed Atta & the 9-11 Cover-up in Florida.* Eugene, Oregon: Mad Cow Press, 2004

Jackson, Devon. *Conspiranoia: The Mother of All Conspiracy Theories.* New York: Plume, 2000

Kick, Russ. *You Are Being Lied To: The Disinformation Guide to Media Distortion, Historical Whitewashes and Cultural Myths.* New York: The Disinformation Company, 2001

Kwitny, Jonathan. *The Crimes of Patriots: A True Tale of Dope, Dirty Money and the CIA.* New York: W.W. Norton & Company, 1987

Lee, Martin A. and Shlain, Bruce. *Acid Dreams: The Complete Social History of LSD—the CIA, the Sixties, and Beyond.* New York: Grove Weidenfeld, 1985

Leveritt, Mara. *The Boys on the Tracks: Death, Denial, and a Mother's Crusade to Bring Her Son's Killers to Justice.* New York: St. Martin's Press, 1999

Marrs, Jim. *Rule By Secrecy.* New York: Perennial, 2000

Marrs, Texe. *Big Sister Is Watching You.* Austin: Living Truth Publishers, 1993

Marrs, Texe. *Circle of Intrigue.* Austin: Living Truth Publishers, 1995

Marshall, Jonathan. *Drug Wars: Corruption, Counterinsurgency and Covert Operations in the Third World.* Forestville, California: Cohan & Cohen Publishers, 1991

Marshall, Jonathan and Scott, Peter Dale and Hunter, Jane. *The Iran-Contra Connection: Secret Teams and Covert Operations in the Reagan Era.* Boston: South End Press, 1987

Martin, Al. *The Conspirators: Secrets of an Iran-Contra Insider.* Pray, Montana: National Liberty Press, 2001

Mayer, Martin. *The Bankers: The Next Generation.* New York: Plume, 1997

McNally, Patrick. *From Chappaquiddick to New York and Washington through Oklahoma City.* Bloomington, Indiana: Author House, 2004

Millegan, Kris. *Fleshing Out Skull & Bones: Investigations Into America's Most Powerful Secret*

Society. Walterville, Oregon: Trine Day, 2003

OKBIC. *Final Report: The Bombing of the Alfred P. Murrah Federal Building*. Oklahoma City: OKBIC, 2001

Palast, Greg. *The Best Democracy Money Can Buy*. New York, Penguin, 2002

Perloff, James. *The Shadows of Power: The Council on Foreign Relations and the American Decline*. Appleton, Wisconsin: Western Islands, 1988

Phillips, Kevin. *American Dynasty: Aristocracy, Fortune, and the Politics of Deceit in the House of Bush*. New York: Viking, 2004

Piper, Michael Collins. *The Judas Goats: The Enemy Within*. Washington: American Free Press, 2006

Reavis, Dick J. *The Ashes of Waco: An Investigation*. Syracuse: Syracuse University Press, 1995

Rappoport, Jon. *Oklahoma City Bombing: The Suppressed Truth*. Los Angeles: Blue Press, 1995

Roberts, Craig. *The Medusa File: Secret Crimes and Coverups of the U.S. Government*. Tulsa: Consolidated Press International, 1997

Scott, Peter Dale and Marshall, Jonathan. *Cocaine Politics: Drugs, Armies, and the CIA in Central America*. Berkeley: University of California Press, 1991

Scott, Peter Dale. *Drugs, Oil, and War*. Lanham, Maryland: Rowman & Littlefield Publishers, 2003

Shattuck, David. *Forbidden Knowledge: From Prometheus to Pornography*. New York: St. Martin's Press, 1996

Simon, David R. *Elite Deviance*. Boston: Allyn & Bacon, 1982

Southwell, David and Twist, Sean. *Conspiracy Files*. New York: Gramercy Books, 2004

Stich, Rodney. *Defrauding America*. Alamo, California: Diablo Western Press, 1994

Tabor, James D. and Gallagher, Eugene V. *Why Waco: Cults and the Battle for Religious Freedom in America*. Berkeley: University of California Press, 1995

Tarpley, Webster and Chaitkin, Anton. *George Bush: The Unauthorized Biography*. Washington: Executive Intelligence Review, 1992

Thomas, Gordon. *Gideon's Spies: The Secret History of the Mossad*. New York: Thomas Dunne Books, 1999

Thomas, Gordon. *Seeds of Fire: China and the Story Behind the Attack on America*. Tempe, Arizona: Dandelion Books, 2001

Thomas, Kenn and Keith, Jim. *The Octopus: Secret Government and the Death of Danny Casolaro*. Portland: Feral House, 1996

Thomas, Kenn. *Parapolitics: Conspiracy in Contemporary America*. Kempton, Illinois: Adventures Unlimited Press, 2006

Thorn, Victor. *The New World Order Exposed*. State College, Pa: Sisyphus Press, 2003

Thorn, Victor. *The OKC Bombing-Elohim City Connection: A Study in State-sponsored Terrorism*. State College, Pa: Sisyphus Press, 2005

Trento, Joseph J. *The Secret History of the CIA*. Roseville, California: Prima Publishing, 2001

Truell, Peter and Gurwin, Larry. *False Profits: The Inside Story of BCCI, the World's Most Corrupt Financial Empire*. New York: Houghton Mifflin Company, 1992

Tucker, Jim. *Bilderberg Diary*. Washington: American Free Press, 2005

Vankin, Jonathan and Whalen, John. *50 Greatest Conspiracies of All Time: History's Biggest Mysteries, Coverups & Cabals*. New York: Citadel Press, 1995

Webb, Gary. *Dark Alliance: The CIA, the Contras, and the Crack Cocaine Explosion*. New York: Seven Stories Press, 1998

Wilson, Robert Anton. *Cosmic Trigger: Final Secret of the Illuminati*. Tempe: New Falcon Publications, 1977

Zepezauer, Mark. *The CIA's Greatest Hits*. Tucson: Odonian Press, 1994

ARTICLES AND WEBSITES

Adams, James Ring. *What's Up in Jakarta?* The American Spectator, September 1995

APFN, *Hillary Directed Waco*, February 10, 2001

Arkancide Clinton Body Count website

Baehr, Richard. *Can TWA 800 Shoot Down Hillary?*

Barsamian, David. *The CIA & the Politics of Narcotics*. University of Wisconsin with Professor Alfred McCoy, February 17, 1990

Blair, Mike. *Oklahoma City Bombing Witnesses Are Dying Fast*. Washington: Spotlight, May 19, 1997

Brandt, Daniel. *Clinton's Long CIA Connec-*

tion. NameBase News Line, October-December, 1996

Brandt, Daniel. *Clinton, Quigley, and Conspiracy: What's Going on Here?* NameBase News Line, April-June 1993

Brewda, Joseph. *George Bush's Opium War.* Executive Intelligence Review, November 26, 1999

Chossudovsky, Michel. *Who is Osama Bin Laden?* Centre for Research on Globalization, September 12, 2001

CBC News. *Afghanistan Leads World in Opium Production: UN Report,* June 26, 2007

Clinton Circle of Death website

CNN. *U.S.: Afghan Poppy Production Doubles.* November 28, 2003

Cockburn, Alexander. *Chapters in the Recent History of Arkansas.* The Nation, February 24, 1992

Connolly, John. *Dead Right.* Spy Magazine, January 1993

Dead People Connected with Bill Clinton

Dee, John. *Snow Job: The CIA, Cocaine, and Bill Clinton*

Denton, Sally and Morris, Roger. *The Crimes of Mena.* Penthouse, July 1995

Donahue, Tom. *Terry Reed-John Cummings Interview.* America's Town Forum, April 27, 1994

Dowbenko, Uri. *Up Against the Beast: High-Level Drug Running.* Nexus Magazine, April-May 2000

Dowbenko, Uri. *Defrauding America* (book review). Conspiracy Digest, 2001

Downside Legacy Research website, February 6, 2001

Duffey, Jean. *The Mena Connection Is Made.* May 29, 1997

Emerson Review. *Clinton Body Count.* Frederic, MI., February 8, 2007

Evans-Pritchard, Ambrose. *Smugglers Linked to Contra Arms Deals.* London: Sunday Telegraph, October 9, 1994

Evans-Pritchard, Ambrose. *Foster Hired Detective to Spy on Clinton.* London: Sunday Telegraph, July 15, 1996

Evans-Pritchard, Ambrose. *Phone Call Rings Clinton Alarm Bells.* London: Sunday Telegraph, October 6, 1996

Evans-Pritchard, Ambrose. *Student Bill Clinton 'Spied' on Americans Abroad for CIA.* London: Sunday Telegraph, June 10, 1996

Farah, Joseph. *The Clinton Body Count.* World Net Daily, September 24, 1998

Franklin, Richard L. *101 Peculiarities Surrounding the Death of Vince Foster.* The Progressive Review

Gritz, Bo. *Letter to George Bush, Sr.* February 1, 1988

Gumbel, Andrew. *The Unsolved Mystery of the Oklahoma City Bombing,* Truthdig, February 21, 2006

Guyatt, David G. *Deep Black: The CIA's Secret Drug Wars.* West Sussex, United Kingdom: Nexus Magazine, February-March, 1998

Hansson, Lars. *A Nation Betrayed (transcript of Bo Gritz interview),* June 1, 1990

Hicks, Sander. *From Vince Foster to Venezuela,* interview with Greg Palast

Hoffman, David. *National Security Council Link in Oklahoma Bombing?* The Washington Weekly, February 3, 1997

Hoffman, David. *The Death of an Oklahoma Bombing Witness*

Hopsicker, Daniel. *CIA Linked to Seal's Assassination.* The Washington Weekly, August 18, 1997

In Aaron's Own Opinion website, December 3, 2005

Insight on the News. *True Crime or Pulp Fiction: Clandestine Operations in Mena, Arkansas.* January 30, 1995

Ireland, Doug. *Partners in Crime.* July 17, 1996

Khun Sa, Vice Chairman Thailand Revolutionary Council (TRC). *Letter to U.S. Justice Department.* June 28, 1987

Kimery, Anthony. *The BCCI Affair.* July 10, 1997

Lee, Martin. *Ex-CIA Agent Calls Drug War a Fraud.* Insight Features, October 1, 1990

Lee, Marvin. *Mena: The Investigation of Barry Seal* (interview with former Arkansas State Police Investigator Russell Welch), March 1996

Lee, Walter. *Vicky Weaver: Fire and Rain*

Leveritt, Mara. *The Mena Airport: Why Arkansas's Biggest Mystery Won't Die.* Arkansas Times, August 1995

Limbacher, Carl. *Clinton-Connected Bribes, Break-ins, Beatings, Death Threats.* October 12, 1998

MacMichael, David. *The Mysterious Death of*

BIBLIOGRAPHY

Danny Casolaro. Covert Action Information Bulletin, Winter 1991

Mizrach, Steve. *Untangling the Octopus: October Surprise, Iran-Contra, Noriega, Iraqgate, and BCCI*. December 13, 2001

Momenteller, Bob. *Deep Inside the Clintonian Reich: Chinese Intelligence, Travelgate, and the Arkansas Connection*. Ether Zone, November 1, 1998

Morrison, Micah. *A Place Called Mena: Just Some Facts*. New York: Wall Street Journal, March 3, 1999

Myers, Lawrence, *Why Did Bill Clinton's National Security Council Fund ATF "Experiments" in Building Home Made ANFO Truck Bombs in 1994?* Media Bypass Magazine, November 1996

Nadler, Eric. *George Bush's Heroin Connection*. San Francisco: Rolling Stone Magazine, October 6, 1994

News Commentary. *Did Hillary Clinton Order Waco Assault?* Winter, 2001

Norman, Jim. *Fostergate*. Media Bypass, August 1995

O'Camb, Michael A. *Unresolved Deaths in Oklahoma*. December 10, 2000

Officer.com website, *Don't You Ever Forget Terrence Yeakey*

The Oklahoma Bombing: Witnesses Allege Government's Prior Knowledge and Complicity

Poe, Richard. *Hillary's Secret War: How Clintons Took Control of Federal Law Enforcement*. World Net Daily, July 7, 2005

Political Friendster, *Connection between Jackson Stephens and Bank of Credit and Commerce International*. November 18, 2005

Progressive Review. *Clinton Legacy: Most Convictions, Crookedest Cabinet, 31 Deaths*. August 12, 2000

Quinn, Jim. *Quinn Interview with Jim Norman*. Pittsburgh: WRRK, December 7, 1995

Revolutionary Worker. *Drug Lords, War Lords and the U.S. Military*

Ridgeway, James. *Software to Die For: Inslaw Lawyer Elliot Richardson Talks About Murder and the CIA*. (New York: *the Village Voice*, September 24, 1991)

Ridgeway, James & Vaughan, Doug. New York: *The Village Voice*, October 15, 1991

Ruddy, Christopher. *Arkansas' Murderous Ways*. Newsmax, October 22, 1998

Shannan, Pat. *OKC Bombshell Implicates Feds in Murrah Blast*. Washington: American Free Press, January 7, 2004

Shannan, Pat. *Who Killed Terrence Yeakey?* APFN

Smith, Sam. *Arkansas Connections: A Timeline of the Clinton Years*

Sprunt, Hugh. *The Third Man*. March 1998

Stelzer, C.D. *Danny's Dead: The Casolaro Files*. 1996

Stratton, Richard. *Altered States of America*. New York: Spin Magazine, Volume 9, Number 12, 1994

Swirsky, Joan. *Hillary Clinton's Culture of Corruption: The Scandal Queen*. The New Media Journal, March 13, 2006

Tumulty, Karen. *Hollywood Scuffle*. New York: Time, March 5, 2007

Valentine, Tom. *Bush-Clinton Have Two Things in Common: BCCI, Iran-Contra*. Washington: The Spotlight, August 31, 1992

Webb, Gary and Kramer, Pamela. *Series on CIA-Run Drug Ring Sparks Call for Probe*. San Jose Mercury News, August 29, 1996

What Really Happened website. *The Activities at Mena*

White, Mack. *Waco, Vince Foster, and the Secret War*. October 24, 2000

William Clinton Memorial Library

York, Byron. *Hillary's Webb—Webster L. Hubbell; Hillary Rodham Clinton*. (New York: *National Review*, July 26, 1999

Index

Abbott, Bruce, 114
Abedi, Hassan, 209
Ables, Alan, 184
Adams, Douglas, 282
Adomitis, Daniel, 152
Allard, Edward, 51
Allen, Gary, 308
Aller, Frank, 285
Altman, Robert, 69
Altman, Roger, 39, 40, 346
Alton, Reginald, 130
Anthony, Beryl, 79
Applegate, Rex, 53
Arthur, Richard, 96, 100, 101
Ashford, Kory, 98, 100

B

Bain, Sarah, 37
Bakatin, Vadim, 334
Bakhish, Abdullah Taha, 210
Banister, Guy, 178
Barak, Ehud, 300
Barkley, William, 272
Barr, William, 260
Barram, Dave, 351
Barry, Steven, 43, 54, 55
Bates, Robert, 287
Battistoni, Lois, 258
Bearden, Boonie, 21, 22
Bell, Harvey, 135
Bell, T. March, 42
Bennett, Robert, 114
Bentsen, Lloyd, 346
Ben-Veniste, Richard, 125
Bessett, Carolyn, 275
Bessett, Lauren, 275
Beyer, James, 100, 128, 129
Bianchi, William, 101
Bickel, Bob, 71
Bin Laden, Osama, 306, 307
Bin Sultan, Pandar, 89
Black, Charles, 66
Blaylock, Wallace, 287

Blythe, Bill, 349
Boorda, Mike, 280
Bowman, Sharon, 75
Boyd, Bob, 30
Bradford, R.W., 37
Braswell, Almon Glenn, 295-297
Braun, Cheryl, 85, 90
Brescia, Michael, 166, 175-177, 186, 286
Brewster, Clark, 182
Brian, Earl, 260, 266
Brightop, Katherine, 19
Brining, David, 259
Brining, Sandra, 258
Brown, John, 18, 21
Brown, L.D., 77
Brown, Michael, 224, 246
Brown, Ron, 121, 122, 205, 207, 216-218, 222-237, 239-251, 263, 265, 268, 270, 277, 282, 328, 329
Brown, Tracey, 231
Brzezinski, Zbigniew, 306-308, 332, 336, 344- 346, 349, 351
Bua, Nicholas, 260
Buck, Brantley, 62
Buckley, William F., 340
Buford, William, 40
Bumpers, Dale, 85
Bunch, James, 269
Burton, Bill, 131
Burton, Dan, 90, 94, 192, 281
Burton, Joseph, 4, 5, 18
Bush, George Sr., 45, 46, 62, 68, 198-201, 207, 253-255, 259, 260, 266, 298, 307-309, 313, 314, 321-323, 325, 326, 331-333, 335, 336, 341, 344, 346, 351, 353
Bush, George W., 313, 314, 332
Butera, Eric, 279
Byrd, Robert, 258, 302

C

Calloway, Davis, 19
Camarena, Kiki, 245
Campbell-Brown, Cynthia, 278
Campolo, Tony, 223
Cardoen, Carlos, 266
Cardoza, Mike & Harolyn, 61
Carroll, Phillip, 65
Carson, Johnny, 333, 339
Carter, Jimmy, 70, 209, 252, 261, 292, 298, 301, 303, 332, 334, 336, 344, 348, 351
Carville, James, 311
Casey, William, 252, 261, 266, 307
Cashill, Jack, 237, 240, 241
Casolaro, Danny, 124, 125, 253-261, 266, 270, 277
Castro, Fidel, 25, 178, 254, 299
Cavanaugh, James, 35
Chandler, Jesse, 14
Chaoying, Liu, 221
Charles, Roger, 165, 186
Chertoff, Michael, 72, 125, 126
Chojnacki, Phillip, 40
Chumley, Don, 283
Chung, Johnny, 221
Christopher, Warren, 326, 346
Cisneros, Henry, 293
Clifford, Clark, 69
Clinton, Chelsea, 81, 234, 236, 247, 248, 329
Clinton, Raymond, 308, 350
Clinton, Roger, 15-17, 59, 139-141, 144, 291, 295, 296, 321
Cogdell, Dan, 48
Cogswell, Steve, 240, 242-245, 250
Cohen, Sam, 160, 162
Colby, William, 74, 272-274
Coleman, Suzanne, 269
Collins, Gregory, 22, 271
Colvert, Jack, 284

INDEX

379

Coney, Keith, 21, 271
Coniglione, Tom, 159
Connolly, John, 257
Cooper, Renee, 152
Coopersmith, Lester, 334
Copeland, Coy, 81
Copperfield, David, 94
Cox, Diane, 12
Criswell, Finnis, 19
Criswell, Paul, 19
Cullen, Gene, 54, 55
Currie, Betty, 279, 280, 328
Cutler, Lloyd, 342, 346
Cwick, Mark, 275

D

Davidson, James Dale, 59, 123, 274
Dawson, Len, 296
Deer, Susie, 11-14
Dees, Morris, 188
Densberger, William, 272
Dershowitz, Allen, 67
Deutch, 281, 293
Dickey, Helen, 81, 82, 107, 108
Dickson, Steve, 270
Digenova, Joseph, 294
Disraeli, Benjamin, 316
Drudge, Matt, 234
Drye, David, 286, 288
Duffey, Jean, 14, 17, 21
Dukakis, Michael, 323
Dulles, Allen, 335
Dwyer, Budd, 100

E

Eastwood, Clint, 62
Edwards, Bob, 127, 128
Eisman, Dennis, 277
Eitan, Rafael, 75
Elder, Larry, 232
Elders, Jocelyn, 9, 13, 277
Ellison, James, 173, 174, 184
Engleman, Ron, 50

Espy, Mike, 293
Evans, Emory, 268
Evans-Pritchard, Ambrose, 43, 100, 186-188, 274
Everhart, Harry, 194, 195, 197

F

Ferguson, Kathy, 267, 269
Ferguson, Larry, 267
Ferris, Shawn Tea, 286
Ferstl, Franz, 127
Finley, Karen, 179-183, 185
Fiske, Robert, 58, 68, 89, 94, 122-126, 128-130, 132
Flowers, Gennifer, 139, 145, 210, 264, 276, 338, 340, 350
Ford, Gerald, 335
Fornshill, Kevin, 90
Forrestal, James, 57
Fossella, 314
Foster, Laura, 64, 85
Foster, Lisa, 55, 61-64, 84, 99, 120, 121
Foster, Vince, 41-43, 55-105, 107-133, 135, 137, 139, 141-147, 152, 157, 201, 214, 239, 242, 247, 262, 268, 272, 278, 318, 327
Foster, Vince III, 64
Foxman, Abraham, 300
Francis, James, 54
Freeh, Louis, 51, 125, 162, 172, 186
Frescia, Aldo, 286
Friday, Herschel, 267
Frost, Jack, 53
Frost, Robert, 247
Fulbright, William, 317, 331

G

Gaddafi, Muhamar, 298
Galbraith, Peter, 236
Gallagher, Neil, 294
Garrett, Richard, 6, 15

Gates, Thomas, 256
Gearan, Mark, 79, 82, 110
Gerberth, Vernon, 87, 96
Gergen, David, 65, 338, 346
Gerson, Stuart, 40, 41
Ghigliotti, 280, 281
Giancana, Sam, 324
Gibbs, Judy, 272
Gigot, Paul, 313
Ginsburg, Ruth Bader, 343
Giroir, Joseph, 213
Giuliani, Rudolph, 301
Gladden, Joey, 283
Gonzalez, George, 91, 98, 100
Goodrich, Aaron, 268
Gordan, J. Dell, 278
Gore, Al, 142, 208, 211, 218, 219, 221, 332
Gorelick, Jamie, 193
Gormley, William, 242-245, 249, 250
Graham, Katherine, 323, 327, 337
Greenspan, Alan, 346, 347
Greer, Frank, 326
Gregory, Dick, 231, 232
Griffin, James, 11, 12
Grobmyer, Mark, 212
Groning, Sam, 162
Gruber, Paula, 270
Guerrin, Larry, 277
Guliani, Lisa, 193, 194
Gunderson, Ted, 255
Guthrie, Richard, 175-76, 284-85

H

Hale, David, 115, 267
Hall, David, 166
Hamilton, Bill, 258, 260
Hamilton, James, 63, 64, 114
Hamilton, Nancy, 258, 260
Haner-Mele, Lynda, 179
Hanley, Brian, 272
Harmon, Dan, 16-22, 59, 144
Harp, Joe, 159, 288

Harriman, Pamela, 311
Hart, Gary, 322-326
Hartzler, Joseph, 191
Haselkorn, David, 351
Hasenfus, Eugene, 25
Hause, David, 242, 245
Haut, Donald, 88, 101
Heard, Stanley, 270
Heather, Randall, 160
Hegel, Frederick, 197, 308, 313
Heidelberg, Hoppy, 178
Helms, Jesse, 59
Henderson, Eric, 282
Henry, Curtis, 3
Henry, Don, 3, 5, 6, 14, 17-19, 21-23, 271, 287
Herndon, Lance, 279
Hewitt, Don, 339, 340
Heyman, Phillip, 131
Hill, Nolanda, 121, 122, 216, 222, 224, 226-229, 231, 240, 246, 257, 282
Hillier, John, 286
Hoffman, David, 161, 163, 178
Hope, Judith, 275
Horiuchi, Lon, 50, 282
Houdini, Harry, 80
Howe, Carol, 164-166, 175, 176, 179-186, 191, 192, 199
Howell, Max, 9
Huang, Johnny, 204, 206, 208, 211, 212, 214-220, 223, 229, 245-247, 270
Hubbell, Webster, 41, 42, 55, 59, 61-65, 68-70, 74, 77, 113, 126, 131, 213-216, 225, 318, 327
Huggins, Stanley, 271
Huizi, Xu, 221, 222
Hume, Brit, 276
Hume, Charles, 64, 118
Hume, Sandy, 276
Humphrey, Hubert, 308
Hunt, E. Howard, 178
Huntington, Samuel, 306, 308
Hussein, Saddam, 46, 307, 308

I

Ickes, Harold, 346
Isikoff, Michael, 277
Ives, Kevin, 3, 5, 6, 14, 17-19, 21-23, 271, 287
Ives, Larry, 16
Ives, Linda, 8, 20, 21

J

Jackson, Jesse, 231, 234, 235, 292
Jamar, Jeffrey, 36, 44, 50
James, Duane, 154
Janoski, Kathleen, 242, 244, 249
Jerkuic, Niko, 237-240, 248, 277
Johnson, Gary, 145, 276
Johnson, Lyndon Baines, 323
Johnson, William, 11
Johnston, Bennett, 90
Jones, David, 33, 34
Jones, Paula, 264, 267, 277
Jones, Perry, 49
Jones, Stephen, 172
Jones, Todd, 295
Jordan, Ann, 327
Jordan, Hamilton, 292, 342
Jordan, Vernon, 65, 268, 304, 325-329, 331, 334, 346, 353
Joslin, Norma, 153
Jun, Wang, 122

K

Kaus, Mickey, 340
Keating, Frank, 151
Kehoe, Chevie, 184
Kellett, Michael, 64, 93, 107
Kelley, Shelley, 240, 280
Kelley (Dwire), Virginia, 10-13
Kelly, Robert, 272
Kendall, David, 112, 115, 117
Kennedy (Onasis), Jacqueline, 64, 327
Kennedy, John F., 98, 179, 254, 261, 315, 323-325,349
Kennedy, John Jr., 275, 276, 289
Kennedy, Robert F., 179
Kennedy, Ted, 276, 320
Kennedy, William, 70, 92, 114, 318
Kettleson, Jordan, 23, 272
Key, Charles, 178, 183
Khomeini, Ayatollah, 298
Kilbane, Edward, 243, 249
King, Larry, 42, 82, 116
King, Robert, 10
Knowlton, Patrick, 104-107, 116, 123
Kohl, Helmut, 168
Kopechne, Mary Jo, 276
Koresh, David, 26, 28-36, 38, 40, 41, 43-46, 48, 49, 52, 54
Kroft, Steve, 340
Kurtz, Howard, 232

L

Lamberth, Royce, 229, 246
Lance, Burt, 209
Langan, Michael (Peter), 174-176, 184
Lapseng, Np, 221
Lasater, Dan, 17, 21, 59, 66, 113, 140, 144, 145, 269, 276, 350
Lawhorn, Johnny, 267
Lawson, Catina, 175
Lay, Kenneth, 223, 228, 299
Lebleu, Conway, 32, 272
Lee, Henry, 124
Lemon, Woody, 288
Leonard, Donald, 278
Leveritt, Mara, 3
Lewinsky, Monica, 78, 226, 231, 233-235, 250, 265, 268, 304, 327-329
Lewis, Charles, 322
Lewis, C.S., 130
Liddy, G. Gordon, 279
Lindsey, Bruce, 41, 61, 220, 346

INDEX

Livingstone, Craig, 92, 114, 116, 117
Longfellow, Robert Wadsworth, 247
Loudenslager, Mike, 283, 284
Lum, Gene, 278
Lum, Nora, 278
Luzzatto, Tamera, 352
Lynch, Larry, 47
Lyons, James, 76
Lyons, Kirk, 169, 170, 172, 184, 187

M

Mahon, Dennis, 164-166, 175, 176, 182, 185, 186, 192
Mahoney, Mary, 268, 279
Majors, Jackie, 284
Malak, Fahmy, 3, 4-10, 12-14, 20, 22, 87, 100, 271
Mankin, Charles, 163
Maroney, Mickey, 278
Marrs, Texe, 315
Martin, Florence, 268
Martin, Wayne, 28, 47
Martz, Lester, 180
Matlock, John, 334
Matos, Adolfo, 293
Matrisciana, Patrick, 287
Matsch, Richard, 183
Matteson, Gordon, 282
Matthews, Chris, 264
Matthews, Robert, 175
McCauley, Alex, 154, 155, 166, 179
McClenny, Gary, 162
McCurry, Mike, 247
McDougal, James, 59, 67, 224, 267, 270, 317, 318
McDougal, Susan, 59, 293
McGovern, George, 351
McGuerin, Dick, 49
McKaskle, Keith, 17, 18, 22, 23, 271

McKeehan, Todd, 32, 272
McLarty, Donna, 63
McLarty, Mack, 41, 63, 82, 84, 274, 320, 327, 346, 348
McMurtry, Larry, 37
McVeigh, Jennifer, 178
McVeigh, Timothy, 150-152, 154, 156-158, 162, 164, 166, 167, 170, 175-180, 182-193, 195-197, 199, 200, 203, 283, 286
Meese, Edwin, 72, 260
Meissner, 207, 223, 245, 246, 270
Mfume, Kweisi, 231
Milam, James, 7, 22, 271
Millar, Robert, 173-174, 182, 184
Miller, Charles Wilbourne, 281
Miller, Ron, 278
Millis, John, 281
Mirzayan, Christine, 277
Mixon, Norman, 258
Moody, Neil, 278
Moore, Frank, 348
Moser, Tony, 282
Moyers, Bill, 305
Moyle, Jonathan, 266
Moynihan, Patrick, 275
Mulford, Clay, 342
Musial, Stan, 296
Myers, Dee Dee, 79

N

Nash, William, 317
Neuwirth, Stephen, 131
Nichols, James, 179
Nichols, Larry, 24, 145, 338, 341
Nichols, Terry, 151, 157, 158, 164, 167, 176, 188, 193
Nixon, Richard, 46, 135, 254, 308, 323, 346
Noble, Kerry, 173
Noriega, Manuel, 46
Norman, James, 67, 68
North, Oliver, 67, 68, 254

Nussbaum, Bernard, 41, 55, 63, 109-112, 116-119, 125, 130-132

O

Oakley, Meredith, 8
Obama, Barack, 290
O'Connor, John Cardinal, 313
O'Halloran, Phil, 197
Olson, Paul, 282
Ortega, Daniel, 25
Orwell, George, 312, 316
Oswald, Lee Harvey, 152, 166, 178, 179, 306

P

Parks, Gary, 138, 139, 144
Parks, Jane, 136-143, 147, 148
Parks, Jerry, 135-139, 141-149, 263, 269
Partin, Benjamin, 54, 161, 193, 195, 196
Patrick, Dennis, 276
Patterson, Larry, 80, 341, 342
Patterson, Thomas, 243
Paugh, Gandy, 269
Peace, Kenny, 171
Pearson, Daniel, 224, 226
Pearson, Kathy, 22
Peeler, Jim, 34
Perot, Margo, 342, 343
Perot, Ross, 336, 341-344
Perry, Bruce, 29
Perry, Roger, 81, 107, 108
Perry, William, 236
Petruskie, Vincent, 170, 171, 177, 184
Petty, Richard, 296
Phillips, Barney, 14
Piper, Michael Collins, 169, 189, 190
Plante, Bill, 341
Pollard, Jonathan, 71, 72, 74, 78

Pond, Betsy, 79, 119
Pridgen, Judy, 20
Prince Bernhard, 330
Princess Juliana, 330
Pryor, David, 65
Purdue, Barbara, 319
Purvis, Joe, 101

Q

Query, Paul, 168
Quigley, Carroll, 315-318, 331

R

Raiser, Montgomery, 267
Raiser, Victor, 267
Rather, Dan, 236
Reagan, Ronald, 72, 252, 261, 307, 322, 324, 332, 346
Reed, J.D., 153
Reed, Terry, 45, 271, 337, 343, 344
Reich, Walter, 300
Reitinger, Joseph, 330
Reno, Janet, 29, 37-42, 50, 54, 69, 114, 123, 124, 126, 167, 192, 193, 206, 213, 225, 232, 270
Reynolds, Scott, 272
Rezai, Ali, 298
Rhodes, Cecil, 314, 316, 318, 344
Rhodes, Gary, 272
Rhodes, Jeff, 22, 271
Riady, James, 206, 208-215, 217-220, 327
Riady, Mochtar, 206, 208, 209
Rice, Donna, 322-324
Rich, Denise, 300-302
Rich, Marc, 293, 298-303
Richardson, Ted, 285, 286
Rickel, Peter, 173
Ricks, Bob, 50
Ridgeway, James, 256
Rivera, Geraldo, 232

Roberts, Craig, 74
Roberts, David, 180
Robertson, William, 272
Rockefeller, David, 306, 330, 332, 336, 344-346, 349, 351, 352
Rockefeller, Jay, 352
Rockefeller, Winthrop, 348-350
Rodham, Hugh, 295-298
Rodham, Tony, 297
Rodriguez, Felix, 25
Rodriguez, Miguel, 101, 123
Rodriguez, Paul, 247
Rodriguez, Robert, 32, 33, 35
Roemer, William, 114
Rogers, Ronald, 274
Rolla, John, 92, 115
Rollins, Ed, 342
Roosevelt, Franklin D., 305, 350
Rosenberg, Susan, 293
Ross, Brian, 216
Rosselli, John, 324
Rothschild, Victor, 330
Royster, Ted, 40
Ruddy, Christopher, 98, 99, 106, 122, 232, 234, 243

S

Sabel, Tim, 272
Sabow, James, 282
Safire, William, 218
Samples, Mike, 287
Sanders, Robert, 183, 192
Sarabyn, Chuck, 35, 40
Scaife, Richard Mellon, 264
Scalice, Vincent, 95
Schneider, Steve, 47
Schroeder, Michael Dean, 49
Schuelte, William, 11, 12
Scott, Marsha, 61, 84, 213
Scully, John, 351
Seal, Barry, 17-18, 143, 268, 270, 271
Sentell, Jeanmarie, 249

Seper, Jerry, 215
Sessions, William, 30, 38, 40, 50, 90, 106, 124-126
Shah of Iran, 254, 306
Sharp, J.D., 153
Sharpton, Al, 231
Shellnut, Finis, 17, 350
Shelton, Bill, 269
Shende, Ji, 221
Sherrow, Rich, 52
Shirley, Don, 257
Short, Don, 280
Simpson, O.J., 2, 124
Sirhan, Sirhan, 179
Skyles, John, 79, 80
Slayton, Laura Lee, 10, 11
Sloan, Cliff, 111
Smiley, Tavis, 250
Smith, Edye, 153, 154
Snell, Richard Wayne, 173, 184
Snider, Harold, 317
Snyder, Steven, 173
Spangler, Tommy, 48
Sparks, Joyce, 49
Spiro, Ian, 277
Stack, Robert, 15
Stafford, Ken, 180, 183
Standord, Alan, 277
Stanford, Karin, 234
Starr, Kenneth, 81, 121-123, 127, 130, 132, 139, 214, 226, 233, 262, 267
Starts, James, 257
Steed, Jim, 14
Steinkamp, Leonora, 287
Stephanopolous, George, 41, 311
Stephens, Jackson, 17, 69, 70, 112, 207, 209-211, 215, 217-219, 281, 311, 349
Stewart, Sonya, 229
Stone, Alan, 55
Strassmeir, Andreas, 164-172, 175, 176, 179, 180, 182-188, 191, 192, 199, 286
Strassmeir, Gunter, 168

INDEX

Styron, William, 327

T

Talbot, Benjamin Franklin, 275
Talbott, Strobe, 191, 248, 337
Tatum, Wilbur, 231
Tempelsman, Maurice, 327
Thomases, Susan, 61
Thomason, Harry, 216, 247, 339
Thomason, Linda Bloodsworth, 216, 339
Thomasson, Patsy, 107, 109-111, 113, 114, 116
Thornburgh, Dick, 260
Timperlake, Edward, 208
Tolley, Tonia, 158
Tomlin, Jerry, 4
Trafficante, Santo, 324
Traficant, Jim, 44
Trentadue, Kenneth, 284, 285
Trie, Charlie, 206, 220, 221
Triplett, William C., 208
Tripp, Linda, 42, 78-80, 82, 146, 265, 328
Tucker, Jim, 336
Tucker, Marc, 351, 352
Tulley, Paul, 269
Turnage, Cheryl, 240
Turner, William, 255
Tyree, Bill, 68
Tyson, Don, 59, 66, 144, 210

V

Valentine, Tom, 189
Vanderboegh, Mike, 167, 185
Van Vleet, Jason, 47
Vaughan, Doug, 256
Vignoli, Carlos, 295

W

Walker, Jon Parnell, 270
Walraven, Calvin, 277

Ward, Pete, 176
Ward, Seth, 15, 17, 350
Ward, Skeeter, 15
Washington, Billy Ray, 11, 13
Waters, Maxine, 231, 232
Watkins, David, 63, 84, 113, 216
Way, Lawrence, 342
Weaver, Randy, 195
Weaver, Vicky, 50, 282
Webb, Maynard, 279
Wecht, Cyril, 243, 249
Weinberg, Morris, 299
Weiss, Philip, 20
Welch, Russell, 15, 279
West, Jolyon, 179
Wheaton, Gene, 95
Whicher, Alan, 278, 279
White, Frank, 319, 320
White, Ken, 246
Whitehurst, Frederic, 47
Wilcher, Paul, 270
Wilhite, Jim, 274
Wilkinson, Beth, 172
Willey, Ed, 267
Willey, Kathleen, 267
Williams, Maggie, 84, 107, 109-111, 116, 117
Williams, Robert, 32, 272
Williams, Theodore, 280
Williamson, George, 258
Williamson, J. Gaston, 317
Willis, Steve, 32, 272
Wilson, John A., 269
Wilson, Sharlene, 15, 16, 18, 19, 23
Wilson, Woodrow, 352
Winters, Richard, 23, 272
Wise, Barbara, 246, 247, 270
Wittman, Tommy, 180
Woodward, Bob, 278, 346, 347

X

Xitong, Chen, 220

Y

Yeakey, Terrence, 200-212, 280
Yeakey, Tonia, 202
Young, Buddy, 139
Youngblood, Buddy, 284

Z

Zimmerman, Jack, 47
Zuckerman, Mort, 337

The Clinton Trilogy: Sex, Drugs & Murder

HILLARY (And Bill): The SEX Volume

In HILLARY (And Bill): The SEX Volume—Part One of the Clinton Trilogy, Bill and Hillary's meteoric rise to success is chronicled. It's a carefully plotted path that eventually led them to the White House. But along the way, a series of compromises had to be made, including a prearranged marriage, clandestine assignments for the CIA, and Hillary's ultimate role as a "fixer" for her husband's many dalliances. Pulling no punches, investigative journalist Victor Thorn paints a compelling portrait of secrecy, deceit, violence, and betrayal that shatters the myth Mrs. Clinton has spent so many years trying to create. This three-book series is the most comprehensive examination of the Clinton marriage ever compiled, with *Hillary (And Bill): The Sex* Volume laying a riveting foundation for the next two books which follow: Part Two—*Hillary (and Bill): The Drugs Volume* and then Part Three—*Hillary (And Bill): The Murder Volume.*

Softcover, 344 pages, $30 for one copy. $28 each for two copies. $27 each for three copies. $26 each for four copies. Five to nine copies are $25 each. Ten or more copies are reduced to just $20 each. Discount carton prices available. Call 202-547-5585.

HILLARY (And Bill): The DRUGS Volume

In HILLARY (And Bill): The DRUGS Volume—Part Two of the Clinton Trilogy some of the most damning examples ever put into print of the U.S. government's crimes and corruption are exposed in glaring detail. Beginning with the Clinton family's long-standing ties to the notorious Dixie Mafia, this book illustrates how billions of dollars of cocaine, cash and weapons passed through Mena, Arkansas during the 1980s—with the the full knowledge of Bill and Hillary—to finance the

AFP PUBLISHING: 1-888-699-NEWS TOLL FREE • MC/VISA

illegal war in Nicaragua. (Tons of this CIA-imported coke help fuel the cocaine epidemic of the 1980s) In short, Bill and Hillary's Arkansas became nothing less than a narco-republic, with little banks near Mena laundering more money than the big banks in New York City.

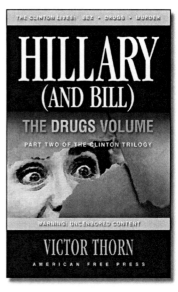

As this thoroughly sourced tale unfolds, the reader encounters a sordid cast of characters including George Bush the Elder (who ran the operation from the office of the VP in D.C.), Oliver North, Manuel Noriega, Webster Hubbell, Barry Seal, Dan Lasater and the Stephens Brothers. In addition, an undeniable amount of evidence proves that nearly every one of Bill Clinton's gubernatorial campaigns—including his 1992 presidential bid—was substantially financed with cocaine money.

The author also includes a wealth of information on the larger implications of Whitewater, the BCCI banking scandal, Travelgate, Filegate and novice stock investor Hillary Clinton's infamous—and mind-boggling—windfall profits derived from trading cattle futures. Also, how the Clintons continually escaped paying for their crimes by firing every U.S. attorney in D.C and appointing friends (many corrupt) as judges.

Softcover, 310 pages, $30 for one copy. $25 each for two copies. $24 each for three copies. $23 each for four copies. Five to nine copies are $22 each. Ten or more copies are reduced to just $20 each. Discount carton prices available. Call 202-547-5585.

Call 1-888-699-NEWS to charge your copies to Visa or MasterCard or send payment to AFP, 645 Pennsylvania Avenue SE, Suite 700, Washington, D.C. 20003.

GET THE COMPLETE TRILOGY FOR $75—reg. $90!

(See following page for "The Murder Volume" . . .)

AFP PUBLISHING: 1-888-699-NEWS TOLL FREE • MC/VISA

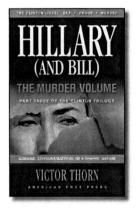

THE FINAL VOLUME IN THE *CLINTON TRILOGY*:

HILLARY (And Bill)
The Murder Volume

In HILLARY (and Bill): the MURDER Volume—Part Three of the Clinton Trilogy, the "Clinton Body Count" is presented in all its gory detail. The most comprehensive study of its kind ever compiled, nearly 120 mysterious deaths are examined, beginning with the grisly murder of two teenage boys who "knew too much" about the illicit drug trafficking operation in Mena, Arkansas, Their murder was then covered-up by Clinton crony, Dr. Fahmy Malak.

After ascending to the presidency in 1992, more atrocities continued with the nationally televised massacre at Waco. Indisputable documents and testimony now prove that not only were FBI and Delta Forces responsible for starting the inferno and killing 80+ Branch Davidians (many of them innocent children), but that Hillary Clinton directed and commandeered the attack to destroy evidence of past government crimes—some related to the manufacture of weapons destined to be included in "Iran-Contra" gun running. Following this nightmare, the public was soon confronted with the "suicide" of Clinton insider Vince Foster. After thoroughly debunking the official version of events, Thorn reveals the identity of Foster's real murderer, as well as treasonous actions against the U.S. government and the involvement of a foreign intelligence agency.

Other high profile cases are also investigated, such as the Oklahoma City bombing, which was in actuality an operation similar to what toppled the World Trade Center towers on Sept. 11, 2001; the murders of Jerry Parks, Danny Casolaro, and former CIA Director William Colby; plus Chinagate and the subsequent political assassination of Commerce Secretary Ron Brown. Despite the corporate media's dismissal of this subject, the Clinton Body Count (i.e. a veritable "Murder, Inc.") is very real and can no longer be discounted as mere coincidence.

Softcover, 393 pages, $30 for one copy. $28 each for two copies. $27 each for three copies. $26 each for four copies. Five to nine copies are $25 each. Ten or more copies are reduced to just $20 each. Discount carton prices available. Call 202-547-5585.

GET THE COMPLETE TRILOGY FOR $75—reg. $90!

AFP PUBLISHING: 1-888-699-NEWS TOLL FREE • MC/VISA

PHANTOM FLIGHT 93 and Other Astounding September 11 Mysteries Explored. By Victor Thorn and Lisa Giuliani. A collection of interviews, articles and on-the-scene investigations by Thorn and Giuliani expose the government cover-up of the fate of Flight 93 (the Shanksville flight) as pure fiction. WHat really happened? Softcover, 150 pages, #1575, $20.

THE CIA IN IRAN: The 1953 Coup & the Origins of the US-Iran Divide reveals how U.S. and British operatives employed every dirty trick at their disposal, including bribery, murder and terrorism, to topple the democratically elected government of Prime Minister Mohammad Mossadeq and maneuvered the infamous Shah of Iran into power. Softcover, 150 pages, #1575, $20.

JIM TUCKER'S BILDERBERG DIARY
AFP editor and reporter Jim Tucker has spent the last 25 years tracking down a group of the richest and most influential industrialists, bankers, media moguls and world leaders that meets every year in complete secrecy in some of the poshest venues the world has to offer. Only Tucker has penetrated these meetings and reported on the nefarious goings on inside despite armed guards, attack dogs and barbed wire fences. Softcover, 272 pages, $25.

DEBUNKING 9-11: 100 Unanswered Questions About September 11
All of AFP's groundbreaking coverage of the event from the beginning: the spies operating in New York; the many theories put forth by independent researchers who reject the government's explanation of many of the events of Sept. 11; alternative theories as to why the twin towers collapsed; detailed informatio of foreknowledge by the government and foreign intelligence agenciest; and much, much more. Large-sized (8.5" x 11" format), 108 pages, $20. Photos.

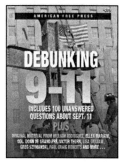

AFP PUBLISHING: 1-888-699-NEWS TOLL FREE • MC/VISA

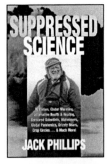

SUPPRESSED SCIENCE: Radiation, Global Warming, Alternative Health & More
Scientist Jack Phillips imparts his lifelong wisdom on a number of suppressed scientific topics including suppressed cancer cures, persecuted alternative health practitioners, the beneficial effects of radiation, the health hazards of vaccines, the real cause of the autism epidemic, the use of divining rods as unexplained—but real—science, and more. Softcover, 125 pages, 176, $17.

Target Traficant: The Outrageous Story of How the Justice Department, the Israeli Lobby and the American Mass Media Conspired to Set Up and Take Down Congressman Jim Traficant—by Michael Collins Piper
The Traficant case is the most outrageous hit-and-run operation ever orchestrated against a U.S. public official. Piper dissects the intrigues of the Justice Department and the FBI and shows that the congressman was innocent of all of the charges. **Softcover, 176 pages, $19.95.**

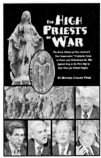

THE HIGH PRIESTS OF WAR: The Secret History of America's Neo-Cons
The High Priests of War, by Michael Collins Piper, tells the secret history of how America's neo-conservatives came to power and orchestrated the war against Iraq as the first step in their drive for global power. Softcover, 144 pages, $20.

DIRTY SECRETS: Crime, Conspiracy & Cover-Up During the 20th Century
Here's a fascinating collection of writings from Michael Collins Piper, transcripts of uncensored radio interviews and reviews of his works—all compiled in one volume. Read where Piper's investigations have led him on such explosive topics as the Martin Luther King and JFK assassinations, the Oklahoma City bombing, the attack on the *Liberty* and many more. Softcover, 256 pages, $22.

AFP PUBLISHING: 1-888-699-NEWS TOLL FREE • MC/VISA

THE NEW JERUSALEM:
Zionist Power in America
This explosive study contains all of the solid facts and figures documenting the massive accumulation of wealth and power by those who have used that influence to direct the course of American affairs—the forces behind America's "New Imperialism." While there are many historical books on "the Israeli lobby," this is unique. Another classic by Michael Collins Piper. Softcover, 184 pages, $20.

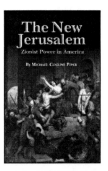

FUTURE FASTFORWARD:
Zionist Anglo-American Empire Meltdown
Is global "Empire Capitalism" about to come crashing down? Will there be a worldwide "people's war" against the Zionists and their powerful minions? Is nuclear war inevitable? What retribution will be meted out to those people who have foisted New World Order slavery upon the people of the world? By Asian political figure Matthias Chang. Softcover, 400 pages, $25.

BRAINWASHED FOR WAR:
Programmed to Kill
From the Cold War to Vietnam and now the so-called "War Against Terror" we have been lied to, mind-controlled and duped by a power elite with the goal of making us mindless supporters of bloody war. Also by Matthias Chang. Softcover, 556 pages, $30.

GEORGE WASHINGTON'S Speeches & Letters:
Here's an inspiring collection of 19 of our first president's most private writings and powerful speeches to firends, family members and colleagues. Includes Washington's Farewell Address and his Farewell to the Army. Letters include ones to his wife, his mother, Gen. Braddock, members of the Continental Congress and more. 12 illustrations. Softcover, 256 pages, $13.

AFP PUBLISHING: 1-888-699-NEWS TOLL FREE • MC/VISA

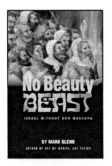

NO BEAUTY IN THE BEAST:
Israel Without Her Mascara
Author Mark Glenn examines Israel from a politically incorrect perspective and comes to the conclusion that the beast of John's Revelation is in fact the beast of Zionist supremacy—a beast that is now devouring the world. Also an amazing chapter of quotes from the perpetrators themselves. Must read for all who call themselves Judeo-Christians. Softcover, 302 pages, $25.

THE PASSION PLAY AT OBERAMMERGAU
How the Thought Police Succeeded in Censoring The World's Oldest Play About Jesus Christ
Find out how the German citizens of Oberammergau, Germany, were forced by the Zionist thought police to change their Passion Play—performed since the 1600s—to make it "less offensive." A shocker. Inclues the full text of the play in novel form. Softcover, 225 pages, $20. Many photos.

THE CITIZENS HANDBOOK:
Pocket-Sized Patriotic Primer for All Ages
Contains the full text of the Declaration of Independence, Constitution, Bill of Rights and ALL subsequent amendments plus a section on every American's rights when called for jury duty. Full color varnished cover to increase life. Pocket-sized softcover, 80 pages, $5. More than 50,000 distributed.

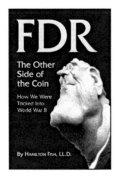

FDR: THE OTHER SIDE OF THE COIN:
How We Were Tricked Into World War II
The author, Rep. Hamilton Fish, felt that had FDR listened to public opinion, millions of lives would have been spared. He documents how FDR refused every prewar peace concession and later refused peace initiatives from anti-Hitler Germans. Mr. Fish traces the roots of the Korean and Vietnamese conflicts to the territorial concessions made by FDR to Stalin at Yalta. Softcover book, 255 pages, $20.

SUBSCRIBE TO *AMERICAN FREE PRESS* NEWSPAPER AND GET FREE BOOKS!

AMERICAN FREE PRESS ORDERING COUPON

Item#	Description/Title	Qty	Cost Ea.	Total
			SUBTOTAL	
	S&H: No S&H inside U.S. Outside U.S. add $6 per book			
	Send a 1-year subscription to AFP for $59 plus 1 free book*			
	Send a 2-year subscription to AFP for $99 plus 2 free books**			
			TOTAL	

*NOTE ABOUT FREE BOOKS: For a one-year subscription to *American Free Press* newspaper ($59), we'll send you one free copy of Michael Collins Piper's *The High Priests of War*. **For a two-year subscription we'll send you *The High Priests of War* PLUS *The New Jerusalem: Zionist Power in America*—almost $40 in free books! (Domestic USA only.)

PAYMENT OPTIONS: ❏ CHECK/MO ❏ VISA ❏ MASTERCARD

Card # _____

Expiration Date _____ Signature _____

CUSTOMER INFORMATION: H3_98

NAME _____

ADDRESS _____

CIty/STATE/ZIP _____

RETURN WITH PAYMENT TO: AMERICAN FREE PRESS, 645 Pennsylvania Avenue SE, Suite 100, Washington, D.C. 20003. Call 1-888-699-NEWS (6397) toll free to charge a subscription or books to Visa or MasterCard.

NEW SUBSCRIBER SPECIAL:

American Free Press
Special Subscription Deal

There is no other paper in America like *American Free Press* (AFP). Every week the hard-driving journalists at *American Free Press* dig for the truth—no matter where the facts may lead. AFP's reporting has been lauded by prominent personalities across the globe, while here at home the controlled media and global power elite try their best to make you believe what you are getting in mainstream publications and on the nightly news is "the whole truth." Nothing could be further from reality!

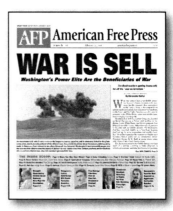

From the unanswered questions about 9-11, the free trade fiasco, the happenings in our corrupt Congress, uncontrolled immigration, to alternative health news and more, AFP tackles the toughest issues of the day with a candid and provocative reporting style that has earned us a host of devoted followers—and powerful enemies.

Isn't it time you started getting a fresh, honest approach to the news that can make or break the future of you and your family?

You'll find all that in AFP plus lots more. AFP is guaranteed to provide all the "sizzle" we promise or we will refund the unused portion of your subscription—no questions asked!

Special "FREE BOOKS" Offer!

Get a FREE copy of Michael Collins Piper's *The High Priests of War: The Secret History of the Neo-Cons* ($20 retail) when you subscribe to AFP for ONE year (52 yearly issues). Get TWO FREE BOOKS—*The High Priests of War* PLUS *The New Jerusalem: Zionist Power in America* (reg. $20)—when you subscribe to AFP for TWO years (104 issues) for $99. Send payment to AFP, 645 Pennsylvania Avenue SE, Suite 100, Washington, D.C. 20003 using the coupon on the reverse. Call AFP toll free at 1-888-699-NEWS (6397) to use Visa/MC.

SUBSCRIBE TO *AMERICAN FREE PRESS* NEWSPAPER AND GET FREE BOOKS!

AMERICAN FREE PRESS ORDERING COUPON

Item#	Description/Title	Qty	Cost Ea.	Total
			SUBTOTAL	
	S&H: No S&H inside U.S. Outside U.S. add $6 per book			
	Send a 1-year subscription to AFP for $59 plus 1 free book*			
	Send a 2-year subscription to AFP for $99 plus 2 free books**			
			TOTAL	

*NOTE ABOUT FREE BOOKS: For a one-year subscription to *American Free Press* newspaper ($59), we'll send you one free copy of Michael Collins Piper's *The High Priests of War*. **For a two-year subscription we'll send you *The High Priests of War* PLUS *The New Jerusalem: Zionist Power in America*—almost $40 in free books! (Domestic USA only.)

PAYMENT OPTIONS: ❏ CHECK/MO ❏ VISA ❏ MASTERCARD

Card # _____

Expiration Date _____ Signature _____

H3_98

CUSTOMER INFORMATION:
NAME _____
ADDRESS _____
CIty/STATE/ZIP _____

RETURN WITH PAYMENT TO: AMERICAN FREE PRESS, 645 Pennsylvania Avenue SE, Suite 100, Washington, D.C. 20003. Call 1-888-699-NEWS (6397) toll free to charge a subscription or books to Visa or MasterCard.